The Best American Travel Writing 2007

GUEST EDITORS OF
THE BEST AMERICAN TRAVEL WRITING

2000 BILL BRYSON
2001 PAUL THEROUX
2002 FRANCES MAYES
2003 IAN FRAZIER
2004 PICO IYER
2005 JAMAICA KINCAID
2006 TIM CAHILL
2007 SUSAN ORLEAN

The Best American Travel Writing™ 2007

Edited and with an Introduction
by Susan Orlean

Jason Wilson, Series Editor

HOUGHTON MIFFLIN COMPANY
BOSTON · NEW YORK 2007

www.houghtonmifflinbooks.com

ISSN 1530–1516
ISBN-13: 978–0–618–58217–4
ISBN-10: 0–618–58217–7
ISBN-13: 978–0–618–58218–1 (pbk.)
ISBN-10: 0–618–58218–5 (pbk.)

Printed in the United States of America

MP 10 9 8 7 6 5 4 3 2 1

Contents

Foreword

A FEW SUMMERS AGO, there was a shark attack at the Jersey Shore. A teenage surfer had his foot bitten by what experts believed was a baby great white shark. Luckily, even though he received sixty stitches, the boy survived and made a full recovery.

Now, shark attacks in New Jersey are rare. Exceedingly rare. This was actually the first attack in decades. I live near enough to the Jersey Shore so that, of course, our local newspaper ran a front-page article about the incident. The headline: "For some, ocean loses appeal after shark attack." The subhead: "But others not as concerned and take the plunge into Atlantic." The reporter quoted a mother with small children who was now afraid to let them go into the water. The reporter quoted other people who said they were not afraid of sharks and would indeed go back into the water.

Alongside that article ran a box of helpful tips under the title "WHAT TO DO: If you come near a shark." Tip #1: "Don't try to touch it." Tip #2: "Get out of the water as quickly as possible." Tip #5: "If a shark attacks you, the general rule is do whatever it takes to get away."

Helpful tips such as these convince me that we have reached a gilded, rococo age of service journalism. The sheer volume of helpful-tip-giving that exists in the world of publishing constantly amazes me. Nowhere is this more evident than in the magazines and newspaper travel sections that I read through every year. Pack light! Use Ziploc bags! Wear a money belt! Stay hydrated on your flight! Be wary of tap water! Watch out for pickpockets!

Not that all of this advice is bad, though much of it is self-evident or common sense or unnecessary. It's helpful in the same way that, when you lose your keys, it's helpful for someone to ask, "Now, where did you last leave them?"

Some travel advice, however, is bad. Take, for example, the advice I've read that suggests Americans should actually pretend to be Canadians while traveling abroad. This is presumably so they might fly under the radar of anti-Americanism. Anyone who's traveled in Europe has seen young Americans taking this advice to heart, prominently displaying little Canadian flags on their backpacks.

Setting aside the fact that rabid anti-Americanism is nowhere near as widespread a phenomenon as reported, or how sad it is to sew a little Canadian flag to one's backpack — the idea that most Americans could ever pass for Canadians is patently absurd.

I have a friend from Toronto who revels in unmasking fake Canadians abroad. She maintains that it's a simple, two-question process. She first asks the fake Canadian if he or she happens to know the capital of Canada. If he or she somehow answers "Ottawa," my friend moves on to the second, more advanced question: Who is the president of Canada? (Note: this is a trick question). "His first name's Pierre, right?" is what one young American recently answered. If the fake Canadian somehow answers the second question correctly, my friend moves on to a bonus round: Name the capital of Saskatchewan. (Hint: it's not Moose Jaw).

Here are three words you will not find in this anthology: *If You Go.*

If You Go — as most readers know — is the standard editorial name for an informational box or "charticle" that accompanies nearly every travel story in nearly every magazine or newspaper travel section you will ever flip through. An If You Go box generally provides the addresses and prices of hotels, opening times and entrance fees of museums, and restaurant suggestions. Presumably, this information is there in case you want to duplicate the writer's trip on your own.

A travel companion recently drove me nuts during a six-hour flight to Lisbon as he read passages, out loud, from his guidebook. He recited: how to locate the most scenic trolley through the Alfama; where we would find the best custard tarts, grilled sardines, and vinho verde; which club was owned by John Malkovich; where we might find the huge Saturday flea market; what the difference between authentic and inauthentic fado music was and where we might find both; where the only place to taste port wine in an eighteenth-century palace happened to be; which hotel had a pool on the roof and a view of the castle. "Remember," he read, "there are very few public toilets in the streets, although they can be found in nearly all museums and it is not that difficult to sneak into a café or restaurant to take care of business."

When we finally arrived in Lisbon, neither of us wanted to carry the bulky guidebook around the city. So I will never know if we rode the most scenic trolley or ate the sardines at the right place. And we never saw John Malkovich anywhere, either.

I have acquaintances who regularly publish several hundred pages of advice on how to vacation in Rome or Amsterdam or Bali or New Zealand, and their hundreds of pages are just a fraction of the thousands of pages of similar counsel on the same subjects. It boggles the mind. And it's all pretty fleeting advice when you really think about it. Much of the information dates by the time the guidebook even reaches the bookshelf. The guidebook writers I know are thorough and detail-oriented, updating their books every other year. Yet they still get cranky letters from readers nitpicking about how stuff has already changed — rates, prices of dinner entrées, opening hours, restaurants that went out of business, bars that had become uncool or changed names, historical sites that were closed for renovation.

Jonathan Stern parodies the explosion of guidebook writing in his very funny piece "The Lonely Planet Guide to My Apartment," collected here. Under the section "What to Bring" he writes, "A good rule of thumb is 'If it's something you'll want, you have to bring it in yourself.' This applies to water, as well as to toilet paper and English-language periodicals. Most important, come with plenty of cash, as there's sure to be someone with his hand out."

Mind you, practical information is all very fine to have, and everybody can use a little advice from time to time. It just has no place in this anthology.

What exactly would be the If You Go for something like Kevin Fedarko's khat-induced adventure in Djibouti? Or Andrew Solomon's exploration into the soul of Libya? Or George Saunders's crazy trip to meet a living "Buddha Boy" in Nepal? No one could duplicate these journeys — or more important, no one could duplicate the travel writing that's come about because of these journeys. That's because, like all great travel writing, each of the stories collected here is born of a singular experience, point of view, and voice. Each of them is a rare achievement.

Perhaps even rarer than a shark attack in New Jersey.

The stories included in this anthology are selected from among hundreds of pieces in hundreds of diverse publications — from mainstream and specialty magazines to Sunday newspaper travel sections to literary journals. I even nominated a fine story from a magazine called *Scrap*, the bimonthly publication of the Institute of Scrap Recycling Industries. I've done my best to be fair and representative, and in my opinion the best travel stories from 2006 were forwarded to Susan Orlean, who made our final selections.

I now begin anew by reading the hundreds of stories published in 2007. I am once again asking editors and writers to submit the best of whatever it is they define as travel writing. These submissions must be nonfiction, published in the United States during the 2007 calendar year. They must not be reprints or excerpts from published books. They must include the author's name, date of publication, and publication name, and must be tear sheets, the complete publication, or a clear photocopy of the piece as it originally appeared. I must receive all submissions by January 1, 2008, in order to ensure full consideration for the next collection.

Further, publications that want to make certain their contributions will be considered for the next edition should make sure to include this anthology on their subscription list. Submissions or subscriptions should be sent to Jason Wilson, The Best American Travel Writing, P.O. Box 260, Haddonfield, NJ 08033.

I really enjoyed working with Susan Orlean on this collection and would like to thank her for choosing the great stories you'll be reading here. I'd also like to thank Will Vincent, among others at Houghton Mifflin.

Finally, I'd like to dedicate this edition to the memory of David Halberstam, who tragically died in an automobile accident just as this book was going into production. You will find his evocative essay "The Boys of Saigon" inside.

JASON WILSON

Introduction

THE SECOND-WORST travel experience I ever had was on a misbegotten trip to a marvelous place that I had gone to for all the wrong reasons. The trip was a few years ago; the place was Bhutan; the reason was love, or what I had mistakenly identified as love, which is probably, technically speaking, the greatest and also the stupidest reason ever to go anywhere. It was not my first time in Bhutan. I had gone there about six months earlier for a story about couples who were attending Bhutanese fertility festivals in hopes of heading home with the ultimate family souvenir. The timing happened to be quite awkward for me — I was writing about happy families fulfilling their dream of having children, but the trip itself, coincidentally, marked the beginning of the end of my marriage. My then-husband had planned to come to Bhutan with me, and we figured a trip somewhere interesting and beautiful might extend the lease on our relationship; instead, I headed off with the fertility group, and he stayed back in New York to start clearing out his half of the apartment. I was pretty blue, but after a few days in Bhutan — where, by the way, most houses are decorated with large, celebratory paintings of penises — I fell madly in love with the tour guide and I started to enjoy the trip a whole lot more. When I returned to New York I was ecstatic. I was convinced that Tshering was my soul mate, notwithstanding the fact that he lived on the other side of the Earth, was somewhat age-inappropriate, and shared with me no cultural, social, intellectual, or religious common ground. Still, I adored him, and I think he adored me, and over the next few months we burned up hundreds of dollars on long-distance phone calls (this was in the pre-Vonage age), planning our future together (doesn't everybody live part-time in Manhattan and part-time in the Himalayas?), trying to figure out how to wangle a visa for him, and reminiscing about every detail of our long (two-week) shared personal history.

Finally, the phone calls didn't feel satisfying enough and Tshering's visa wasn't forthcoming, so I mustered the frequent-flyer miles and the nerve to go back to Bhutan to visit him. My trip itself was a trial: the flight from Bangkok to Bhutan was diverted to Calcutta because of fog or smoke or something, so we were led off the plane, stripped of our passports, and locked in a Grade D Calcutta airport hotel. We weren't allowed to leave the premises because we didn't have visas to enter India, and no one would say when we might hope to get to Bhutan. The owners of the hotel — twin men with what looked like twin wives — doled out skimpy portions of rice for breakfast, lunch, and dinner, and seemed not happy to have us as guests. We had no idea when or how we were going to leave — in fact, we were warned that we were probably going to have to finish the trip over land, a three-day haul via Indian Air Force transport vans, crossing through Assam, which was convulsing with civil war. I was one of only two Americans in the stranded group; the other was a guy who owned a fishing lure company in Minnesota, being flown to Bhutan by the king, who wanted some special flies tied for a spring trout outing.

Finally — probably the hotel was running out of rice and the owners had resolved to get rid of us — our flight was cleared for departure and we made it to Bhutan, and I had what I realize now was the inevitably strained reunion with Tshering. Anyone who has ever fallen in love while traveling — I think it's safe to say it is not a small group — has probably gone through this same jarring experience: the person you so effortlessly and ebulliently connected with while you were traveling requires a little more effort and inspires a little more awkwardness when you see him or her again, and ordinary life intrudes. Tshering and I were fumbling and shy with each other, and I had moments of wondering what on earth I was doing, but what else could we do? We headed off through the ragged gorgeousness of Bhutan, and after a few days the same giddiness we'd felt the first time around started to return. What is it about traveling that inspires that feeling? Is it that when you're with someone and you're not at home, you're in a sort of bubble together, floating through the world, peering out at it together, bound to nothing —jobs, chores, social obligations, dry cleaning that needs to be dropped off — but each other? Is it that when you travel you can invent yourself anew, and the new person you become is freer and more engaged and more engaging than the persona you left at home? And even if you're not in love, is this still what makes travel so seductive — the creation of a new buoyant version of yourself, unpunctured by the familiarity of people who know you and know that you have another self? Whatever it is that makes it feel this way, travel is utterly romantic and the experience of it is the experience of life idealized, and it makes you feel romantic, and romance-able, and this transformation seems more what makes it magical than any particular lovely landscape or fascinating culture you might encounter. Even bad experiences when you travel seem almost mythical — they are bad experiences, but also stories that you will tell around a table sometime later, exotic and fascinating in their badness.

Five days into my trip, Tshering and I arrived in Thimphu, the capital of Bhutan — a town on a mountainside with a scattering of little shops and a paved road or two. It was a Saturday night, as I recall. I thought we might rest a while and then go out for yak tea and some sightseeing. We arrived at the guesthouse, and as I tossed my suitcase on the bed, I noticed that Tshering was lingering in the doorway with an odd look on his face. I asked him why he wasn't coming in, and he finally muttered that he needed to tell me something. He had a girlfriend. And not only did he have a girlfriend, he had a girlfriend whose family owned the guesthouse we were in, and therefore he couldn't be seen with me since . . . well, for all the obvious reasons. He was depositing me in the room and would join me in a day or so. And then he left.

There are always moments during travel when you feel lonely, even when you're traveling with the closest of friends, but those moments are usually subsumed quickly by the moments of delight and fascination and excitement and marvel. This was not one of those moments. I have never, ever felt so profoundly alone. I was in a country where I knew absolutely no one at all except for the jerk who had just ditched me, where I was as far away from home as it was possible to be and still be on Planet Earth; I was in a small country — fewer than a million people — where everyone really and truly knows everyone, where there are practically no strangers and certainly no culture of comfortable stranger-hood, no cafés or pubs where you might unobtrusively spend a day or two people-watching and nursing a cup of coffee. There isn't even any coffee. There weren't any other tourists — Bhutan has always limited its visitors to a thousand or so a year and makes sure they are scattered about, and what's more, I was there during the off-season. I have always winced at the sight of tour buses, but for the first time in my life I really would have welcomed one, and would have been very happy if I could have insinuated myself into a big, loud band of, say, Texans on a tour of Bhutanese souvenir shops . . . anything. Usually when I'm on the road and feeling low, if I can't go to a café, I hole up in my room for a few hours and watch CNN and declare the experience relaxing. This was not an option either: television was, at that time, illegal in Bhutan. Also, there was no Internet. Also, there were very, very few telephones. I didn't have a cell phone that worked in Bhutan, and anyway, it was the middle of the night anywhere I might have called. There was no movie theater, no gym, no shopping to speak of, no diversion to distract me from the profound sense that I was entirely by myself in the whole wide world. In my many years of traveling, I have developed many excellent ways to pass time when I'm bored or a little lonesome. Some are admirable (going to museums and historical sites, talking to local people, exploring neighborhoods) and some are, perhaps, something else (once, when stranded for many days on a story in Mississippi, I spent what seemed like most of my time practicing running on a treadmill with my eyes closed and dyeing my hair different colors). I didn't feel like doing anything useful or edifying and there wasn't much in Thimphu that I could picture as a satisfying time-waster. I thought I might possibly go crazy.

With whatever little energy I still had, I forced myself to leave the guesthouse and walk up and down the little streets. It was early evening. Kids were chasing stray dogs and kicking pebbles; groups of teenage girls, their heads bent together, rushed by whispering and giggling; a small, stout woman with a round-headed baby strapped to her back leaned on a wall and watched me somberly. There was no one, no one, no one to talk to. The few shops nearby were already shuttered except for a small bookstore. A bookstore! Perfect!

I hurried across the street, picturing myself browsing for a few hours until I would be tired enough to go back to the dread guesthouse and sleep. The store was dusty and drafty, with high ceilings and rough wooden floors. The shelves were mostly empty except for English-as-a-second-language manuals, Bhutanese grammar-school textbooks in Dzongkha and Nepali, secondhand Penguin editions of Shakespeare, Indian movie magazines, Buddhist histories. I kept trying to make myself take great interest in pictorials of Bollywood actresses. After a few minutes, I realized that I couldn't even pretend. I gave up, put the magazines back in the rack, nodded my thanks to the storekeeper, and walked out to the street again. It was even emptier, and I was even more aware of my isolation. But somehow, at this point, I gave in to the pure experience of being alone, and while making my way back to the guesthouse I had the distinct sensation of dematerializing. It really was as if I had vanished, become disembodied, and was watching time unspool in front of me, untouched. It was, after I finally yielded to it, kind of fascinating to feel so light and invisible, unnoticed, unremarked upon, unknown.

To make a long story short, I did rematerialize a day later when Tshering sheepishly retrieved me from the guesthouse. By then I had walked every inch of Thimphu, repacked my suitcase, figured Tshering for the cad he was, and determined that my future was probably not going to be as one-half of a Bhutan-Manhattan commuter marriage, but that I would at least make the best of my last few days on the trip, since Bhutan is, truly, the most beautiful place on Earth. I'd also figured out something about the nature of travel. For the first time, it seemed clear to me that travel is not about finding something: it's about getting lost — that is, it is about losing yourself in a place and a moment. The little things that tether you to what's familiar are gone, and you become a conduit through which the sensation of the place is felt. It's nice to see the significant centers of civilization, the important buildings, the monumental landscapes, but what seems most extraordinary is feeling yourself lifted out of your ordinary life into something new. Sometimes, as was the case for me on that trip, there's a little more lift than you're prepared for, and you get that short-of-breath, wide-of-pupil heart skip-thumping that accompanies the powerful feeling that you should have never left home. (I have to confess here that, inveterate traveler that I am, I also feel that before I start a trip, too. As I'm packing I feel myself resisting, resisting, resisting, thinking to myself that I really would prefer staying home, that home is very nice, that I have everything I want at home, that I can just take it easy in my very own living quarters and eat my very own familiar food and have no difficulty using the telephone/getting cash/finding my way around/understanding things, and that this travel business is just a headache.) And yet, I still go, and once I'm on my way I feel like I'm sitting in a Phenomenon-a-tron, where everything is incredibly interesting — the shape of street signs, the clothes people wear, the way things smell. I once took a trip to China with a group of very conservative folks from Utah. They seemed to hate everything about being in China, but most of all they seemed to hate the food, and fortunately (for them) one of the group had brought along several cases of granola bars, which they ate for most of their meals. I was delighted by this, since I got to eat as much of everything as I wanted (not to mention drinking all the beer) while they gnawed on Nature Valley Oats 'N Honey. I wondered — and still wonder — why they had bothered to come at all.

Believe it or not, Tshering and I are still friends. He e-mailed me recently and encouraged me to come visit Bhutan again, which I would love to do. He's married now, and has a daughter, and I'm married and have a son. Our kids are about the same age. I think we'd all enjoy going out together some Saturday night in Thimphu.

But enough about me. The reason I have your attention and the chance to spin my own yarns here is because I have been invited to take the ultimate armchair journey over the last several months, which entailed reading a hundred or so wonderful pieces about other people's travels and choosing the twenty that would make up this book. I read most of them during a long, cold, wet, late, lingering winter, so those of you who wrote about temperate climates, thank you. Each year a different person takes this armchair journey, and I'm sure all of us have different reasons for our choices. My rules were very uncomplicated: one, the stories had to take place somewhere in the physical world, and two, I had to like them a lot. As far as the first rule, I wouldn't even say I adhered strictly to it, since at least one of these pieces takes place in the imaginary world. I am just not a category person, so I had very loose standards for what constituted a travel piece. Description of an interesting place was a plus, but not a necessity; movement from A to B was typical but not required; immersion in an unfamiliar culture was impressive but not sufficient. I have a soft spot for pieces that illuminate places that would never make it into *Luxury SpaFinder* magazine, and for writers who really can make you feel like they saw something with fresh eyes and were truly surprised and interested in what they saw. The best travel writing, in my mind, is just a written document of a conversation with a captivating person who is just a little braver, a little smarter, a little more observant, a little funnier, and a little wiser than I, who has gone places I've either never gone and never will go, or places I've been to many times and never noticed quite the way he or she does, or can talk about the process of going and coming in a way I never imagined before. I'm happy to report that I think all twenty of these pieces have that in common. Otherwise, they are literally and figuratively all over the map.

Travel writing, long ago, didn't have to be much more than a dispatch from the outer reaches; travel writers were the people willing to go to scary places, and what made their work exceptional was the fact that they went there at all. These days, there's nowhere in the world that you can't visit on Google Maps, so the travel writer as explorer is an outdated notion. And yet I still think travel writing matters. Its value now is something much deeper — it's the writer's journey, and the emotional and intellectual weight of the writer's observations, that means something. In a way, these are the exact opposite of the travel you might do on Google Maps — these stories are the world not as it can be plotted by satellite but as it is observed and mediated in a very subjective and personal way. I'm glad for the chance to see the exact layout of Brisbane, Australia, as seen from outer space (the image that has just popped up on my computer's streaming map gadget), but I'm happier to read about Ian Frazier's hilariously bad kielbasa and Reesa Grushka's exquisite and sad stay in Jerusalem and Nando Parrado's unimaginable endurance, even though the satellite map is more comprehensive and more "perfect" and even allows me to zoom in and count the hairs on the chin of the guy sitting on the park bench in the middle of Brisbane. Such details are probably useful sometimes (if you're, say, thinking of opening a barbershop in Brisbane), but they don't have the same power to feed your soul.

Between the time I started writing this introduction and today, when I'm finishing it, a terrible thing happened — David Halberstam, whose beautiful piece "The Boys of Saigon" is included here, was killed in a car accident. He was a great writer, a brilliant reporter, an intrepid traveler. He was one of those writers who fed the soul. When I first read his piece — a memoir from his time in Vietnam — I was struck by how long and exceptional his career had been, and was marveling that he was at work on another book. I was excited to include a piece by a true master of the form in this collection. I didn't know Halberstam personally, but he was a real inspiration to me, and I was heartsick to hear this news. It's a huge loss.

I hope you enjoy the ride through this book. It was a great treat to put it together, and a particularly vicarious pleasure, since I travel a lot less these days now that I have a small person to take care of. Which brings me to one last comment: you now know the second-worst travel experience I ever had. The *very* worst one would have to be any trip I didn't take for one reason or another — sloth, lack of time, lack of imagination, inadequate luggage, whatever. That's why travel writing is so marvelous: now, through these pieces, I've been able to take these trips instead.

Susan Orlean

The Best American Travel Writing 2007

JASON ANTHONY

A Brief and Awkward Tour of the End of the Earth

FROM *WorldHum.com*

A man who's warm cannot understand a man who's freezing.
— Alexander Solzhenitsyn, *One Day in the Life of Ivan Denisovich*

AS I BOARDED A FLIGHT to Vostok Station, Antarctica, to deliver a dozen Russian men, some fuel, and two tons of frozen home fries, I found myself in an ethical crisis: Was it right for me to go? I worked at the time as a fuels operator, part of a crew that managed several million gallons of aviation diesel at McMurdo Station, the hub of the United States Antarctic Program, located twenty-four hundred miles south of New Zealand on Ross Island. We fueled McMurdo's helicopters and planes, we drove fuel trucks, and sometimes ran temporary fueling systems in remote camps. On this trip, I was to help with the transfer of much-needed fuel from the LC-130 Hercules into Vostok's near-empty tanks.

On board, but still on the ground in McMurdo, I was told by our Air National Guard loadmaster that the mission was for cargo only, and would offload no fuel. Here I suffered my brief ethical quandary: should I jump off the plane and go back to work in town, and so miss out on a very rare chance to see Vostok?

The loadmaster solved the crisis for me when, over the growing roar of the turboprop engines, he shouted a request: "We won't deliver any fuel, but there's a chance we'll want you to help us take fuel from the Russians!" I looked at him as if he had told me he hoped to squeeze blood from a snowball. This crew was new to the Antarctic, and they were unclear on the situation at Vostok. Though I explained to him that we had neither the hardware nor the desire to suck up the dregs of Vostok's dirty tanks, and that the Russians couldn't afford to give it away, he remained unconvinced. He was the confused messenger for a confused message. Sensing my opportunity, I decided my duty lay in preventing the aircrew from damaging their engines with (unavailable) bad fuel. Nodding to the loadmaster, I quickly sat down, put in my earplugs, and buckled up for my little adventure.

So this trip was a lark right from the start, but a lark to a place that few humans have seen. It's a trip I would lie to take.

A small research base huddled against the flat white icescape of the East Antarctic ice cap, Vostok is the farthest terrestrial outpost of an impoverished Russian empire. Occupied since 1957, Vostok is also the most isolated of Antarctic bases. Its few old buildings sit in the middle of the godforsaken polar plateau, near the South Geomagnetic Pole, at an elevation of 11,220 feet. It is as far away from the familiar you can go without leaving the planet.

Vostok ("East") is also officially the coldest place on Earth, once reaching a ghastly winter temperature of −129°F. Even now, just past midsummer, −20°F would be a heat wave. Two dozen men work in the cold here each summer, while only a dozen stay for the brutal winter. Still bridging the gap between the old wood-and-canvas "heroic age" of Antarctic exploration and the digital age of modern occupation, the Russians at bitter Vostok contend with conditions long forgotten by other Antarctic workers.

No one visits Vostok. It doesn't exist in the world traveler's currency of *guess-where-I-went.* The odds that someone will find their way there to see it on their own are infinitesimal. No one will stumble onto this weathered colony or follow a guidebook to its doorstep.

Even for U.S. Antarctic regulars, awe is always part of a conversation about Vostok. Our rare glimpses of bearded, hard-worn Russian personnel and the rumors of their working conditions remind us of how easy our own jobs are. For USAP workers, most of whom live in comfy McMurdo, Vostok is synonymous with pain and suffering. For us, it's a mysterious, daunting place that commands our respect.

Buckled into our paratrooper-type webbing benches, we jostled and lurched sideways as the Herc slid down the skiway — a runway for planes on skis — and lifted off. Each bench faced the other, with a line of cargo pallets running down the middle of the fuselage. The mostly silent mix of U.S. and Russian personnel either sloughed off their parkas or sunk into them with their eyes closed.

Every Antarctic flight is like this, each person isolated by the roar of the engines and the earplugs we use to shut it out. Hercs have only a few small portholes on each side of the fuselage, behind the benches. Because the plane is dark and the view is blinding, these are nearly useless. After leveling off, we take turns drifting back to the larger square windows in the rear exit doors.

Most of our guests seemed to be asleep by the time the Herc rose over the Transantarctic Mountains into East Antarctica. Vostok's winter station manager, however, kept his eyes open, staring at the pale-green insulation across the military fuselage. His responsibility for the next year was to keep all twelve men safe and sane. Soon we were droning across an ice sheet the size of China.

Some of the stark Russian faces reminded me of American Civil War portraits staring out from sepia photos. Carved and rugged, dark and impassive: and these were the men who had not yet spent their year on the ice. Then again, the lines on their faces may have been from jet lag. They flew from St. Petersburg to Amsterdam to Singapore to Sydney to Christchurch to McMurdo on an epic one-way ticket.

Over the white emptiness, we veered across Antarctica's bent tapestry of tightly packed lines of longitude. For three hours of our months-long summer day, time zones passed beneath us like crevasses. Imagine flying from Boston to Chicago and seeing nothing but whiteness out the window until suddenly, out of the snowy expanse, a small speck appears, like a distant dark raft.

Vostok looks to the approaching eye like a small broken blister on the ice cap's alabaster skin. Mostly submerged by forty years of accumulating snow, the station (several old small buildings — McMurdo has one hundred) is not a showpiece. Scattered broken-down equipment reminded me of junk-filled yards in rural America. Vostok, the earnest product of an intellectual nation, has the hollow look of poverty.

We landed, on the hard snow of the plateau. Our flight had launched in the balmy 30°F of sea-level McMurdo but landed in Vostok's two-mile-high −30°F. We'd climbed up to the jet stream and only come partway down, as if we'd ascended to a strange life in the clouds. Around the skiway was perfect whiteness, under a perfect blue bell jar of sky. Breaking up the emptiness were an immense radio tower and a "BOCTOK" sign at its foot. Each seven-foot-high Cyrillic letter (red, of course) stood alone, like the Hollywood sign.

The wonder I felt on arrival was interrupted, as it always is in the Antarctic hinterlands, by the noisy, stinky, busy work we do behind the Herc's turboprops. The engines would continue to spin during our entire visit, spewing vaporized aviation diesel and keeping their gaskets warm. We pushed the cargo pallets by hand off the end of the plane's loading platform, because Vostok's forklift had broken down. Their thirty-year-old snowmobile began to ferry loads to the base.

The snow beneath us was like light cement. In central Antarctica, zero humidity, deep cold, little accumulation, and steady winds create tiny snow grains and ice crystals that sinter into an airy white pavement. You can just as easily land a plane on it as cut it with a saw.

One man, just off the plane, with nothing before him but the fringe of the half-buried outpost, pulled off his hat, pulled out a pocket mirror, and checked his mussed black hair. I was reminded of Sir Ernest Shackleton's *Endurance* journey, in which Shackleton, Crean, and Worsley, having arrived at Stromness whaling station after seventeen horrendous months, began to fuss with haggard soot-caked hair and ragged clothes. Their concern, however, was that there might be women: here at Vostok, this was unlikely. Women have on rare occasion done summer science here, but no woman has ever wintered at this small male-only plywood space station.

Wintering in central Antarctica is hardship duty *in extremis.* There is no way out. People can fall apart, with small irritations sometimes mutating into seething disputes. Some winters at America's relatively comfortable South Pole station have ended with a once-joyful community split into enraged factions. And within the thinner walls and deeper cold of a Vostok winter, one of Antarctica's most notorious events took place: a disputed chess game that ended in an ax murder.

Once I'd been assured that the Herc crew wasn't going to try to take fuel, I set off over the white rise — years of plowed-out snow

— toward the station. The visible exteriors of the station buildings were sun-bleached and rusting. Slumped-over tracked vehicles littered the outskirts.

Wearing the USAP parka is like wearing a sleeping bag, but at −30°F, it's helpful. I would have left it in the plane, but it made walking the long path between skiway and base more comfy. On that walk, noisy Herc behind and Russian unknown ahead, I was able to briefly tune in to the immense silence of the continent. I can only compare it to walking over a frozen Atlantic Ocean. Until you've lived at length in the white abstraction of central Antarctica, it's hard not to feel the weight of the frigid expanse crowding in on you. I can't say that Vostok felt more isolated than other camps — one raft in the ocean feels like any other — but the tenuous barrier this facility maintains against the cold unsettles the American mind.

Pushing through heavy wooden doors into the small dark common room of the main building, I stepped into another world. Vostok's residents were gathered around an old billiards table, smoking their raw Russian cigarettes and talking quietly. They sat in a dense smoke that had years ago seeped into cracks in the balls and left a stain the color of sunburned grass.

Murmured Russian syllables followed me into the empty dining room. Spare and plain, the room was clearly Vostok's heart, a repository of old culture and simple food. Years of smoke and grease had browned the high pale-yellow ceiling. Much of the paint on the yellow walls had long ago flaked off, and beneath it an older icy blue spread like frost, as if the snow outside the windows had seeped through.

A mound of boiled eggs glistened in a large bowl like dabs of white paint. Withered window box plants stood silhouetted against the snow. In the dusty light, half a dozen scuffed dark tables held slabs of black bread, a brick of yellow butter, and a plate of sliced pink salami. On the sideboard, a massive cutting board and heavy cleaver wore the deep scars of years: the labor, hunger, anger, and celebrations of men living difficult, cloistered lives. I'd walked into a Russian still life that seemed to breathe in its dark frame.

A transient, I was still bundled up in my parka as I shuffled between the modest invitations of the dining tables. Camera in hand, I was on the prowl for images. The strangeness of entering another culture in central Antarctica was almost dreamlike. How could I walk in from the palpable center of nowhere and find a stained wooden kitchen extracted from the pages of Solzhenitsyn?

The cook, with a blue and white broad-striped shirt and a broader smile, walked in from the kitchen to offer me tea. His arms were open, with a cup held in one hand. To this day, I wish I had accepted.

"Tea, for you?" he said (I think), in Russian.

"No, no, I'm just — I'm looking around. I — no, thank you," I said, lost in my thoughts.

A shrug and another smile said: "As you wish."

He was the only Russian at the camp I spoke with, and it lasted just these few seconds. He gestured to me, and I paused in my bustling exploration — so much to see, a mental map to make — to consider his kindness. Then, to my regret, I declined, so I could spend my last twenty minutes outside where there was enough light to take bleak photos of their industrial graveyard. I wanted to frame Vostok's strangeness, as if I was the empty Antarctic.

And maybe I was. What was this trip? Not work, certainly, and scarcely travel. It was motion without emotion. As I look back, I remember my big red parka as a bubble of self-absorption. My thoughts and experience of Vostok were all exterior. I had found my way to one of the rarer places in the world, but didn't have the insight to take off my coat, sit down, and talk? Pathetic.

As proof of my disconnect, the photographs I took of Vostok are dismal — blurry, fragmented, and boring. One exception is an abstract of the BOCTOK sign seen through a window of the plane, taken on arrival, before I'd replaced awe with an intellectual hobby.

Soon it was time to go. I loaded up silently with the departing Russians as they began their ascent into the warm latitudes. None of them had complaints. Vostok is a place of hardship, but it's also a landscape of their choosing. Like many of us, many of them return to the ice again and again. We all go to the trouble of returning to the Antarctic out of some strange love for the human experience of this inhuman landscape. These exhausted Russians on board the Herc with me, heading north, formed a community that I had not touched. While flying back to McMurdo, my camera stayed in its case on my insulated lap.

Even as I clicked off my roll of film at Vostok, I realized I should instead have sat with their friendly cook to sip some tea, eat an egg, and slab some butter onto the local dark bread. I tried to see this strange place from the outside rather than taking the time to taste it. That was bad traveling. I bypassed Vostok, Russia, and the warm human thread stretched thin between them. I wish very much that I could go back and do it right. But even this wish is a tourist's wish.

RICK BASS

Lost in Space

FROM THE *Los Angeles Times Magazine*

IT KEEPS MOVING, but when I was a child growing up on the outskirts of Houston I believed that it was already all gone, that I had just missed it, the West, by only a single generation, or at the most two — as maybe every generation believes it has just missed the West.

Perhaps not just heat-washed clodhopper farm boys standing discontented hoe-side in gypsum-strangled Utah, or wildcatters dreaming fevered uranium dreams or visions of oil-laden anticlines like sugarplums, but maybe residents of all centuries have stood on a mesa and wondered at a farther, deeper wildness — over the next range of mountains, if not also further back in time. And even then, might they have understood or intuited that their place in that time, believed to be enduring, would in fact prove to be far more prone to disintegration than the physical elements of mountains, forest, plains?

In Cormac McCarthy's novel *No Country for Old Men*, the protagonist, an aging sheriff along the Texas-Mexico border watching his county turn into a drug fiefdom, says, "These old people I talk to, if you could of told em that there would be people on the streets of our Texas towns with green hair and bones in their noses speakin a language they couldnt even understand, well, they just flat out wouldnt of believed you. But what if you'd of told em it was their own grandchildren?"

We can feel it moving now, sliding away; and yet even in its diminishment it is still somehow fiercely present.

(A caveat: I am still, despite my knowing better, dreaming only the Anglo dream of the West. What are the dreams in Indian country, and of Latinos? What dreams do Tibetan and Thai émigrés bring, and Russian orthodoxy, and first- and second-generation Chinese Americans?)

It's a long way from San Diego to Denver, from Seattle to Albuquerque, and yet there remain some undeniable if intangible threads unifying Westerners. A hundred and forty years ago, Major John Wesley Powell, the one-armed Civil War veteran who explored the Grand Canyon and much of the rest of the West, said the unifying thread was water, or the absence of it, and for sure that was, and largely is, one of the major physical threads. But there is something else too, some unseen thread of spirit.

Perhaps it's best not to pick or pluck at that thread too closely — perhaps what we perceive as spirit in the West is really only something as heartless and lifeless as geology, with the rock outcroppings of the East being some several million years older, so that the half-life decay of sun-burnished ions in the West seems still to radiate a bracing and at times intoxicating freshness, able still to be felt and noticed if not yet measured by even a species as insensate and oblivious as our own. Perhaps science will one day ultimately be found to be at the heart of religion, or faith — as almost everything, it seems, is eventually discovered or named or measured or otherwise colonized — but for now, no such explanation or discovery exists, only the inexplicable awareness that there is a difference between the West and rest of the country, and that it is no less profound for its ungraspable immeasurability.

So powerful can be this bond between Westerners and landscape that it's possible to believe that the West might have existed in our brainpans long before the first paleface ever dreamed of conquest, possession, and of that shadowed and seemingly illogical and inconsistent paradox, freedom. As human culture in the Deep South and East is stacked in vertical layers of time, like geological strata, perhaps the building blocks of the West, particularly today's West, the New West, are composed of chunks of physical space — basin and range, sunlight, boulder, forest, river, desert — possessing more of a horizontal breadth.

To say it was always in motion would be conjecture. What can be said confidently is that it is moving now — moving with such alacrity, like an animal getting up from a daybed and traveling for a while, that almost anyone can see it, and that even in those places where we cannot see it, we can sense its movement, its possible going-away or leave-taking, and we are made uneasy by it, even as we are still, at this late date, yet unable to name or measure that going-awayness, that freshness and wildness, that Westernness.

Certainly in 1960s Texas it was going away like a horrific backwash. Each Sunday on our way to church my family would pass the informally named Wolf Corner, where I would lean forward in my seat to see the corner fence post where ranchers had hung that week's bounty, the little coyotes and the larger red wolves, by their heels, for all the honest world to see. It was out by Highway 6, which was once gently waving grassland — it's blanketed now with dazzling superstores, an eight-lane highway, the vertical glittering skyscrapers reflecting the hot Houston sun in myriad directions, like the light envisioned perhaps by the prophets who beheld in their own exalted dreams the streets of heaven (assuming they were not holding the wrong end of the spyglass and witnessing instead the oppositional alternative territory described by those same prophecies). But back then it was only sweet balming tall-grass prairie, yielding weekly its grisly bounty — the little wolves' legs fractured and bloodstained from where they had gnawed for hours or even days at the traps' grip, some of the wolves and coyotes stiffened and sun-dried, hanging like loose shingles after a storm, and others, newly killed, still limp and soft, like sheaves of tobacco hanging in some deathly curing house.

Always, there was something there, placed partly as warning and partly as triumphant victory-show, a marker of how the war against — what? obsolescence, frailty, insignificance, loss? — was faring. Some weeks there were more carcasses than others, and over the years the offerings gradually declined, though almost always there would be at least one, as if the ranchers were trawling the grassy sea, and as if their nets would always find something, some wildness deep within that green grass. As if that country to the west — just beyond the barbed-wire corner fence post — would slow, but never entirely cease, in giving the wolves up.

This was the dailiness and drama of my childhood, situated peculiarly between the Deep South and the far West, in oil-hungry, oil-rich, brash and arrogant and violence-born Anglo Texas. The vertical strata of time mattered, but the story, the myth, of the westering frontier was also present, just over the horizon. There was not just the echo of it, there was still, barely, the real and physical essence of it; we saw it, every Sunday. In those first few years of the 1960s, while the rest of the country — the Southeast, the Northeast, and Los Angeles in particular — stewed and broiled over civil rights issues, we were attending the premieres of movies like *How the West Was Won* and *The Alamo*, in which — not to sound too much like a bleeding-heart liberal — vast territory existed for the taking and, quite naturally, force was the way to take it, particularly since it was inhabited by Mexicans or Indians. Let Mississippi stew over drinking fountains, and Boston and New York argue over segregated schools and busing; in Texas, we were busy looking longingly to the past, and to the West.

Hard country, sometimes. Or once it was, before we set about breaking it, then crushing it. It's an accepted law of biology that in a harsh or austere physical environment, species will often develop elaborate and highly specialized adaptations that allow them to inhabit the various demanding niches in that environment, and thus it is that in a stonier, more arid landscape, one shaped alternately by glaciers, volcanoes, earthquakes, and forest fires, a magnificent and amazing array of creatures evolved to fit that continuous scroll of disturbance, to fit that Big Story of the West. Nimble-footed snow-white goats cling with utter improbability to the sides of steep mountains, and eight-hundred-pound grizzly bears eat butterflies, ladybugs, and lilies, and sleep underground for five months of the year. Golden eagles glide with seven-foot wingspans, and all-seeing condors soar with spans of nine feet.

And upon a landscape dominated by such dramatic disturbance events, which result in the release of stored vegetative energy in wild all-or-nothing amplitudes, magnificent stories of the ultimate prosperity, that of long-term survival, are also created. The myth, the holy grail, of life is *sustainability*, a word so oft-used and malleable as to lose all currency, and yet a word that lingers nonetheless, like a fever or a hope lodged always within us, though buried and forgotten, replaced instead with another word, *tomorrow.*

How much of the West, then — as defined by those things that are found only here — can we retain, and how should we go about it? Too often, still, such discussions have not yet seriously begun. Instead, we mostly just squabble. We scrap over the last crumbs of resources like little boys tussling in a schoolyard, perpetuating the cycle of belligerence and anger and arrogance that is white Westerners' birthright. It's the story of how we got here. Other than the true natives, or, as they're called in Canada, the First Nations people, we all came here from somewhere else: from Spain, looking for gold, or from New England, looking for furs or gold or for more open space, or from anywhere, looking for anything, and as often as not finding it — managing, somehow, to find whatever we had come searching for, finding our heart's desire. Nor were the answers to those desires limited to material things. Sojourners arriving in the West came searching for a new start and freedom — religious and otherwise — or, most nebulous of all, adventure and happiness. Sometimes they came hoping for a better relationship with others; in many instances, they were fleeing unsatisfactory ones, so that part of the West's early destiny was that of emotional refuge, as well as reservoir of hope and opportunity, and physical bounty house.

With the white West's birthright then being established, the course of future expectations was set, with the bell curve of sustainability barely yet beginning its ascent: so much to see, so much to take, so much to receive. Everywhere the eye fell, there was bounty for the taking — sometimes by force, with superior technology, though other times uncontested — and beyond those places where the eye fell, there was imagination.

It was, above all else, a deeply physical place. The heightened delight of the five senses engaged and nurtured a sixth sense, and rather than call it extrasensory perception or imagination, call it perhaps simply *spirit*; and it was a spirit at times as robust and dramatic and at other times as subdued or suspended as the amplitudes of the land itself. As if in a new garden of Eden — or the first garden of Eden, as if that long-ago story had not been history but prophecy, and now, finally, we had arrived — we spilled out onto a landscape the geology of which was still so new that it was as if some gardener had just turned over the earth and stones with a spade and then stepped away for a moment, the new-turned earth still so freshly made or dug that it had not yet begun to gray with aridity or oxidation, and was even still exuding that loamy scent of clarity, pungency, sharpness.

It took me a few tries to land in the West, or the farther, further West — the land lying beyond Fort Worth, where I was born, and the oil-field prairie of Odessa, where I lived in infancy, and the surreal sprawling petrochemical-clotted superstructure of Houston. I studied wildlife science in northern Utah, at Utah State University, then changed my major to geology (after an illuminating internship with the timber giant Weyerhaeuser during which I realized how desk-bound and paper-ridden my boss, a wildlife biologist, was). I got a job in the Southeast — drawn back there as if by some hard-to-escape tide — but then managed to scrabble my way back west, where I fell in love at first sight with the soft muscled humps of the blue-green hills here, the Appalachian-like folds on the U.S.-Canadian border, in the southern terminus of the Purcell Mountains, one of the largest mountain ranges in Canada and the only place where that range comes down into the United States.

The name of the blue-green valley, the garden, into which I fell was the Yaak, a Kootenai word for arrow, named for the way the rushing river in that valley's center charges down out of the mountains to enter the bowed arc of the much larger Kootenai River. The valley lies in a unique and magical seam between the maritime weather influences of the Pacific Northwest — old forests, drippy dark dank mossy fungal rot emerald earth-soak — and those of the Rocky Mountains, with their blazing hot rocky glaciated uplifted spines rising from a land sculpted (and so recently) not just by rot, but by fire and ice. The Yaak, nestled in this cleft between two lands, was, and is, its own place, with its own essence, character, spirit.

I had been in wild country before, not just in the West, but around the world, and yet the Yaak's wildness felt unique to me, substantial, and almost tangible — so much so as to be nearly visible, like the luminous silver-blue rivers of fog that filled the canyons following a cold night rain on sun-warmed earth; so much fog and mist-tatter shrouding the smoothed animal shapes of those mountains, and then revealing them, that always things seemed to be on the move here. And I began, slowly, to think about such things — to imagine what might be the causes for such things — as the root of spirit, as if it were, after all, the unique revelation created by a certain confluence of physical possibilities, as if there might for each landscape, and each moment upon that landscape, be a wavering, pulsing spirit, exuded like breath. Nor would such a confluence be limited to the physicality of the five senses. Instead, it would incorporate the unseen or intangibles — imagination, and history — in such a way as to always be slightly changing, like fog roiling up a series of ravines, and yet always recognizable as belonging to that one place.

There was, and is, a density of spirit in my valley, which I began to envision as being composed, like the strands in a braided rope, of any number of much smaller strands — the relationship between pileated woodpeckers and the centuries-old larch trees in which they hammer out their cavities, the unique microrhizae in the soil beneath those giant larches, microrhizae acting as catalysts in some yet unknown grand soil-building recipe that helps nurture and sustain the old forests, with the woodpeckers' furious chipping-away somehow contributing to that tiny-yet-huge, or tiny-yet-miraculous, recipe . . .

Everywhere I looked, inhaled, listened, touched, there were thousands of such tiny connections, which in turn were connected to one another in an at times phantasmagoric array of radial cross-braidings, more mind-boggling (and dynamic) than any similar but finite array of coaxial or fiber-optic construct. Because of this valley's unique position in the world, curiously caught between at least three different other worlds, there were more species and more relationships than anywhere else in Montana, and, unlike any other valley, any other place, in the continental United States, nothing was known to have quite yet gone extinct here — or not since the last Ice Age. Many of the valley's species were now down to single- or double-digit populations: perhaps a dozen grizzly bears, five or six wolves, a dozen mated pair of bull trout, a handful of lynx and wolverine, an unknown number of Coeur d'Alene salamanders, and even a lone occasional woodland caribou, down from Canada — just barely two of everything, as if upon some reverse kind of Noah's Ark — but even in their diminished representation they were still fully present, still in the here and now, rather than dwelling in some dusty corner of dim memory history-book fade-away.

Here in the Yaak, I was free — one of only about 150 residents in a valley that, counting all the land lying between the Kootenai River and Canada, totals roughly a million acres — to wander the forests and think about such things. It was different from Houston, where such connections had not been visible, and where such pulses had not been felt. Houston had once been the West, but then the West had moved on, drifting, almost as if restless, or searching, seeking its own fit, across the landscape west of the Mississippi. Not separate from that landscape — indeed, formed by it, and being re-formed, slightly, each day, each century — but still, always, in motion.

It would be the grossest of stereotypes to suggest that, given two ways of thinking — as an Eastern industrialist, or as a Western agrarian — two or more different cultural and, ultimately, even religious types might develop, even within the same unified country; to suggest that a yeoman farmer or rancher, arising well before daylight and toiling sweat-browed throughout the long day before crashing into mindless slumber shortly after dark, whenever the season's darkness found him or her, might somehow possess or develop a work ethic more fulsome than that of the lathe operator or conveyor belt technician who watches upright steel cans or glass bottles trundle past in unending phalanx. It would be folly to say that an American Easterner — for purposes of easy contrast — might be more acculturated to producing a soulless product or creation, while some American Westerners might be more acculturated to producing a product (I use the word ironically) that, if not possessing a soul, is more likely to carry the spirit of a living thing, in the organic tradition. In any developed culture of mankind, there have probably always been genes, differences, for city rats and country mice, regardless of whatever physical barrier — a river, a ridge — separated them north and south or east and west. And any of us can imagine or might even have known any number of investment bankers, industrialists, entrepreneurs, and so forth, whose relentless work habits would make the feeding frenzy of sharks seem tame and moderate, while it is just as easy to imagine the gentle noonday slumber of the pastoralist, crookstaff laid across his or her knee as the fatted flock grazes across the endless summer-green pasture beyond, converting the sun's benevolence into free cash, the bounty not of human cunning or ingenuity, nor backbreaking labor, but extracted merely and directly — a gift — from the land . . .

These easy distinctions or false or at least highly permeable borders cannot hold or explain any difference between the West and the rest of this country — all types have always inhabited all regions

— and yet the mind, almost as if under force of myth, is pulled toward an exploration of these themes. And so might there be some faint element of truth in them, or the echo of a once-upon-a-time truth? Both types, industrialist or rancher, automotive assembly worker or logger, would surely have to rely upon or at least have a relationship with mercy, though it's possible that the laborer or captain of industry might believe that he or she could have a slight edge over fate's twists and fortunes via the relatively more predictable behavior of machines versus the vagaries of weather — and from that difference, might a general kind of Westernness develop?

In some ways such a notion is not dissimilar from the idea that "prairie populism" developed first in the agrarian Midwest, and then edged westward, as a direct response to the repeated ass-kickings wrought by angry weather upon the physical lives that sought to cling to a physical land, as did the usual sects, cults, and fundamentalist religiosities that traditionally develop in any culture during hard times — war, famine, pestilence, social and/or economic upheavals — the human comfort found in a hasty retreat to the perceived security of rigid and predictable rules, borders, mores, with (or so goes the philosophy) a commensurate and predictable covenant established between adherence and outcome.

Even for those who did not engage directly in the hands-on extracting of raw materials from the seemingly endless landscape, those extractive occupations were once powerful in the Old West, culturally as well as economically, and would have exerted due influence upon the developing culture of the white Westerners. Again, looking at Texas as one of the early portals into the West — what historian William Goetzmann has termed not just the real and physical West, nor solely the cultural West, but also "the West of the Imagination" — one can find fairly easy clues to what the Old West was, if not yet a full fix on what the New West might be. Legendary Texas historian T. R. Fehrenbach has noted that the republic of Texas had more running wars along its borders, and for a longer period of time, than most other nations in history. In Texas — amid that blood-gotten and blood-held territory or ownership — land, rather than knowledge, was seen as the source of all wealth.

The Old West has been dying more quickly in some places than in others, and for a long time people have been guessing about what will replace it. To say that, like democracy itself, it is a grand experiment in progress is a bit of a cliché, and yet it does speak of a hopefulness that the experiment will continue. The subject of the experiment might be said to be the land, its spirit, our own spirits, and — perhaps closer to the bone here, and to the naming of Westernness — the intersection of not just ourselves with that land, but of our spirits with the land's, so that a made and organic, shifting thing — a third thing or spirit — is formed from that confluence and held in somewhat steady if dynamic equilibrium, like a trout holding its position in the oscillating currents of a quickening stream. If this is the case for Westernness, then as long as the land remains relatively unchanged, such confluence should always yield a product somehow identifiable as Westernness.

What do Seattle residents have in common, then, with those of Denver, of San Francisco, of Salt Lake City, of Libby, Montana? Those five cities, to name any, each possess a specific flavor and identity — indeed, anyone familiar with them would know where he or she was in an instant, upon returning to them — and yet despite their differences, they all feel Western. Despite the landscape's great diversity — old-growth cedar cathedrals, dazzling playas, grassland, rolling hills, Joshua tree deserts, serrated mountains and glaciers — there is, always, among its residents, an attachment to the land. More often these days it is a visual rather than physical attachment, such as the shining blue bay and eucalyptus shimmer rising from the hills around San Francisco, though these visual attachments still engage the other senses as well: the salt-and-fish-and-fog odor, the bay breezes against the skin, the sparrows in the wild rosemary hedges along the sidewalks . . .

The list of sensory attachments could go on and on: Las Vegas defined by its magnificent and overpowering, almost hallucinogenic aridity, Billings with its red rock bluff circumscribing the basin of the town below, Santa Fe with its strange sweet light and piñon essence. The malls are devouring Phoenix-Tempe and even the saguaro stronghold of Tucson — perhaps they will one day soon fall from Western grace, the edges fraying and deteriorating into nothing but mall-land, as Houston fell long ago, and Los

Angeles still longer ago — but surely, still, will not the center always hold?

Many of the West's communities these days are engaged in a land rush to protect, rather than despoil, the open spaces and natural resources that help give the West its identity, and its economic as well as ecological value. A popular report by the nonprofit Sonoran Institute, "Prosperity in the 21st Century West: The Role of Protected Public Lands," cites researchers J. M. Shumway and S. M. Otterstrom, who "found that the greatest number of new migrants to the West are in what they call 'New West' counties, characterized by their recreational nature, scenic amenities, proximity to national parks or other federal lands, and a preponderance of service-based economies. They concluded that in the New West, the importance of mineral, cattle, and lumber production is dwarfed by an economy that is now based on 'a new paradigm of the amenity region, which creates increased demands for amenity space, residential and recreational property, second homes, and environmental protection.'"

If open space remains the breath of the West, then the roadless backcountry, the wilderness, remains the burning spirit within that breath. Never mind that in all of the West — certainly in all of the Lower 48 — there remain only a few places where you can find yourself more than twelve miles from a road, most probably in the contiguous complexes of wilderness acreage in Idaho, California, Montana. A good Brownie or Cub Scout can hike our wildest country in but a day or two. And of the great continental tableau of wildness that was once all of our birthright, and particularly Westerners', only 2 percent of the land west of the Mississippi is protected wilderness. Two percent! As Will Rogers said of land, "They ain't makin' any more of it." Or as the great Western historian and novelist Wallace Stegner wrote so famously in his 1960 "Wilderness Letter":

"Something will have gone out of us as a people if we ever let the remaining wilderness be destroyed; if we permit the last virgin forests to be turned into comic books and plastic cigarette cases; if we drive the few remaining members of the wild species into zoos or to extinction; if we pollute the last clear air and dirty the last clean streams and push our paved roads through the last of the silence, so that never again will Americans be free in their own country from the noise, the exhausts, the stinks of human and automotive waste . . . We need wilderness preserved — as much of it as is still left, and as many kinds — because it was the challenge against which our character as a people was formed. The reminder and the reassurance that it is still there is good for our spiritual health even if we never once in ten years set foot in it. It is good for us when we are young, because of the incomparable sanity it can bring briefly, as vacation and rest, into our insane lives. It is important to us when we are old simply because it is there — important, that is, simply as an idea."

Economists as well as environmentalists have taken to calling these last roadless lands the "Capital of the New West" — not in the sense of financial capital, but rather the seat of political power. How ironic that the thing of which we once possessed the most, the big blank spots on the map, open space and wilderness, sometimes overlaid with a brief furze of timber, or a thin hammered patina of precious metals, or dollops of oil here and there, or flecks of coal studding it in one place or another, or with the bright rushing shafts of clear cold trout-water charging straight down from out of the mountains like an arrow — the excess, the bounty, that we bartered or all but gave away to the industrial East, usually receiving in those barters but a handful of trinkets or coins — might yet still be present in sufficient quantity and distribution to allow us to retain or even regain an identity that very nearly was lost entirely.

Recognizing the ecological value of these last roadless areas on the public lands — some 58.5 million acres in thirty-nine states, though with most of the acreage in the West — the Clinton administration, under the direction of then–U.S. Forest Service Chief Mike Dombeck, spent years receiving input and holding public meetings before crafting a rule that would protect them from logging and road building, though in his first week of office, the new chief executive, George W. Bush, suspended the rule, claiming, among other things, that the two million comments received and the six-hundred-plus public meetings held were insufficient public involvement, and then, without even a single public meeting, decided to turn the decision-making recommendations for these federal lands over to the states, and not just to states, but to one person in each state, the governor — with the White House still being able to veto those recommendations if it disagreed. As if one hundred or more years had never passed, and no lessons had ever been learned; as if the West still existed as but a fiefdom for the corporate and godlike dictum of the East. The Bush administration figuring, perhaps, that given the Republican skew of governors during that four-year cycle of such things (such men and women but a blink in the geological span that involved the creation of these pristine lands, and their forests and prairies, their red deserts and mesas), the good governors would readily hand over those public lands to the corporate liquidators.

Funny things began to happen, however. Republican governors such as Arnold Schwarzenegger came out in full support of the old Clinton-era model — protect all of the public's roadless lands, the last of the last — while pro-Bush states such as Montana replaced Republican governors with Democrats. State leaders in California, Oregon, Washington, New Mexico, Maine, and Montana legally challenged the administration's new rule, which remains in limbo, bouncing among various dueling courts, appellants, and litigants. Meanwhile, in Nevada, Sen. Harry Reid championed a new paradigm linking wilderness designation with economic and community development, and other states — Idaho, Washington, Montana — quickly began adapting and revising their own wilderness dreams, some of which had been overlooked and waiting ever since the Wilderness Act was first passed, back in 1964. Even conservative California Rep. Richard Pombo, long the bane of the environmental movement for his polarizing attacks on the Endangered Species Act and for his resistance, as chair of the House Committee on Resources, to any wilderness designation, announced that he was willing to begin entertaining such proposals as long as they also contained provisions for economic development.

Is all this a heralding, the first flickers of the possible return of the hard-times flames of prairie populism, or is it just a deeper yearning for the increased security brought by old-school bipartisanship? Whatever it is, it seems to be something, not nothing — statistically significant, these beginnings of change — and there are many complicating factors braiding into it, among them the shift away from resource-extraction industries, the increased demographics of Latino voters, the increase of water issues in regions of critical aridity, the rampant loss of open space in a region that was once almost nothing but open space, and the heavy-handed return, in troubled times, of God to politics, forcing the faithful to decide, among other things, which is God's way: to destroy wild nature, or to preserve it as vestigial examples of the sophistry of creation.

Perhaps all countries have their West — their wellspring or at least reservoir of mythic story, their looking glass through which they see, decade after decade and across the centuries, only the images they wish to see, and few others. And bittersweetly, perhaps all countries then have, sooner or later, their New Wests, in which those beloved images do not so much alter as simply fade, giving rise to a No West.

Certainly, there are days when this is my fear. None of the three obvious choices — Old West, New West, or No West — is particularly palatable to me, and so like a hermit I hunker down in a remote valley wired to the World Wide Web, go on hikes in the mountains with their vanishing grizzlies, go to softball games and picnics down in a nearby town, and attend meetings with local environmentalists or community service organizations that labor and conspire to develop collaborative proposals that might protect the grizzlies' last refuges while providing meaningful employment for that last percentage of the work force that still wants to work in the woods. And on good days, in such an unpeopled country, it does not seem like an impossible task.

The larger, metamorphosing, dissolving West is out there, of course, brighter and hotter than ever, beyond my solitary walks through little meadows of wild orchids and beyond the ice cream socials. Alcohol and substance abuse is flooding over the West in breathtaking fashion; in some areas of Montana, more than a third of eighth graders have engaged in binge drinking, and the backwoods proliferate with nickel-and-dime crystal meth labs. One can see the commercialization of the tobacco-chewing, Marlboro-smoking, beer-drinking culture of losers and antiheroes almost anywhere, can hear it in too many of today's country music songs. Immigrants, too, by the millions — some legal, some not — exert a changing force upon the culture and the land. Sometimes it's easy and other times it's hard to find a right and a wrong in these changes, and it is no small irony that doubtless this is how it must have seemed to the native people who were displaced by the current culture, by Europe's shouted echo, even as Latin America and

Asia now answer with story lines and dreams and movements of their own, across the centuries.

How will the landscape receive them? The Next West will certainly and finally be a dewatered West, as Major Powell foresaw. In a country that uses 408 billion gallons per day, the needs or rather desires of industry and humanity are not likely to be sacrificed to meet the needs of forest and wildlife that are interconnected with that water and that humanity. A world different from the one we inhabit now will emerge, along with consequences we have not even considered, but which will, upon their manifestation, their textbook revelation of cause and effect, seem so obvious to us that we will slap our foreheads in dismay at having overlooked their imminent and inevitable forthcoming.

Back during the last days of the fragmentation and cultural eradication, or attempted eradication, of the indigenous people who had lived here for millennia, developing their own fit with the West — was such immense change really only a mere 125 years ago? — the predictable breakdown in ancient and previously intact cultures wreaked havoc upon the native tribes. Smallpox, dislocation, starvation brought about by the extermination of buffalo: as their physical world was destroyed, so too was much of their inner world. Native religions merged, splintered, fell apart; tribes began mixing and matching, borrowing religious and ceremonial and cultural practices from one another as if in a desperate attempt to rebraid, with spirit, into a defensible, identifiable, collected whole, amid such ceaseless and relentless oppression and loss.

Very near the end of the traditional culture of the Plains Indian, a phenomenon known as the Ghost Dance arose in which it was prophesied that the sacred lands would be returned to the people who had for millennia inhabited them, and that the buffalo and other vanished residents would reinhabit the Plains, and whether through a turning back of time or a full revolution forward to that time again, no matter: the vanquished Indian tribes, or that tiny fraction of them, found such solace in the vision, the prophecy, that the U.S. government forbade the dance, censoring even their hopes and dreams and beliefs.

In *No Country for Old Men*, McCarthy writes of that same aging rural sheriff who has been fighting the ever-escalating drug wars along the Texas-Mexico border, and who has witnessed what he perceives to be the final and absolute disintegration of the culture he once knew and had for so long labored to defend: "He walked down the steps and out the back door and got in his truck and sat there. He couldnt name the feeling. It was sadness but it was something else besides. And the something else besides was what had him sitting there instead of starting the truck. He'd felt like this before but not in a long time and when he said that, then he knew what it was. It was defeat. It was being beaten. More bitter to him than death. You need to get over that, he said. Then he started the truck."

There exists, surely, no one measure or definition to describe the West: not its past nor its present, and certainly not its future. This late-summer morning, in the day's first light, I am in the suburbs of a small Western town where the leaves of an apple tree are glowing, illuminated by the rising sun — an image of great and green beauty that could occur almost anywhere — and yet I know, as if by gravity alone, or by some secret and ceaseless whisper, that I am in the West. Perhaps a million other mingled odors, silent histories, and the unnamed or unknown constellations of the night before, with their faint tidal tuggings still imprinted upon my subconscious, conspire to inform me of this fact; there is no measure, there is only the place and the time, and it is now, is still now, but it is also changing, has almost always been changing. The last wolves have long been killed off from the prairies outside Houston (and the prairies dewatered, poisoned, then paved over), and yet in other places wolves are coming back, reappearing, as if following diligently the arc of prophecy.

Why should it surprise us so that such a thing can be true, that one can know one is in the West upon first awakening in the morning, even before one opens one's eyes? That one can know and sense and hear and taste and feel and see Westernness intimately, without being able to measure it? The world is full of inscrutable things — still, and thank goodness — and how much more bereft and fragile we would be than we already are were we not able to discern always and at heart's depth, without a moment's forethought or other knowledge, something as basic as the four cardinal points on the compass: *in the West.*

To not possess such knowledge, one day: I can think of no other better definition for the word *lost.* Which we are not, yet.

KEVIN FEDARKO

High in Hell

FROM *Esquire*

SO IF YOU EVER HAPPEN to find yourself skimming through the troposphere high above the Horn of Africa, the engines of your cargo jet clawing at the currents of sub-Saharan air rolling off the lip of the Ethiopian plateau and down toward the Red Sea, there will come a moment when you'll have to admit that the cockpit of an aging DC-8 with a broken oil-pressure gauge and a washed-out picture of a Ugandan mountain gorilla emblazoned on the tail offers a damn fine view of the most wretched place on the planet.

Off to the right, down along the borderlands extending out toward the very easternmost tip of Africa, stretch the desolate coastal plains that the British used to call the Furthest Shag of the Never-Never Land, and that the Somali camel herders and half-starved bands of refugees refer to as the Guban, which simply means "burned." Off to the left, up against the back end of Eritrea, lurks the Danakil Depression, a salt-encrusted sore on a wrinkled fold of the Earth's hide. The Danakil boasts the lowest point on the continent (more than five hundred feet below sea level) and summer temperatures that frequently hit 120 degrees. Jagged shards of volcanic rock stab through the skin of this land like giant, shattered ribs.

You won't have long to contemplate this bonescape, though, and that's because this is only a twenty-minute flight. So ten minutes after the wheels have lifted from the dusty Ethiopian town of Dire Dawa, your crew of five — a Nigerian captain and a Nigerian loadmaster, a Rwandan copilot, a Congolese purser, and Vincent, your Rhode Island–based Nigerian navigator — will already be making preparations to touch down at the far edge of what L. M. Nesbitt, the British explorer who conducted the first successful traverse of the Danakil in 1927, fittingly christened the "hellhole of Creation."

In fact, there it is now.

Huddling on the southwest corner of the Bab el-Mandeb, or Gate of Tears, the strait separating Africa from the coast of Yemen, sits the tiny nation of Djibouti: horrific climate, endless sand, almost no fresh water, but a strategic cynosure of the first order. Nearly three million barrels of oil pass by this place every day. It also plays host to about fifteen hundred U.S. troops at Camp Lemonier, a former French Foreign Legion post that is now America's sub-Saharan spearhead in the global war on terror. This explains the HC-130 turboprop jets and attack helicopters lining the tarmac of Ambouli Airport — a vaguely unsettling sight, given your payload.

Stacked on the deck of the fuselage on the other side of a thick metal door just behind Vincent's navigation desk sits a mountain of white bags, each the size of a stuffed pillowcase. This is the afternoon's shipment of khat, a psychotropic shrub that provides the overwhelming majority of Djiboutian men with their daily drug fix. Which means that having just vaulted over the Furthest Shag of the Never Whatever, you're seconds away from landing next to a war base bristling with irritable jarheads, accompanied by twenty-two thousand pounds of a Schedule 1 amphetamine that, back in the United States, carries the same penalties for large-scale trafficking — up to life in prison — as heroin, meth, or cocaine.

Jesus, you wonder, could anything be weirder than this?

Why, yes. And damned if it isn't unfolding on the tarmac right now, where a mob of ragged-looking dudes wearing sarongs is sprinting across the runway toward the plane. The good news is that these men seem to be unarmed. The bad news is that they look *really* pissed off.

There are about fifty of them, and they seem to be chasing two open-bed trucks, one of which is pulling a rickety bob-trailer. As the trucks pull up next to the side of the plane, the sarong brigade divides neatly into two groups. The members of the bigger group clamber up the slats on the sides of the trucks, lever open the doors to the cargo hold, and start boosting one another into the plane to attack the payload, furiously flinging out the white sacks. A few of those bundles make it into the trucks, but most are caroming off the heads and shoulders of the men still trying to climb into the fuselage.

Meanwhile, the smaller, slightly more official-looking group is storming up the mobile staircase and appears to be preparing to assault — yes, they *are* assaulting — the door to the cabin. And now the Nigerian loadmaster, who is on his first Djibouti khat run and has thus become so rattled that he's clearly taken leave of his senses, has thrown the latch and removed the only barrier keeping these assailants *out.* So now they're barging into the cockpit, and the leader of this charge, a mean-looking bastard who has shaved his head so close to the bone that his skull looks like an enameled eggplant, has gotten into the face of the poor loadmaster and is screaming —

"Give me the manifest! Give me the manifest!"

This guy's rage is raw, foaming, and totally impossible to fathom. Why is he so *tweaked?* What is his *problem?*

"I need the manifest — *now!*"

"Who the hell is this fellow?" asks the stunned loadmaster, turning helplessly to Vincent.

Vincent looks at his watch and sighs.

"We're three hours late," he notes, and then offers an observation that, in light of this delay, stands as a spectacularly superfluous encapsulation of the obvious:

"These guys really want their drugs."

"If you smoke too much marijuana or drink too much alcohol, you will lose your brain. But with khat, even if you use it for twenty-four hours nonstop, your mind will still be clear. These leaves give you energy — you don't feel at all tired when you chew khat — but they also help you relax. So I really can't put khat in the category of a normal drug, because it is unlike anything else. The only thing I can say for sure is that when I chew it, I feel like my problems disappear. Khat is my brother. It takes care of all things."

That's Khadar Isse Boulale, a Djiboutian we'll meet a little later, holding forth on the merits of *Catha edulis*, a tree with a dull silver bark that is cultivated throughout the highlands of Ethiopia, Kenya, and Yemen, and whose leaves have been used for nearly a thousand years by Muslims throughout East Africa and parts of Arabia as an alternative to alcohol and other mood-altering substances forbidden by the Koran. Khat (rhymes with *pot*) is consumed with droopy-eyed languor at *takhzins*, afternoon chewing parties at which a dozen or so male friends sit around in a circle for up to six hours stuffing fresh leaves into their mouths and chomping away like koala bears. The bitter-tasting foliage is known by a long list of names: *qat, chat, miraa*, the "tree of paradise," the "green gold." It contains minute quantities of cathinone, an alkaloid that stimulates mental activity before ushering the user into a state of stoned-out introspection — the exploration of which is pretty much the entire purpose behind my visit to Djibouti.

Although banned throughout the United States, parts of Europe, and much of the Middle East, khat is perfectly legal in a handful of countries lining both sides of the Red Sea, where it has become as much a national institution as vodka in Russia or wine in France. In Yemen, where legend says the first *Catha edulis* tree was brought from Ethiopia by a Sufi mystic in 1429, roughly two-thirds of the arable land is devoted to khat plantations. In Kenya, taxi drivers, students, and even athletes rely on it to help them stay alert. In Somalia, where the drug was used to pay the militiamen who battled U.S. Rangers and Delta Forces in Mogadishu in 1993, it's a staple among warlords and clan leaders.

But only in Djibouti — where the drug is popular at every level of society, from beggars on the street to President Ismail Omar Guelleh — do these leaves also play the wider role of desensitizing an entire population. Here, the tree of paradise suppresses dissent, helps assuage suffering, and basically keeps the place from coming apart at the seams. Thus Djibouti's passionate affair with khat has elevated this woeful little outpost on the Horn to more than just your average narco-state, like, say, Colombia, Peru, or Afghanistan.

No, Djibouti is something unto itself. Because even though khat isn't a narcotic, Djibouti is perhaps the only country in the world that truly fits the definition of a narco-*society:* a place where a drug is not so much a business as a way of life. And where khat is — quite literally — the opiate of the masses.

Tucked inside the armpit of the Gulf of Tadjoura, where the railhead from Addis Ababa meets the dense, peacock-blue waters of the Red Sea, Djibouti City is the capital of a small, predominantly Muslim republic of 750,000 that won its independence from France in 1977. The once-elegant city — whose colonnaded buildings are now sloughing off scales of stucco like a colony of architectural lepers — suppurates amid a climate of almost unrelieved misery. In July and August, the desert winds kick up and a typical day is 105 degrees. Around noon, the birds begin falling out of the sky, dropping unconscious into the streets, where solicitous pedestrians kick them toward the gutters to prevent them from being run over by passing cars.

The morning after the khat plane deposits me in Djibouti City, I decide to take a stroll through the Marché Central, an open-air bazaar wedged between the European Quarter and the African Quarter in the shadow of the great Hamoudi mosque. It's around 11:00 A.M., and since it's February, the temperature is in the low nineties. In Djibouti, that's a cold snap.

The Marché Central is a vast network of densely packed stalls laden with cheap clothing, sandals, spices, and fruit. Feasting upon this smorgasbord of commerce is one of Africa's more colorful human pageants: tribal elders, eyes milky with cataracts, dodging around lumbering minibuses and through confused herds of goats; henna-handed Ethiopian whores trolling for customers in spike heels, knockoff couture dresses shellacked to their curves; gaunt-faced child beggars, the discarded progeny of the squatter towns and refugee camps, hissing for coins; and Foreign Legionnaires pumping the pedals of their mountain bikes, clad in polished black shoes and absurdly tight khaki shorts. This procession drifts through a roiling river of words — French, Arabic, Italian, Somali, Afar — and a cocktail of odors that is heady and exotic but also makes you want to gag: a whiff of urine and rotting vegetable, a note of frankincense and freshly baked baguette, a trace of diesel exhaust topped with a whimsical finish of donkey fart.

I weave across the Marché and enter an alley, passing a metal dumpster that's throwing off just enough shade to permit two diseased-looking dogs to curl up next to the carcass of a dead goat. It's close to noon now. The temperature is climbing, and as the heat builds into a solid wall, people shuffle out from their tin-roofed shacks and concrete-block shanties, spread pieces of cardboard on the sidewalk, and collapse to the ground like troopers felled by an attack of poison gas.

In front of an open-air barbershop, two khat vendors are perched on stools next to some wilted-looking sprigs left over from yesterday's shipment. One of the sellers informs me in French that a one-day supply of fresh leaves costs anywhere from $1 to $20, depending on quality. Those are formidable prices in a country where the per-capita income averages $450 a year — formidable enough to make me wonder out loud how the hell people can afford it.

"It is because we are addicted!" cries an English-speaking customer, a man in a ratty jacket and torn sandals who has overheard my remark.

He seizes my arm and looks into my eyes with unsettling intensity.

"Do you know the cocaine leaf in Latin America?"

I nod.

"Well, it is exactly the same here: *we must have it!*"

He translates his statement for a group of curious onlookers, at which point everybody opens their mouths and cackles wildly in agreement.

Ha-ha-ha-ha-ha-ha-ha . . .

Their laughter reveals rotting brown teeth embedded in receding gums that are stained to a deep jaundiced orange. Unsettled by the surreal scene, I stumble away from the crowd, duck through a few alleys, and eventually emerge onto a street lined with three-story office buildings. Standing on the sidewalk in the middle of this block is an Indian man in his early twenties. He's wearing a crisply pressed white shirt, and his black hair has been sculpted into a dashing pompadour.

"Why, hello, my friend," he cries out in English, spreading open his arms and flashing a dazzling smile. "What is bringing you to Djibouti?"

Dev Soni is twenty-two years old and is hovering outside the entrance to a colonial-style office building where his family trades goods between Djibouti and Somalia. He hails from the Indian state of Gujarat — more than thirteen hundred miles to the east. He looks almost as out of place as I feel, which probably explains his eagerness to strike up a conversation. Although he doesn't chew khat himself, Dev is delighted to share his views on the subject.

"There is an Arabic word, *tafshan* — it means you're bankrupt," he explains. "Because of the khat, Djibouti and most of its people are *tafshan.*" That's a fairly bold statement, but the facts back him up: according to the United Nations Office on Drugs and Crime, Djiboutians who chew khat spend nearly a fifth of their household budget on the leaves.

"And in addition to the financial problems that this drug creates," Dev adds earnestly, "please keep in mind that if you are eating the khat on a regular basis, your penis will become smaller."

I shoot Dev a look of alarm — an expression he mistakenly interprets as cool journalistic skepticism.

"Oh, it is clear that you are not believing me!" he exclaims. "If you are requiring some supporting evidence, let us obtain confirmation by conferencing with this gentleman standing next to me."

This gentleman, who is one of Dev's employees, is the first in a long line of Djiboutians who agrees to talk to me on the condition that I identify him only as Omar.

"Omar" offers up a dense stream of commentary in rapid Somali, accompanied by some wonderfully evocative gestures. The performance begins with an airy wave of the hand, followed by a delicate finger dance, then segues into a sharp nosedive that mirrors the trajectory of a wounded balloon making its final journey to the floor.

"The penis will definitely become smaller," Dev translates unnecessarily. "The instrument cannot lift itself up, and is unable to keep itself sufficiently firm."

This is more information than I really need, but Omar rattles on.

"Oh, my goodness, this is something new!" Dev says brightly. "Omar is also telling me that the Djiboutian women are needing the sexual intercourse very badly, but their husbands are unable to perform this duty when they are chewing the khat. This is a big problem for the Djiboutian woman. Omar says that khat is the second wife of the Djiboutian man, but that the Djiboutian woman gets nothing from it and therefore, of necessity, she is having to turn to the foreigners and the tourists for the fulfillment of her requirements. This could add a new dimension to your visit to Djibouti, yes?"

Alas, the possibility of exploring this further is abruptly curtailed.

It's now just after 12:30, and a stir is sweeping through the capital. Cell phones are going off. People are picking themselves up from their cardboard Barcaloungers and making bulging signs with their cheeks. In the distance, a faint cacophony of car horns. And all across town, the doors of shops, offices, supermarkets, cigarette kiosks, and restaurants are slamming shut. This burst of energy heralds a glorious piece of news:

"*L'avion! L'avion est arrivé!*"

To fully appreciate the mayhem that's about to ensue, you need to understand that less than forty-eight hours after khat has been harvested, it starts to lose its potency — and by the time the plane lands at Ambouli Airport, the clock has been ticking for about eighteen of those hours. So as soon as the wheels hit the ground, every khat trader in Djibouti is fixed on a terrifying image, somewhere inside his head, of the molecules of cathinone (the good stuff) breaking down, leaving useless cathine (a mild chemical resembling ephedrine, which is found in cold medicines and diet pills). Chained to this unstoppable molecular slide is a price that drops every hour.

My lesson in how this all fits together begins the following morning, when I meet Khadar Isse Boulale (Mr. "Khat-Is-My-Brother-It-Takes-Care-of-All-Things"). Khadar, thirty-nine, is a San Diego taxi driver of Somali descent who's here to visit his ailing mom and to chew as much khat as he can get his hands on. With his rounded jawline and closely trimmed mustache, he looks a bit like Martin Lawrence. After running into Khadar on the street and hiring him as my driver and translator, I inform him that our mission is to follow the drugs.

"Cool," he says. "Let's do it."

Shortly after noon, Khadar parks his uncle's silver Mitsubishi outside the airport and gives me the lowdown on how the khat business works. Djibouti's entire supply is plucked each afternoon from the terraced fields near the ancient walled citadel of Harar, Ethiopia (where legend holds that the magical leaves were discovered almost a thousand years ago by an inquisitive, foliage-nibbling goat), and the country's khat importers all belong to one of three organizations. At one end of the market are about a hundred high-volume traders in the Société Générale d'Importation du Khat (SOGIK), a private co-op that deals primarily in cheap, inferior leaves. On the opposite end are about 180 boutique agents who work under the umbrella of two private syndicates and who are collectively known as the *particuliers*. These are the guys who bring in the high-end product.

As Khadar is explaining all this, the khat trucks exit the tarmac and enter the parking lot. This is the signal for the *particulier* importers to leap into their fleet of souped-up Land Cruisers and Mitsubishi 4x4's and start racing the *particulier* truck (nobody really cares about the SOGIK vehicle) down the tree-lined promenade leading to the main entrance. The moment the *particulier* truck clears the gate, Khadar deftly wedges his 4x4 into the middle of the accelerating entourage.

The Djiboutian drug derby has begun.

We roar out of the airport en masse, bang a hard right, and tear toward the city. On all sides, SUVs are cutting one another off while traders lean out the windows to jeer and bellow insults. Inside the khat truck, the baggage handlers are clinging to the rails to avoid being sling-shot into the street.

Two miles down the highway, we make another right and race toward a dirt lot across the street from the Omar Hasan Construction Depot. This is where the *particuliers'* partners — the next link in the distribution chain — are waiting alongside a hodgepodge of taxis, Land Cruisers, dirt bikes, and scooters. As we rooster-tail into the lot, I look back and see that the baggage guys have already started catapulting the sacks from both sides of the moving truck. The bags land all over the street with moist thuds, and the agents stage a shoving, cursing free-for-all as they scramble to read the names stenciled on the cloth.

Amid this chaos, Khadar spots an acquaintance. His name is Mohammed Hassan Ahamed, but he goes by his English nickname, Blue (his favorite color). Blue, who is twenty-two and is wearing a bright-red Oakley T-shirt, happens to run a delivery route. And yes, for the *specially reduced* price of two hundred dollars — a sum that is swiftly haggled down to twenty bucks — he grants us the privilege of playing chauffeur to him and his leaves.

All around us, khat is being shot-putted through the windows of Land Cruisers, rammed into the trunks of taxis, and lashed onto scooters and dirt bikes. Blue swings his four sacks into the Mitsubishi, leaps aboard, and pounds furiously on the back of the driver's seat:

"Go! Go! Go! Go! *Go!*"

Khadar mashes his foot to the floorboard.

While most of the delivery cars around us are plunging directly into the city's slum districts, a handful are heading straight for Djibouti's port, where the leaves will be loaded onto speedboats and rushed north to the coastal towns of Tadjoura and Obock. There's also a dark-blue Land Cruiser with smoked windows that is supposedly express-delivering Ismail Omar Guelleh's personal stash to the presidential palace. (I.O.G. reportedly likes to get together with his khat posse to chew leaves three or four afternoons a week.)

As we roar down the Boulevard du Général de Gaulle, Blue pulls out a razor blade to gut the cotton sacks and divides the bundles inside into groups. He's also yelling at Khadar to pour on some speed because — *fuck!* — we're getting totally dusted by two solid lines of 4x4's. The phalanx on the right is plowing through the dirt on the berm, the one on the left is half straddling the median strip. The dealers inside these vehicles are all loudly berating Khadar.

"Sorry, man!" he says sheepishly, addressing Blue in the rearview mirror while tossing me an explanation for why everybody's so upset. "I'm only doing eighty-five."

We approach Quartier 4, a warren of cinder-block shacks lining a grid of dirt alleys with open sewers down the middle.

"Where the hell are we going?" demands Khadar.

Blue barks out a flurry of commands in guttural Somali. Khadar chops the transmission into second gear, slides into a right-angle turn, scatters a clutch of terrified goats, plows through a miniature lake of black sewage, and skids to a stop. Blue flings several bundles through the window toward a vendor named Sadho, already besieged by a dozen customers.

"Go! Go! *Go!*"

"Where? Where? *Where?*"

"Right! Right! *Oh, shit!*"

We're hurtling directly toward a Land Cruiser coming from the opposite direction. Both vehicles refuse to give way, so we take the same turn together — and barely avoid a three-way collision with a taxi that's blasting out from the street we're trying to enter. Since everybody's delivering khat, backing up and giving way is completely unthinkable. Instead we face off, grille to grille, and trade insults until everybody scrapes past and roars off.

Our next stop is a stall run by a man in an orange shirt. On

Blue's orders, I hurl some bundles at this guy's head. Khadar has barely slowed down.

We weave through more goats and nearly run over a man who has ventured into the street with a wheelbarrow. By this point, Khadar's horn is blaring continuously. More bundles land in my lap and go sailing out the window at stops four and five. At stop six, Blue himself disappears with his own armful of khat — apparently this is part of the plan — and Khadar thunders out of Quartier 4 onto a paved boulevard, where several dozen vehicles are all jumping the median as they try to enter or exit the slum.

As we pull into our last stop, Khadar stares at the dashboard with a look of stunned disbelief. A bead of sweat the size of a coffee bean is sliding down the bridge of his nose.

"Jesus," he says, mopping his face with his shirttail. "This is nothing like driving a cab in San Diego."

It is now 1:16 P.M.

At 12:30, eleven tons of primo Ethiopian *Catha edulis* were cruising along at three hundred knots inside the belly of the khat plane. In forty-six minutes, it's been offloaded, divvied up, and fire-hosed out to virtually every corner of the country. The only way to move those leaves faster would have been to bring the cargo freighter in over the rooftops, open the doors to the fuselage, and carpet-bomb the place.

"Nothing gets in the way of the opium of the people," observes Khadar. "And now begins the best part of our day. Time to *brouter la salade*!"

Among the Djiboutians who belong to President I.O.G.'s Issa tribe — which forms the elite levels of business and government — "grazing the salad" can be as rarefied and as refined as a Japanese tea ceremony. The ritual begins when participants enter the home of their host toting their *rubtas*, or bundles of khat, and are ushered into the *mabraze*, a special chamber lavishly appointed with Persian rugs and richly upholstered cushions. Pitchers of incense-flavored water and chilled bottles of soft drinks are placed before the guests. Ornate spittoons are set about the room. After everyone settles in, a selection of poetry may be recited, or a piece of music performed on a traditional instrument. And, of course, there is conversation — especially during the first hour or so, before chewers slip into a contemplative phase of dreamy introspection.

I'm anticipating something along these lines when Khadar invites me to his *mabraze.* My hopes sink, however, when he parks the Mitsubishi deep inside the trash-strewn slum of Quartier 6 and we enter a tiny courtyard that seems to be hosting an international convention of houseflies. The floor is littered with cheap rugs and orange plastic water jugs. A poisonous potpourri of odors drifts from an outhouse five feet away. In the alley, two angry women are shouting to be heard over a wailing baby and a bleating goat.

This is the headquarters of L'Association l'Avenir, one of Quartier 6's many khat-chewing clubs. The "Association of the Future" has about twenty dues-paying members, mostly men in their thirties or early forties who grew up in the neighborhood. Those who aren't unemployed hold down jobs as clerks, policemen, security guards, or dockworkers.

"We're kind of like beer buddies in the U.S.," Khadar explains. "We chew until 7:00 P.M. or so, then we go out drinking."

The place quickly fills up as members appear in their *futas* (sarongs), clutching their bundles of leaves. Each arrival glides through the doorway and offers a hearty *"Bonjour, mes amis"* before slipping off his sandals, hitching his *futa,* and folding into the circle. When introductions are made, I learn that in addition to Khadar, I'll be chewing with Awole, Ladir, and eight more Omars.

Khadar builds a nest for himself with three pillows, unwraps the leaves we've bought from Blue, and delivers an off-the-cuff tutorial.

To a connoisseur like Khadar, the varieties of khat are as distinct as chardonnay from tequila. At the bottom end of the spectrum you have *miyal,* a mild, pale-green leaf that has no kick whatsoever (the O'Doul's of khat), and *medetcho,* which is known to cause *dukak,* or khat nightmares. There's also a wide range of midprice options: sweet- or nutty-tasting leaves in which the khat cognoscenti can discern gossamer suggestions of apples, raisins, and almonds. The Dom Pérignon of Ethiopian khat, however, is *warata,* whose virtues Khadar proceeds to extol.

"OK, let's examine this," he says, caressing our twenty-dollar *rubta* of *warata* as if he were smoothing the fur of a small pet. "See how the base of each stem looks like the head of a nail? This shows the branches were taken off the main trunk and are of superior quality. *Warata* is moist and crunchy. Nice and clean, too. Ripe — just like fruit."

He extracts a succulent sprig and carefully snaps each leaf with his forefinger to ascertain tenderness. Leaves that pass this flick test receive a crisp twist where the stem meets the twig. In this manner he rapidly strips the stalk, tossing the rejects to the side while popping foliage into his mouth and building a huge wad in the corner of his cheek. Taking a swig of Coke, he leans back, emitting soft burps of pleasure.

This is the most animated stage of a khat party. Ribald jokes are exchanged. Unsolicited little gifts — a khat sprig here, a cigarette there — go sailing across the courtyard to friends. Somebody touches a match to a stone crucible and the air fills with the astringent aroma of frankincense. The flies begin to subside.

I tentatively cram a few leaves into my mouth and decide that this might be a good moment to inquire about something that's been bugging me ever since my chat with Dev Soni.

"So is it really true," I ask, addressing the group with Khadar translating, "that khat will cause your dick to shrink?"

Four or five arguments simultaneously detonate in French, Somali, and Arabic. At first I'm afraid that I've violated some unknown rule of khat-chewing protocol. But then I realize that, no, this is just a run-of-the-mill, Djiboutian-style debate. Eloquent gestures are being made. Animated expressions are being conveyed. Some complex and possibly quite beautiful ideas are clearly being sculpted and buffed. Ah, yes: here, at last, I am about to witness the penetrating nuances and delicate shades of meaning that form the timeless wisdom of the *mabraze.*

Finally Awole, a policeman who spends half his monthly salary on khat — and who has a trickle of green slime dribbling down his chin — stands up.

"Khat is an aphrodisiac!" Awole shouts at me. "Don't you know what an aphrodisiac is?! It means that after you eat it, all you wanna do is bone the ladies." He performs the Elvis Pelvis while pounding his fist into his solar plexus. "When I chew khat, I gotta fuck all night long. There is no stopping!"

Omars I through IV beat their chests in solidarity with Awole, while Ladir and Omars V through VIII produce cries of indignation and some unflattering remarks about the size of Awole's unit.

"Yes! Yes! Yes!"

"Bullshit!"

"He's telling the truth!"

Eventually the antiaphrodisiacs shout down the chest-beaters and their spokesman presents a rebuttal.

"When you eat khat, you *relax*," declares Ladir, an unemployed dockworker with sharply etched features who's looking decidedly worked up. "When you don't have a job and you chew khat, you are *calm*. You feel like your problems *disappear*. Here in the *mabraze* with my khat brothers, we don't worry about anything. And do you know why? Because with khat, everything is possible. With khat, people stop *fighting*. With khat, there is only *peace*."

A chorus of approving grunts suggests that maybe this is an idea everybody can get behind. Concordance seems within reach—until Awole realizes he's got a problem with where one of the Omars has chosen to sit and attempts to perform an eviction. A shoving match breaks out. The group scrambles to separate the combatants. It takes several minutes to persuade Awole, who already has his shirt off and looks ready to brawl, to get dressed and sit back down.

Khadar turns to me with a wry smile.

"We all know khat's no good," he says. "We spend too much money on it. We don't work. We don't buy shoes for our kids. Divorce, domestic fighting, so many problems . . ."

He sighs, eyes shining with a lacquered liquidity in the fading afternoon light.

"But still, we gotta have khat. What else can I say? This is how we live."

Well, at least they're not in denial.

Then something odd happens. Just as I'm preparing to write off Khadar, his friends, and the entire population of Djibouti as a bunch of drug-addled freaks, I realize that a marvelous feeling is running through my arms, across my belly, and down the backs of my legs.

Well, now . . .

When I'd first crammed the leaves into my cheek and bit down, the sensation had been pretty unpleasant. The taste was acerbic and the texture was coarse, what you might expect if you munched on a pile of hedge trimmings. A film of green scum coated the back of my throat, my mouth turned dry, and for the next forty-five minutes I felt like I was about to retch.

Now, though, the cathinone is finally starting to kick in, and my entire body seems to be marinating in a kind of faint thrum. At first it's so subtle that I attribute the reaction to the lovely lavender light suffusing the courtyard as late afternoon wanes into the pre-evening twilight known as *As-saa'a as-Suleimanya,* or Solomon's Hour. But then I realize that no, it's not the light: a calming vibration is creeping across the top of my head, somewhere around the roots of my hair. Ever taken Vicodin when you didn't really need it? Like that.

It would be overstating things to call this euphoria — the feeling is too delicate for that. I'm relaxed but completely lucid. I find myself savoring long, drawn-out sighs. The mere act of breathing — exhale, pause . . . inhale, pause — has become intensely sensuous and pleasurable. And with this new feeling, the cares and worries that I'm always schlepping around quietly cast off their tethers and drift toward the horizon.

This is what the Arabs call *kayf,* an untranslatable term referring to a blissed-out state of languid, dreamy tranquillity. As the *kayf* steals over me, I realize that the same thing is happening to everyone else. Together we have entered the second phase of our khat chew. Conversation subsides and we all lie back, working our wads and gazing at one another with the heavy-lidded contentment of a herd of dairy cows chewing their cud.

The goat outside is still bleating. The baby continues to wail. The two women haven't stopped screeching at each other, and the courtyard still stinks. But none of this matters in the slightest. In fact, the irrelevance of these nuisances only underscores the luminous truth embedded in an obscure bit of Red Sea folklore cited by Kevin Rushby, author of *Eating the Flowers of Paradise,* the most eloquent testament ever written to the magic of khat:

> *If one's heart is at peace,*
> *Even the asshole of a donkey can be a mabraze.*

For the next several days, I wake up late each morning (one of the leaves' side effects) and wildly irritable (another one), having spent most of the night lying awake and staring at the ceiling (downside number three). I stumble to the market to toss away another chunk of my rapidly dwindling finances (the most notorious side effect of all), purchasing that afternoon's fix. Then I make my way over to Quartier 6 to graze the salad with Khadar and the boys at l'Avenir. At which point Djibouti's wretchedness — its heat, its filth, its odors — smoothly fades away.

After the bitter taste subsides, the mellow tide surges in and suddenly, there I am: floating in a lagoon off some distant archipelago along the outer frontiers of my consciousness. *Yeah, baby . . .*

Yet another characteristic of khat is that your mind remains clear even as you get high. So over the next few afternoons, I stumble upon several *Catha edulis*–lubricated epiphanies:

Day Two, 4:15

For a bunch of deadbeats, these l'Avenir guys have a pretty extensive set of tools.

While munching on an obscenely large wad of ripe and delicious khat, most of which has been stolen from Khadar's share (I seem to have eaten all of mine), I note a mysterious doorway on the far side of the courtyard. A peek inside reveals a storage shed. On the floor are a dozen battered shovels. Lining one wall, a row of picks. There's a blue electric generator on the floor. And piled on a rickety wooden table, a stack of ledgers.

Weird. What the hell does all this have to do with chewing khat?

Day Three, 2:20

Actually, nothing. And everything.

Today the flies are especially bad. As we sit around swatting at them, the guys start talking about a young woman in the neighborhood named Halimo Mohamed Doualeh. Ladir explains that when Halimo died unexpectedly a few weeks ago, they carried her body to the mosque to wash and purify it in the traditional manner, then took it to the cemetery and dug her grave. (It turns out there are no funeral services in Quartier 6.) Then Awole mentions that shortly after Halimo passed away, another neighbor, a sixty-year-old woman named Fatima Hadi, lost power in her home. So the l'Avenir guys hauled out the generator and got Fatima's fans turning until the electricity could be restored. (Each summer, dozens of Djiboutians die from heatstroke during power outages.) At the moment, the members are using their shovels and picks to clear a nearby lot for a soccer championship, and their monthly dues (which are recorded in the treasurer's ledger) are being used to set up some English classes for local kids.

Day Four, 3:03

So, in addition to being a drug den, l'Avenir is sort of like a mutual-aid society for stoners.

Which, let's face it, isn't really *that* big of a deal. As I'm working at the wad of khat in my cheek and marveling at the club's altruism and civic-mindedness, yet another argument starts up between the two women in the alley. And it suddenly occurs to me that the wives behind whose backs these guys are constantly having affairs must surely be less enthusiastic about the social benefits of the green gold. In a country whose infant-mortality rate is 10.4 percent, where half the population is unemployed and 70 percent of children are malnourished, one soccer field, one grave, and one old lady's electricity hardly make l'Avenir the Djiboutian analog to Mother Teresa's Missionaries of Charity. At the same time, however, these minor acts of decency and largess do suggest that what these guys find seductive about khat (in addition to its delightful physical effects, of course) is the excuse it provides to get together and the sense of purpose that these meetings create. Which provokes a rather shocking question:

Day Five, 5:50

Is it possible these guys aren't actually addicted to chewing khat?

Or, more accurately: does the nature of their addiction have as much to do with the alchemy of companionship as with the chemical reactions unfolding inside their brains?

The Djiboutians, as it happens, are way ahead of me on this notion.

"So, my friend, do you finally understand that khat isn't everything?" remarks one of the Omars, whose rounded belly is rolling over the top of his purple-and-green *futa.* "What's important is being together. To talk. To laugh. To help one another out. Without that, we have no community. That's everything, is it not?"

On my final afternoon in Djibouti, Khadar announces that the members of l'Avenir have a gift for me. While Ladir, Awole, and the Omars all smile, he presents me with an object wrapped in tissue paper. It's a bottle of Jack Daniel's, and it must have cost them a small fortune. Deeply touched, I spend my flight home sampling from the bottle while wondering what sort of damage I've done to myself by noshing all those leaves.

While enthusiasts claim khat offers relief from malaria, flu, infertility, and gonorrhea, unpleasant side effects can include hemorrhoids, hypertension, migraines, and chronic borborygmus (a "rumbling noise" produced by wind in the bowels). Oh, and constipation, too. During a short-lived ban on khat imposed by the British in southern Yemen some years ago, sales of laxatives reportedly plummeted by 90 percent.

Confusing? Yep. But that's khat for you. Depending on where you're at and who you're listening to, the drug could either be legal or illegal, an innocuous habit or a toxic vice. It may imbue you with so much energy that you want to bone the ladies all night long, or it could render your nether dimensions even less impressive than they already are. Khat can be none of these things, all of them put together, or hover inside some tangled psychotropic DMZ that only further confounds one's notions of what addiction truly means and what a narco-society actually is.

Which is why, a thousand-odd years after that ancestral Ethiopian goat initiated the long, strange, tempestuous affair that is khat, those emerald leaves remain a deep and abiding enigma.

Sort of like Africa itself. And especially Djibouti.

When I finally made it home, I decided that I truly hated the place. Despite the pleasures of khat, Djibouti, I told my friends, is a reminder that some parts of the world are beyond redemption. Djibouti is awful. Djibouti is the only country I've been where I will never, ever go back.

Eventually, though, that all changed. Slowly and resentfully, I found myself being dragged around to the realization that in the process of hating Djibouti so much, I had somehow managed to fall in love with the place, too. And not for the reasons you might expect.

I did not, for example, fall in love with the way Djibouti's filth and Djibouti's misery can suddenly, at odd and infrequent (and probably khat-induced) intervals, be overtaken by transcendent moments of exculpatory beauty: how the shadow of the minaret on the Hamoudi mosque can caress the broken lines of the Marché Central; the care with which a woman gathers her robes as she prepares to step across a puddle of sewage; or the way the light lies down on the Red Sea just before Solomon's Hour. Maybe those moments were enough to make my heart break for Djibouti, but they weren't enough to make me love her. No, I came to love Djibouti for the chaotic and dysfunctional esprit de corps of l'Avenir.

Never, anywhere, have I encountered human beings who sail the inside of the toilet bowl in such marvelous style — and who do so while displaying such unapologetically defiant, fuck-you élan. And in the act of acknowledging my admiration for this attitude, I realized that the boys of l'Avenir had imparted something else, too.

When I die and am sent to hell as punishment for all the terrible things I've written about the most maligned place in Africa, I'll crawl off into some dark corner to contemplate my sins. And there I'll run into a group of Djiboutians lounging around on a pile of ratty rugs: Khadar, Awole, Ladir, and eight guys who still insist on being called Omar.

There won't be any khat, of course — the plane only lands in heaven. But there will still be a *mabraze,* and that's because these guys will be sitting around speculating about what it would be like if they actually *had* khat. They'll talk about how, when the plane arrives, you can hear the symphony of car horns. They'll reminisce about the tumultuous insanity of the drug derby racing through the slums. And then they'll remind one another what it's like when those who are pure of heart, but also those whose hearts aren't so pure, can all duck through the door, offer up a *"Bonjour, mes amis!"* and settle down together to shoot the breeze and *brouter la salade.*

In so doing, they will have pulled off that most incorrigibly and most triumphantly African of achievements. They will have trumped the devil himself. Because there at the center of Creation's hellhole, inside the asshole of the donkey, they will have managed to chisel out a sliver of paradise.

Even if it exists only in their own minds.

IAN FRAZIER

A Kielbasa Too Far

FROM *Outside*

TRAVEL, AND YOU GET SICK, sooner or later. This truth is universal. I remember reading somewhere that the queen of England, when she leaves her country, always takes with her a certain number of units of her own blood. (Ordinary blood would be unsuitable, I guess, should the queen happen to need a transfusion.) Maybe that's just a myth. The fact remains that if you travel, no matter who you are, eventually you will be brought low.

Even when you're healthy, the dislocation of traveling is itself kind of like being sick. (Of course, this presumes that you're traveling somewhere different from the place where you usually are, a distinction increasingly difficult to make in the U.S.A.) To begin with, in a different place there's the strangeness of time, exaggerated, almost always, by jet lag. Then there are other strangenesses — of smell, of light, of currencies, of the way people dress and walk and smile or never smile. Sometimes just the sparrows flying around inside the terminal are enough to throw me. If you don't speak the place's language, or don't speak it well, a spine-deep queasiness comes with that, too. And when on top of everything you actually *do* get sick in this place, the experience is generally several times worse than it would be at home.

Worse, that is, and then better — when you start to recover, you may feel a weird elation that's as great as your previous sufferings were bad. The only foreign country in which I've traveled much is Russia, and I've been sick there twice. The first time was in a hotel in St. Petersburg, the Oktyabrskaya, a Soviet-era immensity with doorways receding to the vanishing point down bleak halls, and room telephones like flatirons that always rang with calls from prostitutes half a minute after I came in and closed the door. Late one night, lying on the narrow bed pushed up against the wall (Russians love to sleep against the wall), I awoke in the direst kind of renal pain. I was clammy, contorted, and shaking so badly I could barely tie my shoe. Once dressed, I staggered out to the desk of the floor lady, at an intersection where two of the endless halls converged. (Most hotels in Russia have floor ladies, sort of like monitors, on every floor.) I told the floor lady I needed a doctor. Without the least show of sympathy, she said she would call one and ordered me back to my room.

I lay there. The doctor didn't come. I sweated, suffered, writhed. The lamps in the room were of a Soviet modern style, set flush with the wall so they cast their radiance upward like the lighting inside a coffin. At one point, despairing, I put on my coat and set out for a foreigners' emergency room in a far neighborhood mentioned in my Cadogan guidebook, but the floor lady caught me, berated me, and sent me back to wait some more. The doctor, when he finally did arrive, looked like one of the Marx brothers, from their early movies when they were young. He had a long white coat, wacky side hair, and eyes that seemed to rotate in opposite directions in his round black spectacles. He carried not a doctor's bag but a big black box, with shiny metal reinforcements at the corners. Inside it were row upon row of German pharmaceuticals in glass ampoules that could be opened only by breaking the tops. I described my symptoms the best I could (he spoke almost no English), and he took out two ampoules. They looked like something a Nazi would use to kill himself. The doctor broke the tops, administered the bitter, mahogany-colored contents to me, told me to drink lots of water, gave me his card, and left.

Whatever had afflicted me — a constriction of the kidney capillaries, brought on by dehydration, was his diagnosis — began to moderate. The light of dawn rose faintly in the room's high windows. The morning's first trolleybus went by on the street below, the sparks under its wheels throwing reflected flashes on the ceiling. The city's ravens started their morning ratcheting. In my sudden, growing feeling of non-illness, I became so grateful to the mad doctor, and so restored to myself, I almost levitated. Sinister-seeming foreign medicine was actually curing me. My irrational love of Russia returned, and I rolled back against the wall to sleep.

*

What undoes you, usually, is what you gulp. Once, in a bar in Montana, I held my hand against the glass of a case containing a coiled and rattling rattlesnake; if I could keep my hand against the glass when the snake struck, the bartender said, he would buy me a beer. The bet proved a safe one on his part, because it is in fact impossible not to flinch from a striking snake, no matter how thick the intervening glass or strong your will. When you travel, a similar deeply conditioned response occurs: you know the food is bad, the water dangerous. You discipline yourself consciously, stick to bottled water, eat only the mildest, most scrutinized food. Vigilance carries you through one trip, maybe several. But then in an unguarded moment you're hungry, you're thirsty, something smells good, the water from the spring looks refreshing, your reflexes take over — and you gulp.

(Although, strangely, what sickened me that time in Russia was not gulping but caution. I had been so careful about what I drank, I became dehydrated from not drinking enough.)

And the result of gulping, most of the time, is that you come down with a certain ailment. This ailment is in fact the most common one that travelers get. It is so well known that it does not need to be named; you know the ailment I mean. Usually it is caused by food. It is disagreeable and inconvenient but not serious. It sneaks up on you no matter how careful you are. Sufferers usually recover from the worst of it in two to three days. In its commonest form I don't even consider it an illness, technically. It will not kill you. What does kill travelers is accidents (if you're young) and preexisting medical conditions (if you're old). These problems are rarer, thankfully. But in almost all travel stories, an unmentioned amount of the most common travel ailment can usually be assumed.

People who described journeys in former times, when one refrained from being gross in polite company or in writing, indicated attacks of the ailment with the word *indisposed.* A caravan trekker who crossed Asia, reached the Great Wall, entered China, and then ate his first-ever Chinese banquet might report that after the feast he "suffered a most severe indisposition." Many notable journeys involved these indispositions, usually left more or less blank in the tale.

Francis Parkman, a Boston Brahmin and Harvard grad, went west the summer after finishing law school, in 1846, to observe and live with Indians on the Plains. When he and his companion,

Quincy Adams Shaw, reached Fort Laramie, in present Wyoming, Parkman became ill. His "disorder" was so severe he could hardly sit his horse, and of course he made slow progress toward the Sioux camp, having to dismount all the time. Parkman kept riding, on to the Black Hills, so ill at moments out there in the wilderness that he feared he would die. His intrepidity and persistence not only outlasted the ailment but made his book — and, arguably, his later career as a great American historian. Shaw, for his part, came down with poison ivy and spent much of the journey back at the fort "lying on a buffalo robe . . . solacing his woes with tobacco and Shakespeare."

At least Parkman didn't have to deal with the great discrepancy in bathrooms that exists today. Presumably, using the outhouse at Fort Laramie (not to mention simply the bushes) did not differ a lot from similar necessities anywhere. Nowadays, though, if you leave America and travel to someplace interesting like Asia or Africa or South America (I'm sorry, but I don't consider most parts of Europe interesting), you encounter bathrooms that are an unimaginable nightmare. Most countries that are not America occupy a different universe, bathroomwise. A friend who travels in China and Nepal says that what the United States should send to foreign lands is not Peace Corps volunteers or World Bank economists but plumbers and plumbing supplies. In northern parts of Russia, where winter temperatures go to forty-five below, liquids freeze so quickly that a kind of stalagmite effect occurs in the outhouse, rising up through the hole in the floor . . . As the poets say, let us draw a veil across the scene.

The common traveler's ailment causes many of us to see more of this sort of thing than we're really interested in. But, as with a lot of unfortunate circumstances in real life, it could get worse. You could eat bad fish in Thailand and get liver flukes. I'm not even sure what liver flukes are, but you don't want them. You could consume a generous helping of a coral-reef fish that has been feeding on crustaceans rich in some bizarre nerve toxin, and absorb the toxin, and fall into a zombie state (real zombies ingest this toxin deliberately, I believe, in order to become zombies), and lie in a near-death paralysis for who knows how long, as happened to the novelist Saul Bellow. In his seventies at the time, the Nobel Prize winner went out to dinner on the island of St. Maarten, came back to the hotel, felt poorly, and lay catatonic for months. Don't order the grouper is the moral here.

So many maladies for you to catch! Malaria is still quite active in equatorial climates, and drug-resistant strains exist now. Web sites devoted to the disease feature constantly updated maps showing the worst malarial zones. Cholera, a frightening-sounding illness, waits in drinking water and kills by dehydration; if you get it, and can keep hydrated and take antibiotics, it goes away in about a week. Tick-borne illnesses thrive all over, in temperate as well as tropical lands. Serious versions of Lyme disease that can put you in the hospital may be found no farther away than upstate New York. In Russia, a certain kind of tick that lives east of the Ural Mountains carries a fever for which there is no cure. Camping in the summer in Siberia, I awoke one morning to find a tick — the Russian word is pronounced "kleshch," a triumph of onomatopoeia — kleshching to me. I showed it to my Russian companions and they assured me that though it was indeed the kind of tick that carries the fever, the insect is contagious with it only in the spring.

Giardia, a troublemaking intestinal parasite, does well in much of India and can be in untreated water almost everywhere. It turns up sometimes in the tap water in St. Petersburg. A tricky aspect of giardiasis is the time-lapse way it presents: you think at first you merely have the common traveler's ailment, until it goes on too long. Schistosomiasis, another parasitic disease, also waterborne, has similar symptoms. A swim in the Yangtze or the Mekong may give you a dose of it. Dysentery also resembles the common traveler's illness, only it involves blood. Typhoid, hepatitis, polio, SARS, avian flu — I'm getting depressed — and of course the various STDs threaten travelers. A male flight attendant for Air Canada was supposedly the first major international transmitter of AIDS. Even watching the Travel Channel and eating snacks causes arteries to harden and plaque to accumulate in your veins. There is no real hope anywhere.

Travel rules that I have learned, sometimes painfully: Eat no unwashed fruits and vegetables, and no washed ones, either. Salmonella bacteria can persist deep in the crinkles of a lettuce leaf. No fruits or vegetables should be consumed unless they're cooked to a fare-thee-well. Ditto all other food, basically. If it's really cooked, it's probably not bad. Bread is usually OK; also cookies. In general I try not to eat seafood except in the U.S. (and I've gotten horribly sick on it once here, come to think of it). Never drink raw milk, though it looks tasty and bucolic. Carry Wash'n Dris and wash your hands frequently. Once, after visiting the men's room (to return to that grim subject) in the Omsk airport, I used about eight Wash'n Dris, then for good measure asked my Russian friend to pour straight alcohol all over my hands as well as on the soles of my shoes. My God, that place. I never saw anything so gross.

Alcohol, in strengths you drink, does not purify anything. Ice in drinks is always a bad idea; luckily, foreigners aren't as in love with iced beverages as we are. Boiled water is safe for drinking, but opinion differs on the amount of boiling required. I've heard that water needs merely to be brought to a boil, and also that it should boil vigorously for ten minutes at the very least. A travel doctor I consulted before a trip to the Russian Far East strongly recommended the ten-minute rule, and I promised myself I'd abide by it — not a practical plan, as it turned out. After an open-boat journey in wind and rain in early fall with two indigenous Chukchi guys across a fjordlike body of water on the Chukchi Peninsula, the guys beached on a rocky spit, tipped the boat on its side, got under it, took out a blowtorch, and lit it. Then they applied the blowtorch to a teapot, quickly boiled water, made tea, and offered me a cup. At that point I could not really request that they blowtorch it for ten minutes more.

The travel doctor I saw also told me to drink only bottled beverages if possible. "You can get bottled water everywhere," he assured me. Conversations in a clean, quiet anglophone doctor's office in North America don't always give you a clear idea of the actual situations awaiting you. You cannot get bottled water everywhere. In fact, the purpose of many journeys is to go beyond the places where you can. In Russia, knockoffs exist of many products. There's even a watery version of Johnson's Baby Shampoo, eerily similar to the original, down to the bottle and scent. Of course, there's fake bottled water in Russia, too. Russians sometimes laugh at people who insist on bottled water only, and tell them it's just tap water with a cap on.

For more advice on such subjects, I recently called Dr. Mark Wise, graduate of Britain's London School of Hygiene and Tropical Medicine, director of a travel clinic in Toronto, and author of a book about staying healthy while you travel. On the water question, Wise recommends buying bottled water in places where you can see many bottles of it and cases of it still sealed. Failing that, buy fizzy water. "Carbonation is harder to forge," he says. As to boiling, Wise is a bring-to-a-boiler; two minutes of a rolling boil kills most bacteria and parasites, while boiling longer wastes water and fuel at a tiny increase of safety. The Canadian-made water-purifying tablet with the brand name Pristine tastes better than iodine, he says, and may be used when no other means of purification are available. "Sometimes, though, you just have to trust what common sense says is OK," he adds. "You can also go too far being paranoid."

Wise became a travel doctor because of the movie *Butch Cassidy and the Sundance Kid*, which inspired him to take a backpacking trip around South America. Contemplating a volcano in Ecuador while simultaneously enduring an acute onset of the common traveler's ailment concentrated his mind on what could be done for the suffering traveler. Today, Wise is the travel-medicine consultant for several nongovernmental organizations as well as for a number of unaffiliated travelers, and at any one time he has many patients scattered in different parts of the world who are in touch with him by e-mail. "Even on short journeys, a third to a half of all travelers to the poorer parts of the world will get sick," he says. "Usually it's with stomach or bowel problems from dirty water or dirty food. If you can keep hydrated, stay near a bathroom, and let the illness run its course, usually it clears up by itself in a few days. But people e-mail me about many other health problems, too — malaria, animal bites, vehicle accidents, falls. I had a fall myself a few months ago while traveling in Ghana — stepped into a dry, dark sewer as I was walking along at night and screwed up my leg and ankle."

A traveler's problem that Wise deals with more often than you might expect is psychosis. "Psychotic episodes are more common in the younger age group," he says. "The antimalarial drug mefloquine can contribute to them. A kid will be in a faraway country, in a strange environment, maybe taking medications which can cause hallucinations, and he or she will lose touch with reality. These episodes sometimes occur even without an obvious chemical cause. Sometimes we have to send a psychiatric nurse to take care of the person and get him or her out of there. That's one reason I tell people they can't travel without medevac insurance. In a worst-case scenario, you want to be able to have your mother fly over and bring you home.

"When you're sick in a foreign country, there's generally a lot of chatter around you," Wise continues. "You may be treated with presumptive medicine, where a doctor or somebody guesses at the problem and tries to cure you by polypharmacy. Or else people tell you misleading things — local things, herbal things to try. None of that is necessarily bad, but it clutters and confuses your mind. You want to be sure it doesn't cause you to miss something important. In the midst of all that, getting in touch with North American medicine, even by a simple e-mail, can be a bit of a lifeline."

I know what Wise means. Global culture, which carries you along when you travel, is powerful but blunt. It doesn't bother about details, especially human details. As we pass from country to country, we probably have no idea what the people around us are saying, and what they're thinking is ten times more mysterious. Often the best we can do is listen for tones — anger, joy, fear — the way animals do. This ad hoc approach is unreliable and frustrating. I've spent weeks among people where my grasp of what was going on with them, and vice versa, was a scrambled TV signal almost constantly. The mutual obtuseness wears everybody down and makes them mad. When you get sick, your condition isn't generic but specific. Not getting it exactly right can have frightening consequences.

Another alarm in the night in St. Petersburg: this time I was staying at a friend's apartment in the middle of the city. The friend was away. Russian apartments are double-sealed against the world, with double windows and often double doors. The outer of the two doors to this apartment opened with a key — a long and heavy one, like a movie jailer's, which needed the touch of a safecracker to work. The second, inner door had a knob but no lock or key, just a heavy sliding bolt you shot once inside. With this door bolted, a person in the apartment could keep out anyone, even someone with a key. When the first symptoms jolted me from sleep, I wondered fearfully and obsessively about those doors, in between jolts. Should I throw the doors open in advance for the rescue squad? I never had enough of a pause between symptoms to decide.

The pains squarely occupied my middle, like a bull's-eye. This had to be a heart attack. Self-diagnosis is an objective, grown-up skill I lack, but in this case, further symptoms, lower down — rumblings, crampings, and other demonstrations — made the problem seem not cardiac but gastrointestinal. Maybe it was both.

I had come to the city a week earlier to report on its three-hundredth-anniversary celebration. I had walked many miles, seen the elephant, stayed up all through some of the white nights. The day I got sick, I finished the last of my reporting around noon, and then to celebrate bought a two-liter bottle of Baltika Beer — my first mistake, as the kielbasa the color of machine grease that I'd bought to go with it was my second. Later, I went to dinner at a friend's apartment in a high rise on a far edge of the city. My friend's wife made a dinner of which I ate a lot, because she had gone to some trouble and seemed to have a hard life. I took several helpings of salad, possibly not thoroughly washed. Everything I ate that day was suspect, the kielbasa most of all.

Spasms and more spasms — these Russian germs were mean. They grabbed and shook me like a soda can. I'll skip the full details. After an hour or so, I ruled out a heart attack in favor of the common traveler's illness, with all the extras. Or possibly dysentery; I had a symptom of that, too. I tried to drink bottled water to stay hydrated but couldn't keep up. I was hot and shivering. During a short respite after vomiting, I dressed and made it out of the apartment — relocking the outer door took the last of my concentration — and then sort of sleepwalked through the city's strange boreal dawn, down empty sidewalks to a clinic I'd seen advertised in an English-language newspaper. The walk proved harder than I'd imagined, and by the time I reached the clinic, I was all in. I veered across the waiting room to the check-in desk and said to the nurses there, *"Dumaiu, shto ia umriu!"* which means "I think I'm dying!" — an overstatement, but on the other hand they didn't make me wait.

You hear bad reports about every institution in Russia, including Russian medicine. True, this was a clinic for foreigners; but to me, in off the street, it could have been anything. It turned out to be great. A young doctor named Viacheslav Zuev examined me and took my temperature and gave me an EKG. Zuev spoke pretty good English, and when he couldn't think of a word, he would snap his fingers on either side of his face and pull it from the air. He put me in a bed in a single room with the lights dimmed and started an IV. In Russia, sheets are still cotton, not percale or whatever miracle fiber has replaced it here. The sheets on this bed were white, fresh, like in a 1950s bedroom, and the pillowcases the same. Above the bed on the wall hung a clock the size of a steering wheel. I watched it fixedly and barely moved, waiting for this particular moment to be in the past.

The biggest surprise, and the point of this story, was the nurses. Russian women, I should mention in an aside, are beautiful; anyone who has been to Russia recently can verify this. No explanation exists for this phenomenon; it just is. I won't go on about it at too great a length, so as not to seem weird, but there are many, many lovely women in Russia. Anyway, these nurses were up to the standard of their countrywomen and then went beyond it. In America, nurses are brisk, goal-oriented, and upbeat. They don't get paid enough, and they have too much to do, and they want you to recover and move on, and that's fine. But Russian nurses (to judge by these) suffer with you. These wore starched old-fashioned nurses' caps, like the false fronts of buildings, and modest uniforms with pleats. They looked like the nurses little girls used to want to be when they grew up. I forget these nurses' names — Liuda, Sofia, and Elena . . . When they talked to me, their voices cooed sweetly and mournfully. "Oh, yes, life is very hard," their manner seemed to say.

I conversed with them slowly in my limited Russian, the sentences as if taken from the beginning workbook. Where are you from? I live in the state of New Jersey. Have you ever been to the United States? Where do your friends in the United States live? Do your friends like New Haven? Do they like to study at Yale? My wife's name is Jacqueline. She is not a Frenchwoman. She was born near Boston, in the state of Massachusetts. Yes, that is not far from New Haven.

These nurses were of the tradition that compares nurses to angels. They sympathized quietly, wholeheartedly, and from someplace unreachably high. They came and went, and I lay conversing in a disembodied voice. As it became clear that what I had contracted (salmonella poisoning, according to the lab report) was not going to finish me off, I felt embarrassed to have gotten so carried away. Americans are crybabies — that's me. No doubt my nurses had seen similar behavior before.

The window of the room was open, and I could hear the footsteps of passersby on the sidewalk just a few feet away. The steps increased in number as people awoke and the day began. I lay there listening to the steps. Like the nurses, they were different from the American version. They were Russian-sounding, Cossack-dance footsteps, every one of them. I would not have confused them with American footsteps in a million years. For hours I looked at the motion of the clock and listened to the Russian footsteps. By evening I had recovered enough to be discharged. I consider this one of the most satisfactory days I've spent anywhere.

All journeys bring to mind the truck drivers' adage "There ain't no easy run." When we travel, we think we don't want to get sick, but maybe, less consciously, we're not so sure. If nothing of note happens on a journey, was it one? Travel pursues romance, and romance requires the unknown — an element in shorter supply now that technology is encompassing the world with ever-multiplying pings. The goal is not only to arrive at some numinous, far-off destination; it's to return to your usual place clothed in exciting unfamiliarity: you're the boy who lived with pirates, the girl brought back from the wilderness who has grown so accustomed to Indian life she had to be coaxed away. A key element here is the cool impression made on one's friends. Illness is a passage, and when it happens on a journey — a passage within a passage — it leaves you doubly transformed. When you get better, you feel doubly recovered and strong. Getting sick while traveling is one of those tricky accomplishments you simultaneously want to have done and don't ever want to do.

STEVE FRIEDMAN

Lost in America

FROM *Backpacker*

THE TRIP WAS NOT GOING ACCORDING TO PLAN. He knew he couldn't have prepared for everything — you don't get to be a 410-pound ex-Marine, clinically depressed and a quasi-Buddhist and halfway across North America on foot without accruing some wisdom about things like nasty surprises and the necessity of acceptance — but by the time he reached Dayton, Ohio, even for Steve Vaught, things were getting to be a little much.

It wasn't the two rattlesnakes, or the cases of poison oak, or the kidney stone. It wasn't the twenty blisters, or the heat, or even the guy who e-mailed him to proclaim that he could absolutely not, under any circumstances, let Vaught pass Kingman, Arizona, "because it would bring on Armageddon." It wasn't that his wife had told him she wanted a divorce, or that his ghostwriter had complained that Vaught's journal entries were "boring" and "pedantic." It wasn't the clowns who jumped out of the car while he was still in California — real clowns, with noses and floppy feet and everything — and danced around him yelling, then jumped back in their car and drove off. It wasn't the other guy (at least he thinks it was a guy) who e-mailed, "You vulgar maggot . . . you are a fiend and a sniveling backboneless coward."

It wasn't the reporters — "Short and fat and drunk, they all say the same thing. They say, 'Oh yeah, it'll be great to walk with you' and they end up sitting there talking for three hours for two inches in the paper." It wasn't the woman who showed up in three towns and said she wanted to "absorb" him. That was creepy, no doubt, but it didn't make him want to quit. It wasn't the heat of the desert or the cold of the mountains or the loneliness or the rage that came over him after he'd thrown his antidepressants down a sewer drain.

It was all of that and it was none of that. It was as shallow as vanity, as deep as the confusion that can steal into a man's soul at 3:00 A.M. when he looks in the mirror and doesn't recognize the sallow apparition staring back.

He thought about how he would appear the next time he was on TV. He worried that he would look too fat. It was as simple as that. It was also much, much more complicated than people might imagine, because although he desperately wanted to lose weight, he knew that to focus on weight loss was to lose himself. That's the kind of Dr.-Freud-meets-Dr.-Phil puzzle that presents itself to a morbidly obese man as he trudges alone across the deserts of the American West. It's also the kind of insight carried by any man who as a child was ever called fat boy or forced to pull on a pair of Husky jeans. It's the knowledge earned by every teenage girl who is assured by her worried mother, "You have such a beautiful face," then asked, "Do you really need that dessert?"

Everyone is special. In the United States, at the turn of the twenty-first century, that's a truth as self-evident as the ones about life and liberty. Here's another verity of our times: you can make yourself more special. You can get whiter teeth and a nicer car and better job and firmer thighs — all in easy monthly payments. You are a wonderful person. Now here's how to get more wonderful.

It was Steve Vaught's luck — or curse, or both — to captivate a sizable segment of the sizable segment of the American public that has found itself pinned between those two shiny, grinding truths. It hadn't been his intention. He didn't hug and kiss his wife and children and start a twenty-nine-hundred-mile hike to lug with him the hopes and dreams of every chubby — and depressed and lonely and lost and just generally dissatisfied and yearning — adult in the country and worldwide. But by the time he reached Dayton, that's what had happened.

What had started as a plan at once unadorned and profoundly unhinged — to walk across America to drop pounds and find joy — had become a mega–book deal and a publicity scrum and a quasi-corporate enterprise. He wasn't just Steve Vaught anymore. Now he was the Fat Man Walking. He had a website, thefatmanwalking.com. Soon enough, a Mythology of the Fat Man Walking had taken hold. It was this: A man who suffered through things worse than most of us can imagine had eaten more than most of us can imagine until he was more gargantuan than most of us can imagine. Now he was undertaking an epic trek, and it would save him. A variation of an old story, more popular than ever, two thousand years later. Suffering and redemption, writ extra, extra large.

A hike? Hardly. It was Paul Bunyan meets *Pilgrim's Progress.* People checked out his route on thefatmanwalking.com and e-mailed him to tell him if he could lose weight, they could quit cigarettes. Or start exercising. Or lose weight. They could change their lives. Naturally, Oprah's people called.

But how could he save anyone if he couldn't even save himself? By the time he got to St. Louis, right around Christmas, he had been stuck at 318 pounds for more than a month. That's when his wife told him she wanted a divorce. By the time he got to Dayton, he was 345 pounds. Once, he had to use the scale at a truck weigh station to make sure. People e-mailed him, told him to avoid fast-food restaurants. Had those people ever walked along the highways of Middle America? The Fat Man was getting fatter. And desperate. And when word got out that Vaught was calling time-out in the middle of his path to salvation — that the trail to happiness had hit a roadblock in Dayton and he was returning to California for a month to work out with a personal trainer — the Mythology of the Fat Man took a hit. Have gods with clay feet ever been treated kindly? Some of his would-be corporate backers were not happy. His ghostwriter from HarperCollins was not happy. The television folks were not happy. Some of the visitors to his website were not happy. The truth is, Vaught was not happy.

"First, he's this big schlub," says David Mollering, one of two documentary filmmakers who spent twenty weeks with Vaught on his journey. "And then all of a sudden he's Forrest Gump. That's a lot to handle for anybody."

No doubt the schlub-Gump metamorphosis was proving taxing, though Vaught handled it with some aplomb, referring to himself in the third person as "Forrest Lump." But there were other problems, too. He hated being fat. He hated disappointing people. He hated the idea that he might fail. These were all issues that a lot of people could relate to. All were challenges that any man — even a skinny man — could understand. But a man doesn't eat himself to the land of truck-stop scales because he's like the rest of us. Oprah's people aren't holding for you and me. We all have demons. Vaught had a fiend. Or maybe he was the fiend.

"He's been carrying a six-hundred-pound gorilla," says Pierre Bagley, the other filmmaker. "I used to say, 'Steve, if there's a monster in this thing, then you're Dr. Frankenstein.'"

A Bad, Bad Place

He made the decision in a Target store. Friday night, March 25, 2005, in a pharmacy aisle. He was with his wife, April, and his kids, Melanie, then eight, and Marc, then three. Vaught felt a stabbing pain in his back, a tightness in his chest. He struggled for breath. He thought he might be having a heart attack. By the time he made it home and sat down, and realized he wasn't dying, he'd come up with a plan.

It was a big plan, a bold plan. It was the kind of plan we all cook up from time to time — quit the job, hug the wife goodbye, hit the road — but that only a few follow. Vaught had already followed a few.

He had dropped out of high school and joined the Marines at seventeen, gotten married at twenty, divorced at twenty-four. He was living in San Diego then, a muscled 250 pounds, an honorably discharged lance corporal with a new girlfriend and a job as manager of a tow truck company. It doesn't sound too bad. It probably looked good. But people didn't know that his father had left Vaught and his mother when Vaught was three. They didn't know his father had spent much of his life in prison, for crimes Vaught doesn't want to discuss. Vaught applied for a job as a cop after the Marines, and they hooked him to a polygraph and asked if he'd ever thought of killing anyone, and he had said no. The lie stopped the interview. "Not only had I thought about it," he says, "I'd worked it out." He was thinking of his father.

But other children survive abandonment. Other children endure less-than-ideal parents.

Vaught loved drawing. He wanted to be an artist. When he was thirteen, his stepfather told him drawing was for sissies. "I could have sweated gold, and it wouldn't have been good enough," Vaught says. "I could have been playing classical piano, and he would have hated me. It wasn't what I was doing. It was who I was."

Before he became the Fat Man, Vaught was simply a Very Unlucky Boy who became an Unhappy Grownup. But that describes a lot of people. They get by. They don't decide that the answer is a coast-to-coast stroll. Maybe Vaught would have gotten by, too, if not for the accident.

It happened late in the afternoon. He was on his way to pick up a birthday card for his girlfriend. The sun was in his eyes and he was going too fast. Even if he had seen the elderly couple in the intersection, he might not have been able to avoid them. But he was going too fast, and he didn't see them until he was on them. The woman, Emily Vegzary, seventy-five, went through the windshield and died instantly. Zoltan Vegzary, eighty-one, lived twenty-one days before he died. Vaught spent his first night in jail (he would serve thirteen days for vehicular manslaughter), with the dead woman's blood and pieces of her skin in his hair.

A year later, Vaught had gained sixty pounds. He and his girlfriend had split up. After a brief stint in Las Vegas with an uncle, he ended up in an attic apartment in Youngstown, Ohio, where he was born and which he hated, unemployed, barely paying the thirty-five dollars a month rent.

One night, he hears a noise — pop, pop, pop. There's a man outside his window, shooting a pistol. Vaught leans his head out the window, sees the man, starts laughing. He can't stop laughing. The man looks up and sees the fat man leaning out the window.

"What are you laughing at?" the man with the gun yells. "I'll put a bullet through you."

Vaught keeps laughing, then stops. "Go ahead," he says.

"I just didn't care," he says. I knew that eventually something bad was going to happen to me, so why be concerned about it? Maybe I was hoping that would be the night."

Are those the words of a mad scientist, or the monster he created? The Fat Man's not sure. How could he be? Imagine hating your father and stepfather. Now imagine killing two people. Imagine being Steve Vaught. Would you have been able to leave the attic? Vaught speaks about fear and despair with eloquence; he quotes Lao Tzu and the *Tao Te Ching* and Alan Watts with passion and precision. When it comes to what saved him, though, when it comes to love, there's this: "I met a girl, and the girl sort of drug me out of it."

They moved to California, he got a job at an auto repair shop, and one day Vaught came home and the girl said she'd been sleeping with her boss. He sold everything he owned, bought a one-way ticket to England, where his ex-wife was living, and when he told immigration agents he had never been married, they checked their records, saw that his ex-wife lived in England, then sent him back. He took a Greyhound from Newark to Harrisburg, and from Harrisburg back to Youngstown, and from there he managed to fly to Albuquerque, where he stayed with an old friend named Jeff for a few weeks, and from there to San Diego. It was a long, meandering trip undertaken by a man who had nothing better to do than drift, and as anyone who has ever drifted knows, salvation can bob up in the most unexpected places. In San Diego, he stopped to say hello to Jeff's girlfriend. And there he saw a friend of hers who looked familiar.

Vaught knew her from a happier time in his life, when he was twenty, freshly discharged from the Marines and life was filled with possibilities. She had been thirteen then. Now, she was twenty-three, and he was thirty. And three months later she was pregnant, and Steve and April were living in San Diego, expecting.

In the Mythology of the Fat Man, April saved Steve. The love of a good woman and all that. And maybe there's some truth to that. Other men are saved by love, grounded by children. Maybe Vaught was, too. Maybe without April, and without the births of Melanie and Marc, things would have unraveled faster. Maybe things would have been worse. But they were bad enough.

He couldn't stop eating, for one thing. He couldn't stop thinking about how empty he felt, for another. Maybe they were the same thing.

"I said, 'If the next thirty-three years are as good as the last thirty-three, I don't need to hang on anymore.' I thought, 'What kind of father am I going to be?'

"I thought, 'They're almost better off without me.' Once you think that, you're in a bad, bad place. I thought, 'I'm just polluting their environment by being around. If I can't fix myself' — and I was convinced I couldn't — 'then it's better if I'm not around.'"

He couldn't stop the monstrous thoughts. Soon, he was looking like a monster, too. His weight climbed from 300 to 320, and from there to 350, and from there to 375. "Go see someone," April said. "Or just go." So he saw a therapist who put him on Paxil and Wellbutrin, antidepressants. He remembers the day they kicked in, how the smell of the pavement and the colors of flowers "almost knocked me out."

He had a beautiful wife and two great children. He had a therapist and antidepressants that allowed him to function. He'd found work managing an auto repair shop. He had two exercise machines and two mountain bikes in the garage, but he never used any of them. And he ate alone, because he couldn't stand to have people see how much food he consumed. He couldn't stop eating.

"I'm killing myself," he thought, "and I don't know how to stop." The night he left the Target store, he was thirty-nine years old. He weighed 410 pounds. He had gained more than 100 pounds in seven years.

After the children were asleep, he and April sat up for hours in bed talking. "The kids don't get the father they deserve, I don't get the husband I deserve, and he doesn't get the life he deserves," April told Bagley. (April Vaught declined to be interviewed for this article.)

She told him he should hurry up, that he should get started as soon as possible.

On Monday, he quit his job. The same day, he took a warm-up hike. He carried a pack loaded with a fifty-pound plate from one of the weight machines.

"Almost killed me," he wrote in his journal. "The back and leg pain was unbelievable."

The next day, he tried again. "Same route, much less pain." Over the next two weeks, he made it as far as four and a half miles, did a few local television interviews, and lined up two camping stores to donate equipment.

On April 10, 2005, he lumbered away from Oceanside. He carried four flashlights, ten D batteries, two sleeping bags, an electric fan, and no cell phone. He had two hundred dollars in his pocket. His pack weighed eighty-five pounds.

Facing the Truth

The plan was to get from the Oceanside pier to New York City in six months. He walked nine miles the first day, ten the next. Drivers screamed obscenities at him. One threw a Big Gulp cup at him. He developed a blister on his left foot. So he took a day off. Then another day. The fifth day, he managed to make five miles. Not what anyone would call a steady pace. But before he became the Fat Man, before legions of wounded seekers made him their standard-bearer, no one had ever accused Vaught of being the steady sort.

He thought about his feet. He thought about the rain. He thought about different ways of tying his shoes, and his fancy hiking pants that ripped twice and that he sewed twice, and then they ripped again, and he thought more about his feet, and how when he moved up from a size 11 to a size 12 shoe, his whole life improved and how "it is funny how something that is normally a minor incident in one's life becomes epic when you are involved in something like this."

Why couldn't he be happier? He thought about that a lot. Any tortured soul who's ever decided that peace depends on the successful completion of one task knows it's a nerve-racking way to live. "Not because of the pain," he wrote in his online journal on April 27, when he stopped at the Ontario Mills Mall in Riverside County, "but because I cannot face the possibility that I may have a serious injury and this trip might very well have ended for me tonight. I absolutely cannot fail at this, because to do so means that I am going to fail at living, fail my kids and my wife."

April drove to the mall and picked him up, then took him to a doctor. He had a strained tendon, painful but not serious. A week later, she drove back to the mall, and he started again.

He started, and he almost stopped.

"I got to the desert and I thought, 'Oh, my God, what have I done?'" It was 105°F, he was running low on water, and he didn't see a store anywhere. That was in Dagget, near Barstow. "I'm hot and miserable and depressed and sitting in an abandoned Shell station, thinking, 'Why is this happening to me?'" He wasn't even halfway across California.

Another morning, still in the Mojave, short on water again, he came to a cool little creek under a bridge.

"It wasn't that hot yet, but I was tired. I see these little watermelons growing on the side of the road. Turns out they were gourds. I put my feet in the creek for a little while, then I fall asleep, under the bridge."

When he woke, ready to fill his two-gallon water bottles, he noticed something had changed. It was quieter now. The creek wasn't burbling. It wasn't running at all.

"I just kicked myself," he says. "I felt like, that was my life. You find a beautiful creek in the middle of the desert, you wake up, it's gone. You've got to seize the moment."

By the time he made it to Arizona, he was more careful about water, more cautious about mapping his daily route. He had a cell phone, courtesy of a California radio station, and a national following, courtesy of the media. *Today* called. *Dateline NBC* called. One day, he had fifty-one thousand hits on his website. He had groupies. Yet with all that, he was still a man walking across a country. In the Arizona desert, he was daydreaming when he heard a strange noise. In front of him, almost underneath his foot, a diamondback rattler, about to strike. Vaught pulled out his 9mm Ruger P89 and shot it. (Later, a British newspaper would describe how Vaught had dispatched a cobra. What was weirder, shooting a snake in the desert, reading about it in a British paper on your website, or seeing it described as cobra?)

By Winslow, he had a book deal worth almost $250,000.

"When he got book money, he could afford hotels," Bagley says. "That became a problem. It was, 'I got a bath, I got a toilet, I got running water.' It was hard to give that up."

About twenty miles east of Gallup, Vaught wrote in his journal, "I didn't feel like I was going to quit, I just wanted to sit in a comfortable chair, in a warm room, and relax. So I indulged myself and that turned into four days quite easily."

In Seligman, he stopped at a place called the Roadkill Café and tucked into a chicken-fried steak, with biscuits and gravy. A reporter and photographer were there, and the picture went up on thefatmanwalking.com.

April knew how easy it was for Steve — who had already dropped to 346 — to stumble, so she told a group of middle-aged Albuquerque women who'd contacted her online where her husband was. They called themselves the Kat Walkers. The Fat Man called them a "Dr. Phil weight-loss group."

From Vaught's online journal: "Well, they came on like gangbusters, snatching me up from my low point . . . and we hit the road. They eagerly listened to my complaints and excuses, agreed that they were valid, and then said, 'OK then! Let's get to the walking' and they have not let up yet. I would have hidden from them because facing the truth about my weakness and forcing myself to be responsible to myself, my family, and my journey is not what I was looking for. Comfort, sympathy, and macaroni & cheese is what I was looking for . . . self-indulgence, in short. What I needed though was some good support, motivation, and a swift kick in the shorts, which is exactly what they provided."

People surprised him. People were nice. A fruit vendor gave him an orange. A couple offered him a bed and shower. A woman asked him to help her. Her mother was morbidly obese. She was dying. What could the woman do?

People were depending on him. People were helping him. He was losing weight. He was calming down (when he came upon another rattlesnake in New Mexico, he didn't shoot it). He should have been happy. Even the Frankenstein monster had moments of bliss, stretches of solitary, uninterrupted, contented grunting.

But reporters kept calling. Bagley and Mollering wanted to spend more time with him. Before he arrived in Albuquerque, HarperCollins informed Vaught that he would be working with a ghostwriter. The ghostwriter called, and he demanded access. The ghostwriter told Vaught what his journey meant. Vaught thought he already knew what his journey meant.

Was Vaught miserable because people were hounding him, or was it because he was afraid of failing, or was this the garden-variety despair of a man with too many miles to go, too many promises to keep? Or was it that no matter how far he walked, he couldn't escape his childhood? Or was he just constitutionally predisposed to misery and self-destructive behavior, if not an ogre with bolts in his head, then at least a world-class head case? He wasn't sure. He needed to be sure. But how could he be sure of anything with antidepressants clouding his thinking? He decided that was the problem.

He needed to do something bold. Something drastic.

"Why does a four-hundred-pound guy not just go to the gym, not eat right?" asks Bagley. "Why does he think he has to walk all the way across the country? He's not great at making life decisions."

In Amarillo, he threw his antidepressants down a storm drain. Then he filled the bottle with Skittles. When Bagley or Mollering asked if he was still taking his pills — they worried about him — he would shake the bottle and smile.

Over the next few weeks, through the Texas panhandle, he would lock himself in his hotel room for days at a time. He would refuse to talk to anyone. He would cry. Once, he threatened Bagley's teenage son, who was working as a cameraman for the documentary filmmakers. Once, he threw his phone against a hotel room wall.

Things didn't improve in Oklahoma. He was laid up while he waited to pass a kidney stone. He suffered three bouts of poison oak.

By late August, he'd been written about in the *New York Times* and the *Washington Post,* featured in Italy's *Gazzetta del Prione* and Germany's *Stern,* interviewed twice on *Today.* Oprah sent a crew to meet Vaught in Weatherford, Oklahoma. She asked about his diet and exercise and how he was losing weight.

"Oprah was like, 'Call me, it's a weight-loss story,'" says Bagley. "It's not a weight-loss story! He hasn't lost that much weight. I'm not sure what it is, but it's not a weight-loss story."

Was it a quest for clarity? If so, Vaught found it in Elk City, Oklahoma. "It was a day of awakening," he says. "I know it sounds corny, but one day I woke up and a lot of the nonsense seemed to have evaporated. A lot of the noise inside me was gone. The sky was pretty, the people were nice. It seemed like the whole world had lightened up."

How? The isolation, for one. The hiking. And being drug-free.

"I don't say that medicine is bad for everybody who uses it," he says. "I know some people need it. But for me, it dumbed me up, I felt like I couldn't function on it."

The discomfiting thing about heightened awareness is you start noticing things that never made you miserable before. Even though he weighed less than 340 now, and even though he had reduced his pack weight from eighty-five to fifty-five, it was still a lot to carry. He had been talking to people from GoLite almost since the trip began, and they had been imploring him to reduce his load. "If you want to be an idiot," he says an employee told him, "go ahead and keep on with what you've got."

In Oklahoma, a GoLite rep named Kevin Volt flew out and met him. He spread Vaught's belongings out on a tarp. He looked at his two-pound first-aid kit. "Are you going to do surgery?" Volt asked. He nodded at Vaught's three canisters of fuel. "Inviting people over for a barbecue, are you?" When Vaught left Oklahoma City, his pack weighed sixteen pounds. Left behind were flashlights, notebooks, a tape recorder, a digital camera, clothes, and a sleeping bag liner. He kept his laptop computer. He ditched the pistol.

By the time he left Oklahoma, at the beginning of November, he was down to 330 pounds. He got to 325, then 320. By the time he reached St. Louis at the end of 2005, he was down to 318, but he had been at that weight for weeks. He could not break 318. And then he talked to April on the phone and she said she wanted a divorce. (Vaught will not talk about the divorce, but says both he and his wife are committed to being friends and good parents.)

His weight started to climb again. He tried sit-ups. He tried high-protein diets. He heard from eighteen personal trainers, scores of anonymous e-mailers (whose advice started at "Why are you eating a chicken-fried steak, you fat pig?" then got really nasty), and a host of self-professed experts. "One person said, you should eat nothing but egg whites. Another guy kept e-mailing me about diet. He's got a chemical equation that would drive Einstein crazy. A lot of people said, 'Why don't you just start eating less and exercising more.' I said, 'Goddamn it, why don't you have your own fucking show, instead of Oprah?'"

Only one person made sense. His name was Eric Fleishman, though he's better known as Eric the Trainer. Fleishman is a Los Angeles–based trainer who, like more than a few Los Angeles–based trainers, has a website and a vision that goes far beyond good cardiovascular health. He offers, according to his website, "programs [that] provide a holistic approach to fitness that incorporates gender-specific exercises, Eastern philosophy, and diet to achieve a perfect version of you."

"Sign Up," he encourages online visitors. "Call in. Get Fit. Be Beautiful."

Like Vaught, Fleishman is a talker. Like Vaught, Fleishman likes to talk about a wide range of subjects.

They talked on the phone about loneliness and despair, about exercise and eating, about running away from trouble and the search for self.

Fleishman drove out to a truck stop in California, walked around, tried to discover the dietary reality in which Vaught lived. He flew out to Dayton, and they talked some more. An hour later, according to Vaught, Fleishman said, "You're a great guy and a wonderful person and I respect the journey that you're on, but it's a much more complex situation both physically and emotionally than I'd anticipated."

To Fleishman's surprise, Vaught suggested returning to California to work together for a few weeks.

So eleven months into a trip that was supposed to be completed in six, Vaught flew to Los Angeles. He spent twenty-one days in a hotel down the block from Fleishman's gym. Every day he would lift weights for an hour and do martial arts for an hour and walk backward for an hour. He accompanied Fleishman to local schools, where he talked about motivation. He talked about determination and how even when you were feeling helpless and scared, you kept going. He was big and scary-looking and gentle. Is it any wonder that children loved the Fat Man?

"A Little Too Murky"

He flew back to Dayton, started walking again on March 3. He weighed 282.

Some days he made it fifteen miles. On those days, likely as not, he'd walk into a restaurant and order a stromboli for dinner. Some days, he stayed in town. He might have stromboli then, too. He got back to 300 quickly, then to 305, then to 310. "One television producer calls and says, 'You've walked two-thirds of the way across America and you're still fat? Have you considered surgery?' Another one says, 'The story is a little too murky now.'"

Didn't they realize? His life had always been murky. But the saga of the Fat Man — the Mythology of the Fat Man — there was nothing murky about that story. Tragic, maybe, but ultimately redemptive. That's what the public wanted. That's what the TV producers wanted. That's certainly what the publisher wanted. Didn't they realize? He wanted it more than anyone.

The ghostwriter was calling regularly now. He had already written what he called the backbone of the book, sent it to Vaught. "Fill in the rest" is what Vaught says he was told. In the backbone, Vaught breaks down sobbing eleven times in the first chapter, exclaims at one point, "Hey, I'm a big fat loser."

Vaught was not happy about that.

"You know," he says, "a guy who walks across the country is not a big fat loser."

Other long-distance hikers pay attention to landscape, to soft dawns, to the way the birds sound at dusk. Vaught spent much of his journey next to highways, listening to diesel trucks. In Pennsylvania, he suffered two more kidney stones and one more case of poison oak. At night, he stayed in motels, plugged in his laptop, and tapped away miserably at the backbone of his book.

Now Vaught and his ghostwriter were arguing about tone, about structure, about almost everything.

It's doubtful that any ghostwriter would have an entirely easy time with someone as simultaneously driven and lost as Vaught. It's also a safe bet that no one but Vaught would proclaim to a visitor, "It's bad if you have a ghostwriter and you've said to him on more than one occasion, 'You're lucky you're not within choking distance.'"

He was rarely camping out now. He could afford motels. Plus, he had to keep in touch with the ghostwriter, and he had to work on revisions, and there were endorsement deals to consider.

A shampoo manufacturer offered him fifty thousand dollars if he would hold up a bottle of its product every time he was interviewed on television. He declined. A company offered a phone, computer, and RV, if he agreed to sing the praises of its wheatgrass, and "it sounded pretty good," but the company wanted to take over thefatmanwalking.com, so he refused. A company that marketed patches to help people quit smoking asked him to wear its product. "But I had never smoked. The guy says, 'You don't have to say you smoked, you don't have to lie, just that you're wearing a patch, people will assume that's why you don't smoke.'" He turned him down. "Another company wanted me to sponsor their glucosamine product. Same kind of deal — I can't make it across the country without my blah blah. But I don't think you need supplements. So that was no deal."

Some vitamin company people made an offer, too. They would market "thefatmanwalking" vitamins. He said that sounded OK. And they wanted to sell "thefatmanwalking" cholesterol-reduction pills, too. He, oddly enough, had never had a problem with cholesterol, but OK, that was fine, too. High cholesterol was something a lot of people needed help with. And they would sell "thefatmanwalking" diet pills, too. That was a deal breaker. "I'm not going to accept ads that are exploitative of people who are overweight," he says. "They wanted me to prostitute myself."

"I had started to realize there were a lot of people getting a lot of inspiration from what I was doing, and I didn't want to jeopardize that." It's easy to mock a man who makes a grab for the moral high ground just after he admits how delicious it would be to throttle his business partner. But what would you do if someone offered you hundreds of thousands of dollars to expose your most terrible secrets, then hired someone else to make them prettier? And how many people would turn down endorsement deals worth millions?

It's doubtful he was ever a jolly Fat Man. By mid-April, he is weary, eager for the trip to be over. He needs to hurry now. He is in rural Pennsylvania, about four hundred miles from New York City, and if he doesn't make it across the George Washington Bridge by May 15, HarperCollins might cancel the book.

"Sometimes I think I should have turned around at the Mississippi River and just walked back," he says. "Since St. Louis I've had no time to walk around and meet people. I've been dealing with the fucking book. I'm on chapter nine now, and I still have four more chapters to go. A long time ago, this walk stopped being about weight loss and personal redemption. It's about business now."

He just passed his third kidney stone a week ago. He is in the midst of his fourth case of poison oak. He's worn fifteen pairs of shoes, lost four toenails, and suffered twenty blisters "before I got smart about it." It is pouring outside, so he's taking the day off. Maybe he'd be taking the day off anyway. He is back up to 310 pounds. He is seated at a Denny's off the highway in Bedford, Pennsylvania. He orders the pepper jack omelet, with no pancakes, and he eats it in front of a reporter, which is a very big deal to Vaught, because he still doesn't like people to watch him eat.

"We need to medicate ourselves against the hollowness and pain," he says. "We think we can buy happiness, buy a cure or relief of our symptoms, but we can't. This has become crystal clear to me. The solitude of this walk has made this clear to me."

He has dark-brown hair and bottle-green eyes. He flirts with waitresses, complains about being a prisoner of the people who love the Fat Man but don't know Steve Vaught.

He doesn't say much at first, but once he gets going, he says a lot. He quotes from *The Madness of Crowds*, *The Three Pillars of Zen*, *The Best Buddhist Writings of 2005*, and *The Healing Anger*, by the Dalai Lama ("that was a big thing for me") and references the *Girls*

Gone Wild collection; ponders the ubiquity of the Internet and the meaning of Taoism and proclaims that "the inevitability of life is failure." His is the trippy wisdom familiar to anyone who has spent more than a couple days in the backcountry, or the desert, or even a weekend alone shuttling between a Motel 6 and Denny's, cut loose from the moorings of things like jobs and deadlines and family and friends.

The thing about such trippy wisdom is this: it might be trippy, but it's wise.

"Stop looking for the pill or the miracle cure," the Fat Man says. "You know what's going to cure me? Sausage and eggs."

"I tell people, 'You gotta stop watching TV, you gotta unplug.' The news would have you believe you walk out your door, there are gunfights and mayhem. But people are awesome. I've met some angry people, but no evil people. With the exception of a couple weird things here and there, it's been great."

"You can live in the past, you can live in the future, or you can live right now. This is your only true reality. Tomorrow will happen . . ."

It's easy to smile indulgently at the philosophical musings of a man who left his job and his family to find himself, at the proclamations of a guy who rails against the evils of consumerism while being defeated by chicken-fried steaks and stromboli. But can you imagine killing two people, gaining 160 pounds, losing 105, and walking twenty-nine hundred miles?

On May 9, he crosses the George Washington Bridge, and the next day, he appears for his third and probably final interview on *Today*. He weighs 305, but he knows it's just a number and to focus on the number is to be lured back to misery. Soon, the book will be out. After that? He's not sure. He might teach. Oprah might finally air his interview, might even have him in the studio. He might walk across England with Eric the Trainer. Fat Man Walking and Eric the Trainer together. That's a thought.

He will be forty-one on August 1. "What are my plans for the future? Attachment is one of the biggest problems we have as human beings. The stronger you hold something, the more attached you get. Consumerism is just destroying people. They worry about the future, they worry about the past. My only responsibility in life is to take care of my children. That's not a big deal. You feed them, you love them, you guide them. College funds and things like that? Worrying about that stuff doesn't make it happen."

Before he got held up by the rain and poison oak in Bedford, Pennsylvania, he received an e-mail from a girl named Kristin in Sioux Falls, South Dakota. She wanted to tell Vaught that on Easter Sunday, her pastor had mentioned him in his sermon. "It was inspirational," she wrote.

"I get tons of those," he says. "I almost feel guilty for getting them."

Can you imagine what it feels like to be famous for your girth, soon to be divorced, technically unemployed, to wonder what's coming next? Can you imagine the most successful thing you've ever done or are likely to do, about to end? Can you envision what it's like to serve as inspiration to people you've never met, to be a disappointment to yourself?

It's easy to think Steve Vaught is different, that his story is singular. It's comforting to behold his awesome bulk and to decide that his torment and confusion and even his murky triumphs belong to a creature unlike the rest of us. But to do so is to miss what's most important about Vaught's struggle.

He's not a savior. Not a monster, nor a monstrous inventor. Those are all myths. He's just a fat guy trying to lose weight. He's just a self-taught, hyper-articulate, sometimes very cranky person trying to navigate the distance between where he is and where he wants to be.

When it comes to that never-ending, utterly human journey, we could do much, much worse than to heed the wisdom of the Fat Man.

"As far as worrying about next year," he says, "I think about it, sure. I don't want to say, 'Next year I want to be a writer, next year I want to be this, or that.' You set yourself up for failure. No matter what happens next year, I'm going to make it the best possible moment, because that's where I'm living, in my moment. You're going to have good and you're going to have bad, and they're both equally as important. Wherever the road takes me, that's where I'll go."

ELIZABETH GILBERT

Long Day's Journey into Dinner

FROM *GQ*

1. America

SOMETIMES IN LIFE, there is a thing you long for so deeply that you are willing to wait for years — almost lying in ambush! — until you can get it. Suppose there's a woman you've always desired, but her heart belongs to another. You wait with one ear to the ground for the day you hear she's left her fiancé, and then you approach. Or maybe there's a job you've always fancied, or a wristwatch, or a car. You wait for it. Or perhaps there's a sovereign nation that you and your family have always wanted to invade, but the moment never seemed right. What do you do? You *wait*.

For me, that coveted thing was a particular trip to France.

Almost nine years ago, a married couple I knew told me they'd just spent two weeks walking and eating their way through Provence. As they told it, France has a well-kept secret — over one hundred thousand miles of interconnected rural trails called the GR, or Grande Randonnée. These trails run from the Atlantic to the Mediterranean, from the Spanish border to the Belgian, linking almost every quaint little village in the country to almost every other one. My friends walked these paths by day, slept in cozy village hotels by night, and sampled regional cuisine along the way. And every afternoon on their stroll, they would find some pretty spot (perhaps a scenic ditch, near a lavender field) and they would lay out a picnic lunch of baguettes, cheese, sausages, and French wines. Then they'd get a little drunk and doze off together under the warm Mediterranean sky.

The ditch, the cheese, the wine, the nap . . . I wanted all these things, desperately and immediately. But I had to wait. I had a marriage to dissolve first, jobs to finish, bills to pay. Most important, though, I had to wait until I found the perfect traveling/eating/drinking/napping companion. And I did finally find him, two years ago — my Brazilian-born, French-speaking, wine-worshipping, tripe-consuming, uncomplaining traveler of a sweetheart. As soon as we met, I had an instinct about this man. The way another woman might, on a first date, suddenly picture herself having a baby with the guy across the table, what I pictured was this: me and him, eating a duck's liver together in a French ditch.

2. *Paris*

And lo, it came to pass.

For on a recent Thursday morning, my companion and I landed in Paris to commence this journey. And in that small window of time between getting off the plane and hopping on the train to Avignon, we *(1)* bought a corkscrew, *(2)* bought a cheese knife, *(3)* ate two *pains au chocolat*, two *croque monsieurs*, a blood sausage, and a stuffed cabbage, and *(4)* drank an entire bottle of Bordeaux.

Which all might seem a tad heavy for 9:00 A.M., but forgive us. We'd been waiting for this trip for years, and we'd just spent a grim night on American Airlines, where they'd served us two damp meals we'd christened "The Dinner of Tears" and "The Breakfast of Sighs." We were excited, yes, but more to the point: *famished.*

3. *Avignon*

Our plan was to cover about 120 miles, over the course of a couple of weeks, through an area called the Luberon — mountainous, rugged, pastoral, the heart of rural Provence. Basically, we were on the classic multicity tour of Europe. Except that we would do it all on foot instead of on buses. And instead of going through places like Brussels, we would be going through places like Oppedette (pop. 56).

A word about planning: neither my companion nor I is any good at it, nor do we enjoy it, but a trip like this requires some. For instance, while there are certainly worse things in life than getting lost in rural France, we did want to make sure that we ended up every night in a hotel, since we were not carrying tents, sleeping bags, or (obviously) cooking gear. What we *were* carrying was quite minuscule, because what did we really need? One outfit for walking, one for sleeping, and one for dining. And of course — the corkscrew and the cheese knife. Most American fourth graders carry heavier backpacks to school than we carried for two weeks.

We'd selected in advance the region through which we would walk, then acquired a series of incredibly detailed walking maps showing the snaky route of the GR-6, the particular trail that would soon become our home. Thankfully, all this documentation was readily available to us, for the French — who invented bureaucracy and who delight in it still — manage this rabbit warren of paths with maps and guidebooks through a venerable agency called the Fédération Française de la Randonnée Pédestre. The FFRP originated back in the 1930s when some very serious Gauls (whom I imagine riding black bicycles while smoking Gauloises) had grown concerned about preserving France's beautiful rural trails — pedestrian thruways that had flourished for centuries but were falling into neglect as the automobile gradually replaced the foot as man's favored transportation method. Fortunately, though, preservation is something the French adore, and so an agency was charged with the task of saving, mapping, marking, and codifying the paths.

All this we'd learned from an encyclopedic book on the topic called *France on Foot,* written by an American named Bruce LeFavour, who — it turns out — is also the father of the woman who'd put this whole idea into my head nine years earlier. This personal connection was helpful, as it gave me the luxury of phoning my friend's expert dad and asking him simple questions like "Bruce, will you please plan our entire trip for us?" Therefore, and with great pride, I can say that we arrived totally prepared.

Our strategy, then, was to shake loose our jet lag in Avignon and take a bus to our jumping-off point — a town called Fontaine-de-Vaucluse. From there, we would walk all the way to the Durance River, in Sisteron.

So we arrived in Avignon, an old walled marvel of a city. We skipped the tourist attractions and palaces, instead heading straight to the market, which is housed in a municipal building of almost painful ugliness. But inside that building is a culinary bazaar of almost painful beauty — meticulous vegetables, inspiring breads, glistening seafood, and an artful carnage of meat — all served up by French farmers and fishermen and butchers with diligent faces and gnarled fingers.

Now, if you are like me — if you are like practically anybody in America — then you probably hold some negative opinions about the French, based upon movies, rumors, recent headlines, unfortunate run-ins with Parisian waiters, or . . . you know . . . all that unpleasantness surrounding the Vichy regime. Perhaps what you do not like about the French is what we may simply refer to here as "their incessantly Frenchy goddamn Frenchitude." But consider the hard-faced, middle-aged cheese lady at the market in Avignon. We were openly gawking at her gorgeous cheeses when she asked if she could help us with anything. "We're only admiring your cheese," we said timidly, hoping not to get scolded. But she did not scold. She put her hand to her heart and beamed with delight and pride. Then she took up her cheese blade and *skipped* to the far end of her counter, where she sliced into a small disc of Banon — a superb local specialty of ewe's-milk cheese wrapped in chestnut leaves and soaked in eau de vie. Pleased by our pleasure, she also let us sample one version of chèvre dusted with powdery ground green peppercorns and another infused with fresh lavender.

"Do you *really* like it?" she begged. "Would you like to see photos of my goats?"

We ended up buying great armfuls of her happy cheeses, which we ate all the way to Fontaine-de-Vaucluse, on the bus, washed down with a small bottle of homemade thyme liqueur — a fragrant, sweet-tempered drink traditionally used as a digestive aid (which, frankly, we figured we'd need). We'd purchased the liqueur in the market from the cheerful toothless man who worked across the aisle from the amiable cheese lady.

"Typical French jerks," I said to my companion as we feasted.

"Assholes," he agreed.

4. Fontaine-de-Vaucluse

The small, precious, touristy town of Fontaine-de-Vaucluse sits in a valley. This makes for awfully pretty scenery. But what this scenery meant for us was only one reality — however we got out of there the next morning, we were gonna have to climb.

Sustenance seemed vital to our survival.

So we did not deny ourselves at dinner the night before our walk began. No, instead we enjoyed an orgy of escargots and oysters and anchovies and the strangely delicious contents of a veal's head, along with I cannot remember how many bottles of velvety red Côtes du Luberon.

The next morning, we gathered our belongings into our backpacks and set off. The elegant proprietor of our hotel bid us a kind farewell and wished us luck. He knew we were going over the mountains today, so he said: "For such a long trip, I would prefer to use my Mercedes . . . or perhaps a helicopter." (Deliriously pronounced: el-ee-cup-*tair*.)

Not me, though.

It took us a while to get the hang of walking the GR-6. The trail wasn't as well marked as I had hoped (or rather, it was exceptionally well marked when it was marked at all). For this leg of the journey, at least, we were very much alone on the path, so we couldn't rely on the help of fellow hikers, either. At times we even found ourselves consulting our compass — a tool I had never used and which my companion had not seen since the 1970s, when he was, as he describes it, "a fearless lieutenant of the glorious Brazilian army."

But here was the amazing thing: despite our navigational challenges, we promptly realized how much we loved this. Because moving through a country at the pace of a walk is an incredibly intimate way to experience a place. What we encountered during our six-hour hike was simply . . . everything. Every single iris blossom, all the inquisitive local dragonflies and dogs, the chickens who crossed the road nervously, like characters in a joke. We smelled everything, too — the cow pastures, the mustard fields, the wild rosemary and thyme that grew thick in the hills.

Our trail was particularly well-worn; for many centuries, long before the advent of the el-ee-cup-*tair*, this path had been the quickest way for people to travel between Fontaine-de-Vaucluse and Gordes — trading, invading, and marrying, or carrying bad news, revolutionary ideas, plague. In the spirit of all that hard human history, I started to feel like a simple peasant myself, deeply identifying with my footsore pedestrian ancestors . . .

Then, eventually, I would burp and taste a fragrant reminder of last night's escargots. Which sort of blew the whole "footsore peasant" image. But therein lay the beautiful contradiction of this journey: walking like modest serfs by day, we dine like the Sun King by night.

5. Gordes

There is something about entering an ancient town on foot that's radically different from entering the same place by car. Keep in mind that these old French towns were all designed *by* people on foot *for* people on foot. So when you walk in, you're approaching the place as it was intended to be approached — slowly and naturally, the way Dorothy came upon the Emerald City (spires rising in the distance, a sense of mounting mystery: *what kind of city will this be?*). When paved roads were introduced about a thousand years after these towns were built, the macadam sliced artificially across the landscape, stabbing fast into these old parishes at the most convenient (for cars) angles. We, on the other hand, walked there high and alone across the mountains. Then the mountains turned into fields, the fields morphed into a cherry orchard, and the orchard gently spilled us toward Gordes — a city on a hill that, cinematically, we approached from *above*, from an even higher hill. From the moment we first saw the distant church spires until we stood upon those church steps, we walked for almost two hours, as evening approached and the town unfolded its gorgeousness before us. We arrived there the way people were always meant to arrive: awed, tired, grateful.

We checked into a superdeluxe spa-hotel of the sort that can be found anywhere in the world, and then walked around town until we found a small local restaurant of the sort that can be found only in rural France. It was called Comptoir des Arts, and I ate a steak there that had been smothered in morels (the way an American burger might get smothered with fried onions) while the garrulous owner of the place sat with us, sharing our wine and regaling us with stories about the tragic decline of France. He complained that his country was *a full catastrophe* because nobody wants to work anymore. In fact, it was difficult for him to determine who was lazier — the French themselves or the new Arab immigrants. Thank God for the Asiatics, he said, or the country would completely collapse under an avalanche of laziness. (Meanwhile, as he orated and drank, his wife was busy cooking, serving, tending to the other customers . . .)

When I told the man we were walking all the way to Sisteron, he seemed astonished.

"Mais — vous n'avez pas un camping car???"

No, I assured him — we did not have a camping car. Only our feet.

He gave a grand Gallic shrug of defeat, as if to say, "What are you people — *Asiatics?*"

6. Joucas

The silent little hamlet of Joucas — a lovely hilltop warren of golden stone houses piled upon each other — is so small and narrow that most of its streets cannot be navigated by car, even if you wanted to. And yet this community, which does not even boast a supermarket, has two Michelin-starred restaurants. Which is sort of like discovering — in a rural Tennessee mountain town — two rival world-class opera companies.

In the awkward position, then, of having only one night to eat and two equally alluring dining rooms to choose from, we flipped a coin and made our way to Le Mas des Herbes Blanches — a quiet estate restaurant on a hilltop almost two miles north of the town's center (which meant more sweaty climbing for us). There, they offered us a ten-course tasting menu so linguistically complex that my companion, who speaks beautiful French, had to struggle to translate its contents: "OK, here we have a piece of . . . something . . . which has been slow-cooked in the juice of . . . some word I've never seen before . . . and served on a velvety purée of . . . something else."

All the mysterious *somethings* were explained to us, though, by our sommelier — a painfully thin young local man named Michel, with a long and deeply emotive face. The most accurate way I can describe Michel is to say that he cared. He cared about perfection. He cared that we were served our apéritifs on the terrace, while our food must only be served indoors. ("Once the sun goes down, you will become cold, and this will distract from the nuance of your meal.") He cared that the sea bass had been caught on a line and not in a net. He cared that we understood why the only thing one can possibly drink with pigeon served in a penetratingly sharp marmalade of vinegar-infused strawberries is a 2002 Domaine de la Janasse Châteauneuf-du-Pape. ("The tight fibers of the pigeon's flesh must be loosened by the openness of this wine.")

We ate for five hours in this high church of perfected service. That hallowed night, I didn't merely eat salacious blue lobster from Brittany, or svelte asparagus tips, or these little tiny salty niblets that Michel called "tuna bonbons," or a celery sorbet lighter than a fairy's breath, or a cheese plate of regional chèvre paired with five dots of exotic dipping sauces, or a concoction of chocolate served with reduced kumquats in a chilled minestrone of rare fruits . . . I *also* ate the single best thing I've ever eaten, which was the most tender imaginable duck foie gras. It was so tender, in fact, that one might even say that it was falling off the bone (if liver had bones), or that it melted in one's mouth like ice cream (if ice cream were warm and salty and duck-flavored).

When, at the end of the night, we thanked Michel for his excellent care of us, he said (again, with that sad seriousness), "There are people who save money all year just to have a meal like this. If they do not have the experience they deserve, I have failed them." Then he asked if we needed a taxi. We did not. So he made the logical assumption: *"Ah . . . vous avez un chauffeur?"*

No, we do not have a chauffeur.

We had only our drunken human feet, which carried our sated bodies almost two miles down the mountainside. The French countryside was now so utterly dark as to seem a marvel — a darkness unbroken by distant highways, streetlights, or electric suburban sprawl. We stumbled, laughing, miraculously not spraining any ankles, all the way back to our digs in Joucas, which consisted of a cheap backpacker's hostel with a wilting mattress and a shared toilet down the hall. We fell asleep dizzied by the seven different wines we'd consumed that night. And also dizzied, of course, by the bizarre sensory contradiction of having just dined in a place like *that,* only to then sleep in a place like *this* . . .

I woke up at 3:00 A.M., nauseous, sober, and repentant. Why had we eaten *ten courses?*

"Oh, my God, I'm gonna die," I said under my breath.

"I can't eat like this anymore," my companion groaned from the other side of the bed.

"I *promise,*" I told him, "starting tomorrow, we eat nothing but salads and chicken broth."

"No more wine, either," he added.

I clung to him for comfort from my queasiness.

"And please don't touch me anywhere near my stomach area," he requested politely.

7. *Walking*

The next day, as we walked on through the countryside, we stopped at a local market and bought a simple baguette and a bottle of water for lunch. This seemed sane and moderate. But then we saw a really appealing wheel of Camembert, so we bought that, too. Then we picked up a bottle of red wine, because — come on — who wants to eat Camembert with *water*? We had to try the rich local pâté (only because the butcher's wife boasted of it: "You will crawl back here on your knees begging for more of this") and — why not? — we also tried a thick slice of this stuff called *rillettes,* which is a sort of meatloaf, only it's made of shredded goose and covered with a quarter inch of congealed yellow poultry fat. But we only got that because it tastes really good . . .

One of the reasons I'd always wanted to do this trip was on account of this alluring theory: *you can eat as much as you like, because you're just gonna walk it off the next day.* In practice, however, this is not true. If we'd walked every day to, say, Albania, perhaps we could've burned away the effects of our eating, but walking five or ten miles certainly wasn't going to do it. (One mile of walking, I've been told, burns one hundred calories, which, I'm pretty sure, equals about half a tablespoon of congealed poultry fat.)

In the end, though, that wasn't even really the point. The joy of this trip did not come from the exercise or even (despite our love of it) the food. The joy came from the startling closeness with which we experienced France precisely because we were on foot.

There's something vulnerable about walking. We came through this landscape fully exposed, unarmored by anything made of steel or gears. In a reciprocal gesture, then, we were offered up an unarmored version of France, a France that turned no pretense or defenses toward us. Some of these walking trails wound right past people's homes, right through their farms, bisecting their vineyards, and crossing their weathered footbridges. We hung out with people's livestock and talked to children on their swing sets. We saw a one-armed old man pruning his grapevines; he greeted us personably. We walked by a wild pheasant one day; it didn't even startle. Another day, we walked so close to a remote farmhouse that I could not only see the woman washing dishes at her kitchen sink, I could also smell the family's lunch (lamb with thyme) and could hear a child in the background practicing piano scales. The woman smiled. The effect was that of a Vermeer painting, but with fragrance and sound.

And yes (exactly as I'd been picturing for years), we did discover plenty of quiet ditches near lavender fields where we laid down plenty of picnics under olive trees. This became the best part of our daily routine. We refused to eat in restaurants for lunch. Why would we have, when every day was sunny and we were already outside, anyhow? In the little side pockets of our backpacks, where most hikers carry water bottles or cameras, we carried long baguettes and bottles of wine. (It didn't really matter that we drank a bottle of wine every day at noon; it's not like we had to *drive* anywhere.) We would unpack our lunches and admire the day's delicacies like they were Christmas gifts. Once we dined by a stream, cooling our feet in the water as we shared our meal. Eventually, we would always fall asleep.

A balance came upon us from all this slowness in walking, talking, eating, drinking, napping. The journey had an effect on me similar to the rewinding of an old grandfather clock; I felt recalibrated. I felt like I had caught up with Time again.

Or as my companion put it, "For the first time in my life, every single day seems to have the exact right number of hours in it."

8. St-Saturnin-lès-Apt

Because of how dearly France bled during the two world wars, almost every French town has a monument to its fallen soldiers in the middle of the central square. In the center of St-Saturnin-lès-Apt, however, there is a statue of the great nineteenth-century hero Joseph Talon. I'm sorry, have you never heard of Joseph Talon? As any schoolchild around here can tell you, he is the *Père de la Trufficulture* — the man who developed the agricultural miracle of farming truffles. Now, I don't know about you, but when I walk into a town and learn that its greatest hero is the father of truffle culture, I feel that this portends very good things, foodwise.

St-Saturnin-lès-Apt is a beautiful little spot, like to make your heart hurt. Cobbled streets, steep sidewalks, silent stone houses, and a stark absence of tourists. Locals like to tell this story, dating back to the Middle Ages: When God had finally finished creating the world, He took a little walk around the planet to admire His work. He came upon the village of St-Saturnin-lès-Apt and was so astonished by its beauty that He decided — only then! — to invent heaven. Because now He finally had a model for paradise.

Granted, there are holes in this narrative. (Why did God wait until the eleventh century to check out His planet? Why is heaven alluded to in the Bible when France isn't? And what about the truffles?) But logic is not the point of the story. The point is: superpretty place.

We stayed at the Hôtel des Voyageurs. It was run by a gracious married couple who were working their brains out trying to maintain this dear, crumbling little hotel. It was an old French hotel, but it wasn't done up in Old French Hotel Style; it was an *actual* old French hotel, which means it was held together by handsome wooden beams but also by decades of humble linoleum and wallpaper, tacked up by people who had neither the time nor the money to try to make things quaint.

Madame managed the immaculate rooms, and her husband was the chef (specializing in veal with *herbes de Provence*). They were enormously friendly. Although *friendly* is maybe too crass a word. Madame had none of the invasive "Just call me Barb!" faux friendliness of an American B&B owner. In fact, we did not ever learn her name. More incredibly, she never asked for ours. All she did was entrust us with the keys to her property and then serve us as though we were visiting dignitaries.

Again, as with our sommelier back in Joucas, this couple was fighting a heartbreakingly passionate battle to hold themselves to an old-school standard of French perfection in service. Watching them work so tirelessly, I was reminded of the American food writer M.F.K. Fisher and her frustration with her French hosts, back when she was living in Provence in the 1950s. It used to exasperate Fisher that the French (so depleted and defeated after World War II) refused to drop their arduous, arcane manners and simply take shortcuts to more efficient lives. It would infuriate Fisher to observe her cook "stumbling through ten hours of unthinking labor for what might possibly need one hour, just because that was the way her mother and grandmother had done . . ." Why did these exhausted people really care that fish always has to be served with a fish fork and game with a game fork?

Because it *matters*. Because if you see yourself — as so many in Provence do — as the last guardians of a civilization that cherishes artful perfection over bland productivity . . . then it *matters*. Because it's noble. Because if the French do not defend the fish fork, who will?

To our surprise, we ended up spending four days at the Hôtel des Voyageurs. Somehow, we just couldn't bring ourselves to leave. There were lovely long walks every afternoon in the surrounding fields and hills. One day we stumbled upon an old olive mill, where a matronly farm wife with girlish, eager eyes showed us how oil is made. Another day, we found high in the hills the remains of an eighteenth-century abandoned village, all grown over with vines like an Aztec ruin. Plus, there was so much interesting stuff to watch in the town square all day! All sorts of escapades involving local cats and dogs, for instance, which we would observe for hours as we ate our croissants and drank our coffee. And then there was that one lunchtime when we were really considering getting on the road, until Madame handed us a carafe of cool local rosé and said, "You know, the entire upstairs of the hotel is empty right now."

We nodded, not sure how that pertained to us.

With an *almost* imperceptibly sly look, Madame said, "Why don't you two go up there and . . . enjoy your privacy together."

It took us a moment to grasp what this refined lady had just instructed us to do. And then, obediently, we grabbed the wine, headed up the three-hundred-year-old stairs to room no. 10, shut the door behind us, and wasted a perfectly good afternoon entertaining ourselves in various expressions of love.

9. Viens

Finally, we pulled ourselves together and left St-Saturnin-lès-Apt. We took two days to walk the fourteen steep miles to Viens. Along the way, we passed through the tiny town of Rustrel and the even tinier town of Gignac (population — I was told — *ten*). We ate handfuls of cherries as we walked.

Gradually, we came upon the medieval city of Viens — not so much a pretty place as an impressive one. A fortress town teetering over the edge of a great cliff, complete with a menacingly dark tower (which was for *sale*, by the way; the cheerful Century 21 sign proved it). Naturally, we fantasized about buying the tower. Imagine the views! The security! No matter, of course, that yesterday we'd already decided to buy a building in tiny Gignac and open a café there, for the benefit of the town's ten inhabitants. And a few days earlier, we had committed to moving to St-Saturnin-lès-Apt. Also, there'd been a farmhouse last week outside Gordes that had seemed most perfect for us. In each case, we'd made elaborate, serious plans as to how we were going to move to France and be café owners, goat herders, tower inhabitants . . . and in each case, by the end of the day the whole plan would be forgotten. Sometimes the only thing a life's dream needs is one hour of devoted attention before it can expire peacefully and appropriately.

We stayed at the only accommodations in Viens — a fourteenth-century sheep farm owned by a capable woman named Anne, who happened to be a multilingual, retired anesthesiologist from Avignon. She was also a terrific cook who fed us from her own kitchen. All was going well until Anne asked me coolly, as she was dishing out her exquisite cassoulet, "So — how is your Mr. Bush? Do you *love* him?"

It was just a casual remark, but there was something about her tone, her assumption, that made me bristle. I am no lover of George Bush, heaven knows, but what I really wanted to reply was "He's fine, Anne — and how are your Angry Moroccan Car-Burning Youths?"

What is it about France and America that it so often comes to this? Personally, I think it has something to do with our deep, mutual sense of fear. The French have always feared the Americans — feared that someday we shall force them to change their elegant, old culture. And the Americans have always feared the French — feared that someday they shall expose us for what we're secretly afraid we actually are: sorta stupid. It's an old game, but it strikes me as outdated, a waste of time — like when two siblings, who you know really love each other, are still bickering at the age of ninety over who got the green lollipop back in 1928.

Really — *must* we?

So I held my tongue and said only, "Politics are complicated, Anne. But your cassoulet is delicious."

And we all passed safely and politely through the evening.

10. Forcalquier

You can walk from Viens to Forcalquier in one day, but I wouldn't recommend it. We did it, mind you. Though I'm not sure why. (There's another, gentler, southern path, which takes three days, passing through lovely towns all along the way where one could conceivably eat and rest.) But our legs had gotten so strong from all the walking that we wanted to test ourselves, so we decided to cut straight over the mountains. The distance was something between fifteen and twenty miles, depending upon whom you asked. I will discuss little about this exhausting eleven-hour haul, other than to say it was totally worth it for where we ended up — Forcalquier.

What a freaky, wonderful place, Forcalquier! The nice thing about not having done much advance research was that we never had any idea, day by day, what the next town would look like. Quaint valley farm community? Medieval fortress? Monastery on a hill? What we found in Forcalquier surprised us: a rural French Liverpool. A tough, gritty, proud place, filled with tough, gritty, proud citizens. The faces in the cafés around the central square looked like nineteenth-century caricatures of street thugs — there were your rakes, your swains, your swells, your rascals, your cutthroats and ragged rogues. But all of them with a kind of crazy (even sexy) swagger that we found captivating. The architecture matched the citizens — glorious, crumbling, held up by the sheer refusal to fall. There were some lively bars, but we dared not enter them. My companion — a man who is very comfortable in bars, by the way — said he would rather stride into the local cathedral smoking a cigar and cursing in Latin than walk into a Forcalquier tavern uninvited; such places were obviously sacred.

We stayed in a hotel whose wallpaper had not been changed since 1934. We went to see a dubbed version of *Mission: Impossible*

III in Forcalquier's old church turned cinema. And then, the next afternoon, we went to the circus. We knew about this circus because we'd seen a plucky young man driving around his beat-up Renault, calling through a bullhorn that the Cancy Family Circus was coming to town, with all its wonders, including contortionists, clowns, and wild animals.

So of course we went. The old striped circus tent was scarcely bigger than a round suburban backyard swimming pool. The audience consisted of us and perhaps twenty locals. I shall say this for the Cancy Circus: they are a brave and hard-working family. They threw themselves into the task of entertaining us with a desperate, breakneck earnestness. The same young man who'd been driving around town all day with his bullhorn was also, it turned out, the ringmaster, and he made a valiant effort to whip up a froth of excitement, as though he were performing before the great crowned heads of Europe instead of a sparse crowd of scruffy Forcalquerians.

First he introduced the wild-animal act. Out came the pony. Then the goat. Finally, the llama. The pony jogged in circles and stood on his stubby hind legs, resignedly pawing the air. The goat climbed a teetering pyramid of crates. The llama (who carried herself with the vacant dignity of a kidnapped, drugged heiress) jumped over a broomstick. The unflappable young ringmaster could scarcely contain his own astonishment — *Have you ever seen such marvels?*

Then he announced: "And now — our incredible juggler!" He stepped behind a curtain. A moment later, out stepped . . . the same guy, who now commenced to juggling turbulently. (He dropped only a few pins.) Act over, out of breath, he announced: "Prepare to marvel at . . . the Cancy Circus Contortionists!" This act consisted of what I took to be the young man's wife and his sister, gamely executing backbends.

I searched the faces of the performers for signs of awareness that their little family circus was sort of ridiculous, if not totally doomed. The pony clearly knew it; his whole demeanor was like, "This is all so fucked." The goat knew it, too. The llama had checked out ages ago; she clearly didn't even know what town she was in. But the Cancy family showed only sincerity and gravitas as they juggled and contorted their hearts out, as they must have been doing for generations as small-town traveling-circus performers. They did not appear to feel that they were either ridiculous or doomed.

Which got me thinking about France.

Not to say that France is ridiculous or doomed, but . . . OK — in some ways, let's face it: France is both ridiculous *and* doomed. Something about this hopeless, rosy little family circus galvanized in me a question that had been nagging throughout our whole lovely time in Provence — namely: how much longer can all this endure? There was a moment during our trip where we ate — in just an average little town market — a five-year-old cheese (so ripe it made my nose hairs retract in panic) served upon fifteen-minute-old bread, along with a ten-year-old bottle of wine . . . and every component was presented at the appropriate temperature, and each had been crafted by a master. Do you have any idea how labor-intensive that simple snack was? Or how many agricultural tariffs and protective subsidies and generous labor laws and social-security nets (along with deep reserves of cultural stubbornness) are required to maintain such elaborate gentility?

It seems sometimes that France's entire global position is one of instinctive resistance. If something is changing, the French are automatically against it. They're against the war in Iraq, but they're also against the Arabs in their own country. They're against Turkey entering the European Union. They're against McDonald's. They're against children having to go to school on Wednesdays. They're against any words being added to the language that would debase pure *français.* They're against imported Spanish produce. They're against employers being allowed to sometimes dismiss a worker. *Mon dieu,* we'd spent the last nine days hunting around these towns for an Internet connection, but whenever we asked where to find one, the locals would look at us as though we'd asked, "Could you kindly tell us where your village's supersecret rocket-launching space pad is hidden?"

"Oh, no," they would say. "We don't have anything like that *here.*"

Because in rural France, apparently, they are also against the Internet.

Which is a doomed position, an unsustainable battle. And all this defensiveness might seem insane, except for one factor: what the French are defending is something very special. Once it's gone, it won't be replicated anywhere. What they are defending is (in a word they use all the time, with great pride) their *patrimoine*—their beloved herds of goats, the wines they love most, the old hotel in the small town, the ancient rural footpath, the traditional family circus that doesn't happen to be owned by Time Warner. What they are defending is a passionate faith in the refined, the civilized, the local, and the artful. Quaint ideas, perhaps, but the French are the only ones in the world standing up for this kind of stuff en masse. Which is to say, if — two hundred years from now — there happens to be any food left on this planet that doesn't taste like Velveeta, or any township that isn't hash-marked by freeways, we'll probably have a Frenchman to thank for it.

Meanwhile, back at the circus, the young ringmaster/juggler/barker/animal trainer had now commenced a balancing act. Up until this point, the Cancy Circus had seemed funny, campy. But when the young man's sister and wife began to stack old wooden chairs on top of each other, making a rickety chimney over ten feet tall, my companion and I became genuinely anxious. And we grew only more anxious as the kid clambered up there and balanced shakily on one hand upon this fragile old pile of antique chairs. I couldn't look. It was far scarier than any moment in *Mission: Impossible III.*

Finally, he backflipped safely to earth, where — sweaty and tenacious (and perhaps half crazy, but also somehow totally valiant) — he announced: *"Le spectacle continue!"*

The spectacle goes on!

For the sake of all of us, I do hope so.

11. St-Étienne-les-Orgues

The next day, it rained. I'd forgotten that it *could* rain in the South of France, but in fact it poured. We walked through the deluge for about six miles, as far as the little town of St-Étienne. There, we stopped in a small hotel owned by a big, brassy, young Senegalese immigrant, who — when she discovered we intended to walk on over the mountains — put a quick stop to it.

"Non, non, non," she said, in her African-accented French. "Absolutely not. It's going to rain like this for the next three days. I won't let you walk anymore."

She hustled us into her car and drove us — almost before we

knew what was happening — all the way back to Forcalquier, where she had instructed us that we would wait for the next bus to Aix-en-Provence. Her car sped us through the rain over the exact distance we had only just painstakingly covered on foot that very morning. We hadn't been in a moving vehicle in two weeks. Everything felt too fast and sudden now.

The woman chatted on to us about her family in Africa (ten siblings), who she hoped would all someday come live in France. Then — "Voilà!" — she deposited us at the bus stop and hugged us forcefully. We were a bit off-kilter. We'd planned to walk on to Sisteron, but this woman had just finished our journey for us with her decisiveness. (Truly, though, we knew she was right. It was all over.)

We took the bus to Aix and found a dry, deluxe hotel. There we stayed, eating and drinking away our last two days in France, before we would have to head back to the Paris airport and board American Airlines again . . . at which point, we would be obliged to surrender our cheese knife and our corkscrew, in the interests of national security.

REESA GRUSHKA

Arieh

FROM THE *Missouri Review*

1.

SOME PEOPLE EASE into your life as if they have always been there and have only been out mailing a letter. Their chair is still warm. Some people know you, recognize in you immediately what most never see. In the presence of such people the word *no* becomes meaningless. So it was with Arieh. I had been feeling miserable all morning, gummed up with melancholy and bitter thoughts. I had delayed a trip to the *souk,* the covered market, in order to walk aimlessly around the university's residential complex feeling the sun's unrelenting heat, the hard stones of the little paths between buildings, the prickly fingers of rosemary that sprouted everywhere, a dark mute green, releasing a fog of sweet scent when I brushed my hand over them.

There stood an hour's walk between me and the *souk,* a walk that began as a steep decline from the Hebrew University on Mount Scopus, along El Wadi road in East Jerusalem. Then the route wandered in the shade of a nameless street housing lesser embassies and hotels in a state of circumspect decline. This emptied at last onto a wide boulevard of construction and smog, where the blue flag of the United Nations office flapped palely behind a shroud of dust, and where the crowded tenements of Mea She'arim, Jerusalem's Hasidic neighborhood, began. I was still under the illusion that the long white dress I had worn to the *souk* was modest enough for my walk through Mea She'arim, but in fact the light cotton was almost sheer, and the small buttons down the front from neck to hem were far too small to do the work a button should. I would say this was the reason Arieh turned to me, standing before the entrance of the building where I lived, to say: "Ah, my queen, my queen, marry me," but that could not really have been the reason, because Arieh was blind.

I left for Jerusalem because Toronto was cold and I had spent the past year immobilized by an ugly, humiliating illness. I had nearly failed half my courses at the university. The urban mornings, all glass and glint, which usually filled me with energy, now left me cold; everything seemed gray, suffused with fog, heavy and damp. I went to Jerusalem to dry out, to toughen up, to learn to live ardently and spontaneously. That I knew nothing about Israel, had not even a basic mental sketch of its geography or culture, did not bother me. I wrote long journal entries about facing the void and creating art, life, out of emptiness.

It took less than the twenty minutes I spent waiting for my luggage in the Ben Gurion Airport, whose air was damp with August heat, whose snack bars were all closed (didn't I know it was a fast day?), and whose clerks did not believe there were hotels in Arab East Jerusalem, to realize that "the void" was just the name I had given to my own ignorance. No place I had ever been was as full, as crushingly stuffed with life, detail, or other people's desire, as Jerusalem.

Jerusalem shares the logic of dreams. What I mean by this is not incandescent or obscure, only that this is a city in which you believe everything you see and hear. It is nothing like the newspapers make it seem. Not a map with red borders drawn and drawn again, though it is partly that. Not a river of peace, a stream of wealth, or a mother's comforting breast, as the book of Isaiah describes it. Jerusalem is a dream city because there is no blueprint, no draft against which to measure or understand it. The streets are not orderly but twist, as a friend suggested, like the tissue of a brain. And certainly in my first weeks there I felt that Jerusalem was aware of my intrusion and was willfully protecting itself from me. The city undercut reason and the forward flow of time, as well as the functions of a compass — banal laws that I had taken for granted as effective regardless of borders. But to measure and to understand in dreams is meaningless — a busy street becomes a garden. A garden suddenly sprouts a tomb. A tomb reveals a child's lost shoe, a patent-leather shoe with a broken buckle. Beside a bank of pay phones, an argument breaks out about the number that will really, truly, connect you with heaven. Crossing a street leads you to a new language, a new currency, a new god. Bells, sirens, and recorded prayers circumscribe and cross the air. You choke on gasoline and smoke from burning trash, but turn a corner and you smell the dry, gentle olive trees, the aromatic grass. The hawking of wares unwinds past a stand of tall soldiers into a circling Sabbath dance, a white chain of song twisting over flat, old stones, and a girl and a boy with black eyes leading a donkey down a narrow road, the moon in their hair like milk, like silver beads, like crowns.

Jerusalem is also a city of traffic jams and discotheques, banks and vandals, of fashion and shops and terrible coffee. My first night there I paid seventy American dollars for a room with pigeons and a view of a wrecking ball. I was whistled and jeered at by boys no more than twelve years old. I was oppressed by heat, filth, noise, violent politics, and streets that wore modernity like a dirty apron. I did not understand Hebrew or Arabic. And yet, I learned that anything could happen there. The air was thick with the impossible, and the food was saturated by it — such incredible fruits, I thought I was inventing them. And the people, perhaps because they dwell so perpetually in the uncertain and unclear, believe purely, without hesitation, in whatever it is they believe; it is not the content but the form that matters. How many times did an Israeli, Jewish, Muslim, or Christian turn from me, disgusted by the flaccid, bumbling argument I took for logic. "Americans," each would say, nearly spitting. "You don't know what you think." Like figures in a dream, Jerusalemites were powerful, certain, strange, all seeming to know more.

Arieh was legally but not entirely blind. I was never certain what he could and could not see, and he liked it that way. At the time I knew him, he had a magnifying screen that enlarged the letters on a printed page to several inches in height. He always recognized me when I approached him and claimed to see my face, but I don't believe he could distinguish my features. When I imagined his world I saw ghostly planes of faces and hands, as through squinted eyes, reduced to extremes of light and shadow. He could not see inanimate objects very well, and his hands, when he was seated in his university bedroom, always moved over the surfaces of his small dresser and table, hunting out a comb or tin of tea. Blindness had come late in life to Arieh. Before it, he had been an air force pilot and an intelligence officer. He had spied in Lebanon. During the early years of the personal computer he had worked abroad as a communications engineer. He spoke more than ten languages, if you include mathematics and computer codes. He played the guitar incessantly, singing out in Spanish, his favorite, and also in Hebrew, Arabic, Turkish, German, and French. He lived masterfully, knew how to talk to people and to cause laughter. The day we met he had convinced five of his cousins to take him to the zoo to visit the turtles. For this occasion he stood waiting, leaning on a tall staff, wearing a bed sheet, which, due to his enormous stature, barely reached his knees. On his head he had circled a braided vine. His hair hung long, black, and roughly coiled over his shoulders, and his beard pushed jaggedly toward his chest. He seemed to be naked beneath his sheet, and it struck me that, as strange as this man appeared, we were dressed alike.

"Who are you?" I asked, and he answered in a low voice, "I'm the King," as if nothing were so obvious, "I'm the King of kings."

I don't think it is a coincidence that prophecy and faith run parallel to a long history of blindness in Jerusalem. The blind man, losing his access to the visual world, discovers in its place a vision of the invisible. Trachoma, a contagious and cruel scarring of the cornea, still ravages eyes in poor communities; it was endemic in Palestine in the nineteenth century and probably long before. The Viennese ophthalmologist Avraham Albert Ticho was sent to Jerusalem by a Zionist organization based in Frankfurt to open an eye clinic in 1912. He established his home and practice in a house outside the walls of the old city so that he was not confined to any one community and could treat trachoma in the rich and the poor, in Jewish and Muslim patients. Before his death, in 1960, he attained an almost heroic status as he relieved from darkness families who had suffered generations of blindness. Nevertheless, I have never met so many blind men as there, in the gold city. As a result, neither have I met, before or after, so many readers of signs.

The archetype of the blind prophet bears, unfortunately, little resemblance to reality. My own grandfather went blind in his late forties, and he was not a man of vision. He ate and slept and swallowed countless medications. For all the time I knew him, he was very ill. Once, though, when he was in hospital, plugged and tapped into the dialysis machine, his brother-in-law Saul came to visit him, and my grandfather saw him in every detail — pleated pants and red plaid shirt, white hair and broad forehead, square, thick glasses — although the pupils of my grandfather's eyes were solid, milky white.

The story of Saul, how my grandfather had seen him — it must have been early in the course of his blindness — struck me as a true miracle, and I wanted it to happen again. I wanted more than anything for my grandfather, my Zaidy Moe, to see me and see that I had grown much taller, to see the tiny gold star he bought for me hanging from a chain around my neck, and to be less sad. I begged God to help me. I argued that He had managed it once, so He could surely do it again, make Zaidy see the world. Hadn't the Saul incident been a sign, an omen? But on this matter God remained perversely silent, and He did not heal my grandfather's blank, white eyes.

Arieh's blindness never seemed to bind or frustrate him. He was like a magician, always performing, always in absolute control. Under his command ordinary things could sprout wings and fly. He knew how to access the secret compartments hidden in everyday experience, and he taught me how to see them and how to step inside and lose myself in them.

"Like all Semitic languages," he explained, "Hebrew is based on a three-letter root system. Almost every word in Hebrew is an arrangement of three consonants around a pattern of vowels. Once you know the root of a word, it is usually not difficult to figure out how that root will look as a verb, noun, or adjective. Even colors share a form. Red is *adom*, yellow is *tzahov*, and blue is *cakhol*.

"Take a root word, like *kelev*, dog (in the Hebrew: כלב). Now break the root into two parts by doubling the center letter (כל לב). You have two new words now, *col* and *lev*, which in Hebrew mean 'all' and 'heart.' Each word is built out of smaller bricks of words. In these building blocks of language you can decipher true meaning. The world was built of them, and that is why God, the creator, is called the Word." When I was in my room again, I tried it on my own with the word *adam* (אדם), meaning "man." I divided it into its parts (אד דם), *ad* and *dam*, which mean "vapor" and "blood." The blood and the breath, the body and the soul. Each word broke apart into its purer elements. It felt like chemistry or alchemy.

Arieh and I lived in the same student dormitory, his room just one floor below mine. Blind students are invited to study free of tuition at the Hebrew University, and Arieh took advantage of the opportunity. Officially, he was retraining, becoming an academic, but in fact, Arieh was at the university biding his time in Jerusalem, preparing for the moment when the Holy City would be ready for redemption. It is against the Jewish law to proselytize or to convert non-Jews to Judaism, but it is considered a good deed of the highest order to bring a Jewish atheist back to God. Arieh took this duty seriously and fulfilled it, I am sure, beyond the wildest imaginings of the hopeful rabbis who had first convinced him of his purpose.

Unwittingly, I became a fixture in Arieh's show. It began with conversation over a cup of tea, a lesson in Hebrew, visits to his room to look up a text or poem he wanted to share with me. After several weeks of these innocent conversations, Arieh asked me to sit on a chair in the open doorway of his room in the student hall. "When they see you," he explained, "they will be drawn in." And ridiculously, it was true; they came — young Israeli men in soldiers' uniforms, off duty from guarding the gates of the university. They would step into Arieh's room, looking uncertain, which Israelis never allow themselves to be, and look back and forth between me and Arieh and say hello, usually in Hebrew or French.

Then Arieh would introduce himself and light his pipe, a slow process. First, he would have to find the pipe. If he wore a shirt with a pocket, it would be in there. If he wore a T-shirt instead, which was more often the case, the pipe would be leaning against some object on the dresser or little table, where an electric kettle, a hot plate, instant coffee, and a jar of sugar always stood. Because he could not see something as small as a pipe, his hands would wander, touching lightly the surfaces of anything they found, seeking the curved warmth of the pipe. Then Arieh would find the Turkish tobacco in its silver paper pouch with the picture of a ship on the flap. Arieh would dip the pipe into the tobacco, touch it to see that it was packed, scoop a little more, then tap again until everything was as it should be.

All this time he would be talking, asking the name of his guest and discovering who the young man was and how he liked the world through which he moved. They would laugh together as men do who find they understand one another and can be at ease. Then a pause, a scratch, and hush as Arieh lit a match and sucked deeply at his pipe until the tiny shreds began to smolder. Silence; then Arieh would sigh outward a slow, blue breath.

All this would have elapsed over ten or fifteen minutes, during which time I would remain quiet, trying to understand some of their Hebrew. If it was French, which I understood well, or Arabic, which I did not know at all, I looked out the window at the students passing under the shadows of the little trees. By now the room would smell distinctly of the marijuana that rose just under the tobacco smoke. The guest would be asked whether he cared for a cigarette that Arieh had rolled himself, and he would grin because, after all, the guest was only on a break from his post at the gate, or was between classes, but the guest would assent, and I would be introduced, and he would allow himself to stare at me and shake my hand or kiss it because in that small, barren room I was beautiful in a way that I have never been outside it. Men in that part of the world have eyes that range from gold-brown to green-gold, with a liquid quality, making them seem like colored stones beneath the ripples of clear water. Arieh made all of us glow; it was as though we had never seen eyes before, or skin, and we could stare and stare and never have enough.

While he rolled the tobacco and marijuana into a tight paper, Arieh would instruct the guest to read a passage from the Pentateuch, the first five books of the Old Testament, and then to translate what he read into French or English for my benefit. If it was a soldier in the room with us, he first placed his cap on his head and then opened the book Arieh handed to him at a random page, and he would begin to read. An inexplicable number of young men found themselves hesitating on the threshold of Arieh's room and suddenly seated inside it, smoking, reading Torah, baring their naked hearts. In this manner Arieh cultivated a following, even waged what you might call a campaign. They called themselves "the crows" and spent hours between classes making posters that announced Arieh's divine calling, and explaining that the time had come to follow the Messiah into light.

2.

There is a disorder called "Jerusalem syndrome" that affects 1 percent of visitors to Jerusalem each year. Gender and race have nothing to do with it, although a Judeo-Christian upbringing helps. Some of the victims come to Israel with a predisposition for psychosis, but four or five people each year have no previous mental history, according to Dr. Bar-El, the man who first gave a name to Jerusalem syndrome. One day, all of a sudden, normal tourists will begin to dress in white sheets and make proclamations on street corners. They will speak in tongues or spend hours writing prophecies. They will stand motionless, with their eyes rolled heavenward, or wave signs and warnings from bridges over the highway. One travel magazine records that "afflicted tourists have been found wandering in the Judean desert wrapped in hotel bed sheets or crouched at the Church of the Holy Sepulcher, waiting to birth the infant Jesus" or "demanding that humanity become calmer, purer, and less materialistic." The messiahs, John the Baptists, and Marys usually persist in their preaching for five to seven days and then recover entirely, but while the victims are in a delusional state, they will truly believe.

During the year I lived in Jerusalem, I met several messiahs. They were not difficult to find. At Jaffa Gate, in the old city, there is one establishment in particular, the Petra Hostel, that seems to be a magnet for them. The little common room, with its very high, echoing ceilings in the style of the old arched and domed buildings of the city, always holds a few nervous figures at low bridge tables, drinking coffee from disposable cups. These are not young travelers, light with marijuana and the open road, but older men and women who have found their way to Jerusalem despite, or maybe because of, their despair. They reside in the Petra Hostel semipermanently. When I visited there I found Oliver, a man I had encountered in several Jerusalem cafés, talking in an animated fashion about his life as a world-famous economist. His small, round face was pressed close to the face of his companion, and it glowed with a light sweat. "And then they sent me to Geneva to work on the problem of socialist finance," he was saying. The first time I met him, he was an artist creating a series of illustrations for Khalil Gibran's *The Prophet.* The second time he was a war veteran, and he tried to convince me that we had met before on a beach in Malta. Oliver was delusional but very intelligent and also kind. His companion that evening was a newly arrived messiah, quiet and calm, identifiable only by his bed sheet, beard, and solemn eyes.

The genial atmosphere was interrupted when a plump woman with wild hair and a sour look burst through a door at the end of the room. Marching over to Oliver and the messiah, she yelled, "I am trying to get some fucking sleep." She pointed an unsteady finger. "And you . . . *you* . . . keep talking and laughing and keeping me awake." She wore a white nightie with a pink heart painted over the left breast. "Do you know how hard it is to be a female messiah? Do you know what it's like to have to save the whole world?" This last phrase emerged hoarsely. Then, turning on her heel, the female messiah stomped back to her room in a storm of expletives and left us all in a bewildered silence. "Poor girl," Oliver explained, "she's completely mad."

Most of the messiahs have the restless aspect of the lost and homeless; it makes you circle a little wider when you pass them on the street and fills you with a queasy pity. What made Arieh different was that he had received his calling from a group of rabbis and students of Torah who supported him in his endeavor. He did not share the haunted, lonely look of the other messiahs. When Arieh lost his vision, he lost his means of employing his genius. He could no longer see a computer screen. He definitely could no longer fly a plane; he couldn't even read, paint, or shave his beard himself. A genius without a purpose is less than nothing. He is all pent-up energy, no power. In a remote suburb of Tel Aviv, in his parents' apartment, stifled by their attention, by his own incapacity for action, Arieh became disconsolate and mean.

That is how the Chabad found him, and they offered him their vision to replace his own. The Chabad are an order of orthodox Jewry who represent and follow the teachings of the Baal Shem Tov. That revered reformer and leader was born in Poland in 1698, and he devoted his life there to the study of Torah and to a war against pessimism and poverty. He worked to make Torah available and accessible to the "second-rate Jews" who could not read or study, and to infuse a bookish religion with an appreciation for the power and beauty of the natural world. He believed that the happier and wiser people were, the more likely the Moshiach would come. The Chabad make a practice of joy. On the Sabbath, they dress in white and gold and dance and sing for hours by the Western Wall. On Thursdays, at Zion Square in Jerusalem's fashionable downtown tourist district, you can see them dancing to music from a cassette player attached to loud portable speakers. Only men, of course: mostly small, with faces like flowers, flushed and shining, grinning with effort, suffused with love. The Chabad found Arieh, recognized his ability to enchant, his insight and intelligence, and resurrected him in an astonishing form: as a candidate for the messianic throne. There is a tradition of such candidates in Jerusalem. In the crowded streets of Mea She'arim, it is accepted, even expected, that between the wigs, the loaves of bread, the wares of vending stalls, you will see posters, buttons, or bumper stickers bearing the wide smiles of white-bearded messiahs.

In the Old Testament and in the Jewish interpretive and mystical texts, there is an emphasis on the importance of the spoken word. Speaking is the cause, not the antithesis, of an event or action. The words of the prophet become true *because* they are spoken, not the reverse. Prophecy is not witchcraft; it does not foretell the future, but it creates it. The Hasidim, of whom the Chabad are one sect, elect and train messiahs because divine revelation requires human participation, preparation, will, and desire.

In order for the Messiah to come, it is said, all Jewish men must study Torah because the Messiah's birth is not a random event like a meteor but an answer to a plea that must be made by every mouth at once: come to us, oh Lord, our God. This is why the thin, waxy wives of Mea She'arim are willing to bear ten, twelve, fourteen children. The more progeny, the higher the chances that one of them will be the golden one, the savior who will obliterate hunger, exhaustion, filth, and who will raise the lost children, parents, spouses, and siblings from their graves. Is it surprising, then, that a man such as Arieh — three-quarters blind, with his giant, nearly seven-foot stature, his long, black, tangled hair and beard, and his pipe full of blue, sweet smoke — should present himself as a perfect candidate? Or that people accustomed to thinking in terms of the infinite, the majestic and sublime, should see him and believe that yes, yes, he might be the one?

The Chabad opened the mystical books for him. This is no mean honor. A man (only men are entitled) must be thirty-five years old and intimate with the Old Testament before he is even permitted to begin studying the mystical texts, the Kaballah. Access is not easily granted because the powerful ideas of the mystics must be protected from minds that would misunderstand and misuse them. (I met a doctoral student at the Hebrew University who had a grant to masquerade as orthodox and spy on several Kaballah groups in order to report to the university on the texts that were studied.) But Arieh was inducted, initiated. He was made aware of his powers of healing. The infertile daughters of pious men were brought into his presence to kiss his hands. He became the leader of a band of adolescent boys who had left the fold and showed no inclination of returning. It was Arieh's responsibility to bring them back to Torah, back to love.

Why should a city create its own distinct madness? Surely the psychiatrists and scientists suspect that there is more at work in Jerusalem syndrome than a chemical or genetic propensity, more at stake than this rave or that delusion. I want to argue that the messiahs are part of a rich, mystical fabric. Israelis call themselves *sabras,* prickly pears, hard and thorny on the outside but on the inside succulent and sweet. Messiahs, I think, are the blooms on the cactus — infrequent but beautiful, aesthetic rather than practical, miraculous in their own right, bearers of fruit. I believe the city needs messiahs, that the city even cultivates them. How many times did a stranger stop me in the street or a soldier detain me at the gate to the university to ask, seeing my pale skin, when I had come to Jerusalem, and whether I liked it? Better or worse than America? Will you stay here? Are you going to make *aliyah* (literally, to step up or ascend, to immigrate)? Your family is important, but it is more important that all Jews return to the Holy Land so that HaMoshiach will come. These strangers, these soldiers and students, were not speaking to me out of political interest. They were stricken, lovesick for God.

Were they crazy? Maybe. But after all, what isn't crazy? War between cousins? The exchange of one dead or beaten body for another? Inquisitions and military checkpoints? The degradation of peasants whose family farms are claimed randomly by the state? Racial slurs? A countryside ripe with mines, so that anyone walking in the verdant northern hills risks setting off the shards of fire and metal? Hunger and homelessness? That only terrorists are willing to build schools and hospitals for the wretched, on the condition, always on condition, that the wretched sacrifice their sons to blind violence? Isn't this madness? Or is madness the delusion that love and fraternity are possible between nations, the delusion of a peace that is unshakable and true?

The messianic, eschatological history of the Hasidim in Jerusalem stands in opposition to the political history of Zionism. The Zionist ideal was biblical, but it had to do with the secular claims to land and language, not with faith. It was the impulse behind the kibbutz and the *moshav*, communities of farmers, of strong men and women with their hands in the earth. Zionism was romantic, lyrical, physical. It produced the extensive pipelines and pumps that funneled water from the Sea of Galilee and from underground sources out into the unscrolling desert, nurturing life there. Zionist sweat produced the tree-by-tree reclamation of the desert. Its leaders called for an end to the sequestered life of the European shtetl. No more days spent dryly with books and scriptures. No more dark clothing and pale skin. What the world and history had denied them — access to land, to the true, productive work of self-sustainment and communion with the earth — the Zionists sought to establish for themselves.

If you look at early photographs of Jewish settlers in Palestine, you will see a people in love with the sun, bronzed, muscled, dressed for physical work in a uniform of khaki shorts and blue shirts. Men and women worked side by side. On the kibbutz, children were raised together in separate buildings from their parents. During and after the Second World War, when thousands of children came to Palestine without parents, or with parents so broken in spirit they could not care for them, whole kibbutz orphanages sprang up — hundreds of children learning to sing Hebrew songs and till the dry soil. The shtetl wall was the ultimate boundary. Beyond its limits, suspicion dominated. Contact with the world outside the Jewish communities was minimal. These were communities ravaged by pogroms, violence, and fear. The Zionists wanted to break down the barriers between family and family, town and town. How else to create a lasting nation out of a people that had been homeless for thousands of years? How else to teach themselves to die for one another, if it came to that? Sometimes, in a dark mood, I think that is what a modern country is: men and women capable of killing and dying for one another, no more, no less.

The Zionist movement never belonged to Hasidic Jewry because Hasidic Jews do not concern themselves with countries or with wars. Their god is their king, and they weigh each word of every law He has passed on to them. They make no claim to the land or the language except that they may pray on one, and in the other, respectively.

3.

The last time we drank tea together in Arieh's room at the university, we were drawing plans for the Third Temple, drawing with words. A great glass dome. Music at all hours. Gold staircases and rooms for prayer and for dancing. Arieh insisted on helicopters equipped with speakers that would broadcast his music. I had taken a book from the library, called something like *The Phenomenology of Architecture*, because it contained an essay about the claim religious noise makes on a community. I read several passages aloud, invoking the bells of cathedrals and the laments of muezzin, whose music penetrated the walls of houses and even a sleeping person's ear. This had been my experience in Jerusalem, where the week began Sunday at 5:00 A.M. with the first Muslim call to prayer, "God is greater than sleep"; was punctuated by the hourly bells of churches; and fell into a dead silence Friday evening at sundown, following a siren that announced the beginning of the Sabbath. God's music did not request an audience but demanded it.

Arieh was only half-listening. "Yes." His face was dreamy; he was beyond where I could reach him. "There will be amplifiers, speakers. Music will play constantly, guitars, strings singing, and everyone will listen. I will be there in my dome of glass, and she will be there, my guitar. We will sing and sing and sing. And you will have all the gold and the jewels. Women will have their reward when I am king. All the money will belong to you, all the finery you could want."

I tried to explain how useless these things seemed even now, and how much more undesirable they would be after Judgment Day.

"Women want these things," he said, dismissing my objection with a half-wave of his hand; his hand continued on its path, traveling in its blind way toward the neck of his guitar.

I liked to think this way. The imaginary structures of Arieh's Third Temple, which rose frail and graceful out of the bleak landscape of reality, reminded me of hours spent with my Zaidy Moe. He was fearsome, sensitive to and intolerant of loud noises. He was quick to raise his voice, to reprehend and punish, but because I was the first grandchild, the only one he had known before he lost his vision completely, and perhaps because I was the quietest, preferring word or board games to make-believe, he took time to talk to me about my world and how to make it better. One afternoon in my grandparents' white kitchen, my grandfather tapping his perfect fingernails on the white Formica table, we invented a school tens of stories high, with swimming pools and balconies and great windows for the sun. We decided that since teachers only knew about one subject each, and since students knew about each of the subjects, having made plentiful notes in various colored notebooks, there should be time each week for students to teach teachers so that they could learn a thing or two they didn't already know. My grandfather blinked his milky eyes and chuckled but then became quite serious.

"But this is pretend," he said. "You must work very hard in school. Respect your teachers and learn everything you can."

"Zaidy, of course I will." But he was lost again. A deep frown and a crease in his pale forehead. As long as I could remember he had been all whiteness: skin, high forehead, pupils, hair. My grandfather's account of his life, the story he must have told himself again and again, though I never heard it directly from him, I now know was a long catalog of sorrows. He was a poor child in the wintry city of Montreal. His father died when he was seven years old, in the first years of the Depression. So he and his brother woke early in the morning, buttoned their coats, their shirts, and their boots if they had any, and went to the factories to earn what they could.

In the factories every kind of language was spoken: Russian and Polish, Ukrainian, Armenian and German, English and French. And, of course, Yiddish. Most everyone could understand one another in Yiddish. But there was little talking. The machines clattered and hummed, and the workers sang to give meaning to the rhythm of the labor, the stories people tell themselves when they have only half their attention to spare.

There were steam presses for ironing, bolts of cloth to measure and to cut. When he was older he could work the large machinery, watch the flowers and stripes of cotton as they spun through the rollers and the blades, becoming clothes. He stole and sold scraps or mended his own clothes with them. Later he would learn to make hats, shaping felt and fur over wooden blocks. In time he would be foreman, pushing the workers harder, faster; in the evenings he rode the bus home, where he beat success into his children with the hard head of a broom. Then he lay for hours in the close dark of his bedroom, his head still throbbing with the factory's pulse. But before all that, when he was still tender, he worked twelve hours if he could, dropping what he earned into the cupped palm of his mother, who was also working in a factory. Her eyes were tired and red in the morning. After his father died his mother's face became a strange, leathery mask. She mourned forever, never learning how to smile again. His mother's spirit seemed to him like a body badly crushed — she was flattened, broken, waiting stiffly for her end to come.

My grandfather could not sustain his laugh because there was no room in his world for pleasure. Imagination might cause you to lose focus, to lose your footing, and the world would not tolerate mistakes. Arieh stood in opposition, even as a possible solution, to my Zaidy and his world, characterized by meanness and paucity. Arieh loved long, lazy hours; his favorite word was *sababah*, street Arabic for "everything is good, mellow, A-OK." He would drag me to a park overlooking, in the distance, the brown hills of Jordan, and we would sit beside a bronze sculpture of the tree of life, eating falafel, watching the crows shake out their heavy plumage and spiral up in twos and threes and fives. Arieh would smoke his pipe and petition me for stories, especially stories about kings, and I would tell him again about the blind princess in the mountains of Japan who learned to see with her fingers, or about the king of Togatoga, who had to whisper his secrets into a hole in the Earth. It seemed so easy then to lie with the sun on my skin, with my eyes closed, feeling the grass under my neck and the ants filing over my ankles attending to their ant business, noticing our sentences becoming shorter and the pauses between them longer until there were mostly pleasurable stretches of silence and the sun slipped into one of these and drifted off to the far hemisphere that didn't mean anything to us, and yet that meant everything.

That was Arieh's power: if he could not change the world, he could make you see it differently; he could change the story of his life and yours into something enviable, delicate, serene. He created his life from scratch; he invented it. When he told me that he had cured a woman of cancer or that he'd taught a man to speak fluently in Hebrew just by blinking at him, I didn't believe him. But *he* believed, and that was what was so astonishing, and what made his words, on some level, true. He made a reality, or at least a potential reality, of what my Zaidy could not even allow himself to imagine — a life that warmed frigid blood, that melted solid walls of enmity built by war and poverty and cruelty, that reconciled sworn adversaries, that undid knots of hatred. Hatred and fear, Arieh knew, were the bonds that kept Jerusalem — and everywhere — from glory. If Arieh was crazy, it was an admirable, noble kind of lunacy that fed on and generated love. He was free. And if Arieh was free despite his illness, his strangeness, the loss of his job and social status, then everyone could be free, even my grandfather. Even I.

But in the end, imagination failed him, and my Zaidy Moe was right. Although Arieh was a student, I don't believe he ever attended any classes. Complaints were filed and piled up: "He plays his guitar all through the night, and the same song, over and over; the hallway always smells of marijuana; he wears bed sheets in the halls and scares the girls." Arieh received these complaints looking pale, drawn. Reality disfigured him, sallowed his cheeks. In October, I left for a three-week visit to Turkey. When I returned to Jerusalem, Arieh had vanished.

I saw him once more, at his parents' home in the suburbs of Tel Aviv. He telephoned a month after I had returned from my travels. Though he talked about walking by the ocean for hours each day and about a girlfriend he had met there, he sounded lonely. His voice would simply dry up toward the end of a thought, and a long silence would follow. I took a bus to Tel Aviv and then to the suburbs, and I found him terribly diminished.

If you take a bus from downtown Jerusalem to downtown Tel Aviv — less than two hours' ride through the dry hills around Jerusalem, past Bedouin camps made of blankets and stones where donkeys and camels roped to posts twitch their ears and tails, down toward the lush lemon and orange groves, and, finally, toward the salt-blue Mediterranean, where the air is damp and heavy with the sea's sound — you will notice as you step onto the platform of the noisy central bus terminal that your entire body sighs with relief. All the tension from the last few weeks in Jerusalem's narrow, pinched streets slides away. It feels as though you had not taken a breath in so long that you had forgotten about breathing altogether. Then you alight in Tel Aviv, and everyone is sucking in great, wasteful, windy breaths. Everywhere cafés and clubs and street performers. Everywhere sex and skin and sweat. Everywhere crèpes with chocolate, Coca-Cola, flea markets, artists, cats, gardens, and cars. In Tel Aviv, gods take a step back and heroes walk firmly on the boardwalk with the rest of us. In Tel Aviv, messiahs are delusional and nothing more.

Cut off from a community of believers, Arieh had regressed into a mere madman, cursing at his mother because he claimed she was more annoying than a man could bear. Even a man gifted with divine insight? I asked him. But he refused to see it that way. She had betrayed him with her motherly worry, her drawn look. She saw him as the world saw him, and he could not forgive her. To occupy himself and to get out of the house, he spent his mornings visiting the bereaved — there are many families mourning the early deaths of their sons and daughters — and he failed to understand why these strangers did not welcome him as he presented himself, wiry, tangled, blind, at the thresholds of their homes.

Together we stood on the stoop of a suburban duplex, before an empty-eyed mother whose twenty-two-year-old daughter was dead. The air was cool, and we stood in bleak silence. At last she stepped aside and allowed us to press past her into a beige-and-gold sitting room where her family sat together on six or eight low mourners' chairs. They all stared at us as we came in, then turned away, and I felt their wrenching grief. It was in the air as thick as smoke, as real as the clang of bells. Arieh managed to say something in Hebrew and to flash one of his smiles, but it was as if he had said nothing. They paid us as little attention as they would a cold wind that has come in through an open door that is not even worth the trouble to close. I felt trapped, unable to speak or move or look grief in the eye. My blood pumped harder and harder, and I wanted to run from that bright room, from its framed photographs and vases of yellow dahlias, from its two clocks that sounded together like an uncanny tin heartbeat.

In that room, Arieh's impotence, his inability to speak to these people's sorrow, became very clear, and I was ashamed to be there with him, to have intruded. In Jerusalem, Arieh's appearance in a mourning stranger's home would have felt different, natural, an act of love and hope. The unexpected is sacred in Jerusalem, and the city is able to embrace and contain all that is irrational, disorderly, and shaped by blind intuition. Jerusalem could sustain and contain Arieh, who loved the world's — and his own — strangeness, powerlessness.

At the bus stop, where I waited to return to Jerusalem, Arieh and I both knew, in our own way, that we would never see each other again. On the plastic bench in the bus-stop shelter — just posts, really, with a corrugated metal canopy — we talked of the weather, the ride home. When the bus pulled up in a squeal of brakes and an effusion of acrid exhaust, I stood and Arieh grabbed my arm, pulled me close to him, and kissed my cheek. I tried to hide my revulsion and to soften my recoil, but he either didn't notice or didn't mind. He grinned and danced away waving, shouting, "Aha, I got you." And then he was gone.

When Arieh was in the fire of his faith, he made the rest of us, his friends and followers, glow also. He made us feel the heat and power of the mind's possibilities, of the places we were too afraid or too sane to go. But we despised him when he cooled again, and we felt ashamed. Arieh, we saw suddenly, was only half-made, twisted up, the product of neither utility nor art. And because we did not share his vision, because we had only borrowed it, we could not see that he was not halfway between but both at once — that one depended on the other — wise man, fool.

DAVID HALBERSTAM

The Boys of Saigon

FROM *Gourmet*

WE WOULD BARELY be seated inside the Diamond, which was our favorite restaurant in Saigon, when the first platter would arrive, always without our having to order it. Truth is, I recall the entire dinner more or less arriving without anyone ordering it, as if done by a combination of American-to-Vietnamese food telepathy and pure habit, the owner's knowledge of who we were and what we wanted. The first course was always cracked crab. The beer arrived with it, straight from a temporary predinner stay in the freezer, not the refrigerator. The platter bearing the crab was huge — big enough, it would seem, for a table twice the size of ours. Each crab had been broken into about eight or nine pieces. We did not so much eat the crab as attack it. If the first image was of the crab arriving, the next one was of fingers and chunks of crab flying toward our mouths on the upward stroke, and on the downward stroke, a growing and imposing pile of crab shells. Even as we finished the first platter, another one would arrive. We never had to signal for it. The owner watched us and made sure that we didn't go hungry.

The second course at the Diamond was always the baby pigeon. Again, we never had to order. They looked very elegant, all those wondrous little birds, perfectly done, placed with admirable spacing, equidistant from each other, like thirty or forty miniaturized turkeys on a platter. They were, I think, roasted; I know they were not grilled. And again, we did not use knives and forks or chopsticks to eat them — rather our fingers flew, plate to mouth and back. The birds were sweet and exquisitely prepared, but they were devoured quite primitively. We sucked the meat right down to the bone, and we almost always got a second platter. Later, as the pace of the dinner slowed slightly, there would usually be a third course, a giant fish, I think, prepared in a sweet-and-sour style, but even though the fish was good, it did not distinguish the restaurant. The crab and the baby pigeon did that.

The Diamond, I should point out, was not a very prepossessing place. It was in Cholon, the Chinese section of Saigon, and it was about a thirty-minute cab ride from downtown, where most of us lived and worked. It had none of the fading glamour of the Arc-en-Ciel, the great showplace restaurant in Cholon back in the French days, favored as it had been by field-level French officers, and then, in the time between the French war and the American one, by American intelligence officials. I was once taken to the Arc when I was new to the country and saw — not in a private room, but quite openly — an immense table at which were seated about two dozen men, all of them CIA. It was a celebration of sorts, someone going home, or a birthday. So much for covert operations. It struck me then, and it has remained with me since, that Saigon in those days was the most secretive of places and yet, in the end, a place where there were no secrets.

The Diamond was quite ordinary inside. There was just enough inauthentic Asian décor to make it feel slightly exotic to the rare Westerner who liked going there, and not too much to drive away the Vietnamese and Chinese, who generally believed in minimalist interiors — and did not need to be reminded that they were in Vietnam.

I do not know whether we were the most favored customers. The owner was extremely polite and always extremely glad to see us — we came in a large group, which was good, and we were great drinkers, which was better. We were almost all of us war correspondents: noisy, cocky, contentious, and sometimes more than a little bit edgy. We might well have been covering combat that day, or, failing that, have come under attack from American officialdom, either in Washington or Saigon. We were, we already sensed back then, fighting for our professional lives, and we lived very tense, very driven days. There were constant covert investigations by government intelligence units to find out who our principal sources were and to threaten them with suitable punishment (lack of promotion, usually) if they continued to talk to us. And we had learned the hard way to be wary: many visitors, most of them from the World War II generation, had arrived, enjoyed our hospitality, praised the work we were doing, and then gone back to the States and assailed us for being so pessimistic. But we had the confidence of the young; we were wired to a great story with great sources — the men who were actually fighting the war, not toeing the line sent in from Washington — and we knew that one day our reporting would be validated.

The owner of the Diamond took good care of us, but he never fawned, and there is a major difference in that, especially in a country like Vietnam, which was going from a colonial era to one that was much more uncertain. If a group of eight or ten hungry and thirsty journalists liked his restaurant and came back every two weeks as we tended to do, that was all right, and if we never came back again, that was fine, too, and he would probably never wonder where we had gone.

I think it was François Sully who found the Diamond. We would never have discovered it on our own, and the proprietor was not exactly looking for us — there were no advertisements for it that I ever saw. In truth, François found for us almost everything else that was good there. Almost his entire life had been spent in that part of the world; he had entered the French army at eighteen, was sent to fight in Indochina, had survived that war, and mustered out in Saigon. He felt that although he belonged to the former colonial interlopers and the country belonged to the Vietnamese, it was his country too, or at least a country to be shared, as long as he respected their primacy in it. Eventually François morphed into a journalist, working for *Newsweek* and a number of French publications during the sixties.

François knew the old Saigon, a city where the dominant foreign presence was French, though he adjusted easily to the newer one, which was becoming dominated by the Americans. At his parties, there was always a wide selection of Vietnamese, French, and Americans — businessmen, intelligence people, soldiers who never left, and beautiful young upper-class Vietnamese divorcées who were now on their own in the city. That was how most of us met our girlfriends. François was of Saigon as we were not; even when we stayed a long time, we were always simply passing through. He did not want to leave, because he loved the country, so he stayed on, reporting for *Newsweek*, long after most of the Americans started going home. He was killed there in March 1971, at the age of forty-four, when his helicopter was shot down.

From 1962 to 1964, when the war was still relatively small, Saigon was still a very beautiful city. The indigenous culture was ascending, although you could see the French hand in the large villas, the wide avenues, and clubs like the Cercle Sportif, where members played tennis and the girls wore bikinis even as the war went on a few miles away. It was as if the city, with its sophistication and rich nightlife, and the country, with its ongoing bitter civil war, managed to accommodate themselves to each other, as if there were room enough for both, at least for the time being.

The food reflected an extraordinary confluence of cultures, what would now be called fusion but in an age before that term existed. Saigon in 1963 was a wondrous place to eat. There was Vietnamese or Chinese cuisine, often cooked by someone who had been taught by the French, and there was the French cuisine itself, which was also very good. In general, there was amazing seafood — the entire coastline, underutilized in those days, yielded lobster, crab, shrimp, and a vast variety of fish.

I came of age as a food person in Saigon — not just as someone who came to love eating well, but as someone who believes that the very act of eating after a long and difficult day of working is a necessary and well-earned celebration of the day. I am much older now, and if food has become an important part of my life, then the roots of that are in those Saigon years. The pressure of the job was so great, the friendships among colleagues so important, and the food so astonishing that my life changed, and I began to appreciate things that I scarcely could have imagined when I first got there.

The Diamond had about nine or ten tables, and we always took the large round one in the center. We were the veteran reporters on location (you became a veteran reporter after about three months on assignment there), and were never fewer than six, and sometimes as many as ten. The base group included my great pal Neil Sheehan, who was with UPI; Horst Faas, the AP photographer; Peter Arnett, with AP; Ray Herndon, with UPI; Mert Perry, then with *Time*, and his wife, Darlene (Mert was the only one of us who was married); Charley Mohr, also then with *Time*, who was there more and more often as the story grew in importance; and, occasionally, Mal Browne, from AP. In addition, we would take certain sources there — very good ones, people we absolutely trusted, and who were also willing to be seen with us. These were men like Lieutenant Colonel John Vann, later made famous in Sheehan's *Bright Shining Lie*; Lieutenant Colonel Fred Ladd, another division adviser and a gifted, brave, and singularly honest officer; Captain George "Speedy" Gaspard, who ran a Special Forces A-team in the highlands at a place called Dak Pek; and Lieutenant Colonel Ivan Slavich, who commanded the first American armed helicopter company. (I have memories of flying back from a combat operation in the Mekong Delta and Ivan using the commo system in the chopper to alert the others, back in Saigon, that it was the right night for the Diamond.)

By that time, the Diamond was one of our two favorite places to eat. The other was the house that Horst Faas and I were renting on Phan Dinh Phung. Horst and I had been very good friends before we came to Vietnam. We had worked closely together in the Congo, where we had both been stationed — he for AP, me for the *New York Times* — and I thought from the start that he was one of the smartest and bravest people I had ever worked with. He was also one of the most sensitive, although he didn't seem sensitive, not at that moment, anyway, in the judgment of most of my colleagues. He was stolid, quite stocky, and had a relatively thick German accent; a mere sixteen years after the end of World War II, a German accent was not considered an acceptable sign of sensitivity. I usually checked with him when I was working on a story because he always managed to see things that everyone else seemed to miss.

He was not just a superb photographer but a superb teacher. If you were new in a dangerous country like Vietnam, Horst was the person to learn from and go out with on your early operations. In the days before the Americans arrived, we always went out with South Vietnamese troops, and their units varied greatly in ability. Horst was very shrewd, and would carefully check out a unit to determine what condition their equipment was in (a sure sign of how good their commanding officer was). If their gear was well maintained, he would go; if they took better care of their ducks and chickens than of their rifles, he would sit it out. Horst was already in Saigon in the middle of 1962, when I got there, and a few weeks later he told me that the German chargé d'affaires was going on home leave. His villa would be available for three months as a sublet. Did we want to take it? We did.

It was a wonderful old colonial villa. It had no air conditioning, but it did have high ceilings and great fans, so it was always cool — or as cool as you could get in Saigon. If there was a drawback, it was the lack of hot water in the bath, but in time that was taken care of, too. One morning, a jeep pulled up in front of the house, and a young sergeant got out and asked if I was Mr. Halberstam. "Sir," he said, "Lieutenant Colonel Slavich thought you ought to have this," at which point he unloaded a giant hot-water heater and installed it. These days, I ponder the fact that there is probably some Communist official high in the bureaucracy in Saigon who lives in our old house and who, unlike the other Communist officials of his rank in the neighboring houses, can take hot showers courtesy of Colonel Ivan Slavich, U.S. Army (Ret.).

Apparently, the house had been much more sedate in the days when the German chargé was living there — small dinner parties once every two weeks or so, formal and low-key. We changed that almost immediately. The villa came with a staff of four or five, but the most central figure to us was the Bep. (*Bep* is the Vietnamese word for "cook," and that's what he wanted us to call him.) In his mind, the house had become infinitely more exciting with our arrival. On those occasions when we were not out in the field, we had dinner parties at the villa two or three times a week. In the morning, the Bep would ask how many people were coming for dinner and we would tell him six or eight or ten — we had nothing planned — and then we would go through the day inviting friends as we ran into them. In the meantime, the Bep would go pick out lobster or crab at the Saigon market, bring them back to the house, let them walk across the floor of the villa to prove how alive they were, and then cook them for us. He was French trained, and he was very good and very disciplined. He was a wonderful man — he had a combination of sweetness and modesty and pride in his skills — and he was aware from the start how much we appreciated him.

The Bep's specialty — I think he would have cooked it every night of the week if we'd let him, since he was so proud of it and the ingredients were so readily available — was a glorious bouillabaisse. At the end of each meal he would come out, this quite humble man who was so good to us, and be applauded by our guests. Our dinner parties were joyous affairs, and they made for very good reporting: whenever we went out in the field and met someone we liked, we invited him to come for dinner (and often to stay with us), which allowed us to keep up an expert knowledge of the area. We had a kind of ongoing seminar on the war taught by people who had often been fighting it for months. I do not know if it was the kind of training that would have been recommended at a journalism school, but it fit the nature and needs of a reporter in Saigon in those days, and it helped us stay very wired.

In time, our sublet on Phan Dinh Phung ended, and so we took the Bep and moved to another villa, a newer one on Phan Thanh Gian. The water heater stayed behind, as a thank-you to the Germans. The new villa was not as grand as the old, but our evenings were every bit as exceptional, and were made a little less chaotic with the arrival of Horst's fiancée, the lovely Ursula Gerienne.

I sit here today, almost a half century later, and I still remember the pleasure of those evenings, both at the Diamond and at our villa: the passion the war generated, the fierce sense of purpose it kindled in the press corps, the compulsion to talk and argue and analyze what was happening. We needed to understand it all a little better; we needed, more than anything else, to know more and to get it right. We lived like the obsessed.

But there was a richness to our lives then because everything we did seemed to matter so much. We were young and without reputations when we first got to Saigon; we were the front edge of a new generation of journalists covering wars. Our careers were not destroyed. We survived as professionals and friends. Five of us — Neil, Mal, Peter, Horst, and I — won the Pulitzer Prize (Horst won it twice).

Some years ago, the Pulitzer people celebrated the seventy-fifth anniversary of the prize with a giant celebration up at Columbia University. About a week before the party, I got a call from Horst in London, where he was running the AP's European photographic coverage.

"David, we do this Pulitzer thing right, yes?" he said, or, more accurately, ordered. "You are in charge of getting Mal and Peter and Neil, and we all go together! Right!"

"Do we want to go to dinner afterward?" I asked. Columbia, judging by the late afternoon–early evening hour on the invitation, would probably be offering us finger food, and Horst was not a finger-food man. He agreed, and I called up the others. We met at my apartment on the West Side of Manhattan and went up to Columbia, and we entered that giant party all of us together, still friends decades later, still proud of each other and our membership in that small, unofficial club. And there was Stan Karnow, who had worked for the *Washington Post* back then, who looked at us and said simply, "There they are, the boys of Saigon." Which we were, and still are, and, I guess, always will be.

That night, we left together when the party was over, not just the five of us, but a larger group now, with wives and children, and we went downtown to Indochine and had a very good dinner, first rate, really, but not as good, never as good, never could be as good, as dinner at the Diamond.

PETER HESSLER

Hutong Karma

FROM *The New Yorker*

FOR THE PAST FIVE YEARS, I've lived about a mile north of the Forbidden City, in an apartment building off a tiny alleyway in downtown Beijing. My alley, which has no official name, begins in the west, passes through three ninety-degree turns, and exits to the south. On a map, the shape is distinctive: it looks a little like a question mark, or perhaps half of a Buddhist swastika. The alley is also distinctive because it belongs to one of the few surviving sections of old Beijing. The capital, like most Chinese cities nowadays, has been changing fast — the biggest local map publisher updates its diagrams every three months, to keep pace with development. But the layout of my neighborhood has remained more or less the same for centuries. The first detailed map of Beijing was completed in 1750, under the reign of the great Qing emperor Qianlong, and on that document my alley follows the same route it does today. Xu Pingfang, a Beijing archaeologist, has told me that my street may very well date to the fourteenth century, when many sections of the city were originally laid out, under the Yuan dynasty. The Yuan also left the word *hutong*, a Mongolian term that has come to mean "alley" in Chinese. Locals call my alley Little Ju'er, because it connects with the larger street known as Ju'er Hutong.

I live in a modem three-story building, but it's surrounded by the single-story homes of brick, wood, and tile that are characteristic of *hutong*. These structures stand behind walls of gray brick, and often a visitor to old Beijing is impressed by the sense of division: wall after wall, gray brick upon gray brick. But a *hutong* neighborhood is most distinguished by connections and movement. Dozens of households might share a single entrance, and although the old residences have running water, few people have private bathrooms, so public toilets play a major role in local life. In a *hutong*, much is communal, including the alley itself. Even in winter, residents bundle up and sit in the road, chatting with their neighbors. Street venders pass through regularly, because the *hutong* are too small for supermarkets.

There are few cars. Some alleys, like the one I live on, are too narrow for automobile traffic, and the sounds of daily life are completely different from what one would expect in the heart of a city of fifteen million people. Usually I'm awake by dawn, and from my desk I hear residents chatting as they make their way to the public toilet next to my building, chamber pots in hand. By midmorning, the venders are out. They pedal through the alley on three-wheeled carts, each announcing his product with a trademark cry. The beer woman is the loudest, singing out again and again, *"Maaaaiiiii piiiiijiuuuuuu!"* At eight in the morning, it can be distracting — "Buuuuyyyy beeeeeeeeeer!" — but over the years I've learned to appreciate the music in the calls. The rice man's refrain is higher-pitched; the vinegar dealer occupies the lower registers. The knife sharpener provides percussion — a steady click-clack of metal plates. The sounds are soothing, a reminder that even if I never left my doorway again life would be sustainable, albeit imbalanced. I would have cooking oil, soy sauce, and certain vegetables and fruit in season. In winter, I could buy strings of garlic. A vender of toilet paper would pedal through every day. There would be no shortage of coal. Occasionally, I could eat candied crab apple.

I could even make some money from the freelance recyclers. On an average day, a recycler passes through every half-hour, riding a flat-bed tricycle. They purchase cardboard, paper, Styrofoam, and broken appliances. They buy old books by the kilogram and dead televisions by the square inch. Appliances can be repaired or stripped for parts, and the paper and plastic are sold to recycling centers for the barest of profits: the margins of trash. Not long ago, I piled some useless possessions in the entryway of my apartment and invited each passing recycler inside to see what everything was worth. A stack of old magazines sold for sixty-two cents; a burned-out computer cord went for a nickel. Two broken lamps were seven cents, total. A worn-out pair of shoes: twelve cents. Two broken Palm Pilots: thirty-seven cents. I gave one man a marked-up manuscript of the book I'd been writing, and he pulled out a scale, weighed the pages, and paid me fifteen cents.

One day in late April, I was sitting at my desk when I heard somebody call out, "Looonnnng haaaaiiiir! Looonnnng haaaaiiiir!" That was an unfamiliar refrain, so I went out into the alley, where a man had parked his cart. He had come from Henan Province, where he worked for a factory that produces wigs and hair extensions. When I asked about business, he reached inside a burlap sack and pulled out a long black ponytail. He said he'd just bought it from another *hutong* resident for ten dollars. He had come to Beijing because it was getting warm — haircut season — and he hoped to acquire a hundred pounds of good hair before returning to Henan. Most of it, he said, would eventually be exported to the United States or Japan.

While we were talking, a woman hurried out of a neighboring house, carrying something in a purple silk handkerchief. Carefully, she unwrapped it: two thick strands.

"They're from my daughter," she said, explaining that she'd saved them from the last haircut.

Each ponytail was about eight inches long. The man picked up one and studied it closely, like a fisherman who knows the rules. He said, "These are too short."

"What do you mean?"

"They're no use to me," he said. "They need to be longer than that."

The woman tried to bargain, but she didn't have much leverage; finally she returned home, hair in hand. The man's call echoed as he left the *hutong*: "Looonnnng haaaaiiiir! Looonnnng haaaaiiiir!"

Not long after I moved into Little Ju'er, Beijing stepped up its campaign to host the 2008 Games, and traces of Olympic glory began to touch the *hutong*. In an effort to boost the athleticism and health of average Beijing residents, the government constructed hundreds of outdoor exercise stations. The painted steel equipment is well-intentioned but odd, as if the designer had caught a fleeting glimpse of a gym and then worked from memory. At the exercise stations, people can spin giant wheels with their hands, push big levers that offer no resistance, and swing on pendulums like children at a park. In the greater Beijing region, the stations are everywhere, even in tiny farming villages by the Great Wall. Out there, the equipment gives the peasants a new lifestyle option: after working a twelve-hour day on the walnut harvest, they can get in shape by spinning a big yellow wheel over and over.

But nobody appreciates the exercise stations more than *hutong* residents. The machines are scattered throughout old parts of the city, tucked into narrow alleyways. At dawn and dusk, they are especially busy — older people meet in groups to chat and take a few rounds on the pendulum. On warm evenings, men sit idly on the machines, smoking cigarettes. The workout stations are perfect for the ultimate *hutong* sport: hanging around in the street with the neighbors.

At the end of 2000, as part of a citywide pre-Olympic campaign to improve sanitation facilities, the government rebuilt the public toilet at the head of Ju'er Hutong. The change was so dramatic that it was as if a shaft of light had descended directly from Mount Olympus to the alleyway, leaving a magnificent structure in its wake. The building had running water, infrared-automated flush toilets, and signs in Chinese, English, and Braille. Gray rooftop tiles recalled traditional *hutong* architecture. Rules were printed onto stainless steel. "Number 3: Each user is entitled to one free piece of common toilet paper (length 80 centimeters, width 10 centimeters)." A small room housed a married couple who served as full-time attendants. Realizing that no self-respecting Beijing resident would work in a public toilet, the government had imported dozens of couples from the interior, mostly from the poor province of Anhui. The husband cleaned the men's room; the wife took care of the women's.

The couple in Ju'er Hutong brought their young son, who took his first steps in front of the public toilet. Such scenes occurred across the capital, and perhaps someday the kids will become the Beijing version of Midnight's Children: a generation of toddlers reared in public toilets who, ten years after the Olympics, will come of age and bring hygienic glory to the Motherland. Meanwhile, Ju'er residents took full advantage of the well-kept public space that fronted the new toilet. Old Yang, the local bicycle repairman, stored his tools and extra bikes there, and in the fall cabbage venders slept on the strip of grass that bordered the bathroom.

Wang Zhaoxin, who ran the cigarette shop next door, arranged some ripped-up couches around the toilet entrance. Someone else contributed a chessboard. Folding chairs appeared, along with a wooden cabinet stocked with beer glasses.

After a while, there was so much furniture, and so many people there every night, that Wang Zhaoxin declared the formation of the "W. C. Julebu": the W. C. Club. Membership was open to all, although there were disputes about who should be chairman or a member of the Politburo. As a foreigner, I joined at the level of a Young Pioneer. On weekend nights, the club hosted barbecues in front of the toilet. Wang Zhaoxin supplied cigarettes, beer, and grain alcohol, and Mr. Cao, a driver for the Xinhua news service, discussed what was happening in the papers. The coal-fired grill was attended to by a handicapped man named Chu. Because of his disability, Chu was licensed to drive a small motorized cart, which made it easy for him to transport skewers of mutton through the *hutong*. In the summer of 2002, when the Chinese men's soccer team made history by playing in its first World Cup, the W. C. Club acquired a television, plugged it into the bathroom, and mercilessly mocked the national team as it failed to score a single goal throughout the tournament.

Wang Zhaoxin modestly refused the title of chairman, although he was the obvious choice: his entire life had been intertwined with the transformation of modern Beijing. His parents had moved to Ju'er Hutong in 1951, two years after the Communist revolution. Back then, Beijing's early-fifteenth-century layout was still intact, and it was unique among major world capitals: an ancient city virtually untouched by modernity or war.

Beijing had once been home to more than a thousand temples and monasteries, but nearly all of them were converted to other uses by the Communists. In Ju'er, the monks were kicked out of a lamasery called Yuan Tong Temple, and dozens of families moved in, including Wang Zhaoxin's parents. Meanwhile, other members of the proletariat were encouraged to occupy the homes of the wealthy. Previously, such private *hutong* residences had been arranged around spacious open-air courtyards, but during the 1950s and '60s most of these became crowded with shanties and makeshift structures. The former compound of a single clan might become home to two dozen families, and the city's population swelled with new arrivals. Over the next twenty years, the Communists tore down most of Beijing's monumental gates, as well as its impressive city wall, which in some places was forty feet high. In 1966, when Wang Zhaoxin was a six-year-old elementary-school student, he participated in a volunteer children's work brigade that helped demolish a section of the Ming-dynasty city wall not far from Ju'er. In 1969, during the Cultural Revolution, the nearby Anding Gate was torn down to make room for a subway station. By the time Mao died, in 1976, roughly a fifth of old Beijing had been destroyed.

In 1987, Wang Zhaoxin's younger brother accepted his first job, at a Beijing restaurant. Within months of starting work, the eighteen-year-old lost his right arm in a flour-mixing machine. Not long before that, Wang Zhaoxin had gone into retail, hoping to succeed in the new market economy; now he chose a product line in deference to his brother's disability. Fruit and vegetables are too heavy, he reasoned, and a clothes merchant needs two arms to measure and fold goods. Cigarettes are light, so that's what the Wang brothers stocked.

During the 1990s and early 2000s, as the Wangs sold cigarettes in Ju'er Hutong, developers sold most of old Beijing. Few sections of the city were protected, in part because local government bureaus often profited from development. Whenever a *hutong* was doomed, its buildings were marked with a huge painted character surrounded by a circle, like the *A* of the anarchist's graffiti:

Chai: "Pull down, dismantle." As developers ran rampant over the city, that character became a talisman — Beijing artists riffed on the shape, and residents cracked *chai* jokes. At the W. C. Club, Wang Zhaoxin used to say, "We live in *Chai nar.*" It sounded like the English word *China*, but it meant "Demolish where?"

Like many Beijing people I knew, Wang Zhaoxin was practical, good-humored, and unsentimental. His generosity was well known — the locals had nicknamed him Wang Laoshan, Good Old Wang. He always contributed more than his share to a W. C. Club barbecue, and he was always the last to leave. He used to say that it was only a matter of time before the government *chai*'d more buildings in our area, but he never dwelled on the future. More than four decades in *Chai nar* had taught him that nothing lasts forever.

The W. C. Club was near the head of the *hutong*, which ends at Jiaodaokou South Street. That boulevard is busy with streetcars and buses; the nearest intersection is home to a massive new apartment complex, two supermarkets, and a McDonald's. Jiaodaokou represents a border: by stepping onto the street, you enter the modern city.

Every day, most working residents of the *hutong* cross that divide. They pass the bicycle-repair stand of Old Yang, who keeps his pumps and his toolbox next to the Olympic toilet. In a *hutong*, there's no better network than one that combines bikes and bathrooms, and Old Yang knows everybody. Occasionally, he gives me messages from other people in the neighborhood; once he passed along the business card of a foreigner who had been trying to track me down. Another time, he told me that the local matchmaker had someone in mind for me.

"College-educated, 1.63 meters tall," he said curtly. Those were the only specs he knew. For Chinese women, 1.6 is a magic number — you often see that figure in job listings and dating ads. It's about five feet three. I told Old Yang that I appreciated the tip but that I didn't want to meet anybody right now.

"Why not? You're not married."

"Well, I'm not in a rush. In my country, people get married later."

When I started to walk away, he told me that he'd already given my phone number to the matchmaker.

"Why did you do that?" I said. "You have to tell her that I'm not interested."

Old Yang is in his sixties, a tall, stern-faced man with a shaved head. When I tried to decline the invitation, his expression became even more serious than usual. He told me that it was too late: everything had already been arranged; he'd look bad if I didn't go. That week, the matchmaker called me four times. She introduced herself as Peng Laoshi — Teacher Peng — and she had scheduled the date for Saturday afternoon. We met beyond the *hutong*'s boundary, at the entrance to the Jiaodaokou McDonald's. My date was supposed to arrive in a few minutes, but there was something that Teacher Peng wanted to clarify first.

"This is an underground meeting," she said, after we had found seats in the upstairs section of the restaurant.

"Why?"

"It's not official. We're not allowed to work with foreigners."

"Why not?"

"The government doesn't want us to," she said. "They're afraid the foreigners will trick Chinese women."

There was a pause, from which the conversation could have proceeded in any number of interesting directions. But Teacher Peng seemed accustomed to filling awkward silences and she spoke fast. "Of course, I'm not worried about you," she said, beaming. "Old Yang says you're a good person."

Teacher Peng was in her mid-forties, and the skin around her eyes was crinkled from smiling so much — a rare characteristic in China. She wasn't an actual teacher; that's simply a title people use for matchmakers. In China, professional matchmakers still play a role in rural areas and small cities, but they've become less important in places like Beijing. Nevertheless, I occasionally see a sign advertising their services, especially in old neighborhoods. Teacher Peng kept a government-registered office in Ju'er.

At McDonald's, I asked Teacher Peng how much she charged, and she said the fee for meeting someone was usually two hundred yuan.

"But it's more to meet a foreigner," she said. "Five hundred, one thousand, even two thousand."

I asked, as delicately as possible, how much today's client would have to pay for me if things worked out.

"One thousand." It was a little more than $120. Even if other foreigners were worth twice as much, there was some consolation in being double the minimum.

"Does she have to pay anything just for meeting today?" I asked.

"No. It's only if you stay together."

"For marriage?"

"No. For more dates."

"How many?"

"That depends."

She wouldn't give me a number, and I kept asking questions, trying to figure out how the system worked. Finally, she leaned forward and said, "Do you hope to get married quickly, or do you just want to spend time with a woman?"

It was a hell of a first-date question for a single male in his thirties. What could I say? I didn't want the bike repairman to lose face. "I really don't know," I stammered. "But I want to make sure that she's not paying anything to meet me today."

Teacher Peng smiled again. "You don't have to worry about that," she said.

When I first moved to the neighborhood, I regarded McDonald's as an eyesore and a threat: a sign of the economic boom that had already destroyed most of old Beijing. Over time, though, *hutong* life gave me a new perspective on the franchise. For one thing, it's not necessary to eat fast food in order to benefit from everything that McDonald's has to offer. At the Jiaodaokou restaurant, it's common for people to sit at tables without ordering anything. Invariably, many are reading; in the afternoon, schoolchildren do their homework. I've seen the managers of neighboring businesses sitting quietly, balancing their account books. And always, always, always somebody is sleeping. McDonald's is the opposite of *hutong* life, in ways both good and bad: cool in summer, warm in winter, with private bathrooms.

It's also anonymous. Unlike Chinese restaurants, where waitresses hover, the staff at a fast-food joint leaves people alone. On a number of occasions, dissidents have asked me to meet them at a McDonald's or a KFC, because it's safe. When Teacher Peng told me that our meeting was "underground," I realized why she had chosen the restaurant.

Others apparently had the same idea. One couple sat near the window, leaning close and whispering. At another table, two well-dressed girls seemed to be waiting for their dates. Over Teacher Peng's left shoulder, I kept an eye on a couple who appeared to be having some sort of crisis. The woman was about twenty-five; the man seemed older, in his forties. Their faces shone with the unnatural redness that comes to many Chinese who have been drinking.

They sat in silence, glaring at each other. Nearby, the McDonald's Playland™ was deserted. Teacher Peng's pager went off.

"That's her," she said, and asked to borrow my cell phone.

"I'm at McDonald's," she said into the phone. "The Italian is already here. Hurry up."

After Teacher Peng hung up, I tried to say something, but she spoke too fast. "She teaches music at a middle school," she said. "She's a very good person — I wouldn't introduce you otherwise. Good. Listen. She's twenty-four years old. She's pretty and she's 1.64 meters tall. She's educated. She's thin, though. I hope that's not a problem — she's not as voluptuous as the women in your Italy."

There was so much to process — for one thing, my date seemed to be growing taller — and before I could speak Teacher Peng continued: "Good. Listen. You have a good job and you speak Chinese. Also, you were a teacher before, so you have something in common."

Finally, she stopped. I said, "I'm not Italian."

"What?"

"I'm American. I'm not Italian."

"Why did Old Yang tell me you're Italian?"

"I don't know," I said. "My grandmother is Italian. But I don't think Old Yang knows that."

Now Teacher Peng looked completely confused.

"America is an immigrant country," I began, and then I decided to leave it at that.

She recovered her poise. "That's fine," she said with a smile. "America is a good country. It's fine that you come from America."

The woman arrived, wearing headphones. Japanese script decorated her stylish jacket, and she wore tight jeans. Her hair had been dyed a dark brown. Teacher Peng introduced us, crinkled her eyes one last time, and tactfully took her leave. Very slowly, one by one, the woman removed her headphones. She looked quite young. The CD player sat on the table between us.

I said, "What are you listening to?"

"Wang Fei" — a popular singer and actress.

"Is it good?"

"It's OK."

I asked her if she wanted anything from the restaurant, and she shook her head. I respected that — why spoil a date at McDonald's by eating the food? She told me that she lived with her parents in a *hutong* near the Bell Tower; her school was nearby. She asked me if I was from the neighborhood.

"I live in Ju'er Hutong."

"I didn't know there were foreigners there," she said. "How much is your rent?"

This being China, I told her.

"That's a lot," she said. "Why do you pay so much?"

"I don't know. I guess they can always charge foreigners more."

"You were a teacher, right?"

I told her that I used to teach English in a small city in Sichuan Province.

"That must have been boring," she said. "Where do you work now?"

I said that I was a writer who worked at home.

"That sounds even more boring," she said. "I'd go nuts if I had to work at home."

Behind her, the drunk couple began arguing loudly. Suddenly the woman stood up, brandished a newspaper, and smacked the man on the head. Then she stormed out, right past Playland™. Without a word, the man folded his arms, lay his head down on the table, and went to sleep.

A moment later, the music teacher asked, "Do you often go back to your Italy?"

The following week, the matchmaker telephoned to see if there was any chance of a second meeting, but she wasn't insistent. She impressed me as a sharp woman — sharp enough to recognize that my cluelessness might be exploited in better ways than dates at McDonald's. The next time I ran into her in the *hutong*, she asked if I wanted to become an investor in a karaoke parlor. After that, I avoided walking past her office.

When I asked Old Yang about the confusion, he shrugged and said that I once mentioned that my grandmother is Italian. I had no memory of the conversation, but I picked up a valuable *hutong* lesson: never underestimate how much the bike repairman knows.

Good Old Wang was right about *Chai nar.* For years, he had predicted demolition, and, in September of 2005, when the government finally condemned his apartment building, he moved out without protest. He had already sold the cigarette shop, because the margins had fallen too low. And now there was no doubt who had been the true chairman, because the W. C. Club died as soon as he left the *hutong*.

By then, three-quarters of old Beijing had been torn down. The remaining quarter consisted mostly of public parks and the Forbidden City. Over the years, there had been a number of protests and lawsuits about the destruction, but such disputes tended to be localized: people complained that government corruption reduced their compensation, and they didn't like being relocated to suburbs that were too distant. But it was unusual to hear an average Beijinger express concern for what was happening to the city as a whole. Few spoke in terms of architectural preservation, perhaps because the Chinese concept of the past isn't closely linked to buildings, as it is in the West. The Chinese rarely built with stone, instead replacing perishable materials periodically over the decades.

The *hutong* essence had more to do with spirit than with structure, and this spirit often showed strongest when the neighborhood encountered some modern element: an Olympic toilet, a McDonald's franchise. Pragmatism and resourcefulness were deeply ingrained in residents like Good Old Wang, whose environment had always been fluid. The fundamental character of *hutong* life helped prepare for its destruction.

In 2005, the Beijing government finally issued a new plan to protect the scattered old neighborhoods that remained in the north and west of downtown, including Ju'er. These *hutong* wouldn't be put on the market for developers to build whatever they wished, as they would have been in the past. The stated priority was to "preserve the style of the old city," and the government established a ten-member advisory board to consult on major projects. The board's members included architects, archaeologists, and city planners, some of whom had publicly criticized the destruction. One board member told me that it was essentially too late, but that the new plan should at least preserve the basic layout of the few surviving *hutong*. Within that layout, however, gentrification was inevitable — the *hutong* had become so rare that they now had cachet in the new economy.

The change had already begun in my neighborhood. In 2004, bars, cafés, and boutiques started moving into a quiet street that intersects Ju'er, where locals were happy to give up their homes for good prices. The businesses maintained the traditional architectural style, but they introduced a new sophistication to the old city. Nowadays, if I'm restricted to my neighborhood I have access to Wi-Fi, folk handicrafts, and every type of mixed drink imaginable. There is a nail salon in the *hutong*. Somebody opened a tattoo parlor. The street venders and recyclers are still active, but they have been joined by troops of pedicab men who give "*hutong* tours." Many of the tourists are Chinese.

One recent weekend, Good Old Wang returned for a visit, and we walked through Ju'er. He showed me the place where he was born. "There's where we lived," he said, pointing at the modern compound of the Jin Ju Yuan Hotel. "That's where the temple used to be. When my parents moved in, there was still one lama left."

We continued east, past an old red door that was suspended in the *hutong*'s wall, three feet above the street. "There used to be a staircase there," he explained. "When I was a child, that was an embassy."

In the nineteenth century, the compound had belonged to a Manchu prince; in the 1940s, Chiang Kai-shek used it as his Beijing office; after the revolution, it was taken over by Dong Biwu, a founder of the Chinese Communist party. In the 1960s, it served as the Yugoslavian Embassy. Now that all of them were gone — Manchus, Nationalists, Revolutionaries, Yugoslavians — the compound was called, appropriately, the Friendship Guesthouse.

That was *hutong* karma — sites passed through countless incarnations, and always the mighty were laid low. A couple of blocks away, the family home of Wan Rong, empress to the last monarch of the Qing dynasty, had been converted into a clinic for diabetics. In Ju'er, the beautiful Western-style mansion of Rong Lu, a powerful Qing military official, had served one incarnation as the Afghanistan Embassy before becoming what it is today: the Children's Fun Publishing Co., Ltd. A huge portrait of Mickey Mouse hangs above the door.

Good Old Wang passed the Olympic toilet ("It's a lot less cluttered than when I was here," he observed), and then we came to the nondescript three-story building where he had lived since

1969. It wasn't a historic structure, which was why it had been approved for demolition. The electricity and the heat had been cut off; we walked upstairs into an abandoned hallway. "This was my room when I was first married," he said, stopping at a door. "Nineteen eighty-seven."

His brother had lost his arm that year. We continued down the hall, to the apartment where Wang had lived most recently, with his wife, his daughter, his father, and his brother. The girl's drawings still decorated the walls: a sketch of a horse, the English phrase "Merry Christmas." "This is where the TV was," he said. "That's where my father slept. My brother slept there."

The family had dispersed; the father and brother now live in a *hutong* to the north; Good Old Wang, his wife, and their daughter are using the home of a relative who is out of town. As compensation for the condemned apartment, Good Old Wang was given a small section of a decrepit building near the Drum Tower. He hoped to fix it up in the spring.

Outside, I asked him if it had been hard to leave the *hutong* after nearly half a century. He thought for a moment. "You know, lots of events happened while I lived here," he said. "And maybe there were more sad events than happy events."

On the way out, we passed an ad for the Beijing Great Millennium Trading Co., Ltd. Later that day, returning home, I saw a line of pedicabs: Chinese tourists, bundled against the cold, cameras in hand as they cruised the ancient street.

EDWARD HOAGLAND

Miles from Nowhere

FROM *The American Scholar*

In 1966, at the age of thirty-three, the essayist, novelist, and traveler Edward Hoagland spent three months in the remotest parts of northwest British Columbia, west of the Rockies and south of the Yukon. His goal was not only to drink in a landscape beautiful and harsh, but to talk with the old-timers who had sparsely populated that country, to record their stories of prospecting and trapping, and to document their makeshift existence, which had not changed much since the nineteenth century. His journal of that trip, Notes from the Century Before, *published in 1969, would become one of the best known of his nearly twenty books. Having finished the book in 1968, newly married and about to become a father for the first time, Hoagland made a return visit. He found that many of the old-timers had already passed on and that the wilderness, although still rough and beautiful, was disappearing too. But many of the changes he detected were in himself. What follow are excerpts, about one-eighth of his journals from this visit, published here for the first time.*

June 6, 1968

Left New York on a smoggy but hot, cloudless day, from Kennedy Airport — just the day after Robert Kennedy's assassination. Everyone stupid with sorrow, poring over the papers or glued to the interminable radio commentary, and silent. The parting from my wife was doubly disconnected because of the discomforts of her pregnancy (beginning fifth month), though the doctor yesterday said it was all right for me to leave. The baby is wanted, now that our hasty, belated wedding is past, and we have love. We live in a quiet bit of Manhattan, at the eye of a hundred-mile hurricane of suburbs, etc., so that one begins by getting out of and above all this flux. I like living right at the hot center, of course, but I'm also very tired of it. With the baby coming, I expect to be gone only a couple of months; that is our agreement, sealed after she chose to conceive. I'm tired physically and emotionally from an enormously productive spring, and I find, too, less of the boyish readiness that activated my travels to British Columbia two years ago. But the encouraging thing, if you read memoirs, journals, and such, is how very much people accomplish in a couple of months. This was true for some of the major explorers of the past like Alexander Mackenzie, as well as John Muir, and various eccentric side-figures like James Capen Adams, whose adventures I happened to read yesterday. Two concentrated months are potentially a long time. Whoever I see, whatever I write, I'll be exhausted by August. As usual, my plans are informal, except that they open up possibilities — as will fatherhood, next November!

Good flight. Over the Great Lakes, lots of clouds and a really white sun. Outer Edmonton — gray-black fields, as we land, cold air and cloud cover, remote-looking, empty and primitive; parking space downtown is five dollars a month. Farm faces, men's club medallions in the lapels.

June 7

A five-hour train trip toward the heights of the Rockies. Great platform scenes — two kids seventeen having a fistfight, straight from the country — a *fist*fight! Little kids wave, wave, at the train. The prairie runs by in incremental mounds. The soil is black where it isn't green, as we roll through rain squalls, the train whining like a musical dog. People are traveling to visit their kin. A woman is reading aloud to her children, and outside some kids ride two-on-the-bare-back of a horse. It's mostly all forest after Edson, sparse jack pine, poplar, and birch. Then the Front Range of the chock-a-block Rockies appears, and a wider corridor winding in.

June 8

The headlines have followed me here. The flags are at half-mast for Bobby Kennedy and people are telling me that they're sorry for me as an American. The murderer of Martin Luther King was captured today, in London, of all places. Of course there are always going to be those with an impulse toward martyrdom — a murderer's martyrdom — the notoriety and the rigid straitjacket of the law — people who long to be grasped and bound. Art in the past has been concerned with form. Now it involves the documentation of formlessness — ski jumps from the roofs of department stores and visionaries and glamorous personages murdered. Chaos and Brownian motion.

I'm at Maligne Lake, one of the showpiece lakes of the northern Rockies. My father and I stayed here in 1952. It was rather a bore for him because he didn't fish and he couldn't hike as I did; but afterward we took a three-day pack trip on horses with a half-tamed wolf running alongside. I found the tumbled skeleton of a bear that the wolf packs had killed on the mountainside and brought the skull home: also a dead eagle's feet, a set of elk antlers, and a mountain goat's horn I found in a cave. It was all very real, indeed. Animals are becoming figures of speech, or educative symbols that children meet in their picture books. Although I don't like to confess it, my curiosity fails in regard to the future. I turn back from visualizing that life of mere spectatorship, watching the astronauts voyage, perhaps, and the Super Bowl game.

You come into the bush early in the season like this and you feel a little spring rain on your face but you have the trails to yourself. I saw three moose, which with their legs hidden, looked like long-nosed wild boar with bleached manes. Also several deer, patches of whose fur had rubbed off after the winter. They have eyes like a rabbit, but they run like a llama. I talked to the forestry warden and he says that if the coyotes have gathered into a pack and can keep the deer out of a creek or a pool, they can kill them — deer can fight in the water, just as moose can. The wolves don't come through often, because these high narrow valleys, he says, don't give them the space and the meadows they prefer. Moose, caribou, and elk come up, however, and the moose stay in the high country even in winter unless they feel the snow belly-deep. He says that he goes on snowshoes or on skis sleeved with skins for climbing, not with a sled, because the dogs (like wolves) need a more open, windswept type of country, and anyway the service frowns on feeding your dogs Jasper Park moose meat. He's lived alone for seven winters in this park.

"You learn to put up with yourself. You learn to tolerate your own company," he said.

"Do you have hallucinations?"

"No," he said. "If you have hallucinations you get squirrely, and if you're squirrely, you can't tolerate your own company."

June 9

The mountains look dramatic and incisive today. No sun, but a high ceiling, almost windless. I climbed in the Opal Hills, so-called, to the basin under the top ridge. Snow occasionally to my knees in drifts, otherwise gone. Saw some old black-bear tracks on the path — hind foot the size of one of my hands. Very still today, woods quite empty, panorama on top, the lake green and white. I'm enjoying being alone, although thinking about New York literary politics, and the Kennedys, of course. Saw the tracks of a coyote and heard a short bark. Rubbed shoulders with some Maligne mosquitoes. Am glad to know I can climb to the places I climbed sixteen years ago, when I was nineteen. My reactions are quieter and smudgier, though, and the park is developing like Yellowstone.

If a person has just been married, like me, he kicks himself if his new wife isn't constantly in the front of his mind, when, as a matter of fact, it wouldn't be natural for her to be. The symbiosis comes with time. As it is, I think of how pretty Marion was in the three dresses she wore during the weekend of my sister's wedding. We marry for ambiguous reasons, most of us — partly because we're lonely, we've reached a dead end, we feel that we ought to have children already, or perhaps we're afraid of some unfathomable element in our makeup, such as homosexuality, or a more general malaise and panicky despair. It takes a few years for the marriage to rid itself of its beginnings. Two people thirty-five, gradually falling in love, who recognize some of their mistakes of the past and are sick of a sex life of fleeting affairs, start from a better position, but they still need to play it by ear.

I have two strengths in managing my personal life: my reluctance to act and, on the other hand, my beelining directness if I do decide that the time is ripe. I was trained in the world of my gentle father, who never did battle with life, and yet, early on, I seized the principle of living to the hilt, of sampling it all, not shirking. Life is short; so I rise out of my fussy, cautious existence about once a year to *do* something.

June 10

Passed close to moose again, two cows who keep company. Their humps wiggled as they trotted off. They forded the river, legs jutting at angles. The windfalls were so thick as I walked in the forest that it seemed a log fort had fallen down. Moss underfoot — the moss itself was the soil. In the breaks, no marmots but many ground squirrels. And wasteland areas — old rockslides, with marmots. There were footprints of coyotes and moose, though you couldn't tell when they were made. In the soggy June snow even fresh prints like my own don't look very crisp. Since the wolves of the winter are gone, there were no kills. On the steep slopes spruce replaced the lodgepole pine, which have a shallow root-net holding them up.

The heart is an accurate meter, registering every few degrees' change in the pitch of the land, but I was pleased to see how strongly I could still climb. I did get a dim glimpse of the me who climbed for the same goal in 1952 — fearless, an innocent, a rather good woodsman, and even more of an optimist than I am now. At that time I was convinced that no animal was going to hurt an animal lover like me, not with the sixth sense I had. Now, while I'm eager enough to see grizzly tracks, I'd just as soon not see the bear himself. There's that fine line — wanting to be where he was *yesterday*. You try to walk loudly enough so as not to catch him by surprise, though not so loudly you won't see the other game.

After about four hours, I was up on the grand, goaty slope of Leah Mountain where I'd found the goat cave in 1952. Every small knoll was littered with droppings, and sometimes white tufts of hair. This manuring, and the southern exposure, has produced a luscious expanse of grass, but pitched at sixty or seventy degrees. It was slick where the snow was just off and there were intervals, equally slippery, of steep, shaley scree. Only one tree, with the top broken off, and spitting rocks bounded down, as fast as pitched balls from under my feet and also separately. I dislike tricky heights and had some scared moments. Then when I was coming around the corner of an escarpment, something stood up on the ledge just above. All very naturally, there was my neighbor, a bighorn ram. He possessed an immense, muscled neck, a neck as thick as my shoulders — a big wedge-shaped neck — and his ears were lost inside the circles of his huge horns. He was no laggard youngster; he was absolutely prime and heavy and grown. He wasn't twenty yards away, so I could see the cowlicks in his fur, and recognize that he'd give a wolf plenty of trouble. In fact, he was so unafraid I began to wish he were more afraid. It was like one of those sightings in a virgin valley. He was pushing his tongue in and out of his mouth, as a dog will do when prepared to fight, though this was not necessarily his reason. But, hearing my approach, he must have thought I was another sheep. Now, when he wasn't looking for a way up and out, he edged closer to me, magnificent in his musculature and posture, and more formidable than I could have imagined. He had that full heavy curl to his horns, as high as a helmet, a proper, unintellectual face, a Society face, except for the open, flat nostrils, and a clean, white hind end. I talked to him in a friendly voice, partly in hopes that he'd step back a bit. I had my own head thrown back, as one does when talking to somebody on a ladder. He was a living trophy; he was the finest bighorn, and surely the closest, I'll ever see; and yet I was the one who moved off first. He kept coming closer, and I had no trees to play monkey in, only a fall behind me, a drop-off, and my horns and my muscles were no match for his.

The goat cave would have been anticlimactic, if it hadn't been larger than I remembered. The rank smell announces it before you get there, and it has a sweeping, southerly view, good protection from the cold winds, and a grassy green promontory just in front. Smears of black dung go up the walls fifteen or twenty feet, where the goats clamber during the winter. There were some old bones of goats that didn't make it, much matted hair, and empty birds' nests in the stone niches. One is the home of a furry-tailed pack rat who foraged boldly among the goat droppings. He chewed for fleas in his white belly, watching me with his soft eyes while I ate my lunch, with more than a dozen mountains in sight. I remember in 1952 I saw a prowling wolverine from the same spot, and two annoyed eagles swooping at him, and I went to a higher valley, full of boulders, so it looked like a river of rock, and saw two wolves crossing.

June 11

Not only am I not describing the peak-studded view that confronts you when you look down the lake — I don't look at it much. It's too stunning a sight to be useful in a novel. I wouldn't situate a character here because it's about as uncommon a scene as a table of ten movie stars would be, if you are a fellow who likes pretty women. The beauty is so concentrated, excessive, it is slapstick.

June 12

Today the train makes a special stop for me at Vanderhoof. About 180 miles north of here by gravel road is Manson Creek, an old-timer's town. But the first people I asked didn't even know it existed, though that's the reason I'm here. Vanderhoof has a Chinese-owned restaurant, where newspapers are sold, a couple of five-and-dimes, "Smed's Auction Room," a couple of trucking warehouses, and one or two logging supply stores. The raw streets have 1930s cars, and big-brimmed hats, and barrel-chested, melodious-speaking, slow-mannered Indians with crusted boots and unwashed faces. People in winter coats, clodhopper boots, with beleaguered expressions. One burly apparition in his seventies — white hair to his shoulders, and a long beard — walks down the street, his head bent forward, with heavy momentum. That circle of hair is as big as an inner tube round his face, and he has prominent eyebrows and a straight forehead the complexion of beef. He's a prospector from Manson Creek, he says, so the place does await me, like a diamond mine, just as Telegraph Creek did two years ago, any time I want to go there.

June 14

Fort St. James is a very pleasant town physically — open and historical, with Stuart Lake, wide, long, and pretty, and settlements of Swedes and Estonians that have been abandoned along the shore. More meanness lives here than in Telegraph Creek, however, more mockery of the Indians and moneymaking scheming, more summer visitors, and not the same self-contained effervescence. But it's another gold mine of lore and adventure. And these people are the real thing, the real pros in the bush, compared to the Colorado cowboys I met last summer.

Yet there's only a small group of old-timers left — a one-hundred-year-old Indian died just last year, and Fred Aslin and Agate

Alexander the year before that. And now Bob Watson is dying, and also another guy. You cross off your list of locals the names of those who, it turns out, are already dead, or comatose or incoherent.

June 16

It's a little like seducing a girl to get some of these old-timers to talk to you. They *want* to, but they don't want to. The tradition is to be modest and taciturn, so they think they oughtn't to, and there's been so much bullshit told and written that they haven't much respect for the written word — between the boasters and the grizzly-story pulp writers. Yet at the same time they know it's the only way of preserving history. I dangle my maps in front of them like bait — ask them first just to describe a particular river for me, so they won't draw back. Or I use one of the key names, like Skook's, and watch those irresistible smiles spread across their faces. They've drawn back and bridled, but then they put on a studying expression and begin to talk. I huff and I puff with my stutter, and that may help too, because handicapped people have a history of being quite effective here. And since I can't talk, they do. Just like the circus was, this frontier country is a place where misfits gather, and they accept my problem as brotherly.

The old Indians aren't so coy, however. They're natural and hearty. John Prince is eighty-two. He carried the mail to Finlay Forks every month for eight years, a three-week round trip for a couple hundred dollars. He had a toboggan and several dogs (pack horses in the summer), and would pick up extra money packing grub for the trappers and several miners too. When the river opened and the mail went in on boats, he'd work for somebody else on a claim or just carry in food. He'd stay with Billy Steele en route. Then he had a store at Tachie but went broke, and worked on the steamboat at Quesnel on the Fraser River for $1.25 a day. (You could buy a bottle of Hudson's Bay rum for that. Now it's $7.00, he says.) Or he'd trade a bear hide for $6.00 worth of grub at Hudson's Bay and travel round for Hudson's Bay buying furs.

"Billy Steele died long time ago, you know. He didn't die rich; he died poor. The Indians liked him. Lots of bullshit stories; and he drink too, you know. And he buy furs from Indians in the middle of the winter when they running low and sell to him for grub. Indians good then. Now steal, drunk all the time, break into stores, shoot people," John Prince says. "Everybody likes me, especially whites. I never crooked." One of his sons was killed in World War II in Italy. The other seven kids have died by now. "All alone now," he says. Goes to all three masses at church, Sundays, collects the collection, getting ready to die. "Priest couldn't get along — wouldn't hold the service without me."

Schooling, he says, has wiped out the old Indian stories. The kids don't know them, and he has forgot; he used to know a long, long story he'd like to tell me. He says a caribou in the winter can put its nose down and smell when a snowslide is coming and run back — the rest of the herd is waiting in the meantime in the trees. And a beaver knows how hard the winter's going to be. "He cuts lots of sticks for hard one — you go out and see." And, "There are lots of wolves again. Indians aren't trapping them — I don't know what they going to do." He ends the interview by closing his eyes, yawning, and saying he hasn't had his breakfast.

June 17

But I'm in Hazelton again! It's a town steeped with memories of my previous wife and therefore bittersweet for me because we were happy here on our honeymoon in 1960. In the evening sunlight, with the mid-June grass up to my knees, the trees full-leaved, and the luscious Skeena River hustling past, noisy as a narrow ocean, and the horses in the river drinking, the mountainsides still swashed with snow, it's just about the loveliest town I'll ever see. Steep brief roads, log cabins eighty years old, and the happiest childhoods that anyone is spending from here to Hannibal, Missouri — Chinese, Indian, towhead kids. I went up on the hill by the graveyard and felt the most exhilarated — sheer exhilaration — that I've felt for weeks and weeks.

June 20

I wanted this to be an introspective journal and a rather introspective summer, too, what with my first child on the way, and my father twelve months dead. But so many stories and people and facts keep crowding me that I'm simply too busy paying attention and writing them down to do much of anything else. I'd have to lose interest in all of this jump and life and adventure. But if I'd lost interest I wouldn't be here.

The prospecting bug has hit this North Country again. What with the ubiquitous bush pilots and planes for these huge roadless reaches, a flood of investment money, and a boom in the price of metals, everybody who's ever been out in the bush remembers some outcropping he once saw, or that a Caribou Hide Indian took him to, and has flown back and staked it. Tomorrow Jack Lee and Frances, his endearing wife, are taking me out to do just that.

June 21

The planes on the little Bulkley Valley lake look like beetles, but they take off with a bold prolonged roar, like a trombone's blare. Finally it's our turn, and Lee's sipping whiskey to quiet his nerves (Seagram's Special Old — or "ground-softener," as the prospectors call it), and, with Wally, a Love family man, along, we jalopy into the air: the lake brown but sparkling underneath us. I have the usual nervous sore throat and flu stomach this morning, but forget them, looking down at the thousand shades of green and the pale green gullies. The plane is a Beaver and the pilot a bluff blond, Bill Harrison, of Omineca Airlines: charges seventy-two cents a mile. We climb east into an ore-red pass, cutting in close to save gas. There are brilliant snow splatters across the rock, then tiny, aquamarine-colored creeks that braid through the flats. Snow speckles the conifer forest. We cross an irregular burn, our lives filled with the engine's roar, and cross some mountains — Blunt, Netalzul, and Thoen — each striped like a zebra with snow; and see Babine Lake, as long as a river.

The Babine River is brown and seems scaled, lizarding along. Swaying in a silly-dilly fashion, we cross over Mount Lovell and the Frypan Range, not too high but a long snowy line of concise cusps. On the other side is a large flat valley with green shallow rivers around Takla Lake, amoeba-shaped. Beyond is the Driftwood Valley, still larger. Then Bear Lake, which consists of long twists and one loop. Then some green pocket lakes and a low cloud front; a large belt of snowy highlands, and another big churning river with a burn on one side and a forest on the other. Now there's a regular wilderness of mountains everywhere, with the steep irregular valleys between; the gray-green Sustut River, and a lush rug of forest. Then an absolute ocean of mountains strewn and feathered with snow, which the pontoon below me seems to move sedately across. Then a brown muskeg valley, practically treeless, and brilliant snow on the next ridge. Then two expansive green valleys which meet like a carpenter's rule. Thutade Lake is a giant long wiggle of water in a gently sloped valley that is forested heavily except for a burn at the northern end, heading the Finlay River.

We slant over a murderous-looking pass and bank steeply down, yawing, the mountains sunless and black, the choppy land crazily angling underneath us. By a small lake is a neat mining camp of even white tents. Each has a wooden floor built up on logs, when we get inside. This camp is a few hundred feet below timberline. The cindery, blocky mountaintops, Graves and Estabrook, cling close around, streaked with snow. Toodoggone Lake (pronounced *Too*-da-gone) is only a couple of miles long, but simmers with shadow and shine in the wind.

June 22

Jack and his partners have six claims and we're here, quite simply, because thirty-three years ago Jack was working through these valleys above the Indian village of Metsantan as part of a survey crew (four dollars a day) and saw, about quitting time, from where they were camped in the timber, a sort of white stain on the mountainside above him — almost like a stripe that somebody might have made with lime dust. He climbed up there and dug two feet down with his shovel, finding a lead-silver-zinc or galena vein. It was "native lead" that you could peel with the blade of your knife, he thought. With a double ore like that — or tungsten-gold, for instance — the company that works the mine will hope to pay the expenses of the operation eventually out of one of the metals produced, and the other can give you your profit. But he'd covered over his discovery carefully then, even to replacing the tussocks of turf, because in those days, before you started to think about a mining company paying you lots of money for your claim, you were trying to prevent them from beating you out of it. And finally, last year, chartering a plane and running around for six hours, building cairns (or "witness posts"), he did the proper staking, to the best of his recollection. We're here now to try to find the lead again and see if his memory was right, after three decades.

The hill has "got steeper," he says, because one mile is like ten miles was to him then. No white stain shows and he talks about needing x-ray eyes — Superman eyes. There's a thick overburden of soil and turf even above timberline, which is furred with ground scrub, ground balsam, or junipers. We dig down to the frost line several times and chip below that with a miner's pick. The ground is spongy, above, and soft; the snow maybe two-thirds off. Also, the grizzlies had knocked over an interloper's stone cairn, which the guy had built not very much better than a bear would have.

June 23

I spent the day by myself, walking up and partly around a spur of Claw Mountain — nothing too strenuous. It was the first sunny day in a week. I took hotcake sandwiches, and also an ax, for the idea that I was protected, and spent a layabout day, mostly sitting by brooks, looking into the pools, at the moss and the bright-colored rocks on the bottom. There is practically any noise you want to hear embedded in the noise a brook makes — a thin wavering scream; a jolly tuba-voiced conversationalist. I saw lots of moose and caribou sign but started up nothing but ptarmigan — that shallow, quarrelsome cackle. The trees age fast in this brutal climate and don't grow very high, and there are frequent breaks in the forest — mossy, grassy, lichenous clearings link up with one another and are well marked by the caribou as wintering grounds. It's a very open country. All around are unnamed, unnumbered little mountains speckled with snow and enclosing side valleys, too many to explore even if you had the whole summer to do so. The animals have moved out (it's easy to see why so many travelers on these trails have gone without fresh meat for periods of weeks), and since the helicopter from Toodoggone dropped us, no sign of another human, either.

It's such an anachronism in this contemporary world to worry about grizzly bears as one walks in the woods. Here I am, taking a Contac pill with its thousand "tiny time capsules" for a cold and worrying about meeting a bear tomorrow. Yet it's no more strange than walking the streets in fear of a beating, as we do in New York.

They clipped some promising silver-ore fragments today out of a bed on Dedeeya Creek. Wally was busy scratching information on the metal claim tags they will put out tomorrow. I'm stuttering badly, as I generally do with nonbookish people, unfortunately, so I don't say much. And I let lots of misinformation go past unchallenged: than which nothing is more galling. The subjects range from the origins of granite to wolves and snakes to local geography. Seven caribou, including two well-antlered bucks, were seen today by the others.

June 24

Here I am, right where I wanted to be, in the midst of the central experience of this summer that I've looked forward to so. We're approximately a two-hundred-mile walk from the nearest road. We're really alone — almost as alone as it's possible to be physically on this earth nowadays — and is it so different? Of course it's not as savagely lonely as the city can be, because if you're lonely in the city there's no hope. For me it's a period of gassing up. I have to gas up on solitude just as I do on company at other times. But, actually, when you come right down to it, could I do just as well if I were only ten miles from the nearest road instead of two hundred?

When I was nineteen and took care of three or four tigers, I was fearless during the day but dreamed horrendously about them at night. Here it's the opposite. My dreams are placid, but I walk in the woods in considerable trepidation — it's that the grizzly, in what we know about him, is so manlike. As everyone says, "You can come on him everywhere."

June 28

The exuberant friendship and openness of the last day. The plane was due at 6:00, so we began waiting at 4:00 A.M. The rising sun shone for only a moment. Wally stretched out on the grass again to sleep like a farmer boy. When you're expecting to go, you're ready to go; you're primed to go. In this country, with its weather combinations, pilots often don't arrive on the day they are scheduled to. Sometimes they don't arrive at all. One of the helicopter pilots I knew in Atlin in 1966 was killed last year in a crash; and one of the Fort St. James pilots was lost for fifty-nine days a few months ago and froze off the fronts of his feet. As it got toward dusk, Jack cut wood for a long siege — night wood. He hits the log with the blunt end of the blade of the ax to knock it free of the rest.

At 8:30 the next morning, when we were still glumly stuck in our beds with our energy gone, the plane arrived, circling twice. Then, having waited an extra day, we hurry-hurried, like in the army. The pilot, a saturnine, quiet mestizo with a blocky face and a clippered haircut — a stolid face like a dogsled driver's — gunned down the lake and we swayed away. He had been socked in for two days at the village of Stewart, en route to Telegraph Creek, and then on to us.

July 2

I alternate — on the same day — periods of intensive, joyful interviewing and lonely, spinning near-despair: this from being so alone. Today I was over at Mr. Dickinson's comfortable home in Fort St. James, looking at photograph albums. He's got pictures of the hockey and lacrosse teams he played on in the Cariboo country in 1911, and the diamond drilling he did at Germansen Landing in the 1920s. (The bartender was goaltender.) And Peter High Madden himself — an emotive, untidy-looking man, like a Neapolitan organ grinder. And a redheaded commercial traveler, quite an old card, with muttonchop whiskers, who suffered a heart attack by his longboat. (Dickinson speaks of it as though it were a battle wound.) And there's Cap Hood — a big gross fellow of three hundred pounds, the fat folding around his sarcastic mouth, his belt high up under his chest, and a sagging suit coat. And little Billy Steele, with a crewcut, a long nose, a malign face, a little mustache, and the stern, dependable, workhorse Indian wife of an early Hudson's Bay trader. And Cataline's pack train, the predecessor of George Byrnes's on the Telegraph Trail. And Jimmy Alexander, a tall raffish-looking central figure, with a curved pipe, long arms, a flat-brimmed hat, and husky legs, who looks rough and ready to go to work in an instant. Frank Swannell in 1911 has a matinee idol's mustache and wears a bandoleer of bullets. The Chinese cook is there, with a little round bandit's face, unsteady about the eyes, like an Old South slave's. There are pictures of wintering camps, and human pyramids that they used to make on Sundays for fun, and the World War I outfit Dickinson went overseas with. Then there's a late picture of Swannell with some of his shawled lady friends, looking like a plumped-out old roué and showman, a crude P. T. Barnum. And a whole three dozen "clooches" grouped complaisantly about a teamster's trading wagon, dark and giggly in their blankets. And an Indian camp — at Prince's second trapline layover on the Second Nation River — with a white fly and tent, pots, beaver skins stretched on round frames, and beaver meat and trout drying on racks.

July 5

As Bruce Russell says, the Americans have taken over the North without firing a shot. The choicest property is being bought up, and now here I am after even the myths. These people do want their history recorded, however, so they must take the historian offered, New Yorker and stutterer though he is. Six times I've walked to Jack Thompson's house, because of the wash hung out on the lines, but apparently that's only a trick so people will think he's in town — that and the unmade beds. He's been in Manson Creek all the time. Bruce Russell is the trucker who goes clear to Uslika Lake, which is 190 miles north of Fort St. James, about a fifteen-hour trip, if all goes well. Last weekend he trucked Bob Watson's body up for burial, performing the service there himself. About thirty people showed up, which is most of the residents of the Manson area. The only ones who didn't show were Watson's closest neighbors, from across the creek, who of course had feuded with him, as bachelor neighbors will. They did get as far as the store, but couldn't bring themselves into the graveyard. Russell is a sweet-natured, tenor-voiced man; reminds me very much of my college roommate. He's dogged and dusty, humble, appealing, a toobooloo forgetter, and a battler. He has a trucker son and a schoolteacher son; he's a grandfather, although he looks forty. He licks his lips a lot, doesn't charge anyone for their freight if they are poor. A big Canadian Freightways trailer-truck rig comes in regularly, leaves the full trailer in his lot, and pulls away an empty one. He speaks of that delivery as "the dogteam."

July 7

Manson Creek, where I am today, is a wide spot in the road without any particular view but very homelike nevertheless, with its several surviving old-timers, and the Los Angeles expatriates, and a couple of other wanderers or lost souls. Big Massey Ferguson mining equipment left about. Gas is up to seventy cents a gallon. It's definitely a friendly, genial place, and the Owens, the Californians, are chiefly responsible for that. The creeks around have been worked for close to a century, but a young Dutchman brought in a specimen bottle today with an inch of gold grains on the bottom — they looked like grains of tobacco. He had got them by shaking out the mats of old sluice boxes.

July 9

We in the city deprive ourselves of air, light, space, and green complications, a deprivation of such magnitude one can hardly think what could be worse. But people here are denied the delights of food, and the pleasurable soaking of a hot bath, and conversation, and news of the world, and, above all, the softnesses and amplitudes of women — women in the plural, at least, even if they have a wife. I think if I had to choose one place irrevocably, I might choose to live here, but since I don't have to, rather inconsistently, I live primarily in New York.

In the highway era to come, of course, we will drive from one town to another and it will be a matter of minutes and miles. At present, in the bush-plane era, the terminology and the destinations are always stated as *lakes*, even when you are driving along a dirt bush track to get there, not flying and then landing. Before, in the era of hiking, dogsledding, and horse-packing, destinations and geography were generally given as *rivers* and *creeks*; they were the valleys, the home sites, the larders (or obstacles).

Today freighter Bruce Russell and I spent another twelve hours going 140 miles. We saw ravens, and reddish ground squirrels, and baby grouse running and flying up, and two black young bull moose, who looked like donkeys from the rear as they ran away on their stick legs. There is snow falling in the North Country today, so we wondered whether our friends Sam and George, on horses, had gotten safely across the Mesilinka, which is a faster river with more fall to it, until the winter puts the lid on again. Already wild rose petals are starting to fall; by August 15, the birches will be turning yellow. Uslika Lake (a surveyor's joke name?) was ruffled with rain and breezes, and then still again — reflecting the chunky blue mountains to the south — or gray, green, and tawny, with majestically colored reflections from the side hills, the trees like figures in a vastly rich carpet.

Whether it's false or not, there's a sense in this country of contact with ultimates, as though all the world's sources and secrets might be just around the next bend.

July 10

Santa Claus Joe Calper just walked by. He *looks* like the greatest old-timer of all, with his white beard and his bear's build, but he's actually a newcomer and a cipher. Doc Bishop Thurber interests me more. He's a homey, bashful geologist, deep-voiced and unkempt, with white stubble whiskers, doggy eyebrows, and a dirty gray shirt. He looks like the dog in the old Mickey Mouse comic books, and he's named his dog Viking. He was up here on surveys as early as 1937 and has come back at troubled times ever since. Is obviously a woman-oriented fellow; probably with much marital trouble. Has an inferiority complex and a sulfurous, lavalike cough, an incredibly convoluted and serious cough. What he does best is walk. He lives with Johnny Nielsen, who runs a kind of a boarding house for the prospectors who pass through; busily cooks their steaks and gossips with them.

July 11 and 12

I returned from Manson Creek to Fort St. James with Larry Erickson, the ablest, youngest hunting guide in this section of British Columbia. He's personable, enlightened, and educated with regard to game habits and practices, has worked for biologists, trained falcons, and run sled dogs. We stopped to smell wild orchids and roses and pick lupine and paintbrush. Once we nearly had to stop for good because a beaver dam had broken and the road was inundated for two hundred yards with flooding water, two feet deep. We talked about cabin fever, which afflicts isolated partners, and about how these cold, rainy springs sometimes kill off the year's crop of baby grouse with pneumonia. His favorite weeks are those he spends in the summer out with his huskies, hiking. The three of them can carry up to sixty pounds each and, like wolves, need to be stuffed with groundhogs, whole, once every three or four days, and not fed otherwise. He says the grizzlies are doing well on all the moose that people shoot. He's also pro-wolf.

July 17

The newness of our marriage when I started on this trip makes it seem scarcely believable as a fact — rather, it's a relief to remember that I have a tie to go back to, and the memory of a relationship that was good, and that was saving me, that gave life meaning, with the coming child, and that made the future possible, and brought the barrenness to a close. (I remember John Muir, in 1880, returned from Alaska for the birth of Wanda, his first baby.)

July 18 and 19

My trip, by and large, has been a failure. I've learned I no longer like to hitchhike — to subjugate myself to someone else, to have to accept tacitly whatever they say, or let their scheduling be the law. I've learned that my boyish luck and glee have worn out and from now on unhindered satisfaction from life will be harder to obtain. But insofar as I came back to replace the material for a novel that I used up in *Notes from the Century Before*, I may have succeeded rather than failed. And I also came back to "revisit the scene of the crime" of my book, since I may never do so again.

Then, a rainy night tearing down the Alaska Highway from Watson Lake, past the usual grim assortment of trucks, with a French Canadian on the bus who claimed to have fought in the Congo with both Moise Tshombe *and* Che Guevara. Also a pale foreign boy who doesn't speak English; a dumbbell from the Adirondacks; and an "animal." The curiously endless stick forest, with an occasional single cabin with the word *store* on it. British Columbia has put up signs for each river or creek but the mud bespatters them illegibly.

The road runs alongside or in sight of or at the foot of mountains most of the way. At 5:00 A.M. we were at Muncho Lake (Mile 463 — Watson Lake is at 642). The road has no intimacy, but it's wild. There's a valley full of yellow gravel, with a small creek running in it. This is country thirty years raw — country walked on only for thirty years! And I do recommend the journey for gorging on, gulping down, sheer geography.

Lunch at Trutch (Mile 200), on thin soup served with the knowledge that they'll never see us again. It's very painful to leave the bush, and would have been even if I'd accomplished what I had hoped. So this long, numbing, thousand-mile bus trip is a help to ease me out. The whole northern sky is full of a rainstorm and clouds that do everything *except* rain: finally, spitting gusts. Just before Dawson Creek we get into poplared homestead country with soil and green fields and a paved highway — the farmers among us tourists feel relieved. As we pulled into town, the psychosomatics of relief hit me with a sudden sore throat. I stayed overnight in a hotel that has an elevator, and a stoplight outside.

So, down from the mountains to the great plains, with three realizations: that my trip was not as I had hoped it would be; that I've verged into middle age; and that the wilderness really is finished, done for, and in fact is to be more satisfyingly found or explored in my own imagination than in reality.

The Canadians are a muted version of Americans, lacking our worst and also our best qualities. I sat, by a clerical error, in the first-class part of the plane east from Edmonton, and noticed how fat the girth of the seat belt seemed. It was so easy and quick getting from one place to another by now, but the mechanics and maneuvers — gate to gate and desk to desk — seemed intolerably time-consuming, though in fact I was traveling four thousand miles in the amount of time it had been taking me to go one hundred by truck. We had tranquilizing music and then the roar of the jet in takeoff, all of us pausing a moment, with the brief thread of our consciousness in the balance. We lived.

Later, we circled over Bridgeport, Connecticut, for an hour and a half because of a strike of air-traffic controllers. My taxi driver got out of the cab at the toll plaza of the Battery Tunnel and got into a fight with the driver behind him. Then, at last, I was home, finally — a mess on the floor, and little accomplished in the way of moving in — even a brief fight with Marion. Earrings on the floor, a kinky necklace rattling from the doorknob. But oh the delicious complexity! The fullness of life again — pregnancy, difficulty, and beauty.

IAN PARKER

Birth of a Nation?

FROM *The New Yorker*

THE ISLANDS THAT MAKE up the territory of Tokelau are so tiny and remote — and distant even from one another — that their civil servants work out of a more convenient country. Tokelau, a colony of New Zealand in the South Pacific, not far from where the international date line crosses the equator, has offices in Samoa, thirty or so hours away by boat. Although quite small itself, Samoa has a number of things that Tokelau lacks, including an airstrip, a harbor, private enterprise, broadcast television, tourism, cars, dogs, hills, and soil.

One wet, hot morning in February, a few days before Tokelau's sixteen hundred people were to decide, in an unusual referendum, whether or not to remain New Zealand's property, I went, without an appointment, to the building in Apia, Samoa's capital, where much of Tokelau's bureaucracy works. The office was in a bungalow set several feet downhill from a residential road. The rain that day was unrelenting. I walked through the front door into a room apparently emptied of its staff, where, beneath two slowly spinning fans, the desks and filing cabinets were oddly askew. Soggy box files had been piled into a kind of campfire heap on the floor. Everything was damp and stained, unlike the three bright-blue maps of Tokelau's three atolls that I could see hanging on a wall through a doorway: outlines traced in coral of mountains that have disappeared. (An atoll forms when, over time, coral grows at the perimeter of a shrinking volcano, leaving a skinny strip of land — usually broken up into small islets — around a lagoon. A map of an atoll looks like an argument that the sea has almost won.)

A man appeared from the back of the building and introduced himself as Alan Shaw, the general financial manager of Tokelau — in effect, its secretary of the treasury. Although almost every resident of Tokelau is Polynesian, Shaw was born in Glasgow. His reddish mustache forms three gloomy sides of a rectangle.

"I think we need a new office," he said, in a Scottish accent. Rain had collected in the hollow where the office was built, and two nights ago it had risen enough to wash over the desktops. The floodwater had just begun to recede, after seeping into the office safe to dampen part of Tokelau's national reserves. Shaw later showed me blocks of banknotes, dripping through misted plastic.

We went out to the front porch, and, against the sound of rain falling on corrugated iron, talked about Tokelau's referendum. On February 11, Shaw explained, a chartered ferry would carry two ballot boxes and a few dozen officials and observers from Samoa to Tokelau's atolls: Atafu, Nukunonu, and Fakaofo. Each atoll is made up of dozens of islands, but, for reasons of social unity, people live on only one or two islands, leaving the rest uninhabited. A delegation carrying the boxes would visit a village a day — a three-day trip in total — and then a result would be announced and the boat would return. Either Tokelau would take a step toward nationhood — by adopting a new constitution and signing a new treaty with New Zealand — or it would not. Shaw said that he had been due to go on this voyage, but now he had to stay in Samoa to help clear up the flood mess. He was disappointed to miss an important moment in Tokelauan history; at the same time, he knew that the long sea journey could be punishing, especially at this time of year, the cyclone season. He recommended a brand of seasickness tablet.

"Economically, Tokelau shouldn't exist," Shaw said, without disparagement. He described his job: he balances the books of a minute territory, spread over a hundred miles, which has its own language and culture but almost no earned income, and receives most of its seven-million-dollar annual budget from the New Zealand government. We looked down the street through the rain. I asked him about the size of the main island of Fakaofo, the Tokelau atoll that has historically regarded itself as dominant, and where, if I joined the referendum boat, I might be spending the most time. Shaw pointed through the rain. "You see from here?" he said.

"Count the telephone poles: one, two, three, four. OK, from here to there."

The United Nations, in its charter of 1945, identified a category of territory that it tactfully called "non-self-governing." The following year, it published a list of seventy-two such places, ranging from island specks in the Pacific and the Caribbean to large colonial possessions in Africa and Asia. The charter made quite modest demands on the countries that ran the territories. But the UN grew sharper in its anticolonial spirit, as it was joined by member states that had themselves just shaken off colonial control, and in 1960 the General Assembly passed a declaration that called for "immediate steps" to be taken "to transfer all powers to the peoples of those territories." To monitor implementation, the UN formed a committee whose name, when spoken by anyone familiar with it, is usually preceded by a theatrical gulp of breath: the Special Committee on the Situation with Regard to the Implementation of the Declaration on the Granting of Independence to Colonial Countries and Peoples. It is more often known as the Special Committee.

During the rapid decolonization of the world, in the 1960s and '70s, numerous territories became independent — Kenya, Angola, the Bahamas — and were crossed from the list of the Special Committee. By the time the UN's International Decade for the Eradication of Colonialism had begun, in 1991, the list of "non-self-governing" territories was down to seventeen, most of them small islands that did not match any popular notion of what it was to be held in imperial shackles. At the end of the decade, the same seventeen remained: the British territories of Anguilla, Bermuda, the British Virgin Islands, the Cayman Islands, the Falkland Islands, Gibraltar, Montserrat, the Pitcairn Islands, St. Helena, and the Turks and Caicos Islands; two American possessions, Guam and American Samoa; two disputed territories, Western Sahara and East Timor; France's Pacific islands of New Caledonia; and Tokelau, which Britain had claimed as a protectorate in 1877 and passed to New Zealand's control fifty years later.

The only victory that the committee has had since 1990 is East Timor, which was deleted from the list in 2002. Robert Aisi, Papua New Guinea's Ambassador to the UN, and a current Special Committee member, recently told me that UN colleagues sometimes ask, "The committee's not still *meeting*, is it?" While factions within some unlisted territories, such as Puerto Rico, lobby to be noticed, some listed territories lobby to be left alone. "It's fight, fight, fight," Aisi said. "Gibraltans come and throw rocks at us."

Through the years, members of the committee — which today includes representatives from Iran, Syria, and Cuba — set their hopes on Tokelau, eying the islands with the avidity of a drunk watching a slow-moving barman pour his cocktail. It was certainly hard to imagine Tokelau, which has less than five square miles of land, as a fully independent state: not only would it be the world's second-smallest in population, after the Vatican; it would be one of the lowest in elevation, for Tokelau's highest point is a mere fifteen feet. (Imagine a man standing on the beach on a stepladder.) All the same, the UN saw Tokelau as ripe for some degree of decolonization, not least because New Zealand had willingly shed three other possessions, in the 1960s and '70s. Western Samoa — now Samoa — became an independent state, whereas Niue and the Cook Islands became "self-governing in free-association": that is, they arrived at a kind of adolescent version of nationhood, with substantial autonomy but no seat in the UN General Assembly.

The Special Committee made five official mission visits to Tokelau between 1976 and 2002, more than to any other listed territory. (I caught a glimpse of one of these visits on an old Super-8 film, in which the misery of an Iranian delegate, a nonswimmer, his head poking tortoiselike from the top of a very large life vest, is unmistakable.) These delegations were received with courtesy by Tokelau's political leadership, which is made up of a small inter-atoll parliament and, on each atoll, a village council and an elected head, a *faipule*. (To preserve the political equality of the three atolls, the post of national leader, or *ulu*, rotates annually among the three *faipules*.) But the prospect of constitutional change was at first met with little excitement. Patuki Isaako, a former *ulu*, recently gave a speech in which he characterized the local reaction: "Thank you for coming, have a good time, but we are happy to stay as we are."

Over the years, as UN delegates continued to visit Tokelau, and as New Zealand increasingly devolved power on Tokelauans, some enthusiasm for independence emerged. Pio Tuia, the present *faipule* of Nukunonu, a charismatic man with a knack for speechmaking, allied himself closely with the idea of self-determination, as did Falani Aukuso, the head of the Tokelauan civil service, whom one diplomat described as "the power behind the throne" of Tokelau politics. Other islanders remained more circumspect. Not long ago, when Isaako addressed a Special Committee seminar in Papua New Guinea, he asked, "Why would we want to declare to the international community we have self-determination? . . . Is it going to feed our mouths? Is it going to feed our children?"

Last year, Tokelau's parliament voted to hold a referendum: citizens would be asked to choose between the status quo and a level of self-determination that would preserve New Zealand's financial support but grant Tokelau formal control of its affairs and the chance to speak for itself internationally. So, for example, Tokelau would take a seat at the Pacific Islands Forum, a key regional body; and it would for the first time have a flag, a national anthem, and a national symbol. (In advance of the vote, public competitions for these emblems had been announced.) As Pio Tuia said at a UN meeting in New York last June, "Behold, the seas are shimmering with the dawning of the new day. The big fish is about to surface. The journey's end is near."

The referendum group gathered on a rainy Saturday evening at a quay in Apia, in the shadow of a bare-bones blue-and-white ferry, the *Lady Naomi*. Among those present was Neil Walter, the administrator of Tokelau. His title promises an imperial flurry of swords and plumage, but he was wearing chinos and Velcro sandals. He is a fit, straight-backed man in his early sixties, a senior diplomat who has served as New Zealand's ambassador in Indonesia and in Japan. In the 1970s and '80s, he had positions working for Tokelau; a few years ago, he took the job of administrator, wanting to "take a crack" at shepherding the islands to self-determination. He lives and works in Wellington, two thousand miles away.

Walter has a gracious manner, and he made self-deprecating jokes about his own seaworthiness as he moved through the damp, sticky group, which included Falani Aukuso, the civil-service chief, a muscular man with cropped hair and a self-contained manner; Robert Aisi, the UN Ambassador from Papua New Guinea, an almost boyish lawyer in his late forties; and Tony Angelo, a New Zealand law professor, who had helped draw up the referendum's constitutional package. With them were UN vote monitors and development workers, various Tokelauan and New Zealand officials, and half a dozen reporters from New Zealand's daily press, including one who had written a column with the hyperbolic headline "THE UN'S MISGUIDED PLAN TO CUT TOKELAU ADRIFT." This commentary and others like it had spread the thought — seemingly made for broad satire — that Tokelau's vote on self-determination had been imposed from overseas. As a result, the foreigners involved in the process were minimizing their roles as agitators, and pitching the referendum as a primarily Tokelauan initiative. Still, Walter had admitted to me, in a jokey way that illustrated the political trickiness of the moment, that Tokelau had nothing close to a liberation movement. "I'd be glad of an independence firebrand, frankly," he said.

We watched the *Lady Naomi*, which is 150 feet long, being loaded with cargo for Tokelauans, including office chairs, building materials, carrots, and a tricycle. This was a referendum run, but local freight, and a few Tokelau residents, had taken spare space on board. The mood on the quay was festive. Territories have at times shied away from independence — Bermudans, for example, rejected the idea in a 1995 referendum. But, in Tokelau's case, the modest nature of the autonomy plan, as well as the fastidious consultation that had led up to it, had created confidence that, as required, a two-thirds majority would vote "yes." One of the last things loaded on the *Lady Naomi* was a case of champagne.

It was dark when we boarded the ferry, and mid-evening when we left the pier and crashed into the open sea, heading in the direction of Atafu, which is three hundred miles north of Samoa. (The other atolls are a little closer — Nukunonu is sixty miles southeast of Atafu, and Fakaofo forty miles southeast of that.) Short of buying a seaplane, or a fair-sized yacht, the only way to make this journey is on one of two boats, which sail on an uncertain schedule — about twice a month. And it is also only on these boats, when they come, that anyone can travel between the atolls. Of the two ships, one is small and has almost no shelter against rain and spray. "Technically, it meets the safety criteria," Walter told me. The other, the *Lady Naomi*, is larger and has some indoor space, but it was built for short hauls; when the *Lady Naomi* sails to Tokelau, it's as if the ferry to Weehawken had changed course for France.

In the open Pacific, it soon became hard to remain standing. The Tokelauan residents tried to make themselves comfortable by lying across orange plastic seating bolted to the deck outdoors, whereas members of the referendum party had access to a small, air-conditioned cafeteria. But, with ketchup bottles falling to their sides, vacation high spirits soon dissipated, and most people clattered down a metal staircase to take a bunk in one of two communal, sour-smelling cabins. I didn't see Neil Walter again for thirty hours. He has never been what New Zealanders call "a good sailor." When he travels to Tokelau, his policy is to lie down, close his eyes, and not move or talk or eat until arriving.

Weeks before, New Zealand had sent cardboard ballot boxes to the referendum office in Samoa. These had looked too flimsy for Tokelau's high humidity — let alone its surf — so wooden replacements had been ordered. But there had been a miscommunication about size, and Samoan carpenters had delivered two heavy varnished chests, finished with what looked like coffin handles. As a result, although Tokelau's registered electorate amounted to fewer than seven hundred people, there was space in the boxes for tens of thousands of ballot papers — indeed, for a few of the voters themselves.

But the boxes had a fine symbolic presence, and it was rousing to see them reappear on deck in the weak light of dawn on Monday — and not only because they announced the end of the three-hundred-mile journey in rough seas, with a crew that loudly sang predawn hymns in Samoan through the public-address system. The weather had now grown calm, and Tokelau was in front of us. We were moored about a quarter of a mile from the village on the atoll of Atafu, which fills one thin, boomerang-shaped island in a loop of fifty or so islands. (The other islands that we could see were smaller, some with space for only one or two cartoon shipwreck survivors.) Our view of the village was of a strip of pale beach, a dense straight line of palm trees above that, and open sky above. Nothing was higher than a tree growing on the beach, and I felt that an athlete would stand a chance of throwing a tennis ball right over the island, into the lagoon beyond.

Half a dozen decorated wooden canoes came out to meet the *Lady Naomi.* On the beach, about thirty women stood a few feet apart in a line, dressed in long white skirts and white shirts; they had begun an almost lethargically gentle dance, in which long sticks were crossed and uncrossed over their heads. Neil Walter, a veteran of Tokelauan welcomes — which, perhaps uniquely in this region, are never performed in front of Australian tourists eating a buffet dinner — was clearly impressed. "I wasn't expecting the canoes," he said.

An open aluminum tender pulled alongside the *Lady Naomi.* After the ballot boxes and the passengers were handed down onto the boat, it skidded toward shore on the crest of a small wave, arriving at a partly submerged short pier. The senior members of the party were invited to sit, in turn, on a plastic garden chair atop a door-size plank of wood, which was lifted to waist level by four men. They were then carried, like Victorian explorers, onto the beach, a few yards away, and floral garlands were placed on their heads.

As we stepped into the quiet of the village, it was as if a door had closed behind us. Besides having no cars, Tokelau also has no dogs, cattle, or horses — and bicycles make little sense on the rough coral pathways. Atafu does have one small flatbed truck, and, when a boat unloads, it takes cargo from the beach to someplace that is fairly close to the beach. There are also a few all-terrain quad bikes. But now, in the shade of breadfruit trees, there was no sound of these vehicles, or of anything but a cockerel and the crunch of unsteady feet on the coral gravel. I was told that a small brass hunting horn, hanging on a hook near the village offices, was powerful enough to summon Atafu's whole population.

Tokelau has electricity, as well as landline telephones, outboard motors, and flush toilets; but there are no cafés or restaurants, no signs, and no lawn mowers. The island had no evidence of poverty, and little of the flotsam of industrialization that washes over everywhere: the Coke advertisements and old tires. We walked through the grid of Atafu's single-story homes, painted in blues and turquoises that evoke the color of the lagoon; they are primarily one large main room on a solid concrete foundation, and domestic sounds carry through floor-to-ceiling louvered windows. The village felt like a shaded seaside campsite in midsummer.

The atoll's residents were to start voting in an hour. We walked to the atoll's traditional *fale* — an open-sided village meeting hall — to listen to a round of speechmaking. Much of the village was gathered, in crisp Sunday dress; many of the locals were wearing floral crowns, too. In the front row sat the village head and the council of village elders, a body that is usually referred to in English as the "gray-hairs." Falani Aukuso interpreted in Tokelauan, a Polynesian language similar to Samoan, and in English, as Iosua Faamaoni, the pastor of Atafu's one church, which is Congregational, declared that "change" is "the womb from which all progress is born." (In the nineteenth century, the atoll's residents were converted by missionaries.) Faamaoni wore a bright-white jacket and a formal white version of Tokelau's ubiquitous sarong, the lavalava. Walter, sitting cross-legged, spoke soon afterward, and he noted that, among the benefits of a "yes" vote, "other countries would formally recognize Tokelau as a country, and be prepared to offer assistance and support." In the days to come, this paradoxical argument — that a vote for self-determination would expand the reach of Tokelau's dependency — was commonly expressed by "yes" voters, but it never sounded any less odd.

When Robert Aisi, the Papua New Guinean, spoke, he pointed out that he'd been to the islands once before, in 2004. "I said then that Tokelau was like a canoe, and all of us were paddling the canoe of Tokelau," he said. "Self-government is like you're paddling your own canoe. The choice is yours, and we will respect it. If you decide to become self-governing, we will respect it; if you decide not to do that, we will be there to paddle the canoe with you." Aisi's language introduced a troublesome notion: sudden solo paddling. Wouldn't most Tokelauans choose to have as many paddlers as possible, in a place where canoeing has historically carried great risks, and where it has now been abandoned, for all but ceremonial purposes, in favor of outboard motors? (In Tokelau, aluminum boats are guided at high speeds, through barely submerged coral beds, by languid young men who are as coolly removed from the act of driving as are Italian teenagers on Vespas.)

In a large circular room, decorated with a garishly colored tapestry of Leonardo's *Last Supper*, Tokelauans began casting ballots. I introduced myself to Lameka Sale, Atafu's Tokelauan-born and Fiji-trained doctor, who was walking to his clinic, still wearing one of the floral crowns. To his suppressed delight, Sale had been called to treat a member of the *Lady Naomi*'s crew. The patient, when we reached him, was lying on an examination bed, wearing wraparound sunglasses. There was a cut on the sailor's leg, and Sale poked at it in a leisurely way, as if shopping for meat. Two nurses stood by. "We don't need to hurry," he said, turning to me. (Sale attended university in New Zealand and speaks flawless, New Zealand–accented English, as do many Tokelauans.)

However long he might have wanted the procedure to take, the doctor was done in about fifteen minutes. "Four stitches," he said, laughing, as we left. "For me, that's a big one." Living on Atafu is tough for a young doctor eager for traumas. There are only five hundred potential patients; there are no car accidents, no firearms, no traditions of knife-fighting. And, as Sale noted, miming a slap, "They don't even use their fists with any force." He went on, "Outside Tokelau, doctors don't want cases. But not me, I do." He was smiling. "I mean, I don't want people to come to harm. But I do wish the nurse would call me at 2:00 A.M. and say, 'There's a heart attack.' To do resuscitation, to use the defibrillator." We strolled back to the village center, and at that moment we were probably the fastest-moving objects on Atafu.

Vaelua Lopa, a retired schoolteacher and something of a village matriarch, was born on Atafu in the late 1930s, when houses on the atoll were made of wood and thatch. "As a kid, I rarely saw money," she said when we spoke in her living room, sitting on a plushly untropical red sofa. "I didn't know what money was. We were part of the sea, the sky." As she grew up, her only understanding of the outside world came from the boat that arrived a few times a year. "It was a big occasion in the community. 'Sail-ho! Sail-ho!' I had no idea where the boat came from. All I was interested in was whether it brought sugar and flour, which were very special. We lived on fish and coconut." At the age of eight, she was taken out of the local school and sent to study in Samoa, forcing the kind of wrenching separation that has since become common for Tokelauans, most of whom now have family abroad. (Expatriate Tokelauans in New Zealand and Australia now far outnumber island residents.) Lopa lived with relatives in Apia, where she was struck by the gigantic scale of her surroundings, and where she learned that Samoans looked down on Tokelauans: "You know, 'Oh, you coconut-eaters.'" Lopa returned home as a trained teacher, having only recently discovered that Tokelau was not an independent country. This points to the lightness of New Zealand's colonial touch, but also, perhaps, to some level of shared Tokelauan discomfort regarding the islands' economic dependence. (From the current *CIA World Factbook*: "Arable land: 0%," "Permanent crops: 0%," "Natural resources: Negl.")

Lopa had voted "yes." As she put it, "no" voters "think that we can sit, and New Zealand will bring us money. But you have to grow up, man! Learn how to be yourself!" In her view, Tokelauans could best do that by returning to the pre-monetary economy of her ancestors, before the frequent cargo runs created an almost uninterrupted flow of stuff — electronics and canned meat, beer and soda. (Tokelauans have high rates of diabetes and obesity.) New Zealand funds were clearly required for infrastructure and disaster relief, but a self-determining Tokelau could aim for self-sufficiency. "We don't really need money," she said. "We don't want luxuries." As she spoke, my eyes had landed on a large television set. She had followed my gaze. "Yes, I have a TV!" she said, smiling. "But I'm not interested in watching TV!" She said that she had bought it for her children and grandchildren, who watch satellite television — Lopa has Tokelau's only dish.

Before I left Lopa, I asked her about Iosua Faamaoni, the pastor whose speech I had heard earlier in the day. Fifteen years ago, Faamaoni left the atoll after confessing to having sexually abused his adopted daughter, then twelve years old. No charge was brought against him. In 2004, Faamaoni returned and sought forgiveness. And, to the dismay of a large minority of the village, he was elected to serve again as pastor. Although it was not easy for a visitor to tell, neighbor had been set against neighbor, in a place where you can never be farther than a few hundred yards from your antagonist, who is also, almost certainly, a relative.

Lopa looked appalled at the mention of Faamaoni, and her tone, previously teasing and ironic, turned almost fearful, offering a glimpse of the social restraints beneath Tokelau's easy suburban surface. She frowned and shook her head. The people of Atafu had been instructed by village authorities not to talk to the *Lady Naomi* group about anything other than the vote, she said; she would not be a "traitor." I had already gathered that villagers hostile to the pastor were more likely to vote "yes" in the referendum, in the name of shaking up the existing political order, and reforming Tokelau's legal system, which was adept at dealing with episodes of public drunkenness but was ill-equipped to handle any crime besides murder — in which case a defendant would be transferred to New Zealand. (This has never happened; there is no record of a murder in Tokelau since 1881.) For other serious misdeeds, the maximum punishment was a few months' house arrest. Lopa, who opposed the pastor's rehabilitation, would say only that she no longer went to church — this being an almost unimaginable transgression in Tokelau — but instead had begun to worship, with others, at her home.

By lunchtime, all but a handful of Atafu's 183 registered voters had cast their ballots, and the UN election monitors — a young Englishwoman and a large Fijian man — sat patiently in the heat, perfectly still. A local man went to "round up" the final voters. The electorate seemed more conscientious than engaged. There was no sign in Atafu of public political discourse. There were no posters or manifestos, unless one included a number of brief essays in the school magazine. ("Tokelau has not yet become a developed country," a stern fifteen-year-old wrote. "In my conclusion, for those who say Tokelau should be independent, you thought wrong.") The competition to design a Tokelauan flag had drawn fewer entries than anticipated — and some of them were no more than doodles on napkins. Falani Aukuso told me, with disappointment, that a high proportion of the designs made use of the UK's Union Jack, as New Zealand's flag does; he took this to be a frustrating sign of political caution, if not wimpishness. Other designs that I saw were problematic in different ways: some included large crucifixes; and a few had symbolism that clearly referred to four atolls — implicitly annexing nearby Swains Island, also known as Olosenga, which is culturally tied to Tokelau but is, by international treaty, a satellite of American Samoa.

Kuresa Nasau, Atafu's *faipule,* acknowledged, in a roundabout way, that he had voted "no." He asked, "How can you love a country if it's without an airstrip or a ship?" Nasau is unusually candid for an elected official. He is the son of expatriate Tokelauans, who brought him up in Hawaii. He said that when he first moved to the atolls, at the age of forty-one, the only reason he didn't immediately leave was the miserable thought of getting back on the boat. "I didn't like the place," he said. "It took me seven years to get used to it. The pace is so slow. There's always another tomorrow."

That afternoon, Neil Walter and Tony Angelo, the law professor, took a gentlemanly dip in the lagoon. They bobbed up and down in a few feet of warm, clear water; Angelo protected himself from the sun with a hat and a T-shirt. In the *fale* in the center of the island, a group of older women played cards and, at one point, broke into "You Are My Sunshine," sung in English. A large, uniformed village policeman showed me a cucumber patch he had started in the unpromising coral by his back door.

The eastward, island-by-island peopling of Polynesia had reached Tokelau by the tenth century. The atolls, which have a history of belligerence toward one another, as well as traditions of communal living at the village level, were undisturbed by Europeans until 1765, when they were sighted by the British captain John Byron (the grandfather of the poet, and a source of material for *Don Juan*). But, because Tokelau had nothing to trade other than coconut products, the atolls attracted scant outside interest, and fewer than a dozen visits were recorded in the next eighty years. In the late 1850s, Christian missionaries arrived, and they documented one of the most devastating moments in Tokelau's history: the visits of Peruvian "recruiting" ships, in the mid-1860s. Two hundred and fifty-three of the atolls' 541 residents — most of them men — were kidnapped and taken to work as slaves in Peru; most of them soon died of disease. "Sir, all the people of this land are carried off," a missionary on Atafu wrote to his superior, describing how islanders were tricked into the hull of a ship with the promise of a trade in fine cloth. The atolls were left so depopulated that, in the years that followed, boys were encouraged, after reaching sexual maturity, to have children by several different women.

There is little public acknowledgment of the raids in contemporary Tokelau: there is no memorial, no day set aside on the calendar. Neil Walter said that he had never heard the subject raised there. Whatever shared cultural memory exists has not been institutionalized, although Judith Huntsman and Antony Hooper, New Zealand anthropologists who made a long-term study of Tokelau, described playlets that had turned the events into a kind of slapstick. A number of Tokelauans told me about a surprising school fundraiser a few years ago in which children were dressed in rags and held behind a rope, as if they were slaves; their parents had to pay to "release" them. When I talked about the Peruvian ships with

Baitika Aviata, a Tokelauan who trained as an accountant, he began suddenly to weep. "This was not discussed in the past," he said. "It's a very sensitive issue, but what can we do? We can't fight against it. We just pretend to take it lightly."

The episode does manifest itself in one quotidian way — in the European names carried by some Tokelauans. After the Peruvian boats had left, the atolls, which had lost nearly all men of marrying age, sought to boost their population by accepting a few foreign settlers, and Tokelau's electoral register is now dotted with Polynesian Pereiras and Polynesian Pedros.

On the atoll of Nukunonu, which we reached after another night aboard the *Lady Naomi*, I met Luciano Perez, the descendant of a Portuguese trader who arrived in the 1860s. Perez, a man in his late sixties, has a kind of chuckling, restless sociability that I didn't otherwise see on the islands. He lives at the water's edge, by an almost Mediterranean little bay, not far from a point that his neighbor claimed, with some risk of bathos, was the highest spot in all of Tokelau. We talked in a room decorated with a dried-out turtle, a Mickey Mouse cuckoo clock, and a certificate that read "The Holy Father John Paul II Paternally Imparts His Apostolic Blessing to Luciano and Juliana Perez on the Occasion of Their 30th Wedding Anniversary." (Whereas Atafu is exclusively Protestant, Nukunonu is exclusively Catholic.)

Luciano and Juliana Perez are in the unusual position of being Tokelau's village capitalists, in a culture that one Tokelauan characterized as "communist, with a small *c*." Their business is the Luana Liki Hotel and Bar, which opened in 1995. It has seven guest rooms and a balcony that looks out over Nukunonu's lagoon, which is far larger than Atafu's.

Not only do Tokelauans lack a tradition of selling things to one another; they don't sell to visitors, either. (The referendum boat must have had a souvenir budget of several thousand dollars, but none of this potential largess was spent in Tokelau; I overheard one member of the UN team almost plead to be allowed to buy woven fans and bags, but they were only offered to us as going-away presents.) The territory's economy is a monetarized and subsidized variation on traditional communal practices. New Zealand provides 80 percent of the territory's budget; the rest derives mainly from fishing licenses, and a little from the sale of fancy stamps. Out of these funds, the Tokelauan government not only pays its salaried staff — there is a school and a small hospital on each atoll — it also pays some form of stipend to most other adults. On Atafu, women are given the equivalent of fifty dollars a month, while on all three atolls the men must join what is called, in translation, the "able-bodied work force." The men make themselves available every weekday morning in the village center, or show a doctor's note. On a given day, the task might be to unload a ship, or collect garbage, or fish for the village, or there might well be no task at all. In the past, such labor was an unpaid civic duty, but the role now entitles men to an average of two hundred dollars a month.

This accounts for all employment in Tokelau. For the three-quarters of high-school graduates who do not win scholarships to continue studying abroad at a university, the choice is between immigrating to New Zealand, to join its labor market, or withdrawing from any labor market at all; between, on the one hand, economic individualism and social anonymity, and, on the other, scant privacy, long afternoons, and almost limitless tuna. There are no private plumbers or electricians in Tokelau. The one store in each village is cooperatively owned and opens for only a few grudging hours a day. In Tokelau, people go out fishing for themselves, but they don't sell their catch; and, as part of a tradition known as *inati*, if they land more fish than they personally need — fifty small fish, or any sizable haul of marlin or tuna — then the catch will be fairly distributed throughout the village, following carefully preset family quotas. (When I reached Fakaofo, I asked about the temptation to bring in forty-nine fish, and I was given a look of withering pity. But I was touched to be included in the *inati*; a man came to the door and gave me a two-foot bonito. He went on to ask, "Do you have any DVDs of blue movies?")

Luciano Perez has opted out of the system. He was the atoll's school principal for thirty-one years, and he saved some money. When he retired, he was expected to take his place among the able-bodied men, but he resisted. "I said, 'We've got our choices, our feelings. I worked for thirty-one years!' I said, 'I can't work, work, work until my last minute.'" Instead, he ran his hotel. "A lot of people tried to pull me down," Perez said. "They saw someone rising up, and want to bring him down. People want to see the community rise, not individuals."

Perez not only lacks community encouragement; he lacks clients. Tokelau has no more than twenty tourists a year, and has a limited collective appetite for entertaining. (When Billy Connolly, the Scottish actor, and his wife, Pamela Stephenson, recently sailed their yacht to Fakaofo, they were initially asked to leave; in Stephenson's new travel book, *Treasure Islands*, the episode is remembered in a chapter entitled "Told to Fakaofo.") Perez showed me his visitors' book. A decade of guests filled only a few pages, and most entries were written by visiting officials. ("A pleasure to be here as part of the Atafu Tokelau cervical-screening team.") Neil Walter had written, "Many thanks . . . despite the cyclone."

On the day I was in Nukunonu, Perez actually had a guest: a wiry, chain-smoking radio hobbyist from Germany named Udo Moeller. A retired chemical scientist, Moeller travels in remote parts of the Pacific for five months of the year, setting up in each place a little radio outpost that others then take pride in reaching: to talk to Tokelau, in particular, is a coup for any shortwave enthusiast. But Perez's hotel is usually empty, and so is his bar. Perez explained that Nukunonu residents can buy beer from the village shop only on Tuesdays and Thursdays, and each person can buy just three bottles on each day. There is no adjustment for bar owners. Twice a week, Perez buys his beer, as well as the allowance due to his wife and adult children. This adds up to twenty-four bottles a week. When his stockpile has grown sufficiently large, he can open the bar for a night and turn on its karaoke machine.

Perez's pioneering role as an entrepreneur has yet to attract followers, although Baitika Aviata, the trained accountant, led me through what some might regard as premature plans for setting up a Tokelauan chamber of commerce. (He said that he wanted to "create an upper class, a lower class. It's revolutionary!") When I asked a group of children playing Tokelau's version of cricket what they wanted to do as adults, the one who seemed sharpest, a girl in her early teens, said "shopkeeper," which, in this context, was perhaps as ambitious as saying "surgeon" or "pilot."

Tokelau is, in fact, struggling to hold on to its teenagers, who are increasingly familiar with the outside world, through movies, the Internet, and expatriate uncles, but whose detachment from it is painfully physical. Vaelua Lopa told me of a grandson who, at fourteen, had headed out to sea with a friend in an open aluminum boat; they had just a few gallons of water between them. "He was thinking he'd end up on land," she said. "That was the dream. So they just took off—just went *zzzzp*, with an outboard." The New Zealand military sent rescue planes, and after five or six days the boys were found, alive, several hundred miles away. Such episodes are surprisingly common. Doug Brown, the captain of the smaller Tokelau ferry, told me that he had recently helped locate three boys in the open sea who said that they were trying to "reach America" in a little boat equipped with only a few dozen coconuts. While some of these trips are the misadventures of teenagers, others are suicide attempts. A Tokelau suicide drives a boat out to sea until the gas runs out.

On Nukunonu, the population was thought to have voted "yes," by an overwhelming margin. The village had even come up with a referendum song, which translated as "Be happy, the day of the referendum is coming, every Tokelauan is happy." Pio Tuia, the atoll's ebullient *faipule*, made a speech that spoke of "driving away colonial shadows." But on Fakaofo, our third and last atoll, which we reached the next day, there was no singing, no rousing speeches, and the welcoming ceremony was a subdued affair along an alleyway. "The mood here worries me a bit," Walter said. "It doesn't feel quite right."

The main inhabited island at Fakaofo looks like part of a low-rise, tropical town that has been dropped in the middle of the ocean. A seawall rises directly out of the water; at the top of the wall, the village begins. You immediately understand why the five hundred people on this atoll seem to take the threat of rising sea levels more seriously than their neighbors. The island is no larger than twenty-five acres, or about one and a half Ikeas; if you host a party, you disturb everybody. In school sports, a "marathon" is eight hundred meters. Space is so tight that Kolouei O'Brien, the *faipule*, is partway through building a four-story house, which by Tokelauan standards is a skyscraper.

After the polling booths opened, Walter invited me to join him at a closed meeting with the atoll's council of "gray-hairs," which was held nearby in a hot, bare room. These were wary-looking men. One had set his watch to beep for thirty seconds every five minutes—which seemed like a joke on the apparent abundance of time on Tokelau, where, for everyone but schoolchildren, the days seemed to be barely divided between morning and afternoon. At the meeting, Walter made a short speech, and observed that the referendum was "an opportunity that might or might not come twice" — as close to a threat as a diplomat in his position gets to make. When he had finished, he invited questions. For a long while, only the beeping watch disturbed an awkward and unsmiling silence.

Afterward, I walked with Walter back to the polling station, which took us through Fakaofo's tight grid of homes to the village's central patch of clear space: a short strip of concrete in the middle of coral gravel. This is where the village plays cricket with a hard rubber ball; hitting the ball into the sea counts as six runs. Walter is something of a sportsman, and has played cricket here; but he has only watched Tokelauan rugby games, which are played on a similar surface, but with no allowance made for the abrasiveness of the coral. "I've never *seen* so much first aid," Walter said.

He was wondering if Fakaofo, previously thought to be safely pro-referendum, might now tilt the vote to a "no." "The *faipule* has come under some close questioning from some of the more outspoken members of the next generation," he said.

I took a ride on the atoll's aluminum school boat to visit Tino Vitale, a vocal critic of the referendum. We passed one of Fakaofo's two cemetery islands — it is about as wide as its palm trees are high — and within ten minutes arrived at Fakaofo's offshore suburb, which was first settled in the 1960s. The atoll's school and hospital are here, as is the office of Teletok, the government agency that runs the territory's fairly new telephone service, and its even newer high-speed Internet connection, which is available for public use at various points on each atoll, although not in private homes.

Vitale, a worldly, articulate man in his forties, is the director of Teletok. At his disordered office, down a path near the beach at the end of the island, he explained why he had voted "no." In his view, the Tokelau atolls were unprepared for self-government: they lacked infrastructure and management skills. He had been angered by the example of a failed fish-exportation scheme. A few years ago, New Zealand helped fund three small fish-processing centers in Tokelau; they now stood empty and unused, one on each atoll. In Vitale's opinion, the project was ill-conceived — the only way to ship the fish was by the two irregular ferries — and Tokelauans were not ready to commit to a repetitive daily work routine. "We should have had the structures in place, trained the people," he said. His fear was that a newly self-determining Tokelau would receive millions of dollars from, say, the European Union, and then mishandle those funds, humiliating the nation with bad publicity.

Fakaofo's village authorities had held a number of pep-talk public meetings to make the case for a "yes" vote. At one of these, Vitale had asked why the village was not hearing arguments on the other side. He was shouted down — "Everyone's been talking about democracy, but I don't think there is a democracy here," he told me — but what he called "the silent 'no' voters" in the village had begun to rouse themselves.

The polling ended at five in the afternoon. Two police officers dressed in white poured the papers out of the ballot boxes (all the atolls' mixed together) and then held up each box to show that it was empty, like a magician working with unwieldy props; election officials began building "yes" piles and "no" piles in front of them. Boxing-ring ropes had been tied around the perimeter of the *fale*, which was open on all sides to the village, but they held back only a few members of the *Lady Naomi* party, and no one else. "Isn't it odd how the Tokelauans aren't here?" someone said. "You'd have thought they'd be lined up around here. They don't even have TV!" Nearby, a few young Tokelauans were husking a pile of green coconuts; they barely looked over.

During the count, the loudest sound was from a water cooler bubbling in the corner. The result was written on a piece of paper, and was taken first to the Tokelauan election committee, at one end of the *fale*, and then to Neil Walter, at the other. The administrator unfolded the paper and shook his head. "Didn't make it," he said. Walter would not have the satisfaction of ending his career by abolishing his own job.

Tokelauans had signed a declaration of dependence. As one resident, characterizing this mindset, put it, "Only when I'm suffering, then I really want to change. I'm not suffering." Walter stood up and thanked the referendum workers; he turned to the vote monitors and added quietly, in a rather brittle voice, "Great referendum, bum result."

Robert Aisi, the Papua New Guinean, had told me earlier, half-jokingly, that he would return to the UN Special Committee with one of two messages: "It'll be either 'Sorry, we didn't make it' or 'Hey, we're suddenly relevant again!'" Now, he smiled stiffly. "The people have spoken," he said. Falani Aukuso, the civil-service leader, had a look of suppressed fury. (Later, when he met with the representatives from New Zealand and the UN, he mourned the fact that the atolls had squandered so much international goodwill.) And Pio Tuia, the Nukunonu *faipule*, told me, "The Tokelauan public has never been part of the decision-making process, and, now that we've given them a chance, they don't really understand what is going on." He went on, "They don't have a sense of manhood. They depend on New Zealand. They do not realize that being a man has not yet been revealed to them. It's like a baby and a mother. I hate that. I hate that! We are old enough to determine our own future."

There was a ceremony at the *fale* that evening. Kolouei O'Brien officially replaced Pio Tuia as *ulu* of Tokelau, and residents lined up to offer him New Zealand banknotes as a tribute. Formal Polynesian dancing was followed by beer and informal Polynesian dancing.

The next day, the referendum party sailed for Samoa on the *Lady Naomi*, and the people of Fakaofo were again left, for a while, without any means of traveling beyond Fakaofo. The women of the village sat cross-legged in the *fale*, and played a slow, laughing game of bingo for prizes of toilet paper and soda — a game that was, in effect, a way to prolong the process of acquiring household essentials. I walked a few dozen paces to the northern end of the island, where a teenager named Eric Elika was checking on his family's pigs. Fakaofo has so little space that its hundred or so pigs live on a low-lying coral shelf that is mostly underwater at high tide. At those times, lifted by the rising water, the pigs swim, their snouts in the air — and for this they have a fame that has spread at least as far as a New Zealand school textbook. The pigs also eat seafood. I asked Elika how these animals caught fish, and he mimed for me the action of a pig first waiting with its mouth open in the water, then snapping it shut, as a fish wiggled into it. As we spoke, some young children were shrieking and diving off the seawall not far away. Behind Elika — who has left Tokelau only once in his life — I could see, on the far side of the lagoon, high surf silently breaking onto the coral.

NANDO PARRADO

The Long Way Home

FROM *Outside*

IN THE FIRST FEW HOURS THERE WAS NOTHING, no fear or sadness, no thought or memory, just a black and perfect silence. Then light appeared, a thin gray smear of daylight, and I rose to it like a diver swimming to the surface. Consciousness seeped through my brain in a slow bleed; I heard voices and sensed motion all around, but I could see only dark silhouettes and pools of light and shadow. Then, vaguely, I sensed that one of the shadows was hovering over me.

"Nando, *podés oírme?* Can you hear me? Are you OK?"

As I stared dumbly, the shadow gathered itself into a human face. I saw a ragged tangle of dark hair above deep brown eyes. There was kindness in the eyes — this was someone who knew me — but also something else, a wildness, a sense of desperation held in check.

"Come on, Nando, wake up!"

Why am I so cold? Why does my head hurt so badly? I tried to speak these thoughts, but my lips could not form the words. Carefully I reached up to touch the crown of my head. Clots of dried blood were matted in my hair; I felt rough ridges of broken bone beneath the congealed blood, and when I pressed down lightly I felt a spongy sense of give. My stomach heaved as I realized that I was pressing pieces of my skull against the surface of my brain.

"Is he awake? Can he hear you?"

"Say something, Nando!"

"Don't give up, Nando. We are here with you. Wake up!"

All I could manage was a hoarse whisper. Then someone spoke slowly in my ear.

"Nando, el avión se estrelló! Caimos en las montañas."

We crashed, he said. The airplane crashed. We fell into the mountains.

"Do you understand me, Nando?"

For more than two days I'd languished in a coma, and I was waking to a nightmare. On Friday the 13th of October, 1972, our plane had smashed into a ridge somewhere in the Argentinian Andes and fallen onto a barren glacier. The twin-engine Fairchild turboprop had been chartered by my rugby team, the Old Christians of Montevideo, Uruguay, to take us to an exhibition match in Santiago, Chile. There were forty-five of us on board, including the crew, the team's supporters, and my fellow Old Christians, most of whom I'd played rugby with since we were boys at Catholic school. Now only twenty-eight remained. My two best friends, Guido Magri and Francisco "Panchito" Abal, were dead. Worse, my mother, Eugenia, and my nineteen-year-old sister, Susy, had been traveling with us; now, as I lay parched and injured, I learned that my mother had not survived and that Susy was near death.

When I look back, I cannot say why the losses did not destroy me. Grief and panic exploded in my heart with such violence that I feared I would go mad. But then a thought formed, in a voice so lucid and detached it could have been someone whispering in my ear. The voice said, *Do not cry. Tears waste salt. You will need the salt to survive.*

I was astounded at the calmness of this thought and the cold-bloodedness of the voice that spoke it. Not cry for my mother? I am stranded in the Andes, freezing; my sister may be dying; my skull is in pieces! I should not cry?

Do not cry.

In those first days, I rarely left my sister's side, rubbing her frozen feet, talking to her, giving her sips of snow melted in my hands. I was never sure if she was aware of my presence.

"Don't worry," I would tell her, "they will find us. They will bring us home."

How badly I needed my father's strength, his wisdom. Seler Parrado was a deeply practical man who had sacrificed much to build a chain of hardware stores out of nothing, to give his family the life of security and leisure I so casually took for granted. I knew he would not allow himself the luxury of false hope. To survive a crash in the Andes? In winter? Impossible. I saw him clearly now, tossing in his bed back in Montevideo, staggered by his unimaginable loss, and my heart broke for him.

"I am alive," I whispered to him. "I am alive."

Late in the afternoon of the eighth day, I was lying with my arms around Susy when suddenly I felt her change. The worried look faded from her face. The tension eased from her body. Then her breathing stopped, and she was still.

"Susy?" I cried. "Oh, God, Susy, please, no!"

I scrambled to my knees and began to give her mouth-to-mouth resuscitation. I wasn't even sure how to do this, but I was desperate, and I worked at it until I fell exhausted to the floor. Others tried, too, but it was no use — she was gone. I held her all night, and in the morning I buried her, beside my mother, in the snow.

Never had I felt so terribly alone. I was twenty-two years old. My mother was dead. My sister was dead. My best friends had been sucked from the plane in flight, or were buried outside. Most of us were untested young men between the ages of eighteen and twenty-one, lost in the wilderness, hungry, injured, and freezing. With stinging clarity I felt the brute power of the mountains, saw the complete absence of warmth or mercy or softness in the landscape, and for the first time, I knew with certainty that I would die.

But then I thought of my father again, and as I stared out at those ragged peaks, I felt my love for him tugging at me like a lifeline, drawing me toward those merciless slopes. *I will come home,* I vowed to him. *I promise you, I will not die here!*

From my very first hours in the mountains, I felt, deep in my bones, the immediacy of the danger that surrounded us. Nothing in the late-winter Andes welcomed human life. The cold tormented us. The thin air starved our lungs. The unfiltered sun blinded us and blistered our lips and skin, and the snow was so deep that we could not venture far without sinking to our hips.

The initial impact had sheared the wings and tail from the Fairchild, leaving its battered fuselage to plow into a snow-packed glacier flowing down the eastern slope of a massive, ice-encrusted peak. Miraculously, the plane did not cartwheel or spiral; instead its angle of descent matched almost exactly the slope onto which we were falling, and it came to rest with its crumpled nose pointing slightly down the slope. East was the only direction in which we could see for any distance; to the north, south, and west, the view was blocked by towering summits ringing the crash site like the walls of a monstrous amphitheater. We knew we were high in the Andes — later we'd learn that the crash site was at roughly twelve thousand feet — and the slopes above us rose so steeply that I had to tilt my head back to see their tops.

Still, we hoped we had an inkling of where we were in that vast range: we all knew the words our copilot had moaned as he lay dying: "We passed Curicó, we passed Curicó." Curicó was a small city one hundred miles south of Santiago — that meant we must be somewhere in the western foothills of the Andes. Surely, we reasoned, the tall ridges to our west were the last high peaks before the mountains dwindled down to the green pastures of Chile. This became my mantra: *to the west is Chile.*

But first we had to stay alive. If not for our team captain, Marcelo Pérez, we wouldn't have lasted a night. Marcelo was a wing forward — very fast, very brave, and a leader we would trust with our lives. After the crash, as the stupefied survivors staggered about in disbelief, Marcelo had organized the uninjured into a search party to free the dozens of passengers still trapped in the heaps of tangled seats in the plane. Roberto Canessa and Gustavo Zerbino, two players who were also in medical school, had done their best to tend to the injuries, some of which were grisly. A six-inch steel tube had impaled the stomach of a quiet, stoic player named Enrique Platero. When Gustavo yanked the tube from his friend's gut, several inches of intestine came out, but Enrique immediately got to work helping to free others.

As darkness fell, Marcelo turned the Fairchild into a makeshift shelter, stacking loose seats and luggage in the gaping hole left by the tail, then packing the gaps with snow. The living were jammed into a cramped space on the litter-strewn floor measuring no more than eight by ten feet.

Marcelo's wall kept us from freezing, but in the coming nights we suffered terribly from the cold. We had cigarette lighters and could easily have lit a fire, but there was little combustible material. We burned all our paper money — almost seven thousand five hundred dollars went up in smoke — and found enough scrap wood to fuel two or three small fires, but the brief luxury of warmth only made the cold seem worse. Nighttime temperatures plunged to −30°F, and we huddled together, the injured crying out when the jostling of bodies caused them pain. Often, I would lie with my head close to the face of whoever slept next to me to steal a little breath, a little warmth, from him.

But, for the most part, we remained a team. We clung to the hope that rescuers would find us and that all we had to do was hang on. "Breathe once more," we would tell the younger ones and the ones who were losing heart. "Live for one more breath. As long as you are breathing, you are fighting to survive."

By the end of the first week, with no sign of rescue, we began to solve our most pressing problems. Roberto devised ingenious hammocks for the most injured and improvised flimsy blankets from the plane's thin nylon seat covers. Thirst was not an issue, thanks to Adolfo "Fito" Strauch, a quiet, serious former player who had improvised snow-melting basins from square aluminum sheets he found lining the bottoms of the seats.

But we were beginning to starve. One of the first things Marcelo had done was gather everything edible from scattered suitcases or the cabin. There wasn't much — chocolate bars and other snacks, some wine and a few bottles of liquor — and on the second day, he began to ration food. Each meal was nothing more than a small square of chocolate or a dab of jam, washed down with a sip of wine. It wasn't enough to satisfy anyone's hunger, but as a ritual it gave us strength.

One morning, I found myself standing outside the fuselage, looking down at a single chocolate-covered peanut cradled in my palm. This was the final morsel of food I would be given, and with a sad, almost miserly desperation, I was determined to make it last. I slowly sucked the chocolate off the peanut, then slipped it into the pocket of my slacks. The next day I carefully separated the peanut halves, slipping one half back into my pocket and placing the other in my mouth. I sucked gently on it for hours, allowing myself only a tiny piece now and then. I did the same on the third day, and when I'd finally nibbled the peanut down to nothing, there was no food left at all.

We became obsessed by the search for food, but what drove us was nothing like ordinary appetite. When the brain senses the onset of starvation — when it realizes that the body has begun to break down its own flesh for fuel — it sets off an adrenaline surge of alarm as powerful as the impulse that compels a hunted animal to flee an attacking predator. Again and again we scoured the fuselage. We tried to eat strips of leather torn from pieces of luggage, though we knew that because of the chemicals they'd been treated with, they'd do us more harm than good. We ripped open seat cushions hoping to find straw but found only inedible upholstery foam. My mind would never rest. Maybe there was a plant growing somewhere or some insects under a rock. Had we checked all the pockets of the dead? Sometimes I would rise from a long silence to shout, "There is nothing in this fucking place to eat!"

There are some lines, I suppose, that the mind is very slow to cross. Of *course* there was food on the mountain — there was meat, plenty of it, and all in easy reach. It was as near as the bodies of the dead lying outside the fuselage under a thin layer of frost. It puzzles me that, despite my compulsive drive, I ignored for so long the obvious presence of the only edible objects within a hundred miles. But when my mind did finally cross that line, it did so with an impulse so primitive it shocked me.

It was late afternoon and we were lying in the fuselage, preparing for night. My gaze fell on the slowly healing leg wound of a young man lying near me. The center of the wound was moist and raw, and there was a crust of dried blood at the edges. I could not stop looking at that crust, and as I smelled the faint scent of blood in the air, I felt my appetite rising. Then I looked up and met the gaze of other players who had also been staring at the wound. In shame, we quickly glanced away, but for me something had happened that I couldn't deny: I had looked at human flesh and instinctively recognized it as food. I was horrified by what I was thinking, but once that door was open, it couldn't be closed. Finally, one night I confided in Carlos Páez, one of the team's supporters and a friend I trusted.

"Carlitos," I whispered, "are you awake?"

"Yes," he muttered. "Who can sleep in this freezer?"

"Are you hungry?"

"Puta carajo," he snapped. "What do you think?"

"We are going to starve here," I said. "I don't think the rescuers will find us in time."

"You don't know that," Carlitos answered.

"I know it and you know it," I replied, "but I will not die here. I will make it home."

"But what can you do?" he said. "There is no food here."

"There is food," I answered. "You know what I mean."

Carlitos shifted in the darkness.

"Fuck, Nando," he whispered.

"There is plenty of food here," I said. "Our friends don't need their bodies anymore."

Carlitos sat silently for a moment before speaking. "God help us," he said softly. "I have been thinking the very same thing."

In the following days, Carlitos shared our conversation with some of the others. A few of the most practical, including the medical students, Roberto and Gustavo, as well as Fito, believed it was our only chance. Soon we gathered everyone inside the fuselage.

"We are starving," Roberto said simply. "Our bodies are consuming themselves. Unless we eat some protein soon, we will die, and the only protein here is in the bodies of our friends."

There was a heavy silence. Finally, someone spoke up. "What are you saying? That we eat the dead?"

"We don't know how long we will be trapped here," Roberto continued. "If we do not eat, we will die. It's that simple. If you want to see your families again, this is what you must do."

"But what will this do to our souls?" someone cried. "Could God forgive such a thing?"

"If you don't eat, you are choosing to die," Roberto answered back. "Would God forgive that?"

The discussion continued all afternoon. Many survivors refused to consider the idea of eating human flesh, but no one tried to talk the rest of us out of it. We realized we had reached a consensus. Now the awful logistics had to be faced. "How will this be done?" someone asked. "Who is brave enough to cut the flesh from a friend?" The fuselage was dark now, but after a long silence I recognized Roberto's voice.

"I will do it," he said.

Gustavo, whose guts and determination I had always admired, rose to his feet and said quietly, "I will help."

"But who will we cut first?" asked Fito. "How do we choose?"

We all glanced at Roberto.

"Gustavo and I will take care of that," he replied.

Fito got up. "I'll go with you," he said.

For a moment no one moved, then we all reached forward, joined hands, and pledged that if any of us died here, the rest would have permission to use his body for food. Roberto found some shards of glass, then he led his assistants out to the graves. I heard them speaking softly as they worked. When they came back, they had small pieces of flesh in their hands.

Gustavo offered me a piece and I took it. It was grayish white, as hard as wood and very cold. I reminded myself that this was no longer part of a human being, that the soul had already left this body. Still, I found myself slow to lift the meat to my lips. I avoided meeting anyone's gaze, but out of the corners of my eyes I saw the others around me. Some were sitting like me with the meat in their hands, summoning the strength to eat. Others were working their jaws grimly.

Finally, I slipped the flesh into my mouth. It had no taste. I chewed, once or twice, then forced myself to swallow. I felt no guilt. I understood the magnitude of the taboo we had just broken, but if I felt any strong emotion, it was resentment that fate had forced us to choose between this horror and the horror of certain death.

That night, for the first time since we'd crashed, I felt a small flicker of hope. There were no illusions now. We all knew our fight for survival would be uglier and more harrowing than we had imagined, but we had made a declaration to the mountain that we would not surrender. In a small, sad way, I had taken my first step back toward my father.

Early the next morning, our eleventh day on the mountain, I stood outside the fuselage, watching Roy Harley, a tall, gangly wing forward who was the closest we had to an electronics expert, fiddle with a battered transistor radio he'd found in the wreckage. The batteries for the Fairchild's radio were lost along with the tail, but with the transistor we could at least receive some news from the outside world. This morning, like all the others, the signal faded in and out, and Roy was about to turn the set off when we heard, through the buzzing and popping, the tinny voice of an announcer. After ten days of fruitless searching, he said, Chilean authorities had called off efforts to find the lost Uruguayan charter flight that had disappeared over the Andes on October 13.

There was stunned silence. Then Roy began to sob.

"What?" cried Marcelo. "What did he say?"

"Suspendieron la búsqueda!" Roy shouted. "They have canceled the search! They are abandoning us!" Marcelo stared at Roy with a look of irritation, as if he had spoken gibberish, but then Marcelo dropped to his knees and let out an anguished howl that echoed through the cordillera.

My head was swimming. Even though I had always known, deep down, that rescuers would never find us, a part of me lived on that thin hope. Now, if we were to survive, we would survive by our own efforts. The silence of the mountains mocked me, but I knew that sooner or later I would have to climb.

As the days passed, my greatest fear was that we would grow so weak that escape would become impossible — that we would use up all the bodies, leaving us no choice but to languish at the crash site, staring into each other's eyes, waiting to see which of our friends would die and become our food. The thought made me frantic to leave. I knew that I had no chance in those mountains, but what did it matter? I was a dead man already. I would find the courage to do it. But I couldn't go alone. And so I studied the others, imagining which of these ragged, starving, frightened young men I would want by my side.

With Marcelo in despair, my thoughts turned to Roberto — the brilliant, egotistical medical student, strong, clever, and interested in no one's rules but his own. If anyone could stand up to the Andes through sheer stubbornness alone, Roberto was the one.

"We must do it, Roberto, you and I," I said. "We have the best chance of anyone here."

"You're crazy, Nando," he snapped, his voice rising. "Look at these mountains. Do you have any idea how high they are?"

I gazed at the highest peak. "Maybe two or three times the Pan de Azúcar," I said, referring to the tallest "mountain" in Uruguay.

Roberto snorted. "Don't be an idiot!" he screeched. "There's no snow on the Pan de Azúcar! It is only fifteen hundred feet high! This mountain is ten times higher, at least!"

"But what choice do we have?" I answered. "Please, come with me."

Roberto studied me as if he'd never seen me before. Then he nodded toward the fuselage. "Let's go inside," he said. "The wind is picking up, and I am fucking cold."

By the last week in October, I was beginning to feel a small sense of control over my fate. The group had decided to mount an escape attempt, and as we prepared in earnest, our spirits rose. No one else had died since our eighth day on the mountain, when I'd lost Susy. Fito and his steady, levelheaded cousins, fellow team supporters Eduardo Strauch and Daniel Fernández, had devised an efficient system of cutting and drying the meat, and all of us were eating enough now to at least hold starvation at bay. Out of respect for me, the others had promised not to touch the bodies of my mother and Susy, but even so, there was enough meat to last for weeks if we rationed carefully. Many of us were comforted by these thoughts as we filed into the fuselage on the evening of October 29.

As always it was pitch black. I dozed for perhaps half an hour and then woke, frightened and disoriented, as a huge and heavy force thumped against my chest. I felt an icy wetness pressing against my face, and a crushing weight bore down on me so hard that it forced the air from my lungs.

After a minute of confusion, I realized what had happened — an avalanche had rolled down the mountain and filled the fuselage with snow. There was silence, then I heard a slow, wet creak as the loose snow settled under its own weight. It felt as if my body were encased in concrete, I managed a few shallow breaths, but then snow packed into my mouth and nostrils and I began to suffocate. Oddly, my thoughts grew calm and lucid. This is my death, I told myself. Now I will see what lies on the other side.

Then a hand clawed the snow from my face and I was yanked back into the world of the living. I spat the snow from my mouth and gulped cold air.

I heard Carlitos's voice. "Who is it?" he shouted.

"Me," I sputtered. "It's Nando."

Then he left me. I heard chaos above me, voices shouting and sobbing.

"Dig for the faces!" someone yelled. "Give them air!"

"Help me here!"

"Has anyone seen Marcelo?"

"How many do we have? Who is missing?"

"Someone count!"

A few moments later they dug me out, and I was able to lift myself up from the snow. The dark fuselage was lit eerily by the flames of a cigarette lighter. I saw some of my friends lying motionless. Others were rising like zombies.

Our losses were heavy. Marcelo was dead. So were Enrique and six others. The Fairchild was completely covered. How much snow lay above us? I wondered. Two feet? Twenty? Were we buried alive?

It's hard to describe the despair that fell upon us in the grim days following the avalanche. With an aluminum cargo pole, we were able to poke a breathing hole through what turned out to be several feet of snow, but we labored for hours to burrow a passage out of the snow-choked plane, only to discover a blizzard raging outside. Trapped by the weather, we could not sleep, warm ourselves, or dry our soaking clothes. The snow inside the fuselage was so deep that we couldn't stand, and we had to sit with our chins against our chests. Fito's water-making machines were outside, useless to us, and we had to gnaw chunks of the filthy snow on which we were crawling and sleeping. With no access to the bodies outside, we rapidly began to weaken.

We were all well aware that the eight avalanche victims lay within easy reach, but we were slow to face the prospect of cutting them. Until now, a small crew of three or four had cut the meat outside the fuselage, and the rest of us never knew from whose body the flesh had been taken. How could we eat flesh cut from these newly dead bodies right before our eyes?

Silently, we agreed we'd rather starve. But by October 31, the third day of the storm, we couldn't hold out any longer. Someone found a piece of glass, swept the snow from one of the bodies, and began to cut. It was a horror, watching him slice into a friend, listening to the soft sounds of the glass ripping at the skin and muscle below. When a piece was handed to me, I was revolted. It was soft and greasy, streaked with blood and bits of wet gristle. I gagged hard when I placed it in my mouth.

There was something sordid and rank in our suffering now, a sense of corruption that soured my heart. As I shivered in the clammy snow, racked with despair, it was hard to believe in anything before the crash.

*

It took eight days to clear the fuselage, chipping away at the rock-hard snow with broken pieces of plastic. By now we were all convinced that our only chance was to walk out. Three failed attempts had convinced many that escape over the high peaks to the west was impossible, so in mid-November we tried going east. It quickly became clear that the valley did not, as we had hoped, bend around to the west, but we hadn't gone far when we discovered the plane's tail section, filled with an unexpected booty of chocolate, moldy sandwiches, and, most important, the Fairchild's batteries, which we believed could power the plane's radio so we could call out. Yet our jubilation was short-lived: after a week of tinkering, the radio remained lifeless. Meanwhile, we lost two more. Arturo Nogueira, the team's fly half and best kicker, died from infected wounds in his broken legs, and team supporter Rafael Echavarran, who'd suffered bravely through his own gangrenous leg injuries, passed away soon after. Even the strongest among us were fading. I could see hollow resignation in my friends' eyes. I wondered if they could see the same in mine.

Most alarmingly, our food was running low. We were splitting skulls now to get at the brains inside, and eating things we couldn't stomach before: lungs, marrow, the hands and feet. To the ordinary mind, our actions may seem incomprehensible, but the instinct to survive runs very deep, and when death is so near, a human being can get used to anything.

In the first week of December, as the weather improved, we began to prepare for a final westward climb. Fito and his cousins cut meat and stored it in the snow, while the others sewed pieces of insulation from the tail section into a sleeping bag that we hoped would keep the climbers warm at night. Roberto, after much resistance, had agreed to go with me, as had Antonio "Tintin" Vizintín, a front-line forward with the strength and temperament of a bull. For days we gathered equipment: the nylon seat covers we used as blankets, snowshoes that Fito fashioned out of the seat cushions, a bottle to melt water in the sun, and knapsacks Roberto made by tying off the legs of trousers and threading nylon straps through the pant legs.

Tintin and I were eager to set off, but Roberto seemed to find one excuse to delay after another — snapping that the sleeping bag needed better stitching, or he needed more time to gather his strength. But he was cruelly jolted from his mulishness on the afternoon of December 11, when Numa Turcatti, a friend of the team whose courage had won everyone's respect, died from infected sores on his legs.

On the morning of December 12, our sixty-first day in the Andes, I rose quietly. I'd dressed the night before: next to my skin I wore a cotton polo shirt and a pair of women's slacks, then three pairs of jeans and three sweaters. I wore four pairs of socks, covered with plastic supermarket bags to keep them dry. Now I gathered the aluminum pole I would use as a walking stick, a women's lipstick to protect my blistered lips, and bands of cloth to wrap around my hands. I stuffed my feet into my battered rugby shoes, pulled a wool cap over my head, and topped it with the hood and shoulders I'd cut from the antelope coat Susy had worn. Everything I did had the feel of ceremony, of consequence.

None of us had much to say as we followed the glacier up to the mountain's lower slopes. We thought we knew what risks we were facing. Still, our ignorance was staggering. Our bodies were ravaged, and we had no mountaineering skills whatsoever: instead of making our way up a gentle saddle to the south, for instance, we set off straight up the mountain's steepest slopes.

The snow was firm, and the cleats of my rugby shoes bit well into the frozen crust. But soon the surface began to weaken and we were forced to wade uphill through heavy drifts. My snowshoes quickly became so soaked that I felt as if I were climbing with manhole covers bolted to my shoes.

By midmorning we had worked our way to a dizzying altitude. But after five or six hours of hard climbing, the summit seemed no closer. My spirits sagged as I gauged the vast distance to the top. But as my body begged for surrender, some deep instinct forced me into a madman's pace. *Step-push, step-push.* Nothing else mattered. I was a locomotive lumbering up the slope. I was lunacy in slow motion. Soon I had pulled far ahead of Roberto and Tintin, who had to shout to make me stop. I waited for them at an outcrop. We ate some meat and melted some snow to drink. We all knew the kind of trouble we were in.

"Do you still think we can make it by nightfall?" Roberto asked. He was looking at the summit.

I shrugged. "We should look for a place to camp. If we don't find shelter, we will freeze before morning."

Roberto rose and lifted his backpack. "What did we do to deserve this?" he muttered. Then we started to climb.

It was late afternoon now, and the temperature began to fall. By twilight I was starting to panic, and I scaled a tall outcrop to get a better view. But as I pulled myself up, a rock the size of a cannonball broke free.

"Watch out! Watch out below!" I shouted. I looked down to see Roberto, eyes widened as he waited for the impact. The rock missed his head by inches. "You son of a bitch! You son of a bitch!" he shouted. "Are you trying to kill me? Watch what the fuck you're doing!" Then he leaned forward, and his shoulders started to heave. Hearing his sobs, I felt a stab of hopelessness, then I was overtaken by a sudden, inarticulate rage.

"Fuck this! Fuck this!" I muttered. "I have had enough! I have had enough!"

Finally I found a shallow depression in the snow beneath a large boulder, and we spread out the fragile sleeping bag, sewn together crudely with copper wire.

"Did you pee?" asked Roberto. "We can't be getting in and out of this bag all night."

It reassured me that Roberto was his grumbling self again.

"I peed," I answered. "Did you pee? I don't want you peeing in this bag."

Roberto huffed. "If anyone pees in the bag it will be you. And be careful with those big feet."

I tried to get comfortable, but I was far too frightened and cold to relax.

"Roberto," I said, "you're the medical student. How does one die of exhaustion? Is it painful? Do you just drift off?"

"What does it matter how you die?" he said. "You'll be dead, and that's all that matters."

That night the temperature dropped so low that the bottle we were using to melt snow shattered. In the morning we placed our frozen shoes in the sun until they thawed. Then we began to climb. The sun was bright. It was our second day of perfect weather.

With every hundred yards, the incline tilted closer to vertical. The tug of the void was constant. My life had collapsed to a simple game — climb well and live or falter and die. The calm voice in my head had become my own.

Put the left foot there. Now, reach up for the crack in that boulder. Is it sturdy? Good. Lift yourself. Trust your balance. Watch the ice!

I had never felt so focused, so fiercely alive. In those astonishing moments, my suffering was over, my life had become pure flow. How we continued, I cannot say. But all day we struggled toward one false summit after another, only to see the mountain soaring up again toward the clouds. We pitched camp well before sunset, and in the morning decided that Tintin and I would try for the summit while Roberto waited with the packs. After hours, we found ourselves at the base of a cliff towering hundreds of feet. Its face was almost dead vertical, but it was coated with hard-packed snow.

"How can we climb this?" asked Tintin.

I studied the wall. My mind was sluggish, but soon I remembered the metal walking stick strapped to my back.

"We need a stairway," I said. Using the tip of the pole, I began to carve crude steps into the snow. Climbing these like the rungs of a ladder, we continued up. *Dig, climb. Dig, climb.*

Hours passed. Sometime in late morning I spotted blue sky above a ridgeline. After so many false summits, I kept my hopes in check, but this time the slope fell away and I found myself standing on a gloomy hump of wind-scoured snow.

I don't remember if I felt any joy in that moment. If I did, it vanished as soon as I glanced around. The horizon was crowded in every direction with snow-covered mountains, each as steep and forbidding as the one I'd just climbed. I understood immediately that the Fairchild's copilot had been badly mistaken. We had not passed Curicó. We were nowhere near the western limits of the Andes. Our plane had fallen somewhere in the middle of the range.

In that moment, all my dreams, assumptions, and expectations evaporated into the thin Andean air. I had always thought life was the natural thing, and death was simply the end of living. Now, in this lifeless place, I saw with terrible clarity that death was the constant, and life was only a short, fragile dream. I felt a sharp and sudden longing for my mother and sister, and for my father, whom I was sure I would never see again. But despite the hopelessness of my situation, the memory of him filled me with joy. It staggered me — the mountains could not crush my ability to love. In that moment, I discovered a simple, astounding secret: death has an opposite, but it is not mere living. It is not courage or faith or will. The opposite of death is love. How had I missed that? How does anyone miss that? My fears lifted, and I knew that I would not let death control me. I would walk through that godforsaken country with love and hope in my heart. I would walk until I'd walked all the life out of me, and when I fell, I would die that much closer to home. Using the lipstick as a crayon, I wrote the words *Mount Seler* on a plastic bag and stuffed it under a rock. *This mountain was my enemy,* I thought. *And now I give it to my father.*

Soon I heard Tintin's voice from below.

"Do you see any green, Nando?"

I called back. "Tell Roberto to come up and see for himself."

It took three hours for Roberto to climb up. He looked around, shaking his head. "Well, we're finished," he said flatly.

"Look down," I said. "There is a valley. Do you see it?"

The valley wound through the snowy peaks ahead of us, then split into two forks as it neared a pair of smaller mountains. "That must be fifty miles," Roberto said. "How can we make such a trek?"

"Chile is there," I said. "It's just farther than we thought."

It looked hopeless, but we formed a plan. Tintin would go back to the crash site, leaving us his meat, while Roberto and I carried on. That evening, the Andes blazed with the most spectacular sunset I'd ever seen. The sun turned the mountains to gleaming gold, and the sky was lit with swirls of scarlet and lavender.

"Roberto," I said, "can you imagine how beautiful this would be if we were not dead men?" I felt his hand wrap around mine. I knew he was as frightened as I was, but I drew strength from our closeness. We were bonded like brothers. We made each other better men.

In the morning, we stood on the summit. "We may be walking to our deaths," I said, "but I would rather walk to meet my death than wait for it to come to me."

Roberto nodded. "You and I are friends, Nando," he said. "We have been through so much. Now let's go die together."

We eased ourselves over the western lip and began to make our way down.

On December 20, 1972, their ninth day of trekking, Nando Parrado and Roberto Canessa stumbled upon a shepherd's camp in the Chilean region of Los Maitenes. Two days later, Parrado led helicopters to the fourteen remaining survivors.

ANN PATCHETT

Do Not Disturb

FROM *Gourmet*

AS A CHILD I WAS SLIGHT and had a remarkable ability to hold still. These two features, coupled with a good imagination, meant that I was pretty much unbeatable at hide-and-seek. I could stick a pillow in the closet, fold the bedspread neatly over my back, and stay there in a pillow-shape for hours while other children called my name. All these years later it is appalling how much of my fantasy life has to do with hiding. I'm sure the Witness Protection Program would be a terrible thing, and yet I find myself wondering if there isn't some mobster I could rat out in exchange for a false identity. The same thing goes for prison: dreadful, horrifying, surely, but the phone would never ring, and couldn't you get an awful lot of reading done? None of this is to say that I do not love my life. I do. But sometimes it is the wonderful life, the life of abundant friends and extended family and true love that makes you want to run screaming for the hills. It is because you love so many people that you end up incurring too much responsibility.

All those splendid guests who come for dinner and then come to stay for long visits (because they love you, because you love them) until one day you wake to find you are living in an overpopulated Russian novel.

That is the point at which you become very clearly of two minds: one mind that says, "How rich I am to have the pleasure of a full house!" and another mind that says, "If I am ever going to get anything accomplished, I'd better start packing."

And so I am being driven out of my home by the company, the laundry, the mail and the e-mail, and by my own stupid and compulsive need to keep baking the apple pie out of *The Pie and Pastry Bible,* even though it is labor-intensive beyond belief and only ensures that everyone who drops by will drop by again. I make a couple of phone calls, drag the suitcases out of the basement, and offer some brief words of explanation to my husband, who knows me well enough to know that when it's time for me to go, it's better just to stand aside.

Then I fly to L.A. and check into the Bel-Air.

In many ways this is not the best choice: I know a lot of people in the Los Angeles area and many of them are related to me and none of them will be pleased to learn that I have been hiding in their general vicinity without coming to visit. I simply decide not to tell them while temporarily deluding myself into believing that they'll never read this. For a fraction of what I'm spending on my stylish seclusion I could just as easily have booked into a Best Western in Omaha or Toledo, cities where I know not one single soul whose feelings I could hurt. Seeing as how my goal is to soak up some quiet and get a massive amount of work done, what difference would it have made?

Best Western? The Hotel Bel-Air? I'm no fool. Life affords us very few opportunities to run away, and so if I'm going to do it I might as well do it up right. Besides, I love L.A., and, though I didn't grow up there, it is the city I was born in. I love the palm trees and the bougainvillea and the bright blue light of the late afternoons. I find the ways that it is exotic to be both comforting and familiar. Besides, I've been rereading all of Joan Didion's books lately, and she always makes me want to go west. Checking into the Bel-Air for a while seems like exactly what Joan would have done when faced with too many houseguests.

Because I have no plans to go anywhere, I do not rent a car. I do not wish to sightsee or shop. For one brief moment I think it would be nice to see the Getty again, and then I put it out of my head. I am the guest editor for this year's *Best American Short Stories,* and so I have come to the hotel with a suitcase full of fiction that needs to be read and a small computer that contains a half-written novel that should be a fully completed novel by now. My idea of a vacation is getting my work done with privacy and quiet, not driving around. Whatever diversions I require will be provided by the sweet gum trees in the courtyard outside my room.

Californians are never comfortable with the idea of not having transportation. When the desk clerk checks me in, it is late on a Sunday night. He tells me all the places the hotel car will gladly take me for free, over to Wilshire or down Rodeo Drive, where movie stars drink lattes with shivering Chihuahuas on their knees. I shake my head. "I don't want to go out," I tell him. "I've come to work."

"*Work* isn't a word we use at the Hotel Bel-Air," he tells me.

I make a mental note not to mention it again.

I hadn't come to the Bel-Air because I'd stayed there before but because my father had taken me and my sister there for lunch once when we were girls. I remembered how the grounds were like a jungle where steep ravines fell into streams and vines twisted up over every available surface. I remembered the swans, enormous floating ottomans with slender white necks that we watched from our table as we ate. It was where the stars used to go, and later Nancy Reagan, and in between them many others who wanted to be left alone.

Upon my arrival, the Hotel Bel-Air sends over a pot of tea and a lovely fruit plate. My friend Jeanette, who had stayed here fifteen years before, told me they brought you cookies and a glass of milk at bedtime. The cookies were so beautiful she took their picture. But times change. There are no cookie eaters left in Bel-Air now.

The next morning I hit the ground running, which is to say I roll over in bed and start right in on the pile of short stories. I eat the fruit for breakfast and drink the leftover tea cold and it's fine. The silence in the room is so brilliant that I can't bear to leave it. At noon I take a swim in the empty pool, which is kept at a considerate eighty-two degrees.

After unpacking I discover I have devoted much too much of my luggage space to short stories and not nearly enough to my wardrobe. When I turn up at the restaurant for lunch looking neat and presentable and not the least bit stylish, the hostess wants to know about my reservation, which I do not have. It is late. People coming for lunch later than this must be very hip indeed. The terrace has half a dozen empty tables but she seats me in the restaurant, where I have the entire place to myself. I could complain, but I figure if I've come to be alone then I might as well be alone. From my table inside I watch the glamorous women outside who are lunching on Spa Cobb salads without blue cheese or dressing. The man with the bread basket wanders from table to table, lonesome as a cloud. When he comes to me his basket is full and perfectly arranged. He gives me a smile of sincere pleasure when I tell him I will take both the sourdough roll and the cheese stick.

It doesn't take long to catch on to the fact that coming to this particular hotel for anonymity reflects a level of genius that I never knew I possessed. It is a hotel whose reputation was built on catering to people who are hiding, but those other people hide in a much flashier way than I do. They hide beneath hair extensions and giant Chanel sunglasses. The windows of their Jaguars are tinted. It is the kind of hiding that demands and receives a great deal of attention, as opposed to my kind of hiding, which basically consists of staying in my room and frustrating the housekeeping staff. The hostess at the restaurant gives me the word that if I want to try to eat there again tomorrow I'm really going to need a reservation, and so I make one, but when tomorrow comes I find that I don't have the energy for it. I stay at the pool and swim and read stories. The guy who brings the towels lets me eat all the fruit I want from the gorgeous basket beside the bottles of Evian. I'm still a little hungry but certainly not hungry enough to do anything about it. After a while a blond who is somewhere in her late fifties takes up residence on the chaise longue next to mine. Even though there are probably forty empty chairs around the pool, these are the only two that bask in a slight shimmer of sunlight. The plant life at the Bel-Air is so enormous and lush, Tasmanian tree ferns and giant palms, towering camellias and gardenias, that the entire place is locked in a shadow. The woman beside me is very beautiful in the way of an aging Elke Sommer or any of John Derek's early wives. She has pretty legs and a soft middle and wears a tiny pink bikini that is rimmed in what appear to be closely placed pink carnations. Every fifteen minutes or so we pick up our towels and move two chairs down, following the sun as best we can. "It is cold," she says to me in a Russian accent, and then returns to her Sudoku puzzle. These are the only words any nonstaff person has spoken to me in days. For a moment I imagine that she and I have come to the Bel-Air in hopes the air will strengthen our fragile nerves, or that we are guests at the tubercular sanatorium in *The Magic Mountain*, wrapped up in fur blankets and waiting to have our temperatures taken.

There are two sides to the Hotel Bel-Air: on one side is the busy restaurant where well-groomed people have discussions about television shows loudly and with great seriousness. To make a sweeping generalization I would say that men have breakfast meetings and women have lunch meetings and everybody talks about the Golden Globes, Ray Romano, and episodes of *Lost* and *CSI*, or at least those are the words I hear repeated continually while I butter my toast, *toast* being another word that is bandied around a great deal as in "No toast" and "Egg whites, no toast." After several days of being forced into the role of passive audience for everyone else's star turn, I decide I want a little attention of my own. If I were embracing my solitude as fully as I claimed to be I would order the vegetable frittata, but I am so wild, such a fool for spontaneity, I am practically Anita Ekberg walking into the Trevi Fountain in *La Dolce Vita*. I tell the waiter I'll have the pancakes. That was a mistake. It is never wise to order the meal that doesn't move. Still, there are plenty of wonderful things to eat at the Bel-Air. At dinnertime the food is brilliant when it is at its heaviest and most formal; the scallop fondue and the poached Maine lobster are as delicious as they are expensive. If you don't feel up to a very fancy meal you can slip off to the bar where the waiters are friendly, the pianist is charming, and the food is very bad. If you accidentally slip up and order the chicken potpie do not, under any circumstances, eat it.

On the other side of the Bel-Air (you will know it when you see the sign that says "Guests Only Beyond This Point") are the rooms of the hotel. Over there everything is perfectly quiet, so quiet that I sometimes wonder if I am the only person who is sleeping over. (I never see my friend in the pink bikini again.) When I am coming back from dinner alone one night, a man in a suit follows me hurriedly toward this demarcation. "May I assist you with something?" he says pointedly. I feel a little bad about this, because I had gone out of my way to dress up for dinner and I think I bear a remarkable resemblance to a guest, but I must be wrong. I explain that I am staying at the hotel, that I've been staying at the hotel for a while now, and although he doesn't look completely convinced, he allows me to cross over. Here the scent of the purple saucer magnolias blends with the whiff of chlorine coming from the burbling fountains. It is a smell I have always associated with Southern California and one that I dearly love.

What we want out of a vacation changes as we age. It changes from vacation to vacation. There was a time when it was all about culture for me. My idea of a real break was to stay in museums until my legs ached and then go stand in line to get tickets for an opera or a play. Later I became a disciple of relaxation and looked for words like *beach* and *massage* when making my plans. I found those little paper umbrellas that balanced on the side of rum drinks to be deeply charming then. Now of course I strive for transcendent invisibility and the chance to accomplish the things I can't get done at home. But as I pack up my room at the Hotel Bel-Air I think the best vacation is the one that relieves you of your own life temporarily and then makes you long for it again. I am deeply ready to be seen, thrilled at the thought of my own beloved civilization. I have done a month's worth of work in five days. I have filled up to the gills on solitude. I am insanely grateful at the thought of going home.

MATTHEW POWER

The Magic Mountain

FROM *Harper's Magazine*

THE TRAFFIC IN QUEZON CITY — blaring, belching, scarcely moving — seems to be in a permanent state of rush-hour gridlock. Quezon, population 2.2 million, is the largest of the seventeen municipalities that form the megalopolis of greater Manila. Chrome-clad jeepneys, the chopped and airbrushed descendants of World War II army jeeps pressed into public service, engage in a slow-motion chariot race with motorized tricycles, oxcarts laden with scrap metal, and passengerless bicycle rickshaws. A knot of metal and rubber binds every intersection. Ragged children dart between vehicles at lights, selling cigarettes with one hand and huffing gasoline-soaked rags with the other. The tinted windows and air conditioning of the odd SUV create a bubble of sorts for its occupants, keeping the dusty pre-monsoon swelter and the pleas of the riffraff at bay, but do nothing at all to speed them along. The children, hair coppery with protein deficiency, paw like cats against the windows, studiously ignored by passengers a few inches away. Above it all, the chubby, smiling visage of Quezon's mayor, Feliciano "Sonny" Belmonte, beams down with paternal warmth from an enormous billboard, the base of which, strung with wash, has been converted into a tidy home by enterprising squatters.

Nearly half of all Filipinos live on less than two dollars a day, and metropolitan Manila, in its poverty, enormity, utter squalor, and lack of services, perfectly represents the catastrophic twenty-first-century vision of the megacity as most of the world's poor will experience it. I am crowded in the back of a taxi with the photographer Misty Keasler and Klaid Sabangan, our guide and translator. Our driver, a Filipino named Johnny Ramone, blasts seventies singer-songwriter standards on his radio and is not in the least dismayed by the vehicular quagmire we're navigating as we wind our way toward the Payatas dump.

Like most of the outside world, I had first heard of Payatas, the fifty-acre dumpsite on Quezon City's northern boundary, when it flashed briefly across headlines in July 2000. Little else besides people dying in great numbers on a slow news day will bring notice to a place like this. After weeks of torrential rains spawned by a pair of typhoons, a hundred-foot mountain of garbage gave way and thundered down onto a neighborhood of shanties built in its shadow. The trash, accumulated over three decades, had been piled up to a seventy-degree angle, and the rain-saturated mountain had collapsed. Hundreds of people were killed, buried alive in an avalanche of waste. That most of the victims made a living scavenging from the pile itself rendered the tragedy a dark parable of the new millennium, a symptom of the thousand social and economic ills that plague the developing world. I knew that the scavengers had continued living and working at the site even after the disaster, and, thinking there was some human truth to be dug from underneath the sorry facts, I wanted to see Payatas for myself.

Johnny Ramone squeaks his taxi through a gap, and we turn right down a narrow street between rows of tin-roofed shacks, alleys crowded with fruit sellers sitting by heaps of oranges and flapping roosters straining against their tethers. Junk shops line the street, their proprietors living among house-high piles of bottles and sacks of aluminum cans clouded by flies. A parade of dripping garbage trucks jounces along the potholed street, workers clinging to the roofs and young boys chasing after them hoping something salvageable might fall off.

As we come over a rise, my first glimpse of Payatas is hallucinatory: a great smoky-gray mass that towers above the trees and shanties creeping up to its edge. On the rounded summit, almost the same color as the thunderheads that mass over the city in the afternoons, a tiny backhoe crawls along a contour, seeming to float in the sky. As we approach, shapes and colors emerge out of the gray. What at first seemed to be flocks of seagulls spiraling upward in a hot wind reveal themselves to be cyclones of plastic bags. The huge hill itself appears to shimmer in the heat, and then its surface resolves into a moving mass of people, hundreds of them, scuttling like termites over a mound. From this distance, with the wind blowing the other way, Payatas displays a terrible beauty, inspiring an amoral wonder at the sheer scale and collective will that built it, over many years, from the accumulated detritus of millions of lives.

Behind a broad desk, Colonel Jameel Jaymalin looks pressed and combed despite the crushing heat and the bouquet of decomposing municipal waste that drifts in on the breeze. He seems happy in his position, lord of a fiefdom offered tribute by some 450 garbage trucks a day, many of which idle at the entrance gate outside his office as we speak. The colonel recites a history of the site and the government's efforts to clean things up following the disaster in 2000. Thirty years ago, Payatas had been a ravine surrounded by rice paddies and farming villages shaded over with the remnants of the rainforest canopy. As Manila rebuilt in the postwar decades, a great migration from the countryside to the city ballooned the population from 1.5 million in 1950 to nearly 15 million today.

By the 1970s, low-lying Payatas, on the anarchic fringe of a massive city, began by dint of gravity and convenience to be used as a dumping ground. Truckloads of household waste gathered up by sanitation privateers from across the city were poured into the ravine. The site also became infamous as a body dump during the gang wars that raged across the city's slum districts, fought out with spears, machetes, poison arrows, and homemade guns called *sumpak*. Creeks were filled in and the topography shifted; a hill began to grow, accruing layer upon layer and combed over by a population of ten thousand scavengers, junk-shop operators, and garbage brokers who followed the metropolis's waste stream wherever it led. Absent any government oversight, a city of shanties grew up around, and on, the dump. The entire local economy was built on a sort of Trash Rush. By 2000, the Payatas dump was 130 feet high, taller than anything in the surrounding landscape, a dormant and unstable volcano waiting for chance and gravity to run their course.

After the July rains and the collapse, after what bodies that could be recovered had been buried and the television crews went away, there was still enormous political pressure on the Quezon City government to do something about conditions at the site. At first the dump was closed, but the absence of an alternative meant that garbage piled up around the city. Despite the dump's dangers, the scavengers and the dumping cartels wanted Payatas reopened, and within months that is exactly what happened. By year's end the national government had passed an extraordinarily ambitious, if almost completely unenforceable, law called the Ecological Solid Waste Management Act, which called for all open dumps in the country to be closed and replaced with sealed sanitary landfills. According to the act, Payatas was supposed to close by February 16 of this year. When I point out to the colonel that it is now March, and there are several hundred loaded garbage trucks idling outside his door, he admits that, yes, there have been some unavoidable delays in locating a new site. But he insists there have been profound changes at the dump. Payatas is a flagship project: we can go see for ourselves. "Just please don't take pictures of the children."

The colonel hands us off to Rafael Saplan, the dump's chief engineer, who shows us a series of maps and charts illustrating his master plan. Saplan tells me that except for the absence of a liner to prevent waste from contaminating the groundwater, the dump has been largely converted into a sanitary landfill. "It would take three thousand trucks a day eleven years to cart all this garbage to a new engineered landfill," Saplan tells me. The steep face of the pile, which had been nearly vertical before the collapse, has been recontoured to a more stable forty degrees, and terraced steps have been cut into it to prevent slides. Toxic leachate, the heavy metal–laced liquid that percolates down through compressed garbage, is collected and pumped back into the pile. Deep-rooted vetiver grass has been planted to control erosion, and a system of ID cards has been created to document scavengers. No workers under fourteen are allowed.

Saplan is working on a pilot project to mine the millions of cubic feet of methane produced by the pile's decay every year, some of which is pumped into a one-megawatt gas generator. The ultimate goal is to build a generating station that could provide electricity to around two thousand local households for a decade. The government would even be able to receive emissions credits for the methane project under the Kyoto Protocol. And then the site could be turned into an eco-park, maybe even a golf course. In the meantime, the actor Martin Sheen — who spent more than a year in the

Philippines filming *Apocalypse Now* — has built a child-care center at the foot of the pile where the scavengers' children can splash in a wading pool while their parents work above. It looks good on paper: a beneficent, progressive government doing what it can to deal with a huge, toxic, public-health headache. I mention to Klaid that the ESWMA seems like an incredibly forward-thinking piece of legislation. He laughs. "Yes, but in the Philippines the law is only a suggestion."

With laminated passes given to us by one of the colonel's aides, we walk through the gate and down the hill. Truck after truck rumbles by, piled high with household and commercial waste from across Quezon. In the tropical heat the smell of rot and smoke is everywhere; it seeps into the pores and clings to the back of your throat. Our clothes soak through with sweat. We cut through a maze of narrow alleys filled with uniformed schoolkids and men playing billiards, dogs collapsed under the shade of the feltless tables. The neighborhood architecture is cobbled together out of chicken wire, cinder blocks, rusted tin. One rooftop is made entirely out of liberated street signs. Klaid leads us down a narrow trail through the jungle, which in places still edges the slum. We walk across a narrow bamboo bridge and up a steep hill, where a group of people — mothers with babies, men with arms crossed — sit in the shade of a military-style tent, in which a cooking class is under way.

At the foot of the hill lies a half-acre of vegetables: beautifully tended rows of lettuce, tomatoes, carrots, squash, corn. A few people rest under a giant star-apple tree by a small creek. A pregnant woman with a little boy works her way down a row of tomato plants, pulling weeds. Tropical butterflies flit about. It would be an utterly rural and bucolic scene if it weren't for the rusty jumble of houses that begin at the field's edge, towered over by the gray hill of Payatas. The rumble of the bulldozers and the trucks circling the road up its side is a dull grind, and periodically a plastic bag caught in an updraft drifts toward us and descends, delicate as a floating dandelion seed, into the branches of the trees.

"These are all *mangangalahigs,* the scavengers from the local community," Klaid tells me. *Mangangalahig* means something like "chicken-scratcher," after the way the scavengers pick through the trash. For the last six months, with money from the Consuelo "Chito" Madrigal Foundation, funded by one of the Philippines' wealthiest families, Klaid has been running an organic-gardening training program to classes of twenty at a time. Each student was given a plot of land to use and basic instruction.

Klaid, goateed, pierced, with a baby face and a shaved head, looks like a cherubic interpretation of a pirate. He picked up his nickname as a teenage street break dancer with his partner "Bonny." An idealist who struggled for years in his former job at the United Nations Human Settlements Program, he jumped at the chance to do community work without the bureaucratic red tape. "That's why I left the UN," he tells me. "I said, 'For three years I've been hearing you talk, and set paradigms, and talk about frameworks and structures, and not one house has been built.' What we are doing here is the very essence of what the UN is trying to do, but they are limited by bureaucracy and internal politics."

When the class lets out, Klaid introduces me to one of the students, Ronald Escare, a stocky, grinning man with a ponytail tucked under a Mickey Mouse hat who goes by the nickname Bobby. Bobby has scavenged in Payatas for eight years, and he is just about to start his afternoon shift. Among the many new rules implemented by the government, the vast and chaotic population of *mangangalahigs* has been divided into work groups, each with a scheduled shift and a specific assignment of truck numbers whose contents they are allowed to pick over. We pull on knee-high gum boots and walk along a dusty path through the shanties to the dump entrance, trailed by a group of giggling children. On the street by the main gate, perhaps fifty yards from Martin Sheen's drop-off center (the wading pool empty, the children absent), a teenage boy tends to a large pile of burning wires, poking them periodically with a stick, his T-shirt pulled up over his nose and mouth. It is a halfhearted attempt to filter out the carcinogenic smoke, laden with dioxins and furans, which are released when insulation is burned off to sell the copper wire for scrap.

Bobby turns out to be a one-man commodities board of the latest scrap prices. "Red copper, 150 pesos a kilo at junk shop," he tells me. "I sell at factory, no junk shop. Two hundred pesos." His derisive laugh suggests that anyone who does not cut out the middleman in these transactions is a sucker. He gestures at the burning tangle of wire with his *kalahig*, the tool used by all the scavengers to dig through the trash. The *kalahig* is an L-shaped steel spike, perhaps eighteen inches long, with a wooden handle and a needle-sharp point. With a practiced flick of the wrist, Bobby demonstrates how to spear a can on the ground and deposit it into the sack he has slung over his shoulder. When I tell Bobby that aluminum cans in the States can be redeemed for the astronomical equivalent of 2 pesos each, he gives me a look of unalloyed wonder, as if I'd announced that the streets in America are made of chocolate.

We wave the colonel's passes at the guard, a city employee wearing a fluorescent orange T-shirt emblazoned with the word *enforcer*. On the back it bears the message "environmentally friendly" in lowercase script. He waves us through after exacting a toll of a couple cigarettes. On a steep path up the hillside, a line of dusty scavengers, finishing their daytime shifts, stumble down with bulging plastic sacks on their heads. The smell increases as we climb, a miasma of rotting food and burning tires, but before long my sense of smell, apparently defeated, ceases to register the full force of the stench. The ground underneath our boots is spongy, and as we climb, black rivulets of leachate flow down the access road. A black puddle releases methane bubbles like a primordial swamp, and the ground itself shakes when a loaded truck rumbles by. A road cut reveals a gray cross section of oozing agglomerate, shredded plastic bags the only recognizable remnants in the hypercompressed pile.

The colonel's dreams of a grass-covered return to nature at Payatas seem far off as we ascend through the decades-old strata of the pile. Garbage dumps are far from inert. As rainwater percolates down through the pile and organic matter decays, a continuous and unpredictable biochemical reaction occurs, leaching toxins from the various plastics, metals, and organic compounds. The "slow smokeless burning of decay" is a process of centuries: ancient Roman dumps produce leachate to this day. Newsprint can remain legible for decades. Beneath its surface, Payatas is a roiling and poisonous pressure cooker, and any plan to cover it with a green mantle will ultimately have to come to terms with what is buried there.

Trying hard not to slip back down the rancid surface of the pile, we finally clamber to the top. The highest point in the landscape, the "active face" of the Payatas dump is a broad plain of trash, extending to a false horizon so that it seems to contain the entire world. Unlike the gray muck of the mountain's sides, the summit is a riot of torn-open, primary-colored plastic bags in festive profusion, like a Mardi Gras parade hit by a cluster bomb. A line of trucks rumbling up the road drops load upon load, which are sifted and pushed to the edges as the hill grows skyward. The quaking geology of trash beneath our feet is laid down layer by layer, and covered daily with truckloads of dirt, as Bobby explains: *lupa, basura, lupa, basura* — earth, garbage, earth, garbage — in sedimentary gradations, building an utterly man-made landscape. Could they be read, the layers at Payatas — like Mesolithic middens of oyster shells or the trash heaps of Pompeii — might unravel to a future archaeologist some mystery of the millions of vanished lives whose leavings made this mountain.

Hundreds of scavengers, brandishing *kalahigs* and sacks, faces covered with filthy T-shirts, eyes peering out like desert nomads' through the neck holes, gather in clutches across the dump. Gulls and stray dogs with heavy udders prowl the margins, but the summit is a solely human domain. The impression is of pure entropy, a mass of people as disordered as the refuse itself, swarming frantically over the surface. But patterns emerge, and as trucks dump each new load with a shriek of gears and a sickening glorp of wet garbage, the scavengers surge forward, tearing open plastic bags, spearing cans and plastic bottles with a choreographed efficiency. The intense focus and stooped postures of the *mangangalahigs'* bodies recall a postagricultural version of Millet's *Gleaners*. We stand by the side of a fresh pile and watch as it is worked over with astonishing speed. A *kalahig* slits open a bag as if it were a fish, garbage entrails spilling out, and with a series of rapid, economical movements, anything useful is speared and flicked into a sack to be sorted later. The ability to discern value at a glimpse, to sift the useful out of the rejected with as little expenditure of energy as possible, is the great talent of the scavenger.

Cleanliness is relative here. After filling a sack with slop for his pigs — melon rinds, cold spaghetti, some congealed fried chicken at the bottom of a takeout bag — Bobby plunges his greasy hands into a rotting watermelon to clean them off, and then wipes them down with a moldering orange, grinning. He points out the different grades of plastic and their market prices as he walks us around a new heap being combed over by a group of his friends. The group's leader is a striking transvestite with the given name Romeo Derillo, self-christened Camille. Hand on hip, calling out orders to her crew and twirling a *kalahig* like a majorette, she somehow manages an unassailable glamour while standing knee-deep in a freshly dumped load from one of Manila's huge new shopping malls. This is premium garbage, so she has ordered all *kalahigs* sheathed, and the valuable plastic bottles are pulled out by hand. One worker collects nothing but drink straws; another, hundreds of plastic cups. Compact discs catch the sunlight like iron pyrite in a slag heap. A boy runs past, shouting with joy, holding aloft a pair of beat-up roller skates he's just salvaged. A bulldozer rumbles by, the ground quivering, trailing a bloody-looking garland of McDonald's ketchup packets from its rear axle.

Camille, like a great many of the Filipinos who find themselves working in Payatas, came here from the hinterlands of central Luzon island as a teenager. The economic choice between farming in the countryside (all fortunes the whim of the monsoon, of landowners, of the market price of rice or bananas) and mining the wealth of the metropolis's waste was not a difficult one. "In Payatas, they make a better living than they could ever hope to in the countryside," Klaid tells me. Bobby's 50 percent premium (when he cuts out the junk-shop middlemen) means he can make 150 pesos a day; about three dollars, which is 50 percent higher than the Philippine median.

The existence of "garbage slums," where the desperately poor find their economic niche amid the dumping grounds of municipal waste, is by no means a solely Filipino phenomenon. In his terrifying, magisterial work, *Planet of Slums*, Mike Davis cites Beirut's Quarantina, Khartoum's Hillat Kusha, Calcutta's Dhapa, and Mexico City's enormous Santa Cruz Meyehualco as a few of the more egregious examples of this new urban form. Only in the last decade, since it eclipsed Manila's notorious Smokey Mountain (closed by the government in 1995), has the garbage slum in Payatas reached its apogee. Household and industrial trash has become for the world's poor a more viable source of sustenance than the agriculture and husbandry that has supported civilization since the first cities sprang up in the Fertile Crescent.

Occupying a niche like the bacteria and fungi that break down organic wastes in a forest and feed them back into the energy cycle, scavengers have existed in large cities at least since the Industrial Revolution. Victorian London, for instance, had an elaborately structured recycling system, with every subgroup filling its adapted role in the vast city's digestive tract. Night-soil men gathered human waste from privies and sold it as fertilizer. Pure finders gathered dog shit for use in the tanning of hides. Small children called mudlarks scoured the tidal flats along the Thames looking for bits of rope or lumps of coal, and bone grubbers dispatched animal skeletons to the rag-and-bone shops. The advent of plastics in modern industry has changed what the *mangangalahigs* are gathering up, but it hasn't altered their key role in the ecosystem of the city.

Even within the economic bottom-feeding of Payatas there is a self-imposed hierarchy, a funhouse mirror of larger societal inequalities. Scavengers unaffiliated with organized groups are called *ramblistas*, or "ramblers." Like hyenas skulking around a pride of lions at a kill, *ramblistas* circle outside the groups working the newest piles, picking over the dregs. The *paleros*, boys who work on the trucks themselves, making collection rounds of neighborhoods, are in a better position, snatching up the choicest bits before they even reach the dump. Some of the trucks we had seen had huge bags hanging on their sides, and the *paleros* were grabbing what they could from their load and squirreling it away. Before entering the gate by the colonel's office, a truck will pull up in front of one of the junk shops, and the *paleros* heft their day's take onto a scale, dividing up the money to supplement their fifty-peso wage. The jumpers, usually small boys who climb aboard moving trucks and shovel valuable items overboard, have been banned from the dump proper under the new regulations, but that has only pushed them outside the gates. I had spotted them waiting at intersections, where they climb under the tarps of unguarded and idling trucks and grab whatever they can.

Just to the side of the several-acre spot where the trucks are dropping new loads sits a cluster of shacks and lean-tos, shaded by ragged tarps. "That's the food court," says Klaid, "just like the mall." And it is just like the mall, save perhaps the oversight of health inspectors. Small cookstoves heat tea and bubbling pots of stew. For a few pesos the scavengers can get lunch here instead of hiking down to the bottom of the hill. Klaid purchases a *balut*, a fertilized duck egg that has developed for two weeks before being hard-boiled. It is a Filipino delicacy, and with a gold-toothed grin he makes a show of cracking the shell, slurping the juice, and swallowing the fetal duck whole.

Wandering from pile to pile, calling out, "*Piyesa! Piyesa!*" (Parts! Parts!), are brokers of electronic and computer components, a new and lucrative category of waste. I ask Bobby what's worth the most, and he replies without hesitating, "Epson." An empty refillable printer cartridge in working condition can go for as much as 350 pesos. Bobby knows the prices for all these, too: Monitor, 50 pesos. Motherboard, 30. Circuit boards for 25 a kilo, to be melted down for trace amounts of gold. Pentium chips, if the pins can be straightened, 50. A boy approaches the brokers with a scuffed-up printer cartridge, which they glance at before rejecting. It is a buyer's market, and the general sentiment among everyone I talk to is that business has been getting worse.

A year ago, say Bobby and his friends, a *ramblista* might have made one thousand pesos a week. Now she'll be lucky to glean six hundred. Most of the best pickings are intercepted en route or diverted to other dumpsites. I ask Bobby what he'll do if Payatas finally closes down. He shrugs, smiles. His five-months-pregnant wife is working as a *ramblista* a few yards away. "I'll go to Montalban," he says. Klaid tells me that this is the new dumpsite even farther out in the countryside. Many scavengers have already moved there. The enormous waste stream of Manila shifts like the mouth of a river, and wherever it spreads its rich alluvial fan the *mangangalahigs* and *paleros* and *ramblistas* will follow.

The impulse to gamble, the faint hope that the dump might offer up a buried treasure, becomes a kind of religion to the thousands of scavengers. Payatas, which in the 2000 collapse had shown itself capable of taking everything away, can offer up extraordinary bounty. I ask Bobby what is the greatest thing he has ever heard of being found. A Rolex, sixty-five thousand pesos in a box, gold teeth, a half-burned hundred-dollar bill. There are dangers, too: some boys once found a hand grenade and, not realizing what it was, blew themselves up. Just last week Bobby found a huge Styrofoam box containing a 150-pound swordfish, still frozen solid. His group hacked it up on the spot and took it home. He thinks the *paleros* must have grabbed it by accident from outside a restaurant. "Sometimes they don't know what they throw away," he says.

Having come here expecting to see a violent and irrational struggle for existence, I begin to find something reassuring about the efficient dignity with which the *mangangalahigs* go about their work. Bobby tells me that with the new system of collectives, the scavengers share profits within their groups, which leads to more cooperation in the gleaning process, and many participate in a local savings program, from which they can draw small loans. The scavengers seem less victims than rational economic actors, skilled and highly organized laborers who actually provide a sort of public service.

The sun is sliding fast toward the horizon, and we pick our way back down the hill as the next shift's workers begin to make their way up. They will work long into the night, as long as the trucks keep coming, lighting their way with homemade miner's lamps of taped-together batteries. Walking down through the village, I notice several shrines to St. Anthony, the patron saint of poor people and seekers of lost objects, decorated with plastic bottle-ends cut into festive blossoms.

Day after day we return to Payatas, climbing around the pile to talk to people or wandering through the surrounding neighborhoods. There are actually two peaks in the topography of trash here: the newer one, where some thirteen hundred tons of municipal waste are dumped a day; and the older one, site of the 2000 collapse, which was graded and closed shortly thereafter. That part of the dump now houses Saplan's methane-generation project. We pass an outflow pipe coming out of the pile's base next to a small creek. A steady flow of espresso-black leachate, the poison distillate of millions of tons of putrescent garbage, pours out, running downhill directly into the creek, which joins the flow of the toxic Pasig River as it winds through the heart of the metropolis to Manila Bay.

Below a bridge that spans the creek, a group of half-naked boys stand in the gray water up to their waists, rinsing out hundreds of plastic garbage bags, which they bundle up in great bales. Another boy stomps down a truckload of plastic cups that resembles a hay wain. The bag-washers in the river have set alight a pile of waste plastic, which flickers and pops as it sends a black plume across the shacks and frames the scene in Hadean shades. They look up at me, laughing, calling out: "Hey Joe!" "Hey Joe, you're my father!" Laughing and splashing around as they work, the boys are scarcely aware of the health risks to which they and all the scavengers of Payatas are subjecting themselves. Tuberculosis is epidemic, made worse by air pollution and overcrowding. Tetanus, asthma, and staph infections are common. There are a few medical charities that visit, but regular care is rare. Bobby says he's lost three of his children to illness in Payatas: nine years, six years, and three months, "from the methane." He tells me this matter-of-factly, as if he were reciting the market prices of aluminum cans. Personal tragedy is a commodity worth very little in Payatas.

We wander through warrens of shacks, built on blocks to weather the monsoon. The soot-covered houses seem half destroyed, and the people next to the dump don't own the land they live on. Squatters' shacks overhang the banks of the Pasig River, which has been turned into a vast cloaca for the city's waste and yearly rises above its banks to sweep away the most vulnerable settlements. Manila has a severe monsoon, and informal housing among the slum population leaves tens of thousands living in flood-prone, cramped, disease-ridden squalor. Even in the worst locations, or on the periphery where the city fades away into the rice fields and swamps, there is always the threat of a more powerful economic force that can edge squatters out from whatever place they've taken as theirs. They are haunted everywhere by the bulldozers of progress.

Time and again in Manila, huge slums have been emptied to avoid the unwanted notice of the outside world. Imelda Marcos was notorious for clearing out tens of thousands of slum dwellers in the mid-1970s before the arrival of the Miss Universe pageant, the visit of President Gerald Ford, and an IMF–World Bank meeting. Not to be outdone, her nominally democratic successor Corazon Aquino reportedly evicted six hundred thousand squatters during her presidency. When prices rise and landowners want to clear shantytowns from their property, one of the favored methods in Manila is arson, known as "hot demolition." A popular technique involves releasing a rat or cat soaked in kerosene and set alight into a settlement, where the terrified creature can start dozens of fires before it dies.

*

We cut across the narrow valley between the two hills and cross a ditch into the neighborhood that was once known as Lupang Pangako: the Promised Land. This spot, Klaid tells me, is where the hill came down. A woman named Ruth Manadong, sweeping her alley a few yards from the edge of the dump, points us to the exact spot. She and her eight-year-old nephew escaped, climbing the slope behind their house as the saturated garbage surged down like lava. They later returned, she tells me, but were driven away from the site by restive ghosts rattling their windows, knocking pots over in the kitchen, visiting nightmares into fitful attempts at sleep. She does not look up as she tells this to Klaid. She points us down the alleyway, where steps lead to a concrete patio and a memorial on which several hundred names are inscribed: Abalos. Villeno. George. Whole extended families were wiped out in the putrid wave of mud and plastic. No one will ever know for sure how many were swallowed up. More than two hundred bodies were pulled out, but the flow had filled in the ravine thirty feet deep in places, utterly shifting the landscape and making a full recovery impossible.

Not thirty yards from the memorial, a group of mud-covered workers are digging a deep trench into the collapsed hillside. At first I think they are a work detail digging for remains, to give a proper burial to the nameless dead still buried in the site. Klaid speaks with one of them in Tagalog and then explains, "When the dump was first being piled up, the value of aluminum was so low that people didn't collect it for scrap. So they're digging out twenty-year-old cans from the site of the collapse." By the dictates of the open market the decades-old layers of trash were now a relatively rich ore, regardless of the fact that the abandoned tailings the workers now sifted through were laced with their own dead. In a sense, it is all a matter of how quickly one is buried alive in the garbage: in a few terror-filled moments, or by the slow measure of a lifetime's labor.

One Sunday Bobby meets us at a McDonald's in Quezon, where we pile into a motorcycle taxi with a sidecar and bump and rattle down pothole-covered streets into the heart of the slum. Bobby's wife is working a *ramblista* shift today, and women don't often come where we are going. Pulling up into a dusty, open courtyard, we are met by the suspicious stares of a hundred men who are gathered around a squared-off enclosure of rusted sheet metal. Sunday mornings in Quezon are for church or for cockfights, and we have come for the latter.

Men hold their prize birds under their arms, smoothing their feathers, whispering to them quietly, running their fingers down the long green tails as though through a lover's hair. The wall around the enclosure is chest-high and crowded three-deep with spectators. Bobby and I climb up on a corner post, a boy scrambling between my legs to look over. Two scarred men with poorly rendered tattoos enter the dusty ring through a gate, their birds' heads tucked under their armpits to calm them. A hulking man with a notepad stands in the center, sweat running in rivulets down his face, and starts calling out odds in Filipino, waving a splay-fingered hand at the crowd like a magician casting a spell. Surging against the barrier, the sidelines erupt with bets being placed, peso notes held high, men shoving and yelling to get closer to the edge of the ring, sizing up the competitors.

The man taking the bets is called the Cristo — the Christ — and, like an auctioneer, his skill is to build the bidding to a fever pitch. Fistfuls of pesos change hands, odds are given, supplications are made to the heavens. Cockfighting is called *sabong* in Filipino, and as many as 10 percent of Filipinos are active participants in this billion-dollar industry. In some slum economies, as much as a fifth of the average income is redistributed through gambling, and, as with state lotteries in the United States, the poorest people in the Philippines are those most likely to gamble on birds. They are also the primary consumers of *shabu,* a local variety of methamphetamine, and *rugby,* a generic term for glues and solvents with addictive fumes.

Holding the roosters feet up, a handler — Bobby tells me this is often his job — removes the leather sheath from the curved, razor-sharp, three-inch spur tied to the right leg of each bird. The men in the pit clear out a space at the center, giving a wide berth to the cocks, which have been known to kill unlucky bystanders with their spurs. The handlers draw the birds close enough to peck at each other and then back off, repeating this three times before dropping the agitated birds to the ground. The effect is instantaneous and explosive: a blur of color, a broad fan of bright green neck feathers, and a flapping of wings as the birds leap upon each other, lunging with the spurs faster than the eye can follow, seeming to become a single chaotic being. The crowd erupts in cheers, faces contorted, eyes bulging, screaming for their favorites. Bobby, utterly in his element, is swept up in the fervor, pounding against the sheet metal and yelling with the throng. In and out of the ring is a scene of pure, animal aggression, unapologetic and unselfconscious.

As the roosters flail in the dust, the men left in the ring leap to stay out of the way of the flashing surgical steel blades. A bird flaps high into the air and brings a blade straight into the feathers of its opponent's back. Blood flies out in an arc, spattering the barrier. Another lunge and a wing is broken, splayed out on the ground as the injured cock drags itself upright, still lunging after its opponent with the working half of its body. A handler picks both up and swings them together for a last desperate round, trying to stoke whatever smoldering fury they still possess. The crowd leans in, cackling and leering, as the cocks are thrown together. One bird manages to get on top of the other and, even with a broken wing, methodically plunges its spur to the hilt three times in its opponent's throat, just beneath the green fan of neck feathers. Both birds flap weakly, kick, and lie still, breasts pulsing, eyes wide. The Cristo picks them both up, and bright blood drips steadily from a beak, turning black in the dust. The birds are drawn together once more but are too weak to be provoked. The Cristo drops the dying loser onto the blood-caked ground and holds the dying winner aloft. The crowd howls. The whole fight has lasted perhaps twenty seconds.

Around the outside of the pit, money changes hands in an exchange of gloating and recrimination at the defeated rooster. With little ceremony, a man carries the loser, still breathing, out of the pit, and lays it across a bloodstained log, where another man with a cleaver hacks off the spur leg with one swing. A boy unties the steel spur from the severed leg and passes it to the next contestant. The bird is plunged headfirst into a can of water boiling on a trash pile, and it flaps once in the water but within a few moments is defeathered and handed to the victor, a trophy for the soup pot on top of his winnings. The champion bird has its spur untied, and just as quickly is whisked off to the "doctor," who sits on a log near the ring. With a needle and thread and packets of powdered antibiotics, the doctor patches the bird up, probing gashes with a finger for internal bleeding before sewing them up. After a month on the mend the rooster will be back in the pit.

In the afternoon we return to the garden. Bobby, back to earth after the glories of the cockpit, sets to work on his neat rows of tomato plants, watering and pulling weeds alongside his wife, who has finished her shift on the dump. If Payatas closes down, as the colonel has promised, Bobby has no interest in finding a new career. As a scavenger he makes his own hours, he works when it pleases him, and, even with the slowdown at the dump, he earns enough to live. The gardening project is a good diversion, and he'll get food and a bit of income from what he's growing. There's a certain irony, which I point out to Klaid, in retraining migrants who have fled the countryside to be farmers again. "It's true," he replies. "There's no opportunity out there. The city is attractive. For a farmer, life on a dumpsite is comparatively easy. This is not a question of quality of life, but a question of survival."

So what does the garden really do? I ask. "It gives them a place to be quiet, to be patient. To garden instead of gamble. I was a community organizer for ten years, and it did nothing because I tried to save the world. People would get transferred to something even worse, a place with no work and no services, beyond the edge of everything. With this project we decided that if we could reach one person at a time, on an individual level, then it is a huge step."

Whether the garden, whatever it brings to the lives of the scavengers, will even continue to exist is an open question. The property is owned by the Madrigals, but there are many who think the most valuable use of the land would be to build housing for the poor, and that a garden is, at best, a quaint diversion. Ging Gonzales, one of the members of the foundation's board, says as much to me as we are driving through Quezon's traffic to a meeting with Sonny Belmonte, the mayor whose face graces the better part of the city's billboards. "How many children could we send to school for the money we are spending on the garden?" she asks me. "The problem is knowing what is the most efficient means of helping."

When we arrive at his office, Belmonte, as smiley in person as he is on billboards, is receiving hundreds of visitors, interest groups from across his enormous slice of the metropolis. Belmonte sits down with us for a few minutes as Klaid clicks through a slide show about the garden project. "This might be a good thing," says the mayor, in a noncommittal way. "Maybe it will give them skills to take back to the provinces with them." In his rapidly expanding city, an exodus of the poorest newcomers would relieve Belmonte of an enormous social headache. I ask him when Payatas is really going to close. "Now we are hoping for January 2007." A few days later, Belmonte and several other metropolitan Manila mayors are named in a lawsuit by environmental groups for failing to close Payatas and other dumpsites. But no amount of arguing, for or against, seems likely to change the fundamental facts on the ground: every single day, seven thousand tons of metropolitan Manila's household garbage must go somewhere. "If you think Payatas is bad," one of the mayor's aides tells me, "you should go see Pier 18."

Pier 18, on the industrial shorefront of Manila's north harbor, lies half-obscured behind a row of shanties that line a frontage road. We inch our way there, in a solid stream of truck traffic, as the cumulonimbus clouds piled over the western rim of the bay unleash a hot downpour. The low-lying road through the Navotas slum fills with knee-deep puddles in a few minutes. The squatter settlements creep right up to the edge of the road, and even the five-foot-wide median has been littered with squatters' scrap-wood shacks and split-bamboo chicken coops, constant traffic within inches on either side. Passing trucks throw up bow wakes, and waves travel along the narrow alleyways, surging right into the ground floors of the houses. Flotsam butts up against rotted walls, and children splash through the muck, lifting their soaked shirts. Several huts are roofed with the stolen signboards of political candidates, and it seems that the sheltering placards provide a far more tangible benefit to the poor than any unachievable campaign promises printed upon them.

The rain passes, and we get out of the taxi and walk past a sign that reads "Pier 18 North Harbor." Pier 18 is an enormous transfer station the size of several football fields where hundreds of trucks from across Manila dump their daily loads to be picked over and consolidated before being shipped out to Montalban. Hundreds of scavengers, a great many of them small children, swarm over the pile, swinging *kalahigs* wildly as each new load is dumped. Trucks plow in and out through the site, and several times I see children, boots suctioned by the mud, nearly fall beneath their wheels. Jumpers scramble up onto the loads and surf the waves of trash as they slide out of the tilting truck beds. Stray dogs and pigs rove over the piles, rooting out rotting food.

I speak to an eight-year-old boy named Gerald, who has a raw gash over his right eye from the swinging trap door of a truck. I ask him where he lives, and he points across the lake of mud to a row of tarp-covered shacks right on the edge of the pier. His parents work here too, and he comes every day after school. He turns and runs as a new pile gets dropped, very nearly getting plowed under by a bulldozer, and squirms his way to the top of the pile with the adults, filling his sack with shocking speed. People follow behind the bulldozers, spearing anything of value churned up by their treads. Teenage boys burn strings of Christmas lights in an old suitcase. There are no rules, no IDs, no flagship social programs or green reclamation, no sense that there is anyone managing or overseeing this chaos. It is the Darwinian free market in its purest and most ruthless form. To witness this makes all the beneficence of the Madrigals and the economic development programs of the World Bank seem like so much well-intentioned folly.

But even in this swampy hell there is a degree of remove, of levity. At the edge of the pier, under a tin roof, a karaoke machine is running, the words spooling out on a screen beneath a shot of a beautiful girl walking on a beach. A young girl in rubber boots, covered with mud, grabs the microphone and starts singing a Filipino pop song in a cracked but totally heartfelt voice. The *mangangalahigs* have distilled survival, and even joy, down to an essence. That life prevails here is a testament to what can be endured; in the midst of squalor, laughter and karaoke can still be heard. Even the landscape insistently offers up signs of regeneration: when we leave the pier, there is a dim rainbow bent over the piled housing of Navotas. North of the slum, the fenced-off dumpsite of Smokey Mountain lies dormant and abandoned, after ten years its slopes already beginning to be reclaimed by grass and shrubs.

On our last day in Payatas, we accept an invitation to stay at the house of Nanay Remy, a frail, toothless woman of seventy-three, her face half-paralyzed by a stroke. She lives in a five-hundred-square-foot compound with twenty-four family members and still works as a *ramblista* on the pile every day. Dozens of rusty box springs fence off the compound, and inside are several neat huts and a small garden, which Remy planted after her training at Madrigal. As I talk with Bobby and Klaid, Remy serves a feast of fried fish and rice and salad from her garden plots. She has lived in Payatas for fifteen years and doesn't have a clue where they'll all go if the dump closes down. She wants to stay together with her people. The family is the core of Filipino society, and population numbers are often discussed in terms of families rather than individuals. She has two of her tiny, wide-eyed grandchildren in her lap. Their mother, a *shabu* addict, has abandoned them, and Remy feeds them with her fingers as she retells the history of her life: the evacuation from the Visayas islands during the war, the years squatting in the Tondo slum, a husband lost to drink, children and grandchildren raised, the endurance of a long life here. Her story isn't a plea for pity, and she isn't asking for anything except what the trash heap offers up.

Remy has cleared out one of her bamboo and sheet-metal huts for us. I lie on the hard floor, listening as the evening crows of a dozen roosters echo through the village, doomed some Sunday to be called to the pit by the Cristo. At the open window the equatorial darkness falls like a curtain, and across the creek the mountain of the dumpsite rears black beneath a net of stars. Against the silhouette of the garbage mountain, a faint line of lights works its way upward. They are the homemade headlamps of the night shift tracing their way up the pile. Reaching the top, they spread themselves out, shining their lights on the shifting ground to begin their search. Beneath the wide night sky those tiny human sparks split and rearrange, like a constellation fallen to Earth, as if uncertain of what hopeful legend they are meant to invoke.

DAVID RAKOFF

Streets of Sorrow

FROM *Condé Nast Traveler*

SUPERMAN HAS TAKEN THE MORNING OFF. Although appearing among us in mufti, he is immediately identifiable by his square jaw and the comma of dark hair upon his forehead. He greets with an affable hello the other Hollywood Boulevard regulars who have gathered, along with a small crowd of tourists, outside the classical façade of the former Masonic Temple, now the TV studio where Jimmy Kimmel does his evening talk show. The USC Trojan Marching Band, or at least a skeleton crew thereof, goes through its paces, a casually synchronized, loose-limbed routine in which its members instrumentally exhort us to do a little dance, make a little love, and above all, get down tonight. Superman bops his head, enjoying his moments of freedom. In a while he will have to put on his blue tights and red Speedo and go to work, posing for pictures with the tourists in front of Grauman's Chinese Theatre. Maybe he'll stop on the way at the Coffee Bean & Tea Leaf, at the corner of Hollywood and Orange. Batman and the Cat in the Hat go there sometimes.

Suddenly, from the doors of the theater, just behind the Trojans, emerges a chubby and cheerful fellow. Completely unconnected to the proceedings on the street, he is dressed in a cheap red satin Satan costume. Dancing in time to the music, he beckons to us, crowing delightedly, "Worship me! Worship me!"

But we are here neither for the Man of Steel nor the Prince of Darkness. We have come this morning to witness the consecration of the newest star on Hollywood's Walk of Fame. The "star" in question on this dull April morning is local radio personality Dan Avey, who will join the two-thousand-plus others — from the greats to the somewhat-less-than-greats to the downright obscure — in that characteristic luncheon-meat-pink-against-lustrous-black-terrazzo-and-brass immortality. The Hollywood Chamber of Commerce, the organization that administers the Walk, has set up a steel barrier to separate those with a personal stake in the ceremony from the gawkers and hoi polloi. It is a hopeful gesture.

"It's almost like going to your own funeral," says Avey, after the brief tributes from fellow radio announcers. The star is unveiled. Avey's friends and family applaud. A local crazy snaps photos, his straw fedora banded with a braid of blue and white balloons — the kind birthday clowns twist into animal and flower shapes — and his ears sporting very large cubic zirconiums. He is trying to get a knot of puzzled German tourists to move out of the way, but he doesn't speak so much as squeak out high-pitched gibberish, which seems only to increase his frustration, as the Germans simply stare at him. Perplexed Northern Europeans — hereafter PNEs — turn out to be just one of the mainstays of the area, along with leafleting evangelicals, sex workers, harmless ambulant schizophrenics, and beat cops.

There are some places where an intrinsic melancholy might be reason enough to stay away, I suppose, although I can't think of any. I love Miss Havisham places, where a bloodied-but-unbowed nobility valiantly tries to maintain itself in the face of reality. *See?* they seem to be saying, *I wasn't always like this!* Even though Hollywood Boulevard recently underwent a major urban renewal — a charge led by the building of the Kodak Theatre Complex, current home to the Oscars and the *American Idol* finals — the neighborhood's dilapidated, honky-tonk charms are legion. They lie in the vestiges of its storied past, which endure obstinately: Grauman's Egyptian Theatre, currently the home of the American Cinematheque, with its sandstone forecourt and hieroglyphics, looking like something straight out of the Valley of the Kings; the polychrome plaster opulence of the El Capitan Theatre, restored and now owned by Disney; the affronted yet intact dignity of Marlene Dietrich's star, which sits perhaps for eternity in front of Greco's New York Pizzeria; similarly the star of June Havoc, baby sister to Gypsy Rose Lee, which welcomes shoppers to the rubber and fetish extravaganza of Pleasure's Treasures. Only a heartless ogre would fail to be touched by a protective affection for the weary imprecision of the store that announces, "Almost Everything $15 or Less." Hollywood Boulevard makes you want to take care of it.

It was ever thus, it seems. Gleaming new theme restaurants and chain stores fail to get at what has always been the essence of the neighborhood. Like other cultural institutions whose heyday is perpetually a thing of the past — reports of the death of the Broadway musical, which have been around as long as musicals themselves, come to mind — Hollywood Boulevard has always been a little bit sad. The Walk of Fame, for example, was conceived as a means of sprucing up the neighborhood as far back as 1960, when they, *ahem*, laid the first star, Joanne Woodward's. Even further back, the writer Nathanael West lived in a hotel on the boulevard and set his 1939 novel, *The Day of the Locust*, in and around its environs. West's dark tale of Hollywood concludes gruesomely with two senseless murders and a frenzied crowd out of control, whipped into a fervor of lawlessness by the sweeping klieg lights and bottlenecking barricades of a movie premiere at Kahn's Pleasure Palace, a thinly veiled reference to Sid Grauman's Chinese Theatre.

Things are a good deal tamer on the day I visit, as tourists mill about the theater's courtyard, posing with costumed characters — for the most part fictional superheroes as well as a late-Vegas-vintage Elvis — and looking over the hand- and footprints of Hollywood immortals. The tradition supposedly began when silent film star Norma Talmadge was walking in front of the theater and inadvertently stepped in some wet cement. The most popular square remains the joint one of Marilyn Monroe and Jane Russell, an honor presumably conferred by the number of people posing in front of it. No one is standing by the *Gentlemen Prefer Blondes* costars this morning, although a young black woman has her picture taken with her hands nestled in the prints of Denzel Washington. Elsewhere, a five-year-old Scandinavian boy (see earlier reference to PNEs) dutifully places his tiny mitts into the depressions made by Depression-era cutie-pie Joan Blondell. You know how kindergartners go mad for *Gold Diggers of 1933*.

Grauman's Chinese is one of the loveliest and most impressive buildings it has ever been my privilege to enter. If you go to Los Angeles and do not see it, you are a fool, as I was the first dozen-and-a-half times I visited the town. Apparently it's an oversight most people make, because there are only four of us on the tour. Where most opulent movie palaces are great meringues of neo-Versailles frippery, Grauman's Chinese is a lavish exercise in Orientalist escape. The murals that adorn the walls and ceilings of the place, skillful and beautiful traditional Chinese ornamental scenes, were done by Guangzhou-born actor Keye Luke, most famous as "Number One Son" to non-Chinese actor Warner Oland in the Charlie Chan films. It turns out that virtuosic multitasking is part of the Grauman legacy. The east wall of the theater is painted with a silver mural of bamboo groves and palm fronds and assorted other shore-leave ornaments. It was done by Xavier Cugat, of all people, and it's really very charming.

More movie premieres are held in Grauman's than in any other theater in the world; it hosted its first, Cecil B. DeMille's *King of Kings*, in 1927. The prime seats in the theater are in rows seven, eight, and nine, reserved for whoever is starring in that night's film. Indicating a seat in this hallowed section, our tour guide tells us, "Ray Romano sat here for *Ice Age*." Then, so as to assure us that all the seats are good, he points to the front of the house. "For the premiere of *Along Came Polly*, John Travolta and his lovely wife, Kelly Preston, sat down there."

Our guide. Sigh. In his cheap tuxedo, with his mild manner, weak chin, and a face scarified by the ravages of adolescence, he is the embodiment of a doomed and guileless purity; the hapless pawn set upon by the townspeople in a misguided riot of mob mentality. Or perhaps I've got Nathanael West on the brain. But he does seem like the classic victim. Even his evident love for the theater is given short shrift by the powers that be, because throughout the tour the Grauman's sound system vomits out a meaningless and distractingly loud montage of partial commercials, snippets of songs, and movie trailers.

We are led outside and up the outdoor escalator of the minimall/theater complex to the adjoining Mann Chinese 6 theater. We are now being given a tour of a multiplex built in 2001. My underpants are older than the Mann Chinese 6. A greasy usher opens the door for us on the second floor. "Welcome to the VIP area," he says with a leer. (OK, he's not that greasy and not really leering, but there is a smoke-and-mirrors shadiness to the "value-added" aspect of this leg of the tour, and, let me reiterate, we don't have to be here! Grauman's by itself is sublime and sufficient!) The VIP area is neither all that *V* nor all that *I*. It's just a loungy part of the theater where, for twenty dollars, you can sit and order concessions and they'll be delivered to your seat. Or you can play chess or checkers or read a book, our guide tells us, pointing to a wall where there isn't a book in sight. "Go ahead and sit in one of the chairs so you can feel what it's like," he says. We all remain standing.

The tour ends, as such things do, in the gift shop, where we see two old projectors from Grauman's, which are kind of cool, and also two wax figures of Chinese mannequins that once stood in the theater lobby. Rubbing them used to be considered good luck. Our guide then lets us in on a secret. "There are many people who come to the theater and see how authentic it is and are under the mistaken impression that Sid Grauman was himself Chinese. He wasn't," he says, disabusing us of an apparently oft-held Hollywood myth. "He was Irish and Jewish." Who, I wonder, are the genius demographers who think that someone named Sid Grauman was Chinese? But my unspoken outrage is drowned out by "Sugar Pie Honey Bunch," which blasts over the gift shop sound system throughout his talk.

A little spent, I return to my hotel. Luckily, I am staying right across the street at the Hollywood Roosevelt, a beautiful building erected in 1927. A cool, dark Spanish colonial folly of a place, with a central lobby that has a tile floor and a splashing fountain, it's like Norma Desmond's house in *Sunset Boulevard*. The similarities don't stop with the architecture. There are moments when it distinctly feels like things are being run by a delusional Gloria Swanson. The frustrations are minute but widespread. The wooden ledge that runs the length of my room and doubles as my headboard is gray with dust and remains so throughout my stay. Every time I ask reception to call me a cab, I am told affable words to the effect of "Right away"; my request is then radioed out to one of the attendants in the driveway not twenty feet away, indicating my imminent arrival in, oh, about five seconds, along with a description of what I am wearing. I emerge from the hotel into a veritable scrum of attendants with headsets and whistles, all ready to be of service, and I am invisible. The sense one gets at the Roosevelt is that they have bigger fish to fry. Or cuter and younger fish, at any rate. The very first Academy Awards ceremony was held at the Roosevelt in 1929, and the hotel is once more at the burning center of movie star currency. At the time I was staying there, young women in skinny jeans and stilettos, accompanied by their men in untucked striped oxford shirts and premium denim, were flocking each night to Teddy's, the Roosevelt's bar, a hopping establishment that has since been closed down. The writing was on the wall even during my stay because, just prior to my arrival, Teddy's had been embroiled in a minor scandal when "nightlife producer" Amanda Scheer Demme was dismissed, ostensibly for allowing (I am shocked, shocked!) underage drinking by young celebrities. There were further accusations against the impresario that she had made the actual guests of the hotel feel unwelcome at Teddy's (again, permit my organs to rupture in surprise). I wouldn't know, since I couldn't find the place no matter how many hallways I tried. I could hear the thumping of the sound system each day starting at dusk. I entered many a disused ballroom thinking that this must be the way, but no luck. To this day, I cannot tell you where it is, or was. Does the Roosevelt have a gym? I have no idea. I do know that there is a pool, apparently one whose bottom and sides were painted by David Hockney. I've seen pictures in magazines, and it's quite pretty — plus, the juxtapositional joke of Hockney applying paint to the very object he's famous for rendering in paint is amusing — but again, no sign in the elevator telling me where it might be and a staff that can seem downright ivory-billed in its elusiveness.

The exclusion I feel at the Roosevelt Hotel is not unlike living in the apartment directly beneath Valhalla, a feeling only amplified one morning when I go across the street to Coffee Bean & Tea Leaf, where Thor is standing outside holding a latte. His helmet is a plastic rendition of beaten metal and animal horns, with a fall of synthetic flaxen hair sewn onto the inside edge. The locks spill over his "bare" shoulders, which are in reality the sleeves of his costume, a shiny flesh-colored fabric. The musculature, meant to mimic the bulging biceps and ropy forearms of the Norse god of war, is sewn directly into the garment. But the stitches around the pillowy inserts are visible, and the whole thing bags and wrinkles around his skinny arms. "You guys drinking later?" he asks his friends, his mouth a checkerboard of missing and intact teeth.

He could use the kind of makeover once promised in the Johnny Mercer song (". . . if you think that you can be an actor, see Mr. Factor, he'd make a monkey look good. Within a half an hour, you'll look like Tyrone Power. Hooray for Hollywood"), and he'd be in luck, because the original Max Factor Building is just down the street. A perfect pink Deco boîte of a building, picked out here and there with golden plaster detailing of fabric swags, it is terribly chic and female and looks like an enormous jewel box from a Busby Berkeley number, whose lid might at any moment open to reveal five hundred pairs of legs dancing on a mirror-finish floor. To look around it is to smell pressed powder and Final Net with your eyes. The ancient woman who methodically takes my money and hands me my change with a painstaking if glacial precision is still sporting a hairstyle straight out of *Swing Time.* She might well have been one of the marcelled beauties who paraded these halls back when it was still a salon. It has since been turned into a museum dedicated to Hollywood history, the ground floor concerning Max Factor's specific role in the dream factory. A series of small rooms is devoted, respectively, to a different hair color and that shade's most iconic stars. The For Blondes Only room claims Lana Turner and Marilyn, among others. Brunettes boasts Liz Taylor as its figurehead. The For Redheads Only room loves Lucy, naturally. And then I come upon a room reserved for "Brownettes," which is a new one on me and sounds like nothing so much as the affectionate name one might give a beloved and highly effective barbiturate. How fitting then that the Brownette for the ages is none other than Judy Garland.

I keep up the period perfection and take lunch at Musso & Frank's, a grill a little farther east. Opened in 1919, the restaurant makes an appearance in *The Day of the Locust.* The interior is a relief from the California sunshine outside, with dark-wood booths and a mural of a leafy New England in autumn. By all rights, I should order something authentically carnivorous and insouciant, like a rare steak and a gin martini, but it is midday in late spring and I opt instead for a somewhat healthier Caesar salad with chicken, electively excluding myself from a true Musso & Frank's experience. I speak too soon, because my waiter, Manuel, who has worked there for thirty-plus years, makes my salad from scratch right at the bar, a courtly procedure involving a bowl wiped with a garlic clove, the flourished brandishing of a raw egg and anchovy fillets. Throughout the theatrical preparation, Manuel continues his conversation with a woman sitting a few seats down, clearly a regular. The years have taken their toll, and her back is curved over toward the wood of the bar, perhaps a tribute to the curling prawns in her cocktail glass. Osteoporosis hasn't dampened her spirits any. Her laugh is freely and frequently unleashed. It is the sound of rocks in a blender, a granite smoothie.

An afternoon rain has dispersed the tourists along the street. The gray light smooths out the edges and polishes the street beautifully. As evening approaches, I take a taxi (no thanks to the Roosevelt) to see friends. The fresh green breast of the Hollywood Hills rises just to the north of Hollywood Boulevard, and the cab winding its way up the roads of Laurel Canyon is an antidote to the clatter of the street. The houses aren't the behemoth pleasure domes of Beverly Hills or Brentwood but rather storybook sweet, with eaves overhung with flowering clematis. In the violet dusk, the vegetation seems to become an even more inviting velvet green, with the magenta bougainvillea and vivid red flowers of the bottlebrush trees standing out. It is all as calming and luxuriant as a Rousseau painting: the perfect break. When it is time to return later that night, the city lies just over the escarpment like a jeweled carpet. It seems so exciting, I can't wait to get back down the hill.

When I first arrived, I found the Walk of Fame, with its embarrassment of unrecognizable names, the very breadth of the enshrined, unutterably depressing. At every step was a cruel reminder of the heartlessness of time and tide. For every Hedy Lamarr to remind you of what a brilliant, patent-holding beauty she was, there is a Barbara LaMarr to keep you cognizant that someday you, too, will be dead and the subject of a great cosmic shrugging "Who?" (Barbara LaMarr, "The Girl Who Was Too Beautiful," best friend of ZaSu Pitts, was one of the first in Hollywood to succumb to drugs, in 1926. She was already dead more than thirty years before they even started the Walk.) But as the days have passed and I have spent more and more time with the pavement, I have revised my opinion. I suppose the way to think of it is as if the pipe fitters' union were honoring one of its own. It's just by happy accident that some of its members happen to be globally famous and recognizable. The custom has sprung up elsewhere: on Fashion Avenue in New York, I walk over Claire McCardell's and Norman Norell's plaques; in the Brooklyn Botanic Garden, that borough's native-born Ruby Stevens, better known as Barbara Stanwyck, has a paving stone among the greenery; on Toronto's King Street is Canada's Walk of Fame, about which 'nuff said. And in each place, the overriding sense one has is of, if not having intruded exactly, then at least being witness to something that ultimately doesn't involve one. A Walk of Fame by its nature turns out to be a very local phenomenon.

I take one final stroll over to Vine on my last morning on the Boulevard. Most of the businesses are still shuttered. The tourists have yet to arrive at Grauman's. I pass Dan Avey's star once again. It is all of four days old, but I see that it is patched. No doubt it left the workshop patched. There, against the salmon pink of the five-pointed star, is a cloud of darker red, like a bruise or the small beating heart of a tiny creature. There is such hope and poignancy, an almost animal frailty in that blemish, that I stop in my tracks for a minute. People have been coming out West with stars in their eyes for so long, and for just as long, some have returned to where they came from, their hopes dashed. But if the fulfillment of one's dreams is the only referendum on whether they are beautiful or worth dreaming, then no one would wish for anything. And that would be so much sadder.

GEORGE SAUNDERS

The Incredible Buddha Boy

FROM *GQ*

LAST DECEMBER, I got an e-mail from my editor at *GQ*. A fifteen-year-old boy in Nepal had supposedly been meditating for the past seven months without any food or water. Would I like to look into this?

I went online. The boy's name was Ram Bahadur Bomjon. He was sitting in the roots of a pipal tree near the Indian border. The site was being overrun by pilgrims, thousands a week, who were calling this boy "the new Buddha." He'd twice been bitten by poisonous snakes; both times he'd refused medicine and cured himself via meditation. Skeptics said he was being fed at night behind a curtain, that his guru was building himself a temple, that his parents were building themselves a mansion, that the Maoist rebels, in on the hoax, were raking in tens of thousands of dollars in donations.

I e-mailed my editor back: I was pretty busy, what with the teaching and all, besides which Christmas break was coming up and I hadn't been to the gym once the preceding semester, plus it would be great to, uh, get an early start on my taxes.

Then we embarked on the usual Christmas frenzy, but I couldn't get this boy off my mind. At parties, I noted two general reactions to the statement *Hey, I heard this kid in Nepal has been meditating uninterruptedly in the jungle for the past seven months without any food or water.*

One type of American — let's call them Realists — will react by making a snack-related joke ("So he finally gets up, and turns out he's sitting on a big pile of Butterfinger wrappers!") and will then explain that it's physically impossible to survive even one week without food or water, much less seven months.

A second type — let's call them Believers — will say, "Wow, that's amazing," they wish they could go to Nepal tomorrow, and will then segue into a story about a transparent spiritual being who once appeared on a friend's pool deck with a message about world peace.

Try it: go up to the next person you see, and say, *Hey, I heard this kid in Nepal has been meditating uninterruptedly in the jungle for the past seven months without any food or water.*

See what they say.

Or say it to yourself, and see what you say.

What I said, finally, was: This I have to see.

Austrian Airlines is big on hot rolls. Red-clad flight attendants continually tout their hot rolls in the accents of many nations, including, one feels, nations that haven't actually been founded yet. ("Hod roolz?" "Hat rahls?" "Hoot rowls?") The in-flight safety video is troubling: it's animated and features a Sims-like guy with what looks like a skinless, skeletal death's-head who keeps turning to leer at a slim Sims lady who keeps looking away, alarmed, while trying to get her long legs tucked away somewhere so Death can't see them. Later she slides down the emergency slide, holding a Sims baby, Death still pursuing her.

Ancient Mariner–style, my seatmate, a Kosovar, tells me about a Serbian paramilitary group called the Black Hand that left a childhood friend of his on a hillside, "cut into tiny pieces." During the occupation, he says, the Serbs often killed babies in front of their parents. He is kindly, polite, awed by the horrible things he's seen, grateful that, as an American citizen, he no longer has to worry about murdered babies or hacked-up friends, except, it would appear, in memory, constantly.

Story told, he goes off to sleep.

But I can't. I'm too uncomfortable. I'm mad at myself for eating two roolz during the last Round of Roolz, roolz that seem to have instantaneously made my pants tighter. I've already read all my books and magazines, already stood looking out the little window in the flight-attendant area, already complimented a severe blond flight attendant on Austrian Airlines' excellent service, which elicited an oddly Austrian reaction: she immediately seemed to find me reprehensible and weak.

On the bright side, only six more hours on this plane, then two hours in the Vienna airport and an eight-hour flight to Katmandu.

I decide to close my eyes and sit motionless, to make the time pass.

Somebody slides up their window shade and, feeling the change in light on my eyelids, I am filled with sudden curiosity: has the shade really been lifted? By someone? Gosh, who was it? What did they look like? What were they trying to accomplish by lifting the shade? I badly want to open my eyes and confirm that a shade has indeed been lifted, by someone, for some purpose. Then I notice a sore patch on the tip of my tongue and feel a strong desire to interrupt my experiment to record the interesting sore-tongue observation in my notebook. Then I begin having Restless Leg Syndrome, Restless Arm Syndrome, and even a little Restless Neck Syndrome. Gosh, am I thirsty. Boy, is my breath going to be bad when this stupid experiment is over. I imagine a waterfall of minty water flowing into my mouth, a waterfall that does not have to be requested via the stern flight attendant but just comes on automatically when I press a button on the overhead console marked MINTY WATER.

The mind is a machine that is constantly asking: What would I prefer? Close your eyes, refuse to move, and watch what your mind does. What it does is become discontent with that-which-is. A desire arises, you satisfy that desire, and another arises in its place. This wanting and rewanting is an endless cycle for which, turns out, there is already a name: samsara. Samsara is at the heart of the vast human carnival: greed, neurosis, mad ambition, adultery, crimes of passion, the hacking to death of a terrified man on a hillside in the name of A More Pure and Thus Perfect Nation — and all of this takes place because we believe we will be made happy once our desires have been satisfied.

I know this. But still I'm full of desire. I want my legs to stop hurting. I want something to drink. I even kind of want another hot roll.

Seven months, I think? The kid has been sitting there *seven months*?

*

We arrive in Katmandu just before midnight. The city is as dark a city as I've ever seen: no streetlights, no neon, each building lit by one or two small bulbs or a single hanging lantern. It's like a medieval city, smoke-smelling, the buildings leaning into narrow unsquared roads. It's as if the cab has been time-transported back to the age of kings and squalor, and we are making our way through the squalor to the palace, which is the Hyatt. A garbage-eating cow appears in our headlights. We pass a lonely green-lit mod ATM kiosk that looks like it's been dropped in from the future.

The Hyatt lobby is empty except for rows of Buddha statues: a maze with no guests. The Business Center manageress not only has heard of the boy but is also of the opinion that he is being fed by snakes. Their venom, she says, is actually milk to him.

I go to bed, sleep the odd post-trip sleep from which you wake up unsure of where, or who, you are.

I throw open the curtains, and there is Katmandu: a sprawling Seussian city where prayer flags extend from wacky tower to strange veranda to tilting spire-of-uncertain-purpose. Beyond Seuss City: the Himalayas, pure, Platonically white, the white there was before other colors were invented. In the foreground is the massive, drained, under-repair Hyatt pool, in a field of dead, dry Hyatt grass, and a woman tending to the first of an endless row of shrubs, in a vignette that should be titled Patience Will Prevail.

I take a walk.

The level of noise, energy, and squalor of Katmandu makes even the poorest section of the most wild-ass American city seem placid and urban-planned. Some guys squat in a trash-strewn field, inexplicably beating the crap out of what looks like purple cotton candy. A woman whose face has been burned or torn off walks past me, running some small errand, an errand made heartbreaking by the way she carries herself, which seems to signify: I'm sure this will be a very good day! Here is a former Pepsi kiosk, now barbed-wired and manned by Nepalese soldiers armed for Maoists; here a Ping-Pong table made of slate, with brick legs. I cross a mythical bleak vacant lot I've seen in dreams, a lot surrounded by odd Nepali brick high rises like a lake surrounded by cliffs, if the lake were dry and had a squatting, peeing lady in the middle of it. Averting my eyes, I see another woman, with baby, and teeth that jut, terrifyingly, straight out of her mouth, horizontally, as if her gums had loosened up and she had tilted her teeth out at ninety degrees. She stretches out a hand, jiggles the baby with the other, as if to say: *This baby, these teeth, come on, how are we supposed to live?*

Off to one side of the road is a strange sunken hollow — like a shallow basement excavation — filled with rows of wooden benches on which hundreds of the dustiest men, women, and children imaginable wait for something with the sad patience of animals. It's like a bus station, but there's no road in sight. Several Westerners huddle near a gate, harried-looking, pissy, admitting people or not. A blind man is expelled from the lot and lingers by the gate, acting casual, like he was not just expelled. What's going on here? Three hundred people in a kind of open-air jail, no blind guys allowed.

I go in, walk through the crowd ("Good mahning how on you I am fahn!"), and corner a harried Western woman with several mouth sores.

"What is all this?" I say.

"Soup kitchen," she says.

"For . . .?" I say.

"Anybody who needs," she says.

And there are many who need: two hundred, three hundred people a sitting, she says, two sittings a day, never an empty seat.

This, I think, explains the expelled blind man: he came too late.

Life is suffering, the Buddha said, by which he did not mean *Every moment of life is unbearable* but rather *All happiness/rest/contentment is transient; all appearances of permanence are illusory.*

The faceless woman, the odd-toothed woman, the dusty elderly people with babies in their laps, waiting for a meal, the blind guy by the gate, feigning indifference: in Nepal, it occurs to me, life *is* suffering, nothing esoteric about it.

Then, at the end of a road too narrow for a car, appears the famous Boudha stupa: huge, pale, glacial, rising out of the surrounding dusty squalor like Hope itself.

A stupa is a huge three-dimensional Buddhist prayer aid, usually dome-shaped, often containing some holy relic, a bone or lock of hair from the historical Buddha. This particular stupa has been accreting for many centuries; some accounts date it back to 500 A.D. It is ringed by a circular street filled with hundreds of circumambulating Buddhist pilgrims from all over Nepal, Tibet, Bhutan,

India: wild costumes in every hue of purple, red, and orange; odd piercings and hairstyles. A shop blares a version of the *om mani padme hung* chant over and over, all day. A woman with a goiter the size of a bowling ball gossips with some friends.

The stupa is multileveled, terraced; people circumambulate on each level. Pigeon shadows flee across multiple planar surfaces, along with the shadows of thousands of prayer flags. Barefoot boys lug buckets of yellowish whitewash to the top level and sling these across the surface of the dome, leaving jagged yellow thunderbolts. The only sounds are birdsong and the occasional clanging of a bell and, in the distance, a power saw.

I do lap after lap, praying for everybody I know. For me, this has been a tough year: a beloved uncle died, my parents' house was destroyed by Katrina, a kindhearted cousin shipped off to Iraq, a car accident left my teenage daughter sobbing by the side of the road on a dark, freezing night, I've found myself loving my wife of eighteen years more than I'd even known you could love another human being — a good thing, except that it involves a terrifying downside: the realization that there must someday come a parting.

Today, at the stupa, it occurs to me that this low-level ambient fear constitutes a decent working definition of the human: a human being is someone who, having lived a while, becomes terrified and, having become terrified, deeply craves an end to the fear.

All of this — the stupa, the millions of people who have circumambulated it during the hundreds of years since it was built (in Shakespeare's time, while Washington lived, during the Civil War, as Glenn Miller played), the shops, the iconography, the statues, the *tangka* paintings, the chanting, the hundreds of thousands of human lives spent in meditation — all of this began when one man walked into the woods, sat down, and tried to end his fear by doing something purely internal: working on his mind.

As I'm leaving the stupa, a kid drags me into a little room to the side of the main gate. Inside are two massive prayer wheels. He shows me how to spin them. Three laps is recommended for maximum blessing. In one corner sits a midget in monk's robes, praying.

"Lama," my guide says as we pass.

On the second lap, he points out a collection of images of great Buddhist saints, stuck above a small window. Here is the Dalai

Lama. Here is Guru Rinpoche, who first brought Buddhism to Tibet. Here is Bomjon, the meditating boy.

The photo shows a boy of about twelve: a chubby crewcut smiling little guy, shy but proud: like a Little Leaguer, but instead of a baseball uniform, he's wearing monk's robes.

"Bomjon," I say.

"You are very talent!" says my guide.

Back at the Hyatt, I meet Subel, my translator, a kindly, media-savvy twenty-three-year-old who looks like a Nepali Robert Downey Jr. We take a terrifying ride through Katmandu on his motorcycle to a darkened travel agency, where we buy plane tickets by candlelight; Katmandu is under a program called "load shedding," which, in the name of conservation, cuts power to a different part of town every night. The agent processes our tickets sacramentally in the light from three red candles tilted on sheets of newspaper.

Given Nepal's political situation, there's something ominous about the darkened travel agency, a suggestion of bleaker conditions soon to come.

More than ten thousand Nepalis have died in the past ten years in an ongoing war between the monarchy and the Maoists. Over the past three years, the new king has basically canceled the burgeoning but inefficient democracy and seized back all power. A week after I leave, he will arrest opposition leaders, and the most serious attacks yet on Katmandu will take place.

Over dinner, Subel (like some prerevolutionary Russian intellectual, a Herzen or Belinsky, personally offended by the cruelty of his government) gets tears in his eyes telling me about a twenty-year-old Nepali woman who died in a distant airport, unable to get to the Katmandu hospital because the inefficient airline canceled all flights for three days straight; tells about the arrogant Nepali soldiers who pulled over two friends of his, singers, and made them sing on the street as the soldiers laughed at them. He doesn't want to ever leave Nepal, he says, unless in doing so he can acquire a useful skill and come back and "make some differences."

The country is scared, wired, suffering, dreading an imminent explosion that will take a catastrophically poor country and turn it into a catastrophically poor country in a state of civil war. In Katmandu it seems everybody knows about the meditating boy, follows news of him avidly, believes he's doing what he's said to be doing, and wishes him luck. They feel him, you sense, as a kind of savior-from-within, a radical new solution to festering old problems. Political pragmatism exhausted, they're looking for something, anything, to save them.

A friend of Subel's tells me he hopes the meditating boy will do "something good for this country," meaning, to my ear, *something good for this poor, beaten-down country, which I dearly love.*

Next morning we fly to the southern village of Simra in a submarinelike plane that has, for a sun visor, a piece of newspaper taped to the windshield. The seats are webbed and metal-framed like lawn chairs, the floor made of carpetless dented metal. We pass, barely, over one-room farms perched atop cartoonishly steep mountains, entire spreads consisting of just a postage-stamp-sized green terrace dug out of a gray mountainside. From Simra we take a jeep to Birgunj and spend a restless night in a Gogolian hotel where the bathroom lights buzz even when off, and I am perplexed by a mysterious panel of seven switches that never seem to control the same light twice.

Next morning we're off to see the boy.

We head back through Simra by minivan and then beyond, through a swirl of the maddest poverty: girls plod out of deep woods with stacks of huge leaves on their backs to feed some animal; a woman squats to piss, yards away from a muddy pond where another woman draws water; men pound metal things with other metal things; dirty kids are sniffed by dirty dogs as dogs and kids stand in trash.

After a couple of hours, we pull off into a kind of gravel staging area overhung with red welcome banners. On a large billboard — the only one I've seen all morning — a personified condom gives an enraptured young couple some advice out of its jauntily tilted receptacle tip: "Please, enjoy safe sex!"

"Is this it?" I say.

"This is it," Subel says.

Beyond the staging area, the road goes single-vehicle, double-rutted. I try taking notes, but the road is too bumpy. *CRWLFF!* I write, *FHWUED??*

The jungle gets denser; a dry riverbed on the right disappears into the trees. Finally, we reach a kind of minivillage of crude wooden stalls. Boy-related postcards and framed photos and pamphlets are for sale, along with flowers and scarves to present as offerings. We leave the van and walk along a dirt road. Pilgrim-related garbage lines the ditches on either side. A TV on a rickety roadside table blares a Bollywood video: a woman so sexy she captivates a shipful of genial sailors. At a climactic moment, she drops backward into a giant cup of tea, causing a blind man to lose his treasured burlap sack.

A mile farther on, we leave our shoes in a kind of Shoe Corral, take a narrow path worn smooth by tens of thousands of pilgrim feet. The path passes through the roots of a large pipal tree hung with pictures of the boy. A quarter-mile more and we reach a tree-posted sign in Nepali, requesting quiet and forbidding flash photography, especially flash photography aimed at the meditating boy. Beyond the sign, seven or eight recently arrived pilgrims stand at a gate in a barbed-wire fence, craning to see the boy while stuffing small bills into a wooden donation box mounted on the fence.

Though I can't see him from here, he's *there*, right over there somewhere, maybe five hundred feet away, in that exact cluster of trees.

I step through the pilgrims, to the fence, and look inside.

Online accounts say that at night a curtain is drawn around the boy. This is presumably how he's being fed: at night, behind the curtain. So I expect to see the drawn-back curtain hanging from . . . what? The tree itself? Or maybe they've built some kind of structure into the tree: an adjacent room, a kind of backstage area — a place where his followers hang out and keep the food they're sneaking him at night.

In my projection of it, the site resembles the only large-capacity outdoor venue I'm familiar with: a rock concert, with the boy at center stage.

I step through the pilgrims, to the fence, and look inside.

The first impression is zoolike. You are looking into an Enclosure. Inside the Enclosure are dozens of smallish pipal trees festooned with a startling density of prayer flags (red, green, yellow, many faded to white from the sun and rain). This Enclosure also has a vaguely military feel: something recently and hastily constructed, with security in mind.

I scan the Enclosure, looking for That Which Is Enclosed. Nothing. I look closer, focusing on three or four larger trees that, unlike the smaller trees, have the characteristic flaring pipal roots. This too feels zoolike: the scanning, the rescanning, the sudden sense of Ah, *there* he is!

Because there he is.

At this distance (about two hundred feet), it's hard to distinguish where the boy's body ends and the tree roots begin. I can make out his black hair, one arm, one shoulder.

The effect is now oddly crèche-like. You are glimpsing an ancient vignette that will someday become mythic but that for now is occurring in real time, human-scaled, warts and all: small, sloppy concrete blobs at the base of the fence posts; an abandoned treehouse-like platform near the boy's tree; a red plastic chair midway between the two fences.

No secret tree-adjacent room.

No curtain, and nowhere to hang a curtain, although there is a kind of prayer-flag sleeve about ten feet above the boy's head that could conceivably be slid down at night.

There's nobody inside the Enclosure but the boy.

And a young monk standing near the gate. The monk's bangs appear bowl-cut. He's wearing a St. Francis–evoking robe. There is something striking about him, an odd spiritual intensity/charisma. He appears very young and very old at the same time. There is a suggestion of the extraterrestrial about his head-body ratio, his posture, his quality of birdlike concentration.

Between the gate and the inner fence is a wide dirt path leading up to where the boy is sitting. Only dignitaries and journalists are allowed inside the Enclosure. Subel has assured me we'll be able to get in.

I sit on a log. What I'll do is hang out here for an hour or so, get my bearings, take a few notes on the general site layout, and —

"OK, man," Subel says tersely. "We go in now."

"Now?" I say.

"Uh, if you want to go in?" Subel says. "Now is it."

Meaning: Now or never, bro. I just barely talked you in.

The crowd parts. Some Village Guy — head of a Village Committee formed to maintain the site and provide security for the boy — unlocks the gate. The young monk looks me over. He's not suspicious exactly; protective, maybe. He makes me feel (or I make me feel) that I'm disturbing the boy for frivolous reasons, like the embodiment of Western Triviality, field rep for the Society of International Travel Voyeurs.

We step inside, followed by a gray-haired lama in purple robes. The lama and the young monk start down a wide path that leads to the inner fence, ending directly in front of, and about fifty feet away from, the boy.

Subel and I follow.

My mouth is dry, and I have a sudden feeling of gratitude/reverence/terror. What a privilege. Oh God, I have somehow underestimated the gravity of this place and moment. I am potentially at a great religious site, in the original, mythic time: at Christ's manger, say, with Shakyamuni at Bodh Gaya, watching Moses come down from the Mount. I don't want to go any farther, actually. We're in the boy's sight line now, if somebody with eyes closed can be said to have a sight line, closing fast, walking directly at him. It's quieter and tenser than I could have imagined. We are walking down the aisle of a silent church toward a stern, judging priest.

We reach the inner fence: as far as anyone is allowed to go.

At this distance, I can really see him. His quality of nonmotion is startling. His head doesn't move. His arms, hands, don't move. Nothing moves. His chest does not constrict/expand with breathing. He could be dead. He could be carved from the same wood as the tree. He is thinner than in the photos; that is, his one exposed arm is thinner. Thinner but not emaciated. He still has good muscle tone. Dust is on everything. His dusty hair has grown past the tip of his nose. His hair is like a helmet. He wears a sleeveless brown garment. His hands are in one of the mudras in which the Buddha's hands are traditionally depicted. He is absolutely beautiful: beautiful as the central part of this crèche-like, timeless vignette, beautiful in his devotion. I feel a stab of something for him. Allegiance? Pity? Urge-to-Protect? My heart rate is going through the roof.

The gray-haired lama, off to my right, drops, does three quick prostrations: a Buddhist sign of respect, a way of reminding oneself of the illuminated nature of all beings, performed in the presence of spiritually advanced beings in whom this illuminated nature is readily apparent.

The lama begins his second prostration. *Me too,* I mutter, and down I go. Dropping, I think I glimpse the boy's hand move. Is he signaling me? Does he recognize, in me, something special? Has he been, you know, kind of *waiting* for me? In the midst of my final prostration, I realize: his hand didn't move, dumb-ass. It was wishful thinking. It was ego, nimrod: the boy doesn't move for seven months but can't help but move when George arrives, since George is George and has always been George, something very George-special?

My face is flushed from the prostrations and the effort of neurotic self-flagellation.

The gray-haired lama takes off at a fast walk, circumambulating the boy clockwise on a path along the fence.

The young monk says something to Subel, who tells me it's time to take my photo. My photo? I have a camera but don't want to risk disturbing the boy with the digital shutter sound. Plus, I don't know how to turn off the flash, so I will be, at close range, taking a flash photo directly into the boy's sight line, the one thing explicitly prohibited by that sign back there.

"You have to," Subel says. "That's how they know you're a journalist."

I hold up my notebook. Maybe I could just take some notes?

"They're simple people, man," he says. "You have to take a photo."

I set the camera to video mode (no flash involved), pan back and forth across the strangely beautiful Enclosure, zoom in on the boy.

It's one thing to imagine seven months of nonmotion, but to see, in person, even ten minutes of such utter nonmotion is stunning. I think, Has he really been sitting like that since May? *May?* All through the London bombings, the Cairo bombings, the unmasking of Deep Throat, Katrina, the Israeli withdrawal from Gaza, the Lynndie England trial, the Bali bombing, the Kashmir earthquake, the Paris riots, the White Sox World Series victory, the N.Y.C. transit strike, through every thought and purchase and self-recrimination of the entire Christmas season?

Suddenly, the question of his not eating seems almost beside the point.

The young monk says that if we like, we may now do a circumambulation.

Meaning: Time's up.

We start off, the young monk accompanying us.

His name, he says, is Prem.

Prem grew up with the boy; they're distant cousins, but he characterizes them as "more friends than relatives." They became monks at the same time, just after fourth grade. A couple of years ago, they traveled together to Lumbini, the birthplace of the Buddha, for a ten-day Buddhist ceremony being led by a renowned teacher from Dehra Dun, India. There the boy was invited to undertake a three-year retreat at this lama's monastery.

But after one year, the boy left the monastery — *fled* is the verb Prem uses — with just the clothes on his back. Prem doesn't know why. Nobody does. The boy came home briefly, vanished again, after a dream in which a God appeared to him and told him that if he didn't leave home he would die. His distraught family found him under this tree, rarely speaking, refusing food. The family and the villagers were mortified, embarrassed, demanded he stop. He was teased, poked with sticks, tempted with food, but still refused to eat. Three months into his meditation, he called for Prem, asked him to manage the site, minimize the noise. Prem is now his main attendant, here every day from early morning until dusk.

"Who is inside the enclosure with him at night?" I ask.

"Nobody," Prem says.

Prem shows us an area just inside the fence where, per the boy's request, Prem performs Buddhist rituals: a puja table, incense pots, texts.

It was just here, he tells us, that the first snake, crawling in, got stuck under the fence. The monks assisting at the time couldn't kill it, for religious reasons, and were struggling inefficiently to free it. Finally, the boy got up from his meditation, walked over, and freed the snake. As he did so, the snake lunged up and bit him.

"What kind of snake was it?" I ask, trying to be journalistic.

"It was . . . a big jungle snake," Subel translates.

"Ah," I say.

The snakes, Prem says, were "arrows" sent by older lamas, jealous because they'd practiced all their lives and hadn't attained this level of realization.

I ask about the boy's meditation practice. What exactly is he doing? Does Prem know?

Prem hesitates, says something to Subel in a softer voice.

"His belief is, this boy is God," Subel says. "God has come to earth in the form of this boy."

I look at Prem. He looks at me. In his eyes, I see that he knows this statement sounds a little wacky. I try, with my eyes, to communicate my basic acceptance of the possibility.

We have a moment.

Does the boy ever move or adjust his posture?

Prem smiles for the first time, laughs even. The sense is: Ha, very funny, believe me, he *never* moves. People accuse us all the time, he says. They say, This is not a boy, it is a statue, a dummy, something carved from clay.

What was the boy like as a cousin, as a friend?

A good boy. Very sweet-hearted. Never cursed. Did not drink alcohol or eat meat.

He would always smile first, then speak.

Back near the Shoe Corral, we talk with the Village Guy. He seems frazzled, overworked, cognizant of the fact that anybody with a lick of sense would suspect him and the Committee of being at the heart of any hoax, anxious to address such concerns in a straightforward way. He reminds me of one of my down-to-earth Chicago uncles, if one of my Chicago uncles suddenly found himself neglecting everything else in his life to tend to a miracle. His attitude seems to be: *Why should I lie? You think I'm enjoying this? You want to take over?* So far the Committee has collected approximately four hundred forty-five thousand rupees (about sixty-five hundred dollars). A portion of this is used for site maintenance and the small salaries of eighteen volunteers; the rest is being held in a bank for the boy.

Something occurs to me: it's one thing to, from afar, project a scheming, greedy group of villagers in a faraway land, but when you actually get to the land, you see that, before they were scheming, they had intact, in-place lives, lives that did not involve scheming. They were fathers, husbands, grandfathers, keepers-of-backyard-gardens, local merchants. They had reputations. For someone to risk these preexisting lives (lives which are, in this case, small, impoverished, precarious) would take a considerable level of forethought, risk, and diabolical organization. Imagine that first meeting: *OK, so what we'll do is get a kid to pretend to be meditating and not eating, then sneak him food and water and get the word out internationally, and before long — bingo — we've got six grand in the bank! Everyone in agreement? Ready? Let's go!*

After lunch, bound for the boy's village, we cross a dry riverbed of coarse gray sand, like cremated ashes, into which some men are sinking a water well.

When a fairy tale says, *He left his village and set out to seek his fortune,* this is the village you might imagine the hero leaving: a cluster of huts along a dirt track. Mustard and corn growing on rounded slopes, higher than your head. Kids racing in dust clouds behind the minivan, baby chicks skittering off into high weeds, as if dropping out of the children's clothes.

The boy's mother is home but unhappy to see me. I would describe her reaction as a wince, if a wince could be accomplished without a change of facial expression: as Subel introduces me, she undergoes a kind of full-body stiffening, then plucks three glasses off a tray with the fingers of one hand and disappears brusquely inside the house.

So much for that, I think.

But then a little girl comes out with the three glasses, now full of tea. The mother sits, submitting to torture in the name of politeness. She's an older woman, pretty, with a nose ring, answers my questions without ever once looking at me.

When he was born, he didn't cry the way other babies do. Instead, he made a different kind of sound, a sound she describes as a sharp scream.

He kind of shouted out, she says.

As a child, he was totally different from her other children. He was a loner, always wandering off on his own. When people would scold or bully him, he would just smile. When he came back from the monastery in India, his speech patterns had changed: if he kept to small sentences he was fine, but when he tried to talk in longer sentences he would get anxious and agitated and descend into gibberish; no one could understand him. She thought maybe some kind of curse had been put on him by the lama he'd fled. But now she understands: he was going through a profound change. The main problem at this point, she says, is the noise. He can't concentrate on his meditation. They have gone so far as to outlaw one group from coming to the site, a sect from a particular part of the Tarai, known for being loud. (Subel later relays a common slur about this group: you can't tell if they're laughing, or screaming in agony.)

All of this is happening for a reason, she says. There is a God in him that is helping him feed himself. She sits quietly, grieved, flies landing on her face, waiting for this to be over.

She puts me in mind, of course, of the Virgin Mary: a simple countrywoman, mother of a son who appears in a time of historical crisis representing a solution and a hope above politics.

We walk back to the van, followed by the flock of kids, who still seem to be miraculously sprouting baby chicks.

Our plan is: Go back to the hotel, get some rest. Come back tomorrow, spend the night, see if some kind of Secret Eating is taking place.

It's misty, getting cold. There are open fires along the road, and local governments are distributing free firewood, concerned that people will freeze to death tonight in the countryside.

And they do. During this night, over a hundred people die of exposure across India, Nepal, and Bangladesh, including one old man in this district. Temperatures in Delhi reach their coldest recorded levels in over seventy years.

And tomorrow night, the driver tells us, it's going to be even colder.

Next evening the driver drops us at the Shoe Corral.

He'll return tomorrow morning at eight.

Nearby is a kind of crude tent: four trees hacked into tent poles, with what looks like a parachute draped over them. This is the Committee Tent, where volunteer members of the Committee stay overnight to provide security. But tonight there's no Committee, just the boy's brother and a friend. Though not expecting us, they have no objection to our staying. Three lamas from Eastern Nepal will also be here, meditating all night. Will we need mats? Do I want to sleep near the lamas down by the gate, or up here at the tent near the fire?

We leave our shoes at the tent. The lamas are seated in front of the gate on a single mat, canoe-style. The brother puts my mat ten feet or so behind them, placing it carefully so leaf moisture won't fall on me.

Prem has left for the night. The brother checks the padlock on the gate. Sitting, I can't see the boy, but if I crane around the monks, I can see his tree. I'm wearing thermal long johns under a pair of khaki pants, a long-sleeve thermal undershirt, a sweater, and a sleeveless down vest.

This won't be bad, I think.

It gets dark fast. A big moon rises, just short of full. The brother and his pal hiss angrily back and forth, then launch off on a perimeter check, their flashlight bobbing away in the dark.

From inside the Enclosure, or maybe the far side of it, I hear what sounds like a cough. Sound is traveling strangely. Was that the boy? Did the boy just cough? To note this possible cough in my notebook, I devise a system: I take out my mini flashlight, mute the light with my hand, so as not to disturb the boy, record the time, make my note.

At 7:20, oddly, a car alarm goes off. How many cars in deep rural Nepal have alarms? It goes on and on. Finally it dawns on me, when the car alarm moves to a different tree, that the car alarm is a bird.

The Car-Alarm Bird of Southern Nepal keeps it up for ten minutes, then falls silent for the rest of the night.

In this quiet, even the slightest posture adjustment is deafening. If a tiny breeze picks up, you notice. If a drop of moisture falls, you jump. So when one of the lamas stands up and goes to the fence, it's a major event. The other lamas whisper, point excitedly. The first lama paces back to me, gestures by touching his fingers to his forehead and flinging something outward. I don't get it. He has a headache? His head is really sweating? He motions for me to return with him. Soon I'm sitting canoe-style between Lama One and Lama Two. I can hear Lama One mumbling mantras under his breath. Suddenly he turns to me, again makes the gesture, points into the Enclosure. I get it now: the gesture means, *Look, there is something emanating from the boy's forehead!*

Do I see it?

Actually, I do: vivid red and blue lights (like flares) are hovering, drifting up from approximately where the boy is sitting, as if borne upward on an impossibly light updraft.

What the heck, I think. My face goes hot. Is this what a miracle looks like, feels like, in real time? I close my eyes, open them. The lights are still drifting up.

A noise begins, a steady drumlike thumping from inside the Enclosure, like an impossibly loud heartbeat.

For several concept-free seconds, it's just: colored up-floating lights and the boy's amplified heartbeat.

I look through the binoculars. Yes, red and blue sparks, yep, and now, wow, green. And orange. Then suddenly, they're all orange. They look — actually, they look like orange cinders. Like orange cinders floating up from a fire. A campfire, say. I lower the binoculars. Seen with the naked eye, the sparks look to be coming not from inside the Enclosure but from just beyond it. Slowly, a campfire resolves itself in the distance. The heartbeat becomes syncopated. The heartbeat is coming from off to my right and just behind me and is actually, I can now tell, a drum.

I stand up, go to the gate. That, I think, is a campfire. I've never seen, it's true, red/blue/green cinders, but still, that is, I am almost positive, a campfire. I'm embarrassed on the boy's behalf for his motley, boisterous, easily excited entourage.

But maybe, part of me protests, this is how a miracle happens?

Another part answers: it has all the marks of a Sunday school.

I return to my assigned spot, resolve to ignore all future faux-excitement, and just watch.

At 8:30, I take my winter hat and gloves from my pack. Abruptly the lamas rise and exit in a group. What, I think, the lamas are chickening out? I'm tougher than the lamas? Soon they return, laden with mattresses and fat sleeping rolls and plump pillows. What, I think, the lamas are incredibly well prepared for what is shaping up to be a damn cold night?

Subel goes back to the Committee Tent to sit by the fire.

Now it's just me and the snoring, sleep-moaning lamas.

From near the source of the drumming, I suddenly hear dozens of barking dogs. The drum patterns morph into Native American patterns from old Westerns, as if what they're doing over in that village is planning to attack and overrun our little outpost here, using their constantly barking attack dogs.

Before long the dogs and drums fade and I'm lapsing into odd exhausted waking dreams: The boy sticks a pole into my chest, which is made of fiberboard, so the pole goes in easily and painlessly. *Don't go for the heart,* he says. I don't get it. *Should I write about you?* I ask. *Sure,* he says, *go ahead, just tell the truth, doubts and contradictions and all. I don't mind.*

Soon my legs and feet are freezing. I take my socks out of my pocket and put them on. The vest/sweater combo is keeping my torso warm, but my neck and legs are becoming problematic. I drape a pair of dirty sweatpants around my neck, take out my coat (a shell that's supposed to have a fleece lining, which I've somehow managed to lose), arrange it over my legs. Subel returns from the fire and stretches out behind me, trying to sleep. I think of him back there: no socks, just a flannel shirt and a light windbreaker. I have an emergency blanket in my pack, a tinfoil-ish thing in a small cardboard box. I throw it back to him, he unrolls it for what seems like hours: the noisiest thing I've ever heard.

"Am I being too loud?" he asks sweetly.

By 10:30, he's asleep. I'm fading fast. The dogs sound distant, gooselike. The drummer seems tired. I try to feel the boy sitting out there, and really I can't. How are you doing this? I think. Forget eating, how do you *sit* so long? My back hurts, my legs hurt, the deep soreness in my ass seems to connote Permanent Damage.

At 10:58, a jet passes overhead, bound for Katmandu.

At 11:05, I take the dirty sweatpants from around my neck, stand up, put them on over my khakis. I put the coat/shell on, drawstring it tight, tuck my chin down, so none of my face is exposed. With a rush of happiness, I remember there are two more dirty pairs of pants in my pack! I drape them like blankets over my legs and feet. What else do I have? Two pairs of dirty underwear, which I briefly consider putting on my head.

By 11:22, I can see my breath.

Even in my socks, my feet are freezing. I sit still; any move may cause an increase in Coldness, and any increased Coldness is, at this point, unacceptable. I remember a certain yoga move that involves tightening the rectum to get a heat tingle to surge up the spine, and do this, and it feels better, but not better enough to justify the exhausting rectal flexing.

At 11:55, dozing off, I wake to the sound of a woman's voice, possibly my wife, shouting my name from near the Committee Tent.

Time slows way down. I wait and wait to check my watch. Three hours go by, slow, torturous hours. It is now, I calculate, around three in the morning. Excellent: next will come predawn, then dawn, then the minivan, the hotel, America. As a special treat, I allow myself to check my watch.

It's 12:10. Fifteen minutes — fifteen minutes? — have passed since my wife called my name. Damn it, shit! I find myself in the strange position of being angry at Time.

Subel stirs, gets up, says he's going back to the tent: his feet are too cold.

I take out the flashlight, carefully write: *If it gets colder than this I'm fucked.*

It gets colder.

Soon I'm making no effort to stay awake or, ha ha, meditate: just trying not to freak out, because if I freak out and flee into the Nepali darkness, it will still be freezing and I'll still have eight hours to wait (eight hours? Christ!) before the minivan returns.

At 12:15, time officially stops. My current posture (sitting up cross-legged) becomes untenable. I can't help it. I fall over on my side. This is going to invalidate the whole idea of: stay up all night, confirm no Overnight Feeding. Oh, fuck that, I think. The ground is hard and cold through the thin mat. I ball the dirty pants up around my frozen feet. The drums start again, accompanied by the inexplicable smell of burning rubber. Wherefore burning rubber? I can't figure it.

It starts to rain.

To say I fall asleep would be inaccurate. It's more like I pass out: unwilled, involuntary, unstoppable. Out I go, totally, like a wino on whom a clothes hamper has exploded.

I would characterize the quality of my sleep as: terrified/defiant. I am think-dreaming: hypothermia! People died out here last night, people who were probably wrapped in blankets. People are probably dying right now. This is serious; try and wake up, really.

I won't wake up, I won't, I answer myself. Because if I wake up, I'll be back where I was before, trapped in that freezing endless torment of a night.

But finally I do wake up, with a start, shivering, colder than I've ever been in my life. I struggle back to a sitting position, find my flashlight, groggily check the time.

It's 1:20.

I've slept an hour.

Shit shit shit, the night is still young.

It starts to rain harder. The flashlight makes a little hiss-pop and goes out — possibly, it occurs to me, the boy's way of saying: Lights out.

Looking into the darkness, I think: Still there? Through all of this, and much more, so many other intolerable nights, before I even knew you existed? If Snake One bit you on a night like this, did you hear it coming? Did you think of bolting, screaming out, calling for your mother?

Poor kid is just sitting in the dark all alone. Tonight, anyway, nobody seems to have the slightest interest in feeding him.

Something powerful starts to dawn on me.

No one has entered the Enclosure all night. After a couple of early checks, the brother and his pal hightailed it back to the Committee Tent. The only entry, the front gate, has been locked since we arrived.

The fact that the Powers That Be (tonight, just the brother and his pal) let us spend the night with no advance notice argues against the existence of a Secret Feeding Plan, because any such Plan would therefore constantly be at the mercy of Drop-Ins, i.e., would have to be aborted anytime anyone showed up to spend the night. There could theoretically be days in a row, weeks even, when it would be impossible to perform the food sneakage.

A suave, logical Devil's Advocate arrives in my mind.

Come on, think aggressively, he says. Don't be a sucker. Is there any possible way they can be sneaking him food?

They could theoretically, I answer, be hiding food in the woods and bringing it in over the fence at a position far from the gate.

Could a person get over that fence without making any noise? he says.

I don't think so, I say. I can hear it anytime anyone leaves the tent, even to pee. And besides, how does an earnest hyperreligious monk who dreams of a God telling him to flee his home become a boy who willingly and sneakily accepts food and water when he has publicly forsworn these?

Good point, says the Devil's Advocate.

Doesn't ring true, I say.

No it doesn't, the Devil's Advocate says, and fades away.

No light appears in the distance to signal dawn, not at all; it just keeps getting darker. I'm shivering, desperate for the paradise of that sad little gray van. I'll put my feet up on the seat, have the driver crank up the heat! We'll stop for tea; I'll pour the tea down my freezing three pairs of pants! I hallucinate a Georgia O'Keeffe flower that opens and closes in megaslow motion while changing colors. I walk downhill into some sacred cave, part of a line of chanting Eastern Holy Men. One of the Holy Men asks a ponderous Zen question, which I answer in a comedian voice via some kind of fart joke. A laugh track sounds in my mind. The Holy Men are not amused. The boy intervenes: *That is his way of being profound,* he says, *leave him alone.*

I'm so tired, says the Devil's Advocate, who has now come back.

Oh God, me too, I say.

Finally, I give up on getting comfortable, and this seems to help. It's a strange thing, staying up all night in the jungle to see if a teenager pulls a fast one via eating. The pain I am feeling at every sensor is making me kind of giddy. Being beyond tired, beyond cold, completely stripped of control, I'm finding, has the effect of clearing the mind.

You know that feeling at the end of the day, when the anxiety of that-which-I-must-do falls away and, for maybe the first time that day, you see, with some clarity, the people you love and the ways you have, during that day, slightly ignored them, turned away from them to get back to what you were doing, blurted out some mildly hurtful thing, projected, instead of the deep love you really feel, a surge of defensiveness or self-protection or suspicion? That moment when you think, Oh God, what have I done with this day? And what am I doing with my life? And how must I change to avoid catastrophic end-of-life regrets?

I feel like that now: tired of the Me I've always been, tired of making the same mistakes, repetitively stumbling after the same small ego strokes, being caught in the same loops of anxiety and defensiveness. At the end of my life, I know I won't be wishing I'd held more back, been less effusive, more often stood on ceremony, forgiven less, spent more days oblivious to the secret wishes and fears of the people around me. So what is stopping me from stepping outside my habitual crap?

My mind, my limited mind.

The story of life is the story of the same basic mind readdressing the same problems in the same already discredited ways. First order of business: feed the trap. Work the hours to feed the trap. Having fed the trap, shit, piss, preparing to again feed the trap. Because it is your trap, defend it at all costs.

Because we feel ourselves first and foremost as physical beings, the physical comes to dominate us: beloved uncles die, parents are displaced, cousins go to war, children suffer misfortune, love becomes a trap. The deeper in you go, the more it hurts to get out. Disaster (sickness, death, loss) is guaranteed and in fact is already en route, and when it comes, it hurts and may even destroy us.

We fight this by making ourselves less vulnerable, mastering the physical, becoming richer, making bigger safety nets, safer cars, better medicines.

But it's nowhere near enough.

What if the boy is making this fight in a new way, by struggling against the thousands-of-years-old usage patterns of the brain? What if he is the first of a new breed — or the most recent manifestation of an occasionally appearing breed — sent to show us something new about ourselves, a new way our bodies and minds can work?

Could it be? Could it?

Part of me wants to hop the outer fence, hop the inner fence, sit knee to knee with him, demand to know what the hell is going on.

I get up, but just to take a piss. It's so dark I can't tell where I've left the trail. There are dim shapes on the ground, but I can't tell if they're holes, shrubs, or shadows. I think of snakes, I think: Bring them on. Then I think: Hoo boy, no no, don't bring them on. I try to get deep enough into the woods that nobody will, tomorrow, step in my piss. When I do go, it's Niagara-esque, so loud the boy must hear it, if in fact he's still hearing things.

Sorry, sorry, I think, I just really had to go.

I look up into the vast Nepali sky. Night, I conclude, is a very long thing. Is he suffering in there as much as I'm suffering out here? I wonder.

If so, then what he's doing is a monumental, insane feat of willpower.

If not, it's something even stranger.

Hours later, at a moment that (in the quality of light, a slight shift in the ambient sound) feels like the Beginning of the Beginning of Morning — the colored lights appear again.

I struggle to the fence, trying not to tread upon any sleeping lamas. Scattered across the ground inside the Enclosure are thousands of snowflakelike silverish glittering flecks. I perform a test, developed back in my acid days: Are the flecks also on my hands? They are. Are they still visible when I close my eyes? They are. Therefore they are an optical illusion, albeit one I have never had before or heard of anyone else ever having.

Oh man, I think, I have no idea what's going on here. The line between miracle and hallucination is all but gone. I am so tired. The center is not . . . What is it the center is sometimes said not to do? Hanging? Having? The center are not hanging.

The lights go white, then orange. Definitely orange. I visually compare this new orange bulk of light to the orange bulk of light I know is the fire back at the Committee Tent.

Again I conclude that the miracle is a campfire.

And yet.

And yet.

Undeniably, over an indefinite period of time, during which time continues not to pass, it gets lighter. The canoeful of lamas rises up, confers briefly, rushes off on a good-morning circumambulation.

I go to the fence.

The sun comes up.

The boy is revealed, sitting, still sitting, in exactly the same position as when I last saw him, at sundown. How did you do it, I think, in your thin sleeveless garment? All night bare to the cold, matless on the cold ground, in full lotus: no coat, no gloves, no socks, no hope of an early-morning rescue.

It seems impossible he's not dead. He looks made of stone, utterly motionless, as impervious to the night as the tree he appears to be part of. Can I see his breath? I can't. Does his chest expand and contract? It doesn't, not that I can see.

Because this night was hard for me, part of me expects it was hard for him and won't be surprised if he stands up and announces he's quitting.

But then I remember he's already spent on the order of two hundred nights out here.

I take what I know will be my last look at him, hoping for . . . I'm not sure what. Some indication that he's alive, that he's operating within the same physical constraints as I am: an adjustment of posture, a clearing of the throat, a weary sigh.

Nothing.

I feel, to gravely understate it, the monumental distance between his abilities and mine.

Pilgrims begin arriving. They step to the fence, gape in wonder, dash off along the circular path, chatting loudly, speculating on what he's doing and why he's doing it.

In short, a new day begins.

I rejoin Subel at the Committee Tent.

"I salute you," he says.

"I salute you," I say.

Both of us are in a state of sleep-deprived paranoia. It has separately occurred to us that the boy must be dead or in a coma. When Subel brought this up last night at the fire, the brother's only explanation was that since the boy sits leaning slightly forward, if he does die, he'll topple forward. Subel asks me how long it takes a body to decay. We try to remember: didn't Prem tell us that he goes to the ditch every morning and checks to make sure the boy is breathing?

We are relatively sure he did.

The family, Subel tells me, desperate to prove that this is real, is livid with the government and the media for not arranging appropriate scientific tests. They will do anything to help; their only condition is that the boy not be touched, since this would interfere with his meditation.

We experience the deep delight of putting our shoes on again. At one of the stalls, we stop for tea. We have breakfast at another. We are escaped from the boy, from his asceticism, like guilty holiday-makers, lowering ourselves back into the deliriously physical, the realm where any discomfort is instantly reckoned with.

We drive back to Birgunj. Subel is thoughtful: he came out here doubting this boy, he says, but now thinks there is something there, the boy seems to have some power . . .

An early-morning fog is on everything. In the heavy traffic, we have several gravel-crunching close calls. But soon enough, we're sleeping through even these.

Back at the hotel, under every blanket I can find, including the reclaimed emergency blanket, I sleep all afternoon, a deep, dream-drenched sleep: more O'Keeffe flowers; more secret communiqués from the boy; finally, a series of impossibly detailed *tangka*-like patterns in reds and yellows, constituting themselves into being from right to left. The patterns are intricate, encoded, terrifying in their complexity, full of love and challenge and cocky intelligence, beautiful and original in ways I wouldn't have believed possible if I weren't seeing it right in front of me, with my own eyes.

Two months later, on March 11, 2006, I get an e-mail from Subel: "A very bad thing has happened. The Buddha Boy suddenly vanished last night. He is not there anymore. There are so many reports and stories, but nothing is certain. He might have shifted to another location, but no one knows. The Committee has no idea where he might have gone. They have denied the possibility that he has been abducted. They are all, including the police and the local administration, looking for the boy."

I'm kind of blown away by this. It occurs to me that I've developed a faith in this boy, a confidence that, six years from now, he'll have just finished his sitting, and I'll be able to come back to Nepal and ask him what he learned, what I should do, what we all should do, based on what he's learned.

Over the next week, more rumors: The fence was cut. His clothes were left under the tree. He was seen by a villager, walking slowly into the jungle. The boy turned, placed his hands together in greeting, continued. Hundreds of people were out searching for him but had so far found nothing.

Then, on March 20, the BBC reported that the boy had briefly reappeared for a secret meeting with the chairman of the Village Committee. He said he was going into hiding and would reappear again in six years. He asked that monks perform purification prayers at the spot of his meditation. He was quoted as saying, "I left because there is no peace here. Tell my parents not to worry."

So it's a mystery, even more than it was a mystery before, when it was already pretty damn mysterious.

But I imagine him the night of his escape, making his way through the woods in the moonlight, weak on his feet from months of fasting and sitting, his eyes really open for the first time since May. The world, the beautiful world, is fleeing past, and he's seeing it in a way we can't imagine. He's come so far and is desperate to get somewhere beyond the reach of the world, so he can finish what he's started.

He hasn't eaten in ten months, and isn't hungry.

GARY SHTEYNGART

Brazil's Untamed Heart

FROM *Travel + Leisure*

THE *BUNDA*. In its female incarnation it is the soul, the moral sustenance, the very psychic infrastructure of Brazil. It is the subject of song, of innuendo, of contention and violence, of worship and delight. At a literary conference in workaday São Paulo, I brood about the future of the novel, the state of American publishing, and the rise of the made-up memoir, until a young man in a sparse goatee leans forward and whispers loudly and rhetorically: "Our women have nice *bundas*, yes?"

"Yes."

"Very large *bundas* . . ."

"Muh-huh."

All of the men breathe a sigh of relief. The state of American publishing — whatever. The visiting writer likes the *bundas*. He seems to smile and smack his lips. He is at one with the Brazilian experience.

A few days later, I head to Salvador, capital of the great black state of Bahia — the first colonial capital of Brazil and now a topsy-turvy modern city of more than two million. The statue that greets me by the city's center is an innocuous-enough Modernist piece entitled *Fountain of the Market Ramp*. But no local would ever call it that. The fiberglass symbol of Salvador is known simply as "Bunda." And it's a *bunda*, all right. A great double-fisted one, lit up at night, with water spilling over it like sweat on a dance floor. Unlike many visitors, I did not come to Salvador, or Brazil in general, looking for gigantic asses. But here I am, drenched in the tropical heat, beneath this weighty, salacious object, and all I want to do is understand what this life is about, what makes these people — say, the old blue-skinned man carrying a sack of flour on his head while whistling a catchy *forró* tune — suffer and love. We have no wings, and yet we take to the air. We are not fish, and yet we snorkel. I have no discernible behind, and still I head for the Bahian dance floor if only to observe and learn something about the physical life, which I enjoy mostly in my dreams.

The samba place is called Fundo do Cravinho, which means "Back of O Cravinho." At the actual O Cravinho, which looks out on Terreiro de Jesus, the main square of Salvador's Old Town, one can get soaked to the gills by way of different types of *cachaça*, the national firewater, but in Fundo do Cravinho the drink of choice is ice-cold beer, tall dark bottles of it. In the front, dapper locals and the occasional over-soused foreigner trade conversation and clink caipirinhas; in the back it's all *bundas* and beer and biology and gleaming white teeth. A month has passed since my trip to Brazil and I'm sitting in an overly tidy East Coast apartment looking out over a landscape of nothing. But in my ears some immovable, wordless melody from Fundo do Cravinho is fluttering about like an anxious bird. I can't transcribe the beats, but the tinny ringing in the back of my mind sounds like *tiri puh-piri, piri wiri; tiri puh-piri, piri wiri; uh, uh, uh,* [very emphatically] *uh.*

And when I close my eyes, I see a hangarlike space, bad lighting, blue plastic chairs, moist green walls, and hip-hugging couples dancing with minute precision, as if their lives depended on it. I recall the *bundas*, more with awe than with lust, because in Salvador da Bahia, the ass is not an ass. It has legs and arms and a mouth; it spins and shimmies; it rotates counterclockwise, one cheek leading, the other accompanying. It does all this naturally, without bidding; it does this atop glistening black thighs, within cheap white shorts, sometimes below the quarter-moon of early pregnancy. The giant green *tantan* drum leads the way, and the ukulele-like *cavaquinho* strums to me things I cannot understand, except that the life cycle here is fluid and tragicomic, and that I am enchanted and curious but utterly assless in Brazil.

The city of Salvador juts out into the Bay of All Saints, but the *baia* is just preliminary, for Salvador stretches clear across the Atlantic into the heart of Yoruba culture, into modern-day Nigeria, Benin, and Togo. The story of Salvador, indeed of the northeastern part of Brazil, is in large part the story of the transatlantic slave trade and its consequences. Pretty much everyone here is black. The food is bathed in palm oil, an African staple. The popular mode of prayer is candomblé, a fusion of Catholic rites and elaborate ceremonies centered on offerings. The result is a curious authenticity that diasporas often carry with them from one part of the world to another. When I wish to visit the Russia of my youth, I don't take a plane to Moscow or St. Petersburg, cities that have changed completely since my salad days. I go to Brighton Beach, Brooklyn, where the year 1979 has been frozen in amber. Salvador, in its culture and religion, similarly casts a glance back at the Old World. When you're watching a performance of capoeira Angola — a mixture of nonviolent martial arts, interactive ballet, and musical comedy — or biting into a fritter of black-eyed peas, Brazil can seem more African than Africa itself. And when you look at the restored colonial architecture, at the azure tiles in the beautiful convent of São Francisco depicting Lisbon before the earthquake of 1755, Salvador appears to the eye somehow more Portuguese than its old, tired parent across the sea.

The lay of the land is startling. The Upper City, where most of the colonial treasures are scattered, perches high atop a 236-foot-high bluff overlooking the bay and the sunburned commercial buildings of the Lower City (the Lacerda Elevator, in all its Art Deco glory, connects the two). But Salvador stretches in all directions to encompass the human condition, high and low. Here are favelas, or shantytowns, that are as poor as any place on Earth, clinging impossibly to eroding hills, oddly attractive from a distance, spirit-shattering when seen up close. There is the wealthy neighborhood of Barra, bristling with sleek, heavily guarded skyscrapers that evoke Miami on a shoestring. And in all directions out of the city and across the bay are sparkling white-sand beaches that, taken with a chilled beer or a well-macheted coconut, evoke a kind of fundamentalist paradise, minus — and I can't stress this enough — the virgins.

Most visits to Salvador start in the Upper City neighborhood called the Pelourinho, which means "the Pillory." In the prominent squares of Pelourinho, African slaves were whipped and humiliated — their reward for carrying up the cobblestones that line the Upper City, not to mention erecting the churches and municipal buildings that sparkle to this day. The local Jesuits, in fact, once asked that the whipping post be moved to another part of town — the cries of the victims were interfering with their meditation and prayer.

On this journey I am fortunate enough to have a Portuguese-speaking companion, my friend Albertina. We arrive at the popular Redfish pousada, and check into a tall, airy, brightly colored room with lots of toy turtles and fish, Brazilian Indian "nightmare catchers," hanging from the rafters.

Once out on the Pelourinho streets we stumble for Iberian comparisons: Seville with black faces? Salamanca with a rhythm? Baroque and Rococo façades look down at us, saints and angels point their fingers, slender Art Deco townhouses flake paint onto the crowded sidewalks, everywhere samba and reggae accost the visitor out of man-size speakers, and the heartless noonday sun presides. If you dim your eyes a little the colors you see floating before you are blue, yellow, green, and black. The streets slope down without warning, then ramp up into the sky. One minute the bulbous spires of the Igreja de Nossa Senhora do Rosário dos Pretos are at your feet; the next thing you know, you're staring up at the sky-blue façade of the church, built for slaves, by slaves (they were not allowed to worship with their masters), and still bursting with the sounds of the Yoruban-language mass.

The Museu Afro-Brasileiro on the main square of Terreiro de Jesus gives you a good overview of Bahia's unique Afrocentric culture, touching upon the three *C*s: candomble, capoeira, and the *Carnaval,* which is said to rival Rio's, although some locals bemoan a slide into commercialization. But our most moving visit is to Igreja da Ordem Terceira do Carmo. In this outwardly imposing structure, the African slaves were held downstairs in inhuman conditions, next to an even darker hole where they would hide to escape punishment. The former slave quarters are now home to a solitary squatter, a ninety-five-year-old woman with one tooth, whose laundry hangs in the breeze. "I'm ninety-five years and ninety days old," she tells us, speaking out of a withered face that appears to hang off the peg of her skull. Her eyes are surprisingly agile and blue; her smile is genuine. She points out where the slaves slept and ate, nondescript parts of the room that only take on meaning once you realize that this woman is a descendant of the very men and women whose quarters she occupies. She speaks lovingly of Princess Isabel, who freed the slaves in 1888, as if that milestone had happened yesterday, as if perhaps we hadn't heard the news. She was, after all, born only two decades after emancipation.

Next door, in the Igreja de Nossa Senhora do Carmo, is an eighteenth-century life-size statue of Christ at the whipping post by the half-Indian slave Francisco das Chagas. Christ's blood is made up of hundreds of rubies inlaid into the wood — but it is his expression of deep suffering and otherworldly resignation that catches the eye — the clenched, upturned hand, the masterful rendering of the calloused feet, the elasticity, and shock of physical pain. This is Christ as could be conceived only by a slave. The statue endures, unchanged — unlike the neighboring Carmelite convent, which has been converted into a high-priced boutique-style pousada, complete with butler service and spa.

Ten years ago, none of this was possible. Pelourinho was a dangerous, forsaken area. Then gringos started helping themselves to the most scrumptious Baroque tidbits and opening up quaint Redfish-like inns. Now the area is policed to within an inch of its life, but much of the authenticity is gone, too, replaced by Internet cafés and Jamaican-style hair-braiding places that have monopolized many a pastel-colored street corner. One is reminded of Salvador's realities — I am told that 60 percent of the population lives in favelas — mostly by the parade of street kids begging us for every little thing we own. One tiny boy even begged for the last drops of water in Albertina's plastic cup, a pathetic gift she gladly handed over.

After a few days in Pelourinho's stunning but contrived colonial wonderland, we look forward to seeing the rest of the city. Salvador is not a small metropolis, so we decide to use our stomachs as a compass. First, I should mention the most notorious staple of Bahian cuisine: *dendê*. Daily ingestion of *dendê*, or palm oil, as saturated as a slick of heavy crude winding its way down Lake Erie, is a delicious way to die slowly and with major complications. The best place to start the process is Yemanjá, located on a highway spiriting past Salvador's northern beaches and named, appropriately, after the Yoruban goddess of the sea. The décor is decent enough, but you'll mostly be looking at the waitresses, with their smooth brown skin (pity your own sunburned hide) and cheekbones from here to ya-ya. A friend later tells us that Yemanjá hires the most beautiful *mulatas*, as the locals unabashedly call mixed-race women. Albertina and I split a *moqueca*, the Bahian seafood stew loaded with onion, garlic, parsley, and *pimenta* (hot-pepper sauce), and cooked in coconut milk. Yemanjá produces a version with crunchy soft-shell crab and fatty lobster, to be spilled over rice and chased with long drafts of beer. You can send your fragrant *moqueca* into overdrive with a little extra pepper sauce and a dusting of smoky *farofa*, the toasted manioc meal Brazilians dump on just about everything.

Satiated, but mostly excited for more, we strike out up the beach to get a taste of some real Bahian street cuisine. In the main square of the nearby seaside village of Itapuã, a very busy woman named Cira, dressed in the traditional *baiana* white head wrap and full dress, dishes out her famous *acarajés*, deep-fried, mashed-bean "sandwiches" that she fills with such delicacies as dried shrimp, *vatapá* (a homey yellow porridge of shrimp, garlic, cashews, coconut, and *dendê*) and *pimenta* to taste. What makes Cira's *acarajé* so brilliant is the crispness of the outside contrasted with the softness inside — it's like a giant street knish filled with striking flavor, such as that of the thermonuclear *pimenta* (the phrase *sem pimenta* apparently makes the madness go away).

Next, we take a long taxi drive to the other, more working-class, side of town, heading for the Sorveteria da Ribeira, a bare-bones ice cream shop where we gorge on flavors such as *coco verde*, squeezed out of the freshest, youngest green coconuts; *umbú*, a somewhat plumlike fruit with an addictive tang; and the all-tart *maracujá*, or passion fruit, which leaves my mouth throbbing and refreshed, my sun-addled brain rightfully chilled and greatly subdued.

After a week of fried peas, palm-oiled seafood stews, and tropical ice cream, we have dinner with my friend Dr. Albert Ko and his wife at Paraíso Tropical, in the chic seaside neighborhood of Rio Vermelho, which serves a modern take on Bahian cuisine. Compact, humming with energy, and trained at Harvard Medical School, Albert is possibly the most honorable gringo in Salvador, having dedicated the past ten years of his life to fighting infectious diseases in the favelas. Befittingly, the food at Paraíso Tropical is healthier and lighter than any we've tried so far, and the restaurant's outdoor garden is lovely. There's less palm oil here; even the *farofa* lacks the usual *dendê* heaviness. We feast on shrimp and octopus with rice and guava, and I make the acquaintance of a fruit I've never met before: the sour pickle–like *biribiri*, which is as fun to eat as it is to pronounce.

The conversation turns to Albert's work and to the situation in Salvador and Brazil's northeast, which is significantly poorer than the southern parts of the country, where the world-famous beaches of Rio and the megalopolis of São Paulo are located. He offers to take us to the favela that he is researching, to show us how the majority of Salvador's residents live.

The next morning we head for the Pau da Lima neighborhood, so far away from the city's high-rise beachside towers in terms of ambience and wealth that it might as well be in Chad. I have come across many poverty-stricken areas, but I am not completely prepared for what turns out to be a descent to the *n*th circle of hell. The favela is composed of shacks of red-orange brick and mortar, which cover a hillside (the frequent mudslides are inevitably deadly), and each step down into the valley unearths a different level of despair. I learn that even the favelas are stratified: the rent on the shacks is higher at the top of the hill, near the paved streets and the stunted services the government provides.

At the bottom of the hill we are completely off the grid as far as the rest of the world is concerned. Stuff, as they say, flows downhill, and here the smell of raw sewage is overpowering. There is a midday quiet, dogs sulk, a rooster struts, ducks waddle, boys kick around a football with easy grace, and, to Albert's anguish, a barefoot child plays in a mound of waste. The disease Albert is working to prevent is leptospirosis, a bacterial infection that causes liver and kidney failure and is spread from the urine of infected rats. Playing barefoot in an open sewer is the last thing a child should be doing here.

We talk to a woman of seventy-two who complains of high blood pressure. "A lot of rats," she says, "very big ones, they come inside the house sometimes." She lives at the very bottom of the hill, in a shack that serves as the *terreiro*, a house of candomblé worship.

Wooden statues of male and female African deities stare at us amid the muck. I spot Exú, with his big red penis: he is one of the prime movers of the universe, without whom there could be no life. I have to breathe slowly. I am experiencing that familiar Western sense of losing control, that crumbling of the elaborate façades our civilizations have put up to keep the knowledge of this kind of inequity at bay. And then I realize that I misheard this ancient woman's age. She's not seventy-two, but fifty-two. The average life expectancy in Brazil's favelas is around fifty years.

"It's a privilege to work here with these people," Albert tells me as we are driving up to Pau da Lima. I thought he was being overly noble. But after a day spent following him around the neighborhood, I understand why someone would feel blessed to be of help in a place where cruelty seems to trump kindness at every turn. "Because of the drug dealing, the violence, many of the favelas in Rio are already lost," Albert says, after introducing me to the members of a local association whose meetings he chairs. "But here in Bahia there's still hope we can turn things around. In ten, twenty years it may be too late." The members of the Pau da Lima association meet in a little community center on the neighborhood's main drag. There are teenagers here, along with middle-aged men and women in T-shirts and sandals, and an old man with few teeth who is dressed in freshly pressed trousers and shined shoes. A seventeen-year-old girl in dreadlocks, wise beyond my years, let alone hers, presents a report on distributing powdered milk to children with disabilities. The local botanical garden will give a lesson in recycling. In unique, self-contained moments, the desolation and hopelessness outside is flooded with an intensity of spirit that overwhelms the easy cynicism I have carried with me from New York. It is hard not to feel at least a pinch of optimism in Pau da Lima. It is hard not to want to help.

I have seen Salvador's smiling face, calloused fingers, and quivering *bunda*, but now I want to understand her heart. One of my last evenings in the city could pass for a clandestine operation. A young man shows up at my hotel. I am put into a small Renault with my fellow traveler, a quiet Colombian doctor with a voodoo fetish, and soon we're speeding through the decrepit suburbs of Salvador heading for a house of candomblé. In the simple whitewashed *terreiro*, I meet Luis, our guide, who is a thoughtful acolyte of the African religion. The Colombian and I are slotted amid a row of locals, incense clouds my eyes, and soon men and women of all ages clad in Bahian white (they are all black-skinned, except for one fat white Brazilian, wearing what looks like a toque) start a slow, ponderous procession around the room to the beat of drums and an undulating Yoruba chant. They welcome the sixteen *orixás*, spirit guides who connect each worshiper to the high god, Olorun. Each *orixá* has his or her own dance, liturgy, and colors. Tonight we are celebrating Xangô, the *orixá* of justice, the guardian of lawyers, judges, and government workers. Personally, I like the pregnant Oxum, mistress of rivers, who stares vainly in her own mirror and protects those toiling in the arts and crafts.

As the drumbeats crescendo, people occasionally fall to kiss the ground or stretch out their arms in veneration of a particular *orixá*. White dresses swirl around me; sweat erupts in geysers. The bodies are round and strong. It may seem profane, but I am taken back to the samba I saw at Fundo do Cravinho on my first night in Salvador. A huge *pai de santo*, or resident holy man, emerges in a bright orange robe. He dances gently with a small child. Suddenly it is 1538, and we have returned to the time when the first unfortunate African feet touched the ground these modern-day Bahians are now kissing. Women come out with the offerings. They are dancing with huge plates of *acarajé*, *carurú* (an okra dish), and yellow and white corn. Then I notice a pretty young woman convulsing, possessed by the spirit of her *orixá*, her very body speaking in tongues. The *pai de santo* quickly intervenes; she is wrapped in white cloth and carried off. I nervously finger the round Ativan pill in my shirt pocket. But the dancing continues. Women walk around with towels, wiping sweat from the congregants. We are welcomed to eat the sweet and salty foods with our hands.

Candomblé was banned by the Portuguese masters, but as far as anyone can remember drums have echoed through the night in Salvador's African quarters. In this religious worldview, I am told, there is no guilt. There is no hell and no paradise. Respectful and communal, *terreira* is one of the last redoubts of purely oral tradition in a world speeding along with flashes of image and garbles of sound. Like everything else in Salvador, I leave it reluctantly, worried that tomorrow I will not find anything to take its place.

ANDREW SOLOMON

Circle of Fire

FROM *The New Yorker*

HERE'S A STORY THEY TELL IN LIBYA. Three contestants are in a race to run 500 meters carrying a bag of rats. The first sets off at a good pace, but after 100 meters the rats have chewed through the bag and spill onto the course. The second contestant gets to 150 meters, and the same thing happens. The third contestant shakes the bag so vigorously as he runs that the rats are constantly tumbling and cannot chew on anything, and he takes the prize. That third contestant is Libya's leader, Colonel Muammar Qaddafi, the permanent revolutionary.

Libya is about the size of Germany, France, Italy, and Spain, combined, but its population, just under six million, is roughly the same as Denmark's. Oil revenues make Libya, per capita, one of the wealthiest countries in Africa, and yet malnutrition and anemia are among its most prevalent health problems. It is an Islamic country where alcohol is illegal and most married women wear the *hijab*; it is a secular country where women are legally allowed to wear bikinis and Qaddafi is protected by a phalanx of gun-toting female bodyguards. The version of socialism promulgated in the mid-1970s by Qaddafi's political manifesto, *The Green Book*, is honored; the country is in the throes of capitalist reform. The head of the Libyan Publishers' League says that the books most often requested in his store are the Koran and Bill Clinton's *My Life*. Then, of course, there's the official line that the country is ruled by its citizens, through Basic People's Congresses, and the practical reality that it is ruled by Qaddafi. Libyan officials must far outstrip the Red Queen in her habit of believing six impossible things before breakfast.

For Americans, there's an even more salient contradiction. A regime led by a man President Reagan dubbed "the mad dog of the Middle East" — a regime that, throughout the 1980s, sponsored such groups as the IRA, the Abu Nidal Organization, and the Basque ETA, and was blamed for the explosion that, in 1988, downed Pan Am Flight 103, over Lockerbie, Scotland — is now an acknowledged ally in America's war on terror. Libya's governing circles are beset by infighting between those who think that this alliance is a good thing and hope for closer ties to the West and those who regard the West with truculent suspicion.

Qaddafi came to power in 1969, at the age of twenty-seven, when, as a junior military officer, he helped stage a bloodless coup against the pro-Western King Idris, who had been installed by the Allies after the Second World War. Now Qaddafi claims that he has no formal role in Libya and is simply an avuncular figure dispensing wisdom when asked. Yet Libyans are afraid to say his name, except in official contexts, where it meets with predictable cheering. The general euphemism is "the Leader." Informally, people refer to Qaddafi as the Big Guy or the One, or just point an index finger straight up. Saying "Qaddafi" aloud is thought to invite trouble. So is questioning his sometimes absurd policy proposals. He once insisted that families should use only one bar of soap a week. On another occasion, he proposed that currency be eliminated in favor of barter. "He believes in desert culture, even though the desert has no culture," one cosmopolitan resident of Libya's capital, Tripoli, told me. "He is trying to take life to its childhood."

The name of Qaddafi's second-oldest son and possible successor, Seif el-Islam al-Qaddafi, is seldom spoken, either. The inner circle refers to Seif, who is one of eight children, as the Principal, but he is also called the Son, the Brave Young Man, Our Young Friend, and the Engineer. The relationship between father and son is a topic of constant speculation. The Principal holds no title and, in keeping with his father's decree, maintains that the position of Leader is not hereditary. He does, however, sit comfortably close to power. The Leader, for all his opposition to royalty, looks a lot like a king, and the Principal is his crown prince.

Seif's role is to be the face of reform, "to polish his father's picture," as one prominent Libyan writer suggested to me. His academic papers at the London School of Economics, where he is pursuing a doctorate in political philosophy, are said to show a solid grasp of Hobbes and Locke. He founded the Qaddafi International Foundation for Charity Associations, which fights torture at home and abroad and works to promote human rights. He appears to be committed to high principles, even though real democratic change might put him out of the political picture. One of Seif's advisers told me that Seif would rather be the first elected head of the Libyan state than the second unelected leader of the revolution, but that he could go either way.

"Qaddafi claims that he is not the Leader, and Seif claims that he is the opposition, and they are both liars," Maitre Saad Djebbar, an Algerian lawyer who has worked on Libyan affairs for many years, said. Others see a personal agenda. "The Leader is a Bedouin from the desert and simply wants power and control — he is content to rule a wrecked country," the expatriate poet Khaled Mattawa told me. "But his sons are urban; they have traveled, studied abroad, learned sophistication. They go falconing in the Gulf states with the princes of royal families. They want to drive BMWs and rule a country that is accepted in the panoply of nations."

Seif's office is in Tripoli's tallest and fanciest tower — a hulking glass building topped by a gigantic circular apparatus that was intended as a revolving restaurant but neither revolves nor serves food. The foundation's suite is modest and sparsely furnished, and its staff members appear to be the busiest people in Libya, bent over computers, talking simultaneously on several phones, surrounded by papers. The walls are covered with posters for Seif's causes: one shows a man with his face wrapped in barbed wire, with the caption "International Campaign Against Torture: Middle East Area: Libya the First Station."

Seif, however, is usually elsewhere, and I met him last fall in Montreal, where he was opening an exhibition of his own paintings. These are rendered with expressionist enthusiasm in a variety of familiar styles and may feature images of horses, desert skies, the face of the Leader, or one of Seif's beloved pet Bengal tigers. Seif has bestowed his pictures on urban centers from Paris to Tokyo, where they have been received as documentary curiosities, like the personal effects of the last czarina. Whether the primary function of these exhibitions is political, social, or artistic is never discussed.

We met at the Sofitel, which had given over the top floor to Seif and his entourage. Various deputies and advisers had gathered there in a large, nondescript suite. When he came in, everyone sat up straighter. Though Seif tries to be intimate and casual, his presence, even his name, makes other people formal. He wore a well-cut suit, and moved with grace. At thirty-three, he is good-looking and hip, with a shaved head, and he speaks intelligently, though with the vagueness about self and reality that afflicts royalty and child stars, and that comes from never having seen oneself accurately reflected in the eyes of others. He has more than a trace of the paternal charisma, but it has yet to harden into genius, incoherence, or his father's trademark combination of the two.

When I asked why Libya was not proceeding more rapidly toward democratic reform, Seif said, "In the last fifty years, we have moved from being a tribal society to being a colony to being a kingdom to being a revolutionary republic. Be patient." (After centuries of Ottoman rule, Libya was occupied by Italy between 1912 and 1943.) But, like his father, Seif relishes extravagant pronouncements, and soon proposed that Libya give up its entire military.

"The whole faith and strategy has changed," he said, looking to his courtiers for nods of agreement. "Why should we have an army? If Egypt invades Libya, the Americans are going to stop it." During the Reagan years, he said, Libya was "expecting America to attack us anytime — our whole defensive strategy was how to deal with the Americans. We used terrorism and violence because these are the weapons of the weak against the strong. I don't have missiles to hit your cities, so I send someone to attack your interests. Now that we have peace with America, there is no need for terrorism, no need for nuclear bombs." Seif dismissed any comparison between the terrorism that Libya had sponsored in the past and the kind associated with Al Qaeda. "We used terrorism as tactics, for bargaining," he told me. "Mr. bin Laden uses it for strategy. We wanted to gain more leverage. He wants to kill people. Fundamentalism in Libya — it's always there, though not so strong as before, in the 1990s." Seif did not mention that in the 1990s his father's security forces routinely imprisoned fundamentalists.

Religious extremists had "created a lot of problems in Libya," Seif said. "They tried to destabilize the whole society. But not anymore. Now they are weak. But the threat is there, the potential is there." Seif noted that three Libyans had been involved in suicide bombings in Iraq last year. "They are being recruited by Zarqawi," he said, "who wants to create cells and attack American interests in Libya — oil companies, American schools, and so on. It's a disaster for us, because we *want* the American presence. There aren't so many of these extremists, several dozen, but even that in a country like Libya is a big headache." As for American security interests, he said, "We are already on your side, helping the American war on terror. It's happening, and it's going to happen."

Seif's rhetoric may beguile his Western admirers, but to the hard-liners in Libya's government it remains anathema. Seif, for his part, refused to acknowledge the substantial Libyan opposition to reform: "Maybe there are three or four citizens like this. Not more."

That was the most outlandish of his declarations. An American congressional aide who has worked closely with Seif accurately described him as "80 percent sophisticated." Seif's prospects, of course, will depend not upon his profile abroad but upon his ability to orchestrate support at home. Despite his political presence in Libya, his father's legacy will not be easily assumed; there are too many competitors for the next generation of power. But Seif is a canny fellow. "The Principal knows that one secret of leadership is to see where the parade is headed," one of his advisers told me, "and rush in front of it before it gets there."

In 2004, two decades of American sanctions came to an end, after Libya had agreed to pay compensation for the victims of Lockerbie and renounced weapons of mass destruction. (Seif, who has spent a good deal of energy trying to rehabilitate Libya's image in the world, was involved in both negotiations.) Since then, the great question in Tripoli has been how deeply reform will penetrate a country that has been largely isolated for decades. Within the government, the fighting is bitter. The National Oil Company (reformist) and the Department of Energy (hard-line) are in constant conflict, as are the Ministry of Economics (reformist) and the Libyan Central Bank (hard-line). Since Qaddafi makes the ultimate ideological decisions, the spectacle calls to mind the worst aspects of multiparty democracy, albeit without parties or democracy.

According to Ali Abdullatif Ahmida, a Libyan expatriate who chairs the political-science department at the University of New England, in Maine, Qaddafi "plays his biological son Seif el-Islam against his ideological son Ahmed Ibrahim." Ibrahim is the deputy speaker of the General People's Congress, and the most public of an influential conservative triumvirate that also includes Musa Kusa, the head of Libyan intelligence, and Abdallah Senoussi, who oversees internal security. (About a year ago, Ibrahim declared that the United States, under orders from President Bush, was "forging the Koran and distributing the false copies among Americans in order to tarnish the image of Muslims and Islam.")

The infighting helps Qaddafi moderate the pace of change. "He thinks reform should come 'like a thief in the night,' so that it is hardly noticed," one family friend said. In some areas — notably with respect to civil liberties and economic restructuring — the rate of change is glacial. "What's the hurry?" A. M. Zlitni, the country's chief economic planner, asked when we spoke, with the careful blandness that Libyan officials affect in order to avoid affiliation with either camp. "We are not desperate." In other areas, change has occurred with startling speed. Although the country is still afflicted with the legacies of its two colonial powers — Byzantine corruption and Italian bureaucracy — it has opened up to international trade with dispatch: there are foreign goods for sale, even if few Libyans can afford them. You can buy Adidas sneakers and Italian shoes, along with local knockoffs like a brand of toothpaste called Crust. In bookstores once devoid of English-language titles, you can find editions of *Billy Budd*, *Invisible Man*, and the works of Congreve. The private sector is back in force. Hundreds of channels are available on satellite TV, and Internet cafés are crowded. One senior official said, "A year ago, it was a sin to mention the World Trade Organization. Now we want to become a member." The editor of *Al Shams* (the *Sun*), a leading state-owned paper, described a newsroom policy shift from "expressing struggle against the West to advocating working with foreign countries."

"Qaddafi understands the tribal structure and has the ability to play one person against another, one group against another," one Libyan official explained. "He's a strategic genius. He is doing with the reformers and hard-liners what he has done with these tribes, playing the pro-Western element against the anti-Western element."

For a foreigner, there's no better illustration of the push-me, pull-you quality of the new Libya than the process of getting in. An application for a journalist's visa that I submitted last year went nowhere, although the Libyan representative to the United States assured me steadily for five months that the visa was nearly ready. (When I met with Seif in Montreal, he volunteered to take care of it, with no evident results.) Next, I joined an international party of archaeologists who had been promised entry — but as we were waiting to board a Libyan Arab Airlines flight in Rome we were abruptly denied access to the plane. One source in the Libyan government told us that the Ministry of Immigration had moved recently and our papers had been mislaid. Another said that the head of the visa section had sabotaged files during the move. A third said that the story about the move had been floated as an alibi; the Leader had decided not to let in any Americans. Indeed, a tour group from the Metropolitan Museum arrived by ship in Tripoli in October and was not allowed to dock; the next month, five other ships met the same fate.

As a dual national, I applied using my British passport, again as a member of the archaeologists' delegation, and, as advised, wrote on the form that I was Anglican. Finally, I received a document marked "sixty-day invitation," though no one knew whether that was sixty days from the date of the letter, sixty days from the date the visa was stamped in my passport, or sixty days from the date I entered the country. I called the Libyan consulate in London every day about my visa. In the morning, there was no answer. In the afternoon, someone answered and said that consular services were available only in the morning. I flew to London, where the consular officer explained that I could enter Libya anytime in the next forty-five days for a stay of up to ninety days. I arrived at Tripoli airport in mid-November. Through a Libyan travel agency, I had arranged for a car at the airport, and, just as I'd joined a nearly motionless line for immigration, a man from the agency came by with my name on a placard, and walked me straight through; the immigration officer never even looked to see whether I matched my passport. "Your visa expired — you were supposed to enter within thirty days," the man said. "Fortunately, the guy at immigration is a friend, so it wasn't a problem."

It was an apt introduction to a country where the law is always open to interpretation and personal connections are the principal currency. I was in as a British Christian archaeologist rather than as an American Jewish journalist, but I was in. I promptly went to the

International Press Office, where I declared my journalistic purpose, and where the man in charge lectured me for thirty minutes about why Libyan democracy was better than American, the terrible untruths that American journalists had heaped on Libya, and America's imperialist tendencies. Then he volunteered that the officials I'd wanted to speak to would be too busy for me, and that I shouldn't have come.

This was standard procedure. Last April, after months of planning, the Council on Foreign Relations, in New York, sent an august delegation — including David Rockefeller, Peter G. Peterson, Alan Patricof, and Leonard Lauder — to Libya, with appointments to meet both Muammar and Seif Qaddafi. After they arrived, they were told that the Leader was unavailable and that the Principal had made a scheduling error and was on his way to Japan.

Officials in Libya seldom say no and seldom say yes. Libyans use a popular Arab term: I.B.M., which stands for *Inshallah, bokra, moumken,* or "With the will of God, tomorrow, maybe." All plans are provisional, even at the highest levels of government. You can see the head of the National Oil Company with an hour's notice; you can also spend weeks preparing for an appointment that never materializes.

I requested a meeting with the Prime Minister, Shukri Ghanem, before I went to Libya and every day for three weeks while I was in Tripoli. On my last day, I was in the middle of a meeting when my cell phone rang. "The Prime Minister will see you," someone said. I said that I hoped he could see me before I had to leave. "The Prime Minister will see you *now,*" he replied. "Oh, OK, I'll get my tape recorder —" I began. "He will see you *right now,*" the voice interrupted. "Where are you?" I gave the address. "A car will pick you up in three minutes."

The drive to the Prime Minister's office was terrifying, as most Libyan driving is. Tripolitans seem to think that traffic lights are just festive bits of colored glass strewn randomly along the roads, and they rebel against tightly regulated lives by ignoring all driving rules, blithely heading into opposing traffic on the far side of a two-way road, turning abruptly across five lanes of streaming cars. "No shortage of organs for transplant here!" a Libyan acquaintance remarked during one excursion. The driver dropped me at the wrong building. It took two hours of calls and confusion to reach my destination.

Dr. Shukri, as he is called by those close to him and by those who pretend to be close to him — he has a Ph.D. in international relations from the Fletcher School, at Tufts — has a certain portly grandeur. With a neat mustache and a well-tailored suit, he exuded an effortless cosmopolitanism that seemed more conducive to facilitating Libya's reentry into the world than to winning over the hard-line elements at home. When I arrived, he was sitting on a gilded sofa in a room furnished with Arabic reimaginings of Louis XVI furniture, before many trays of pastries and glasses of the inevitable mint tea. In the Libyan empire of obliquity, his clarity was refreshing, and his teasing irony seemed to acknowledge the absurdity of Libyan double talk.

I mentioned that many of his colleagues saw no need to hasten the pace of reform. This was clearly not his view. "Sometimes you have to be hard on those you love," he said. "You wake your sleeping child so that he can get to school. Being a little harsh, not seeking too much popularity, is a better way." He spoke of the need for pro-business measures that would reduce bureaucratic impediments and rampant corruption. "The corruption is tied to shortages, inefficiency, and unemployment," the Prime Minister said. "Cutting red tape — there is resistance to it. There is some resistance in good faith and some in bad faith."

Nor was he inclined to defer to the regime's egalitarian rhetoric. "Those who can excel should get more — having a few rich people can build a whole country," he said. Qaddafi's *Green Book* decreed that people should be "partners, not wage workers," but it is not easy to make everyone a partner, the Prime Minister observed. "People don't want to find jobs. They want the government to find them jobs. It's not viable."

The civil service, which employs about 20 percent of Libyans, is vastly oversubscribed; the National Oil Company, with a staff of forty thousand, has perhaps twice the employees it needs. Though salaries are capped, many people are paid for multiple jobs, and, if those jobs are overseen by members of their tribe, failure to show up is never questioned. On the other hand, because food is heavily subsidized, people can get by on very little money, enabling them to refuse jobs they consider beneath them. Heavy labor is done by sub-Saharan Africans, and slightly more skilled work by Egyptians.

"We have a paradoxical economy, in which we have many unemployed Libyans" — the official unemployment rate is almost 30 percent — "and two million foreigners working," Ghanem said. "This mismatch is catastrophic." The combination of an imported work force with high domestic unemployment is typical of oil-rich nations, but the problem is especially urgent in Libya because its population is growing rapidly — it is not unusual to meet people with fourteen children in a single marriage. Roughly half the population is under the age of fifteen.

On the subject of Islamic militants, the Prime Minister's views were close to those expressed by both the Leader and the Principal. "Radical fundamentalism is like cancer," he said. "It can strike anyplace, anytime, and you can't predict it, and, by the time you discover it, it has usually spread too far to be contained. Is there such fundamentalism here? I honestly don't think so. But it could be hatching quietly, unseen by us all."

The predominant form of Islam in Libya is Sunni Maliki, a relatively supple creed that is remote from the fundamentalisms espoused by the jihadis. Some Libyans, though, have pointed out that conditions that seem to have bred terrorism elsewhere — prosperity without employment and a large population of young people with no sense of purpose — currently prevail in the country.

The Prime Minister was more circumspect on the prospects for U.S.-Libyan diplomacy. "We would like a relationship, yes, but we do not want to get into bed with an elephant," he said, laughing, and spreading his hands wide in a gesture of innocence. "It could roll over in the night and crush us."

I mentioned public statements he'd made about being unable to bring about reform when he had to work with a cabinet assembled by Qaddafi, and asked about the constraints on his authority. Ghanem assumed the air of one confiding a great personal truth. "My ministers are like my brothers," he said, wrapping his hands around his knee. "I didn't choose them." He paused and added with a smile, "My father chose them."

At the center of Tripoli lies Green Square. Now mostly a parking lot, it's one of those vast anonymous spaces which military regimes favor. East of Green Square lie the surviving Italian colonial buildings. To the west is the old city, a warren of tiny streets and shops, crowned by the ancient Red Castle, which houses a distinguished archaeological museum. In front is an esplanade beside the sea. The modern city stretches out in all other directions, with some neighborhoods of private villas, and many of Soviet-style housing developments; it reflects both the optimism and the shoddiness of more recent Libyan history.

I was invited, one day, to the opening of a special exhibition on volunteerism, in a tent in Green Square. Addressing a gathering of a hundred or so people, an official said that tribute had to be paid to the greatest volunteer of all: Colonel Muammar Qaddafi, who, unlike the American President, does not draw a salary but out of "love and honesty" graciously consents to rule. "There is one God, and Muhammad is his prophet, and Qaddafi is his modern incarnation!" someone in the crowd cried. Such public avowals are of a piece with the billboards you find throughout Libya, showing a beaming Qaddafi, as triumphant and windswept as Clark Gable. Those billboards are the first thing a visitor notices; the second is the ubiquity of litter. Wherever you go — including even the spectacular ruins of the Hellenistic and Roman cities of Cyrene, Sabratha, and Leptis Magna — you see plastic bottles, bags, paper, chicken bones, cans; a film covering the landscape. "It's how the people of Libya piss on the system," one Libyan academic told me. "The Leader doesn't actually care about this country. Why should we keep it beautiful for him?" It is the most arresting of the country's many paradoxes: Libyans who hate the regime but love Libya cannot tell where one ends and the other begins. You can take this as a tribute, by way of inversion, to the state ideology.

In the early seventies, the Leader, disappointed by his countrymen's lack of revolutionary fervor, withdrew to the desert to write *The Green Book*, in which he advanced his Third Universal Theory as superior to capitalism and Communism. Individuals were to own their homes; other land was to be held in common. In 1977, he issued a Declaration of the Establishment of the People's Authority, launching the Jamahiriya, or "state of the masses," and the Libyan system of "direct democracy," in which the country is "ruled" by the People's Congresses: what *The Green Book* calls the "supervision of the government by the people." The Great Socialist People's

Libyan Arab Jamahiriya — memorably abbreviated as "the Great SPLAJ" — was born. *The Green Book* proposes that, to avoid internal disputes, every nation should have one religion, but it makes no mention of Islam. Qaddafi claimed that his manifesto enshrined the basic tenets of the Koran (freely equating, for instance, the Koranic notion of alms-giving with his redistributive social-welfare policies), and that it therefore had the status of Sharia. His relation to Islam has two aspects: he draws upon it to buttress his authority, but he is hostile to the Islamists because he will countenance no rivals to that authority.

The two radical decades that ensued — televised public hangings, burnings of Western books and musical instruments, the sudden prohibition of private enterprise, intense anti-Zionism, official solidarity with terrorist and guerrilla groups — met with sharp international disapprobation. Libya's rogue status allowed Qaddafi to consolidate power and play protector of his besieged population, a role in which he excels.

One Libyan in early middle age who had lived in the United States until September 11, and who missed America, spoke of what was wrong with Qaddafi's Libya, and then said, "But I wouldn't be where I am without the revolution. They paid for my education, sent me to America, and gave me a life I wouldn't have dreamed of without them."

In part, that's a reflection of the fact that prerevolutionary Libya was poor. The Jamahiriya benefited from the dramatic increase in petroleum prices that began in the seventies, and from the more aggressive revenue-sharing deals it imposed on foreign oil companies, so that oil earnings in the mid-seventies were roughly ten times what they had been in the mid-sixties. Oil money made possible major investments in education and infrastructure. The literacy rate in Libya has risen from about 20 percent, before Qaddafi came to power, to 82 percent. The average life expectancy has risen from forty-four to seventy-four. More than eighty thousand kilometers of roads have been built. Electricity has become nearly universal.

And Qaddafi has become, for most Libyans, simply a fact of life. Of Libya's nearly six million citizens, more than 70 percent have been born since he came to power. During that period, the cult of personality has sparked and dimmed, in a way that has a certain congruence with the phases of Soviet leadership: a heady moment of Leninist-style revolution when many people believed in the ideals; a Stalinist period of cruel repression and deliberate violence; a long Khrushchev period of mild thaw; and now a Brezhnev-style period of corruption, chaos, and factionalism. Many of Seif Qaddafi's admirers hope that he will prove to be the reforming Gorbachev of the story.

The fact that an essentially repressive society can be characterized as being in the midst of reform reflects just how grim things used to be there. In Tripoli, I heard stories about life inside prison from many people whose only offense against the Jamahiriya was to be critical of it. In 2002, a former government official who publicly called for free elections and a free press was jailed; he was released in early 2004 — only to be sent back to prison two weeks later for criticizing the regime to foreign reporters. There is no opposition press; an Internet journalist who had published stories critical of the government spent several months in prison last year on trumped-up charges. There are "social rehabilitation" facilities — effectively, detention centers — supposedly for the protection of women who have broken the laws against adultery and fornication, some of whom are in fact rape victims rejected by their families. A woman in these compounds can leave only if a male relative or fiancé takes her into his custody.

More widely covered is the case of five Bulgarian nurses who were accused in 1999 of deliberately infecting 426 children in a Benghazi hospital with HIV. The nurses were tortured until they confessed, and were sentenced to death in May 2004. Among people outside Libya, the accusations seem bizarre and concocted; among most Libyans, it's taken for granted that the children were deliberately infected and that the Bulgarians are the likeliest culprits. (Whereas Western investigators have blamed the infections on poor sanitation, a Libyan doctor close to the case maintains that only children on the ward where the convicted nurses worked were infected, and that, when the Bulgarians left, the infections ceased, despite the fact that sanitary conditions, in all the wards, remain far from ideal.) Seif has said that the convictions were unjust, a brave stand given how important it is that he not appear to be capitulating to Western pressure. "Sure, the Big Guy let Seif say the nurses were innocent — to see how it would play," a junior government official explained. "And it played badly." A few months later, Qaddafi reaffirmed the hard line, declaring that the infections were caused by "an organization aiming to destroy Libya." Negotiations with the Bulgarians are ongoing, however, and Libya's supreme court has granted the defendants a new trial, which is to begin in May.

Qaddafi is no Saddam Hussein or Idi Amin. He has been brutal and capricious, but he has not killed a large part of his own population. It is illegal to slander the Leader, and Law 71 makes a capital offense of any group activity opposed to the revolution, but this has been less strictly enforced lately. Libya has signed the UN Convention Against Torture, and the Minister of Justice has said that he will bring Libyan law in line with international human-rights standards. Some of this is window dressing. "They closed the People's Prisons, where all our political prisoners were," one Tripolitan lawyer told me. "And what happened? The political prisoners got reassigned to other prisons." The Foreign Minister, Abdurrahman Shalgham, told me with pride that four hundred policemen had been arrested for human-rights abuses — then admitted that none have been found guilty.

Last year, Omar Alkikli, a highly regarded fiction writer who was a political prisoner for ten years in the seventies and early eighties, sued the Libyan government for excluding former prisoners from the Libyan Writers' League. "I lost, and I knew I would lose," he said. "But I made my point." A medical student at Tripoli's Al-Fateh University told me, "OK, they've fixed maybe 4 percent of our serious problems, but I guess it's something." An official in Benghazi said, "The laws that were made of stone are now made of wood."

Few Libyans are inclined to test what civil liberties they may have. Giumma Attiga, a human-rights lawyer and one of the founders of Seif's Qaddafi Foundation, said, "The fear is very intense, very deeply ingrained. The highest official could tell people to speak freely and openly, with every guarantee that it was safe to do so, and the words would stick in their throats." In fact, it is a felony entailing a three-year prison sentence to discuss national policy with a foreigner, and, although such offenses have been less frequently prosecuted recently, most Libyans speak of such matters anxiously. The atmosphere is late Soviet: forbidding, secretive, careful, albeit not generally lethal. I was asked not to mention names on the phone or in e-mail. Several people asked me not to write down their phone numbers, lest my notebook be "lost." "I am speaking from my heart," an outspoken woman told me. "Carry it in your head."

Surveillance is pervasive in Libya. I was warned that the cabdriver who had been helping me get around was reporting to the security services, and I understood that my cell-phone conversations were not to be considered private. All the same, I was surprised when a press officer questioned me about shades of meaning in a personal e-mail I had written home a few days earlier. Someone from Seif's office called me indignantly one day and said, "You were heard in the hotel unfairly saying that you were unhappy with the help we've given you."

One night, I had dinner with a bureaucrat who complained about local politics. He told me that he had been questioned at length after a recent conversation with a foreigner. "Our interrogators were trained in brutality, cruelty, and sneakiness by the best — people from Cuba, East Germany, Syria, Lebanon, and Egypt," he explained.

When we had finished our meal, the waiter cleared all our dishes, then came back and redeposited the sugar bowl.

"What's with the sugar?" I asked the bureaucrat.

He gave me a bleakly mischievous look. "The other one ran out of tape," he replied.

For the most part, when Libyans talk of democratization they envision not elections but more personal privacy, greater educational opportunities, and expanded freedom of speech. "*Democracy* here is a word that means the Leadership considers, discusses, and sometimes accepts other people's ideas," Zlitni, the chief economic planner, said.

Qaddafi views electoral democracy as the tyranny of 51 percent — he has memorably written that citizens of Western-style democracies "move silently toward the ballot box, like the beads in a rosary, to cast their votes in the same way that they throw rubbish in dustbins" — and recently announced, not for the first time, that Western democracy was "farcical" and "fake." "There is no state with a democracy except Libya on the whole planet," he declared. "Countries like the United States, India, China, the Russian Federation are in bad need of this Jamahiriya system." For most Libyan pragmatists, political reform is about changing the mechanisms of Qaddafi's control, not about relaxing it. One government minister told me, "In most European countries, there are many parties, and in the U.S. only two. So here it is only one! It's not such a big difference." Even reformers seldom express much enthusiasm for electoral democracy. Most aspire to a sort of modernizing autocracy: their ideal is closer to Atatürk or the Shah of Iran than to Václav Havel. "There are no democracies in the Arab world," said Ahmed Swehli, a young businessman who had recently moved back to Libya from England, where he was educated. "We aren't going to go first. What we need is a really good dictator, and I think Seif al-Islam might be just that. And maybe he'll be that and be elected, too, though I can't think why he'd bother." Others are less cynical about electoral democracy as an ideal, but no more hopeful about its implementation.

One reason that many Libyans are leery of elections is their fear that, in a highly tribal society, the larger tribes would win control and everyone else would be squeezed out. Less intimate and specific than families, tribes are a second layer of identity, stronger for some people than for others. Especially among the less well educated, groups based on kinship and descent — tribes and their various subsets (subtribes, clans) — provide both a social network and a safety net: members of your group will get you a job or help you if you have money problems or mourn you when you die even if they didn't like you much while you were alive. "Better Qaddafi, a tough leader from a minor tribe, than one who represents his own tribe 100 percent," one Libyan intellectual said.

Meanwhile, the Basic People's Congresses provide at least a theater of political participation. They are open to any Libyan over eighteen, and meet for a week or two, four times a year. In principle, you can discuss anything at a Congress, though an agenda is set from above. There are 468 Basic People's Congresses, and, when in session, they meet daily. Afterward, a brief report is sent from each Congress to a Central Committee. (Libya is committee heaven — there is even a National Committee for Committees.) A typical Congress includes about three hundred members; most educated people who are not trying to climb the political ladder do not go. The format is town hall with touches of Quaker meeting and Alcoholics Anonymous.

The Basic People's Congresses were in session while I was in Libya, and I repeatedly asked, in vain, to visit one. Then, by chance, I mentioned my interest during an interview with the director of the National Supply Corporation (NASCO), which administers the subsidies that are a mainstay of the Libyan economy; he said that there would be a meeting at its offices at noon and invited me to attend.

I had hoped to sit quietly in a corner; instead, I was escorted to the front row, and someone scurried in to serve me tea. A voluble woman made an impassioned speech asking why Libya imported tomato paste when there was enough water to grow tomatoes. A discussion of tomatoes ensued. The officials introduced issues of economic reform. My interest was more in the session's dynamic than in its content, so I was paying scant attention when my translator shifted from phrases such as "openly traded equities" and "reallocation of subsidy funds" to something about how "we are lucky to host a prominent American journalist"; and just as I was registering this new topic he said, "who will now address the Congress on the future of the U.S.-Libya relationship," and I was handed a microphone.

While each of my sentences was being translated into Arabic, I had a fortunate pause in which to think of the next, and so I gave a warm and heartfelt speech, saying that I hoped we would soon see full diplomatic relations between our countries, that I had loved meeting the Libyans and hoped they would feel similarly welcome in the United States, and so on. I received a protracted ovation, and thereafter every speaker prefaced his remarks with kind words about me. I was just settling into the comfortable glow of new celebrity when my translator said, "We have to go now," and took me outside, where three journalists from *Al Shams* wanted to interview me. We wandered through fairly predictable territory and then they asked my opinion of Qaddafi's efforts to broker peace in Darfur. (Qaddafi has publicly met both with rebel leaders and with the Sudanese president, Omar al-Bashir.) I said that anyone working on that situation deserved support. I also said that Qaddafi's opposition to terrorism would appeal to Americans.

The following day, *Al Shams* ran a nearly full-page story with three large photographs of me at the Congress, under a double-banner headline that said, "THE WORLD NEEDS A MAN LIKE MUAMMAR QADDAFI TO ACHIEVE GLOBAL PEACE," and, below, "THE AMERICAN PEOPLE APPRECIATE MUAMMAR QADDAFI'S ROLE IN EASING THE PAIN INFLICTED BY SEPTEMBER 11TH" The morning that the piece was published, I received my long-awaited invitation to the Qaddafi compound.

A minder from the International Press Office called to tell me that I was in for "a surprise" and that he would pick me up at my hotel at 4:00 P.M. At the International Press Office, near Green Square, I joined some twenty other "international" journalists, all from Arab countries, and talked about why Qaddafi might want to see us. I was solemnly told that one never knows what the Leader wants: "One comes when asked." Finally, at about 6:45, a minibus appeared; we drove twenty minutes and then stopped by a vast concrete wall, at the perimeter of Qaddafi's compound. The car was searched and we were searched, and then we drove through a slalom course of obstacles and another security gantlet before being ushered into an immense tent with a lavish buffet. Within the next half-hour, four hundred or so people piled in, many in traditional robes.

One of my new journalist friends said that "the event" was about to start, and so we went over a knoll and into a polygonal structure with exposed rafters, which bore some resemblance to a rec hall at a summer camp. Hanging on the walls were sayings of the Leader's in huge Arabic and English type ("The United States of Africa is Africa's Future" and "One African Identity"), flanked by poster-size photographs of Rosa Parks. It was the fiftieth anniversary of her refusal to move to the back of the bus, and that, we finally understood, was the occasion for the gathering. At the front of the room, on a dais, stood a gigantic Naugahyde armchair, with three microphones beside it. A man in medical scrubs came out and swabbed down the chair and the microphones with gauze pads, to protect the Leader from infection.

Some African-Americans were seated in the row in front of us. I introduced myself to one, and he dourly explained that he was Minister Abdul Akbar Muhammad, the international representative of the Reverend Louis Farrakhan, who had been in Tripoli earlier but had returned abruptly to the United States for health reasons. Qaddafi has long been one of the Nation of Islam's funders.

Then the speeches began. The speakers stood at a lectern off to the side, keeping the dais free for Qaddafi. The first speaker was a former Deputy Minister of Foreign Affairs. "We Libyans cannot accept the prejudice of Americans against Africans," he began, to applause. "Those who were seven or eight when Rosa Parks was being shoved to the back of the bus are now fifty-seven or fifty-eight, and are leaders of the United States. They still carry this mentality. The new generation inherited this, and it is still going on." He worked himself up into rhetorical paroxysms, as though Jim Crow laws were still in effect. "We must fight the hatred of America for Africa," he said.

When he stepped down, Abdul Akbar Muhammad took the lectern to speak about American racial injustice, mentioning that, under segregation, blacks and whites had had to use separate *hammams*, or public steam baths, a detail previously lost on me. "We cannot count on the Zionist-controlled American media to tell our story," he said. "Zionists in the U.S. won't show how the leader of the Al-Fateh revolution is in sympathy with us and us with him."

The Leader never emerged, apparently having decided that, if Farrakhan wasn't making an appearance, he wouldn't, either. Still, the event reflected his fixation on establishing Libya as more an African than an Arab country (even though most Libyans are contemptuous of black people, who do the manual labor that Libyans disdain, and who are blamed for all crime). Qaddafi's early dream of pan-Arab unity fizzled, and when other Arab nations observed the UN sanctions in the 1990s, while many African countries did not, he turned southward. By African standards, Libya seems wealthy and functional; Arab nations, even North African neighbors, have little affection for Qaddafi. He has backed groups opposed to the Saudi regime, and Libyan agents were implicated in a 2003 plot to assassinate the Crown Prince of Saudi Arabia. (Seif suggested to me that the Libyans involved were hoping, in his coy phrase, for "regime change" but didn't necessarily know that the agenda of their Saudi partners included physical attacks on the royal family.)

When Qaddafi went to Algeria recently, a local cartoon showed a tent pitched at the Algiers Sheraton; Qaddafi sleeps in a tent, true to his Bedouin roots. One man is saying, "Let me in, I want to go to the circus!" The other says, "There's no circus here." The first rejoins, "But I was told that there's a clown in that tent!"

For modernizing reformers such as Shukri Ghanem, Libya's major problems are poor management and isolation, and the solutions are better management and global integration. "The world has changed," as Ghanem put it, "and, like other socialist states, we recognized that we had limited means and unlimited needs." The Internet and satellite television — the dishes are so plentiful that landing in Tripoli is like descending on a migrant storm of white moths — have brought further pressure for reform, by making that larger world visible. "The change has been inevitable since Oprah came on our televisions," a leading Libyan poet said to me ruefully. What Libyans mainly relate to, though, is the standard of living in other oil-rich states, as displayed on Al Jazeera and other Arab channels. Libya seems dusty and poor in comparison, and they wonder why.

Earnings from oil exports account for about 80 percent of the national budget. In the heyday of Libyan oil production, the country produced 3 million barrels a day. That number has dropped to 1.7 million, but the National Oil Company plans to get it back up by 2010. Libyan oil is of high quality, low in sulfur and easily refined. Libya has proven reserves of about 40 billion barrels of oil, the largest in Africa, and may have as much as 100 billion. Several major oil companies have ranked Libya as the best exploration opportunity in the world; the Libyans have lacked the resources to conduct extensive explorations themselves. In the fifteen years since foreign companies left, Libya's resources have been seriously mismanaged. "If Dr. No were trying to muck up the Libyan oil economy," a British adviser to the Libyan government said, "there is nothing he could think of that hasn't been done."

Still, oil money continues to make possible Libya's subsidy programs — the socialism in the Great Socialist People's Libyan Arab Jamahiriya concept. NASCO pays twenty-six dinars for a 110-pound bag of flour and sells it to bakers for two dinars; you can buy a loaf of bread for two cents. Rice, sugar, tea, pasta, and gasoline are also sold for a fraction of their cost. Economic reform will involve scaling back these subsidies (which currently amount to about six hundred million dollars a year) without impoverishing or starving people — which is all the more difficult given that wages have been frozen since 1982. Meanwhile, there is little credit available in Libya: no Libyan-issued credit cards can be used internationally; no financial institution meets international banking standards.

"The oil absorbs all the mistakes, of which there have been many," one Libyan official told me. "The oil money means that there is stability, and it makes the country easy to run. It's this little country with all this oil — it's like if you decided you wanted to open a 7-Eleven and you had a billion dollars to back it." The oil is a curse as well as a blessing. The SPLAJ system has produced a population that is unhampered by a work ethic. Libyans work five mornings a week, and that's it — assuming that they have jobs to go to. "If they were willing to take jobs in, say, construction, there would be jobs for them," Zlitni said sternly. "But we're a rich country, so the youngsters don't want to work hard." The fact remains that economies based on resources such as oil generate few jobs unless they diversify. Many university students I spoke to were convinced that, for all the talk of reform, their talents would remain unexploited. "When I finish my MBA, chances are that I won't be able to get a job," one complained to me. "The whole country runs on oil, not on employment. The wealth doesn't come out of anything you can get by working hard, which I am prepared to do, but what's the point?"

"If we hadn't had oil, we would have developed," the Minister of Finance, Abdulgader Elkhair, told me. "Frankly, I'd rather we had water."

For him, and for aspirants to Libya's emerging private sector, the main outrages are represented by a sclerotic ministerial bureaucracy and its endemic corruption. The nonprofit organization Transparency International gives Libya a Corruption Perceptions Index of 2.5, ranking it lower than Zimbabwe, Vietnam, and Afghanistan. The Heritage Foundation's 2006 Index of Economic Freedom ranks Libya 152nd out of 157 countries evaluated. "You need twenty documents to set up a company," Elkhair told me, "and even if you bribe all the right people it will take six months."

One day, I sat in bumper-to-bumper traffic with a Libyan human-rights activist, who gestured in despair at the roadwork, and said, "They dig it up and close it and dig it up again, for enormous sums of money every time and with no other purpose. This corruption makes me late for my meetings. Necessary things are not done here, and unnecessary things are done over and over." I met the previous head of the National Cancer Institute, described to me by other doctors as the best oncological surgeon in the country, who had been removed from his job to make way for a friend of the Leader's. The displaced doctor is now working at a small clinic, without essential equipment. The administrator who served under him sells fish at a roadside stand nearby.

"Qaddafi is very happy to have corrupt people working for him," a Qaddafi insider said to me. "He'd much rather have people who want money than people who want power, and so he looks the other way and no one threatens his total control of the country." (Tribal loyalties, which intersect with simple cronyism, also play a role here: Qaddafi has filled many high-level military and security posts with members of his Bedouin tribe, the Qathathfa, along with members of a large tribe to which the Qathathfa have long been allied, the Warfala.) A Tripoli lawyer added, "Corruption is a problem, and sometimes a solution."

I attended the opening of a United Arab Emirates trade fair in Tripoli, which was held in a tent and was full of international goods presented with a smile. You could get samples of everything from medication to cookware and industrial equipment, and a select crowd of Libyans passed through with shopping bags. Many business cards were exchanged. "Look, this country is so rich you can't believe it," Ahmed Swehli, the English-educated businessman, told me, glancing around. "Right now, it's like we're the kids of the richest man in the world, and we're in rags. The corruption, the bloat, is impoverishing."

Compounding the problem of graft is a shortage of basic operational competence. I went to a session of a leadership training program in Tripoli, organized by Cambridge Energy Research Associates and the Monitor Group, two American consulting firms that are advising the Libyan government. The foreign organizers had been determined to include the people they thought had the strongest leadership potential, but some local officials wanted to choose on the basis of connections. The compromise was neither wholly meritocratic nor purely corrupt. To some in the group, capitalism was still a novelty; others were ready for corner offices at Morgan Stanley. They role-played. They made speeches through crackly microphones under gigantic portraits of the Leader. Some described sophisticated financial instruments and drew flow charts; there was talk of "leveraged buyouts" and "institutional investors" and "a zero-sum game." On the other hand, one participant, dressed in a shabby suit and a bright tie, was asked how he would fund a construction project, and replied, vaguely, "Don't banks do that?" Another was surprised to learn that international backers usually expect interest or profit-sharing in return for risking their money. Libyan business, it's clear, will be led by people of impressive competence and by people of no competence.

At the end of the conference, the prize for the best presentation went to Abdulmonem M. Sbeta, who runs a private company that provides oil and marine construction services. He was suave and cultivated, with darting, lively eyes. "We need not leaders but opposers," he said to me afterward, over an Italian dinner in the Tripoli suburbs. "Everyone here has had a good model of how to lead. But no one has ever seen how to *oppose*, and the secret to successful business is opposition. People want prosperity more than emancipation, but, in any case, social reform can be achieved only through economic development."

But does Qaddafi wish to teach his subjects to oppose him? An expat businessman told me, "Qaddafi is afraid that the emergence of a wealthy class might inspire a so-called Second Revolution." Wealth is a relative term; by world standards, the wealthy people in the country are the Qaddafis, and, if anyone else has truly substantial assets, he's smart enough not to show it. In the meantime, the Leader's vagaries have kept Libya's elites off balance, sometimes in almost absurd ways. In 2000, Qaddafi lifted a longtime ban on SUVs, and prosperous Libyans went out and imported Hummers and Range Rovers. Three months later, the Leader decided that he had made a mistake, and he outlawed them again, leaving a large number of privileged Libyans owning vehicles that it was illegal to drive. "You can tell if you've reached the top," a young Libyan told me, "if you listen to a lot of conversation about SUVs rusting in the garage."

"Don't say 'opening,'" the Foreign Minister, Abdurrahman Shalgham, said, waving his hands in protest, when I asked him about the new Libya. "Don't say 'reintegrate.' Libya was never closed to the world; the world was closed to us." But the cost of Libyan paranoia has been an isolation that feeds this paranoia and keeps Libyans in the fold of the Leader. The idea of a world that wants to engage with Libya is dangerous to Qaddafi's hegemony. "America as an enemy would cause him trouble," Ali Abdullatif Ahmida, the political scientist, said. "But he doesn't want America as a friend, either."

Relations between Libya and the United States remain shadowed by history. Qaddafi's most vigorous opponent was President Reagan, who in 1980 closed the Libyan Embassy, then suspended oil imports, then shot down two planes over the Gulf of Sidra, where the U.S. disputed Libya's sovereignty. Ten days after the Libya-linked bombing of a West Berlin nightclub frequented by American servicemen, in 1986, Reagan bombed Tripoli and Benghazi, dropping ordnance on Qaddafi's compound in an apparent attempt to assassinate him. Qaddafi claims to have lost an adopted daughter in the raid. "His grip on power was sliding and then there was the bombing and it united the Libyans behind him," one Libyan official told me.

The total isolation of Libya began in 1991, when the United States and Britain indicted two Libyans suspected of involvement in the downing of Pan Am Flight 103, and the French indicted four Libyan suspects in the 1989 explosion of the French airliner UTA 772 over the Niger desert. Libya refused to surrender any of the suspects, and, the following year, the United Nations approved economic sanctions. Only in 1999 did Libya allow the Lockerbie suspects to be brought to trial, under Scottish law, in The Hague. (A financial settlement was reached that year with French authorities as well.) The Scottish court convicted one of the suspects and acquitted the other. Libya long denied any wrongdoing but eventually accepted that it had to admit to it, as a pragmatic matter, though Libyan officials see it as a forced confession. Qaddafi never accepted personal guilt.

The Lockerbie question, a closed book to most Americans, was brought up repeatedly while I was in Libya. One official said, "I can't believe the Libyans at that time could have pulled off something that big. Something that stupid — that is completely believable. But not something that big." Western investigators continue to argue whether Libya had direct involvement in the event. Initial inquiries suggested that the bombing was the work of the Syrian-led Popular Front for the Liberation of Palestine–General Command, a terror group funded by Iran, and both a former Scottish police chief and a former CIA officer later submitted statements claiming that the physical evidence inculpating Libya had been planted. Because of such problems, Robert Black, the Q.C. and Edinburgh law professor who helped set up the trial, told the *Scotsman* this past November that the Lockerbie verdict was "the most disgraceful miscarriage of justice in Scotland for one hundred years," and would "gravely damage" the reputation of the Scottish criminal-justice system. The case is now under consideration by the Scottish Criminal Cases Review Commission. Because Libya supported foreign terrorist groups, though, the regime could have been implicated even if it was not the main author of the disaster.

In recent years, U.S. diplomatic relations with Libya have thawed to tepid. In 1999, the United States agreed to the suspension of UN sanctions, but not its own, which it renewed in August 2001. Then came 9/11. Qaddafi condemned the attacks, called the Taliban "Godless promoters of political Islam," and pointed out that six years earlier he had issued a warrant for Osama bin Laden's arrest. In August 2003, the Libyan government pledged to deposit $2.7 billion in the Bank for International Settlements, in Switzerland, to compensate the families of those lost on Pan Am 103. Four months later, after secret negotiations with a British-led team, Libya agreed to renounce its WMD program, and American sanctions were eased.

In fact, Qaddafi had made similar overtures to both George H. W. Bush and Bill Clinton but was spurned — in part, according to Martin Indyk, who was Clinton's Assistant Secretary of State for Near Eastern Affairs, because Libya's weapons programs were not considered an imminent threat. This has been borne out. Mohamed ElBaradei, the head of the International Atomic Energy Agency, described Libya's nuclear program as "at an early stage of development" — many of the centrifuges had evidently never been uncrated. But John Wolf, who, as George W. Bush's Assistant Secretary of State for Nonproliferation, played a key role in dismantling Libya's program, maintains that something of real value was secured — more by way of information and evidence than by the removal of a present threat. "The Libyans had the design of a nuclear weapon, sold by the A. Q. Khan network," he told me, referring to the former head of Pakistan's nuclear-weapons program. "Libya's decision to turn over not only equipment but also the documentation, shipping invoices, plans, et cetera, provided a treasure trove of materials that were instrumental in establishing the credible case that mobilized countries against implicated individuals and companies abroad. We would not have been able to convince many of these countries or the IAEA of the cancerlike nature of the festering A. Q. Khan network without that documentation. The information that enabled us to break up the network was critical."

After the 2003 agreement, President Bush said that any nation that gave up WMDs would "find an open path to better relations" with the United States and that "Libya has begun the process of rejoining the community of nations." By late 2004, the United States had revoked the travel ban, established limited diplomatic relations, and lifted many remaining trade restrictions. What Seif calls "this cocktail of problems and sanctions" had, it seemed, been largely addressed. Certainly the Bush administration was eager to see American companies compete for oil-exploration rights in Libya, and it has facilitated economic engagement. But issues such as the 2003 anti-Saudi plot and the affair of the Bulgarian nurses have stalled the entente, and Libya remains on the State Department's list of state sponsors of terrorism. Until the country is taken off the list, the United States must vote against IMF and World Bank loans to Tripoli, and substantial sanctions remain in place.

"It's almost the same as during the embargo," the head of the National Oil Company said. Libyan hard-liners point out that U.S. officials have acknowledged that no act of terrorism has been linked to Libya in years, and they complain that, while Tony Blair, Jacques Chirac, Gerhard Schröder, and Silvio Berlusconi have all visited Tripoli, the United States has sent no one above the undersecretary level. The United States has no official consulate in Libya; Libyans who want visas apply in Tunisia, and the United States does not grant them freely. Libyan reformers who thought that settling Lockerbie and renouncing WMDs would allow the resumption of normal relations talk about "receding goalposts."

David Mack, a former high-ranking U.S. diplomat who has served in Libya, told me, "It's been useful to us to be able to engage in intelligence exchanges with Libya; it's quite clearly been useful to them." He pointed out that the United States had agreed to list the dissident Libyan Islamic Fighting Group as a terrorist organization, and got it banned from Britain, where some of its members had been based. "Having made all this progress," Mack said, "if we now just let things drift, inevitably there will be relapses."

So while the Bush administration holds up Libya as a role model for disarmament — "If Libya can do it, Iran can do it, too," John Bolton, the U.S. Ambassador to the United Nations, has said — some policy analysts think that the administration has done too little to promote that example. Ronald Bruce St John, a Libya scholar at the International Relations Center, observes that America's priority has been to control WMDs and get support for the war on terror; Libya's priorities are the rationalization of commercial and diplomatic relations. American goals have been met; Libyan goals have not. In Tripoli, hard-liners seethe that Libya gave away the store, while the reformers feel undermined.

The reformers' own diplomatic efforts have had limited success. Representative Tom Lantos, of California, and Senator Richard Lugar, of Indiana, both have visited Libya, where they met with Seif, Shukri Ghanem, and Qaddafi himself, and have taken an optimistic view. "Qaddafi has clearly made a 180-degree turn," Lantos said to me, "and we are turning around the aircraft carrier that is U.S. policy." But when Lantos sought a cosponsor for the United States–Libya Relations Act, which was meant to strengthen bilateral relations, nobody was interested. Mack said, "We need to show the world, particularly governments like Iran and North Korea, that there is an alternative paradigm for dealing with the United States, and much to be gained by having a normal relationship with us," and suggested that American interests would be served by improved relations with an Arab leader who opposes fundamentalism and has substantial oil reserves.

"Deep down, the Libyans think the U.S. will not be satisfied with anything short of regime change," one of Seif's advisers said. "And, deep down, the Americans think that, if they normalize relations, Qaddafi will blow something up and make them look like fools."

Everywhere I went in Libya, opposition to U.S. policy was tempered by enthusiasm for individual Americans. Among the older generation of Libyans, the reformers were eager for news of the towns where they had once studied, in Kansas, Texas, Colorado. (Most of the hard-liners I met had never visited the United States.) Many Libyans hoped for improved relations with the outside world simply because the pariah experience has been a lonely one.

I spent a morning with the human-rights lawyer Azza Magour, a striking woman with cascading hair and a warm laugh, who had just returned from a humanitarian conference in Morocco. Her father was an important figure in postrevolutionary Libyan politics, and this has given her leeway; she seemed almost oblivious of the constraints that keep most Libyan women in headscarves and at home. I asked her how she felt about the U.S., and she told me that it was hard for her to be pro-American in the wake of the news reports about Abu Ghraib and Guantánamo. "You cannot imagine how we worshiped the idea of America," she said, and she looked down at the floor, as though she were talking about a relative who had recently died. "We wanted nothing more than to be with you, this rich, fair democracy. But now we ask who is giving us this lesson of freedom? I mean — if you caught your high priest in bed with a prostitute, would you still count on him to get you in the door of heaven?" Magour is still hoping to show her young daughter the United States, though. She said that, at least once a week, her daughter asks how things are going between Libya and America, and Magour says, "It's going, sweetheart." And her daughter wonders, "So can we visit Disneyland yet?" and she has to say, "Not yet, sweetheart, not yet."

For a culture that is politically and socially underdeveloped, Libya has a surprisingly active intelligentsia, who view their own society with tenderness and irony. People I met and liked invited me out over and over and introduced me to friends and family. I went to a birthday party at the house of one Libyan; his wife cooked a feast for us, and I stayed up half the night with them and their children, watching movies. The day before I left, friends took me out for late-night tea and gave me full traditional Libyan dress — a long shirt, an embroidered vest, and a little black hat — as a going-away present.

The social life of Libyans is essentially private. Tripoli is latticed with wide highways; gasoline is subsidized, and, because there are no bars or clubs and few cinemas or theaters, the most popular pastime is driving; people cruise around for hours. The privacy of cars enhances their charm, but mostly the Tripoli highways, busy through the night, provide diversion for citizens desperate for entertainment or novelty. When they aren't driving, most Tripolitans socialize at home rather than in cafés, partly because of the absence of women and alcohol in public places.

I had my first drink in Libya after a friend called an army colonel and asked, "Do you have any pomegranate seeds?" (It is wise to use euphemisms in police states.) He did, and we drove to the outskirts of a small city, to a large white house with a long veranda, beside a dirt road. In the Libyan way, the house was built of concrete and painted white, but it was beginning to show signs of wear. We sat on a wide, bright-colored banquette under fluorescent lights in an enormous room. The place was decorated with souvenirs from Central Asia, where our host had trained, including many carvings of bears with fishing rods. We listened to a medley of Shirley Bassey hits played on the zither, and took turns smoking from a five-foot-tall hookah. The colonel, a beaming, extroverted Libyan of sub-Saharan ancestry, served the local home brew, eighty proof and rough enough to remove not just fingernail polish but quite possibly fingernails as well, on a table covered with a lavishly embroidered cloth and laden with Fanta and Pringles. The atmosphere was reminiscent of a high-school pot party.

I asked my friend how he would feel about his sons drinking, and he laughed, replying, "It's inevitable." Then I asked about his daughters, and he grew serious: "If my daughters were drinking, I would be very, very upset — furious, in fact. Because, if people found out that they had been drinking, they would think they might also be sexually active, and their marriage prospects would be shattered."

I met a Libyan woman who worked for Alitalia, a job that she loved but that she felt no Libyan husband would tolerate. "I have to choose between a marriage and a life, and I have chosen a life," she said. "Most women here choose a marriage. It's a question of taste." The restrictions are a matter not of laws — on issues like gender equality, the laws are more progressive than in most Arab countries — but of social norms.

Qaddafi accepts such customs, but he frequently describes his own society as "backward" (his favorite term of disapprobation); one Libyan intellectual complained to me, "If you listen to his words, you will agree that he hates the Libyan people." While Qaddafi represses the democratizing forces from the left, he is far more brutal with the Islamist ones on the right. Indeed, most of the regime's political victims in the past few decades have been members of Islamist groups that he has banned, including the Muslim

Brotherhood. Libya's Islamic institutes, almost fifty of them, were shut down in 1988. When clerics protested Qaddafi's "innovative" interpretations of the Koran and his dismissal of all post-Koranic commentary and custom, Qaddafi declared that Islam permitted its followers to speak directly to Allah, and that clergymen were unnecessary intermediaries. A year later, he likened Islamic militants to "a cancer, the black death, and AIDS." As if to vex Hamas, once a beneficiary of his largesse, he has even argued, in recent years, that the Palestinians have no exclusive claim to the land of Israel, and called for a binational state — he dubbed it "Isratine" — that would guarantee the safety of both Palestinians and Jews, who, far from being enemies of the Arab people, were their biblical kin. ("There may be some objections to the name," he allowed, "but they would be unhelpful, harmful, and superficial.")

"You ask us, 'Why do you oppress the opposition in the Middle East?'" Qaddafi said in March, speaking via satellite link to a conference at Columbia University, dressed in purple robes and seated in front of a map of Africa. "Because, in the Middle East, the opposition is quite different than the opposition in advanced countries. In our countries, the opposition takes the form of explosions, assassinations, killing . . . . This is a manifestation of social backwardness." On this point, at least, the hard-liners and the reformers tend to converge. Foreign Minister Shalgham told me, "The fundamentalists represent a threat to your security. They represent a threat to our way of life. They are against the future, against science, the arts, women, and freedom. They would drag us back to the Middle Ages. You fear their acts; we fear the ideology behind those acts. OK, read the Koran for an hour a day, and that's enough; if you don't also study engineering, medicine, business, and mathematics, how can you survive? But people have figured out that, the tougher your Islam, the easier to find followers."

The fear of radical Islam helps explain why authorities cracked down so forcefully when, in February, protests erupted in Benghazi over the Danish cartoons of the prophet Muhammad and the decision of an Italian cabinet minister to wear a T-shirt featuring the images. Eleven people were killed by the police, and violence spread to at least two other cities in the eastern part of the country, where Qaddafi's hold on power has always been relatively weak.

Seif gave local voice to international opinion, saying, "The protest was a mistake, and the police intervention against the demonstrators was an even bigger mistake." His father, too, repudiated the "backwardness" of the police response, but mainly wanted to insist that the riots hadn't arisen from Islamic fervor, much less discontent with his regime; rather, they were spurred by anger at the history of Italian colonialism. (More than a quarter of a million Libyans — perhaps a third of the population — are estimated to have perished as a result of the Italian occupation, many in concentration camps.) "Unfortunately, there could be more Benghazis," or even "attacks in Italy," if Rome didn't offer reparations, Qaddafi warned, saying that he would be mollified if Italy were to build a highway across Libya, for some three billion euros. The Italian Foreign Minister, Gianfranco Fini, said that this was "a not too veiled threat," adding, "We have already said that we want to put the colonial past definitely behind us in our relations with Libya. We maintain this position in a clear and transparent way. We expect a similarly coherent position from the Libyan leader."

When I read this statement to a Libyan acquaintance, he burst out laughing. "Good luck, Mr. Fini!" he said. Expatriate opposition leaders have claimed that Qaddafi staged the riots to extract concessions from Europe, and that they then escalated out of control. In Libya, the issue was widely seen to be economic — a disgruntled population of unemployed youth needed an outlet for their anger.

The most immediate sequel to the riots was the dismissal of Prime Minister Shukri Ghanem. (He was given a post at the National Oil Company.) There were already rumors when I was in Tripoli that Ghanem was going to lose his job in a cabinet reshuffle; the openness that seemed so refreshing when we met had not pleased the Leader. "He made three basic mistakes," one Qaddafi adviser said to me. "First, he associated reform with his own name and complained publicly about the Leadership. In Libya, if you want to accomplish things you make yourself invisible, you sublimate your ego. Second, he thought that a strong position with the West would guarantee his hold on power and didn't understand that the West counts for very little here. Third, he failed to win over the Libyan people; he never seemed to be concerned about their suffering . . . . In the street, there is relief that he is gone — though there is no affection for the alternative." Ghanem's successor was the taciturn hard-liner Baghdadi al-Mahmoudi. "For the Leadership, it will be easier to make economic adjustments now that the reform will come clearly and directly from the Leadership, and not be seen as admissions that the Leader was wrong, as concessions to some kind of competition."

The change of Prime Ministers was, of course, a reassertion of Qaddafi's power: more tumbling of the rats. Several ministries — including oil and energy — were shaken up, with people removed from jobs they had held for decades. The U.S. State Department's decision, in late March, to keep Libya on its terrorism list both reflects the problem and contributes to it, and has outraged Libyans in and out of power.

Because Ghanem's strong suit was supposed to be his ease with Western powers, his failure to get Libya removed from the U.S. terrorism list helped insure his replacement by a hard-liner. Baghdadi al-Mahmoudi has been described to me as financially corrupt but wily, calculating, and extremely industrious. He is "a technocrat out of the Revolutionary Committees who works hard to glorify the Leader's policies," a Libyan-American academic said. "Will reform slow? Well, Shukri Ghanem talked a good line about reform but accomplished so little that there's not much backsliding to do. Mahmoudi realizes that economic reform has to move forward and will do that for the Leader. He has absolutely no interest in political or social reform, and he will leave it to the Leader to have a relationship with the West." It has been suggested that, with the appointment of a hard-liner, some of the infighting will subside.

"Ahmed Ibrahim's power will wane, too," one of Seif's advisers told me hopefully, referring to the deputy speaker of the General People's Congress. Seif will now be his own man: "He's old enough to carry that off."

"We call the world close to the Leader the Circle of Fire," one Libyan intellectual said. "Get close and it warms you up; get too close and you go down in flames. The Circle of Fire includes both reformers and hard-liners; Qaddafi likes the chaos that creates." He spoke with irony, almost with disdain, and yet he was not above warming himself at the fire. The class of educated Libyans — a class that includes poets, archaeologists, professors, ministers, doctors, businessmen, and civil servants — is tiny. Given the way that tribalism intersects with class alliances and political identities, social relationships exist in Libya among people who in a larger society would probably be kept apart by mutual opposition. Political enmity is often crosshatched with social amity. In Tripoli, I had dinner at the home of an older writer who spoke passionately of the injustices of the Qaddafi regime in both its absolutism and its new capitalism. "He has to go," he said. "This colonel has eaten the best years of my life, poisoned my soul and my existence, murdered the people I loved. I hate him more than I love my wife. He and his government and everyone who has anything to do with him must go. Enough is enough. We have no souls left. Do not let yourself be fooled by this talk of reform. What kind of reform is it when this man is still sitting in Tripoli? I cannot say it to you enough times. He must go. He must go. He must go." A few minutes later, when I mentioned a high-ranking member of the regime whom I hoped to interview, he said, "Ah, he was here for dinner earlier this week." He added, with a shrug, "I don't agree with him, but I like him."

The coziness between the authorities and many of those who railed against them continually surprised me. Some of this was simple pragmatism, but not all; it was more intimate than that. A person's network of loyalties and connections was never predictable. I had a drink (of nonalcoholic beer) in the Tripoli planetarium with a professor who had previously claimed that the Prime Minister and Seif got drunk together and raped the country — and they were the good guys. We had joked about the government's inefficiencies, and he had said darkly that no one who wasn't Libyan had any good reason to endure this kind of chaos. He had asked how I could hold on to my sanity when I was dealing with government offices.

Now he was beaming. "Hey, I've been given a job with the Ministry," he said. He raised a hand up over his head in a gesture of pride and triumph.

I said I was surprised that he was so eager to join a regime that he loathed.

"Well," he replied, "it also happens to be the only game in town."

JONATHAN STERN

The Lonely Planet Guide to My Apartment

FROM *The New Yorker*

Orientation

MY APARTMENT'S VAST EXPANSE of unfurnished space can be daunting at first, and its population of one difficult to communicate with. After going through customs, you'll see a large area with a couch to the left. Much of My Apartment's "television viewing" occurs here, as does the very occasional **making out with a girl** (see "Festivals"). To the north is the **food district**, with its colorful cereal boxes and **antojitos**, or "little whims."

What to Bring

A good rule of thumb is "If it's something you'll want, you have to bring it in yourself." This applies to water, as well as to toilet paper and English-language periodicals. Most important, come with plenty of cash, as there's sure to be someone with his hand out. In My Apartment, it's axiomatic that you have to grease the wheels to make the engine run.

When to Go

The best time to travel to My Apartment is typically after most people in their twenties are already showered and dressed and at a job. Visits on Saturdays and Sundays before 2:00 P.M. are highly discouraged, and can result in lengthy delays at the border (see "Getting There and Away").

Local Customs

The population of My Apartment has a daily ritual of **bitching**, which occurs at the end of the workday and prior to ordering in food. Usually, meals are taken during reruns of *Stargate Atlantis*. Don't be put off by impulsive sobbing or unprovoked rages. These traits have been passed down through generations and are part of the colorful heritage of My Apartment's people. The annual **Birthday Meltdown** (see "Festivals") is a tour de force of recrimination and self-loathing, highlighted by fanciful stilt-walkers and dancers wearing hand-sewn headdresses.

Health

Rabies and hepatitis have almost completely been eradicated from My Apartment, owing to an intensive program of medication and education. However, travelers must still be wary of **sexually transmitted diseases**. While abstinence is the only certain preventative, it is strenuously not endorsed by the My Apartment government. Condoms and antibiotics are available on most evenings (see "Medical Services").

Society & Culture

The inhabitants of My Apartment tend to be insecure and combative. This is likely the result of living under the thumb of a series of **illegitimate dictators** (see "History") that have dominated the citizens in recent years. Since the Breakup of 2004 and the ensuing electoral reforms, the situation has become more democratic.

Women Travelers

Solo female travelers are often subjected to excessive unwanted male attention. Normally, these men only want to talk to you, but their entreaties can quickly become tiresome. Don't be afraid to be rude. Even a mild polite response can be perceived as an expression of interest. The best approach is to avoid eye contact, always wear a bra, and talk incessantly about your "fiancé, Neil."

Dangers & Annoyances

The ongoing economic recession has led to a large increase in **petty crime**. For the most part, this is limited to the "borrowing" of personal items and the occasional accidental disappearance of the neighbor's newspaper. However, the U.S. Department of State has issued a warning about several common cons — such as the "I'm out of small bills" scam, typically perpetrated when the delivery guy arrives.

Volunteer Organizations

Various international agencies can place volunteers in projects working on areas such as job training, doing my laundry, election monitoring, developing opportunities for young women, running to the deli for me, and therapeutic massage.

Things to See & Do

A ten-foot walk to the nonworking fireplace brings musically inclined visitors to the popular **collection of novelty records**, which includes *Leonard Nimoy Sings*. The north-facing section of My Apartment is divided into two districts. In the lively Bedroom District, the excellent **drawer of snapshots of ex-girlfriends naked** is a good way to gain a deeper understanding of the history of the people, and is open for guided tours on most Saturdays between 2:00 A.M. and 3:00 A.M. The Western Quarter is home to the **bathtub with one working spa jet**, in which the recreation commissioner of My Apartment plans to hold an **international jello-wrestling tournament** in the spring of 2007.

Places to Eat

Tourists often flock to the **salvaged wooden telephone-cable spool** in front of the TV as a convenient dining spot. More adventurous eaters might try **standing over the sink**, as the locals do. If you're willing to venture off the beaten track, there's **balancing your plate on the arm of the couch** or **using the toilet lid as a makeshift table**.

Night Life

The music on offer tends toward late-seventies disco recordings, but they are sometimes embellished with impromptu live vocal performances. There was once a cockfight in My Apartment, though it was unplanned and will likely never happen again (see "Law Enforcement").

Sports & Outdoor Activities

The **air-hockey table** probably still works.

Excursions

A short trip in almost any direction will bring travelers to one of many unique **Starbucks** outlets. Or try one of the nightly walking tours to the sidewalk in front of the brownstone across the street to watch **that redhead** getting out of the shower with her curtains open. And tourists are often sent around the corner to visit the **ATM machine** in order to stock up for the rigorous financial demands of a trip to My Apartment.

Mule Rental

Mules can be rented by the hour or the day and are situated near the **main closet**. Prices vary with the season and it's best to reserve in advance, since My Apartment's stable of twenty-six mules books up fast. They may not be the quickest form of transportation, but they provide a wonderful way to see My Apartment up close.

Wildlife

The dog's name is **Sadie**. Don't touch her.

CYNTHIA ZARIN

Fantasy Island

FROM *Gourmet*

AT FIRST IT WAS THE NAME: Swans Island. The ad was tucked away in the back of an alumni magazine, among others for monogrammed tartans and plates painted with collegiate scenes. *Charming house on cove, three bedrooms, beautiful views; ferry from Bass Harbor.* Secretly, upon reading the ad, I embarked on a fantasy. We'd abandon city life and tend a garden laced with salt spray. At dusk we'd watch swans gliding under mackerel skies. I had read the children Robert McCloskey's *One Morning in Maine.* I, too, would make chowder with clams my children found; the harvest would be that much sweeter because the growing season was short. I imagined a plate of tomatoes scattered with wild mint, cobblers made from just-picked blueberries.

There are people who understand the nature of travel. I am not one of them. My approach shares the same pitfalls of imagination — unrealistic expectations, inevitable disappointments — that others bring to love affairs. Anywhere I go, I imagine myself setting up house. At the local market, using sign language, I pester the vendors until they tell me how to cook *morue* and tiny artichokes. I choose the pebble-dash house or sunstruck villa where, growing old, I will spend out my days. My vision of Swans Island was so encumbered. I called the owner of the house. He sent pictures, which I had no way of knowing were misleading in the extreme.

It was our second summer together as a family, and that may have accounted for its feeling of frantic fancy. We were trying to fit halves of two different families together: my daughter and me, and my husband and his two children. The summer before, we had taken ourselves to Cape Cod, to the village where I had spent every summer as a child. The ease of a familiar place (my stepchildren had spent holidays on the Cape, too, albeit on a different strip of sand) had seemed the most reasonable course: sorting ourselves out would be adventure enough. Every day after the beach we drove to the farm stand, where in wooden bins near the register were pyramids of topaz tomatoes, huge lettuces with the dirt still on them, ruby radishes. In the cool gloom of the fishmonger's we chose between bluefish and cod, and from the local butcher we bought hamburger and flank steak, which the children doused happily with ketchup. In our rented cottage's tiny kitchen with its turquoise-painted floor, I made fresh tomato sauce, ratatouille, and peach tart. The little girls made a sign out of an old shingle and wrote "Star Fish Café" on it with red nail polish.

The year had been full of bewilderment. I think now that I was trying to build us up and turn us into a family by feeding us the same bits of cellulose and peptide chains. We had no idea then that that cottage would become the fulcrum of our new-made life, but that first summer we knew that the month had been a success. So much so that by winter we decided to trifle with it. A new family, we thought, should try new things.

I have a very clear memory of that ferry trip to Swans Island, notable for its absence of foreboding. The children, excited and famished, are standing in the prow of the boat, their hair blowing backward in the wind, and I sit nearby wearing a large straw hat, pinned down against the breeze, unwrapping chicken salad sandwiches. I remember that there was lettuce in the sandwiches. We also had a plastic container of cut-up melon and strawberries: a smashed fruit salad. As we neared the dock I noted, idly, that a number of cars were packed with grocery bags and that one or two day-trippers seemed oddly weighted down with marketing, but my eye moved on. After all, I had provisions, too: a week's worth of imported pasta, two pounds of Parmigiano-Reggiano and another of farmhouse Cheddar, a tin of good olive oil and some wrinkled olives packed in rosemary, a bag of pistachios to have with drinks, a few bottles of decent wine.

The ferry docked. We drove off into the sharp air, which was pungent with diesel fuel. About a mile down the road we found the house, a trim white cottage set back from the water on a long hill.

The pictures had omitted the four-foot-high working replica of a lighthouse on the lawn next door, which, we learned shortly, switched on automatically at dusk and strafed the night with its high beam. The inside of the tidy house was as described — a clean-swept living room with a utilitarian kitchen: a spotless Sears stove, a big white refrigerator, and a washing machine. The cupboards were bare. Unlike in other houses I'd rented, the previous tenants had left not even a bag of sugar or the sticky remains of a jar of barbecue sauce. I missed these traces of other lives. The cottage was so empty the effect was antiseptic. Upstairs, the beds in the children's room were extravagantly high. When they jumped on them, they hit their heads. That done, we went out to scavenge for supper.

The owner of the cottage had left a map marked with the location of the grocery store and the historical society. (Later, I was to reflect that these were, in some respects, one and the same.) We piled into the car, still packed with our swimsuits and summer reading, our towels and orange peels. A few minutes later, after navigating the candy rack, I stood in front of the vegetable bin, which contained three molting cabbages and a few wormy potatoes. Too late, I read the message of those grocery bags on the ferry. Dismay hit. *What would we eat?*

I have spent most of my life in Manhattan, and the feeling was akin to that moment when, in a very tall building, the elevator doors close with a shudder, indicating they may not open again anytime soon. This trip had been my idea, and my ideas about it had been extravagant. In particular, I had a reverence bordering on fetishistic for the food we would eat together on summer holidays. I tended this reverence over the winter, when the children were with us only two nights a week, and slumped at the table, tired from traveling, like small pilgrims, between two households. The food we ate during the summer needed to sustain us all year.

While the children nudged each other over by the comics, I reconnoitered. A quick survey of the edible contents of the store yielded two gallons of milk, Rice Krispies, a quart of reconstituted orange juice, a pound of salted butter, a dozen eggs, frozen peas, two packets of ham, ketchup, and a bag of chips. No joy was to be had from a question to the clerk about fresh meat or chicken. A tentative inquiry about fresh vegetables met with a shrug. Pressed, he admitted that Mary, down the east side of the island, sometimes sold tomatoes, but she'd gone off island to see her sister. After a pause, he offered that the island's one restaurant was only open Wednesday until Sunday; a storm, he added, had broken its windows.

Back at the house, we found a corkscrew, opened the wine, and ate the pistachio nuts. The children were delighted with the chips. For supper we tucked into pasta with peas and grated Parmigiano-Reggiano. Afterwards I considered the options. Cheese omelets. More pasta. Peanut butter. I had not yet realized, as I would at 4:00 A.M., that our next-door neighbor was a lobsterman.

No snapshot could have conveyed that our neighbor, whom I will call Frank, revved his engine at four in the morning and played Elvis tunes full blast on his tape deck. When he returned — it was still very early — hoisting traps onto the dock, my husband greeted him. They bargained. In the six days that remained to us in Maine, we ate lobster five times. Perhaps because Frank realized he was ruining our sleep, the lobsters came cheap. We ate them boiled, sautéed, and grilled. We ate lobster salad with mayonnaise I made from the olive oil and ancient grocery-store eggs. I returned to the grocery and bought the blowsy cabbage, and we ate lobster medallions on peppered slaw. It is true, I think, that if you like to cook, you can make do with almost anything, but monotony is trying. I recalled the Pilgrims, bemoaning their diet of oysters and salmon. I worried we were eating nothing fresh, but the children didn't mind. They existed on peanut butter and plain pasta and Rice Krispies. I tried frying the shellacked grocery-store apples in butter, but they were too starchy; as for cooking kelp, my nerve failed. We were a family that always ate at home, but on Wednesday, when the restaurant reopened, we went.

We were the only customers. It was a little shack, perched precariously above a stony inlet where the sea was dashed on the rocks, green and black, the glorious slapdash of a John Marin print. The eldest dutifully read aloud from the plastic menu, and we discovered the dismal fact that there was absolutely nothing we wanted to eat. I'm not sure what I'd had in mind: Maine bouillabaisse? Oysters with wasabi? Fish fingers? Fried chicken? The hot dogs that we finally ordered — a better bet, we imagined, than burgers — arrived obscenely bare, accompanied by cottony white rolls and seemingly encased in plastic. We tried gnawing at them.

After that sad supper, I gave in. We demolished the pistachio nuts, broke off hunks of Cheddar, and drank up the wine. The children had recoiled from lobster's waving tentacles, its garish red hue, and by Thursday, so did we. Whatever point I wanted to make at the table dissolved in the thick salt air. There was something to be said, even I could see, for ice cream for supper. Feeding the ducks in the pond with store bread *(duck,* I thought, and considered the strength of my hands), we met a woman I had known in another life, who had inherited a beautiful stone house on the island. She invited us in and fed the children almond brittle from a tin box. Though I remembered her as a generous gourmand, she didn't invite us to stay for supper; in retrospect, I think she was hoarding her stores. What would an impromptu dinner party look like on the island, I thought? Lobster canapés on saltines, followed by *homard à l'américaine,* sans tomatoes, tarragon, and parsley, with Pop-Tarts to follow?

The next day, we bade adieu to Swans Island. We had not seen even one swan; at the local museum, amid the antique lobster traps, we discovered the island had been named for one James Swan, Revolutionary War colonel.

That week in Maine we hadn't, of course, had nothing to eat. What we didn't have was food grown in the earth, with the sun on it, or work for a cook with time on her hands and a family to grow and feed. When, a few years later, because of an eye injury, I was told I could do anything I liked for a week except read, I cooked instead, and thought of Maine, when the reverse had been true, and I could see but not taste.

When we got to the Cape after the daylong drive, we went straight to the nearest farm stand, where I bought five pounds of late tomatoes to roast in the battered oven, for the smell. While they cooked, I sat on the splintery porch and looked down on the dune covered with late roses and rose hips out of which the children, I knew, would soon make undrinkable tea, and I thought of the silvery beach on Swans Island, with its minaret carpet of sea urchins like a tiny St. Petersburg, the oyster-shell houses, and the straight pines like furred fish bones. The children raced out of the house like furies, begging for marshmallows. When we go back, I thought, we'll bring provisions. But we have not.

Contributors' Notes

Notable Travel Writing of 2006

Contributors' Notes

Jason Anthony's Antarctic essays have been published in the *Missouri Review, Seneca Review, Isotope, Alimentum* (forthcoming), and in the anthologies *In Pieces: An Anthology of Fragmentary Writing* (Impassio Press) and *Antarctica: Life on the Ice* (Traveler's Tales). One was a Notable Essay in *The Best American Essays 2006,* and his 2006 work was nominated for the Pushcart Prize. He would like to thank Jim Benning of *WorldHum.com* for his edits on the piece that appears here. Jason Anthony's Antarctic writings and photographs are online at www.albedoimages.com. He teaches English at the Deck House School in Edgecomb, Maine.

Rick Bass is the author of twenty-three books of fiction and nonfiction, including, most recently, a story collection, *The Lives of Rocks.* He lives with his family in northwest Montana's Yaak Valley, where he has long been active in efforts to help designate as wilderness the last roadless areas of the Kootenai National Forest.

Kevin Fedarko is a freelance writer who lives in northern New Mexico and works as a river guide in Grand Canyon National Park. He has been a correspondent for *Time* and now contributes to *Outside, National Geographic Adventure,* and *Men's Journal,* reporting primarily on mountaineering, backcountry skiing, and other aspects of outdoor adventure.

Ian Frazier writes essays and longer works of nonfiction. His books include *Gone to New York, Great Plains, Family, Coyote V. Acme, On the Rez, Dating Your Mom,* and most recently *The Fish's Eye.* He lives in New Jersey. He is working on a book about Siberia.

Steve Friedman's stories have been published in many national titles and anthologies, including, six times, *The Best American Sports Writing.* His third book, *The Agony of Victory,* will be published in October 2007. A Saint Louis native and graduate of Stanford University, Friedman lives in New York City, where he is Writer at Large for the Rodale Sports Group.

Elizabeth Gilbert was born in Connecticut in 1969 and was raised on a small family Christmas-tree farm. Her first book, a collection of short stories called *Pilgrims,* was a *New York Times* Notable Book, received the Pushcart Prize, and was a finalist for the Hemingway Foundation/PEN Award. Her novel, *Stern Men,* was also a *New York Times* Notable Book. *The Last American Man,* her biography of Eustace Conway, an eclectic modern-day woodsman, was a finalist in 2002 for both the National Book Award and the National Book Critics Circle Award. Her most recent book was the *New York Times*–best-selling memoir *Eat, Pray, Love,* about the year she spent traveling the world alone after a difficult divorce. It was chosen by *Entertainment Weekly* as one of the best ten nonfiction books of the year. Much of her writing has been optioned by Hollywood. Her *GQ* memoir about her bartending years became the Disney movie *Coyote Ugly.* Paramount Pictures recently has acquired screen rights to *Eat, Pray, Love,* in which Julia Roberts will star.

Reesa Grushka was born in Toronto, Canada. She currently lives in New York City, where she is working toward a PhD in Jewish studies. Her prose and poetry have appeared in *American Poetry Review, Gulf Coast, Five Points,* and the *Missouri Review.*

Just before this anthology went into production, **David Halberstam** was tragically killed in an automobile accident. Perhaps no other writer has so faithfully chronicled the profound changes in America in the second half of the twentieth century and the challenges of the twenty-first century as Halberstam did. He won a Pulitzer Prize at age thirty for his prophetic reporting in the early days of the Vietnam War and thirty-eight years later his bestseller, *War in a Time of Peace,* was a runner-up for the Pulitzer Prize. His classic, *The Best and the Brightest,* is the definitive book on how and why we went to war in Vietnam. His other books include *The Powers That Be,* about the rise of modern media; *The Reckoning,* about the challenge of Japan to the American automotive industry; and *The Fifties,* about a decade he regards as seminal in determining what our nation is today. *The Fifties* was made into an eight-part television series on the History Channel. Halberstam was never confined to one small piece of territory. Five of his fifteen bestsellers have been about sports, and it reflects the breadth of his work and the public's response to it that both *The Best and the Brightest* and *Summer of '49* (on an epic pennant race between the Yankees and the Red

Sox), were number-one *New York Times* bestsellers. Halberstam lived in New York City. He is survived by his wife, Jean, and their daughter, Julia.

Peter Hessler came to China as a Peace Corps volunteer in 1996. After working as a teacher in a small city called Fuling, he moved to Beijing in order to write. He became *The New Yorker*'s China correspondent, and he also contributes to *National Geographic.* He is working on the final book in a trilogy that spans the decade he spent in China. The first two books are *River Town* and *Oracle Bones.*

Edward Hoagland's first book, *Cat Man,* won the 1954 Houghton Mifflin Literary Fellowship. Since then he has written nearly twenty books, including *Walking the Dead Diamond River* (a 1974 National Book Award nominee), *African Calliope* (a 1980 American Book Award nominee), and *The Tugman's Passage* (a 1982 National Book Critics Circle Award nominee). In 1982 he was elected to the American Academy of Arts and Letters. Hoagland was the editor of *The Best American Essays 1999.*

Ian Parker is a staff writer at *The New Yorker.* He is British and lives in New York.

For seventy-two grueling days in 1972, **Nando Parrado** and fellow members of a Uruguayan rugby team fought for survival on a mountain peak in the Andes following a tragic plane crash that changed their lives forever. Since his ordeal, Parrado has gone on to achieve great personal success. He is the president of six companies in his native Uruguay and founder of two television production companies. In addition, he has won numerous motorcycle, auto racing, and watercraft awards, including the European Team Cup for stock car racing. In 1991 Parrado spent twenty-eight days crossing the Sahara Desert, a journey of more than eighty-five hundred kilometers from Morocco to Tunisia. Parrado resides with his wife and their two daughters in Montevideo, Uruguay. He is the author, with Vince Rause, of *Miracle in the Andes.*

Ann Patchett is the best-selling author of the novels *Run, Bel Canto, The Magician's Assistant, Taft,* and *The Patron Saint of Liars,* as well as the memoir *Truth and Beauty: A Friendship.*

Matthew Power has reported on places ranging from post-tsunami Thailand to post-Taliban Afghanistan, ridden motorcycles through the Kashmir Himalayas and the Andes, hopped freight trains across Canada, and drifted down the Mississippi on a homemade raft. He tells his mother about these things only afterward, so as not to worry her overly. An interest in the detritus of civilization, from dumpster diving in New York to computer recycling in China, drew Power and the photographer Misty Keasler to the Payatas dumpsite in Quezon City, Philippines. Power is a contributing editor at *Harper's* and *National Geographic Adventure,* and his writing has also appeared in the *New York Times, GQ, Men's Journal, Discover,* the *Virginia Quarterly Review, Slate.com,* and *The Best American Spiritual Writing 2006.* He grew up in Vermont and lives in Brooklyn, New York.

David Rakoff is the author of the books *Fraud* and *Don't Get Too Comfortable.* A regular contributor to Public Radio International's *This American Life,* his writing has also appeared in the *New York Times Magazine, Outside, GQ, Salon, Harper's Bazaar,* and *Slate.com,* among others.

George Saunders is the author of the short story collections *Pastoralia, CivilWarLand in Bad Decline,* and, most recently, *In Persuasion Nation.* He is also the author of the novella-length illustrated fable *The Brief and Frightening Reign of Phil,* the *New York Times*–best-selling children's book *The Very Persistent Gappers of Frip* (illustrated by Lane Smith), and a forthcoming book of selected nonfiction, *The Braindead Megaphone.* A 2006 MacArthur Fellow, he teaches in the creative writing program at Syracuse University.

Gary Shteyngart was born in Leningrad in 1972 and came to the United States seven years later. His debut novel, *The Russian Debutante's Handbook,* won the Stephen Crane Award for first fiction and the National Jewish Award for fiction. It was also named a *New York Times* Notable Book, a best book of the year by the *Washington Post* and *Entertainment Weekly,* and one of the best debuts of the year by the *Guardian.* His second novel, *Absurdistan,* published in May 2006, was named one of the Best Books of the Year by the *New York Times Book Review, Time,* the *Washington Post Book World,* the *Chicago Tribune,* and the *San Francisco Chronicle.* In 2007 he was named one of the Best American Novelists by *Granta.* His fiction and essays have appeared in *The New Yorker, Granta, GQ, Esquire, Travel + Leisure,* the *New York Times Magazine,* and many other publications. He lives in New York City.

Andrew Solomon studied at Yale University and Jesus College, Cambridge. He is a regular contributor to *The New Yorker, ArtForum,* and the *New York Times Magazine.* He is the author of *The Ivory Tower: Soviet Artists in a Time of Glasnost* and a novel, *A Stone Boat,* which was a finalist for the *Los Angeles Times* First Fiction Award. He is the winner of the 2001 National Book Award and was a finalist for the Pulitzer Prize.

Jonathan Stern is a screenwriter and film producer.

Cynthia Zarin is a staff writer at *The New Yorker.* She is the author of three books of poetry, including *The Watercourse,* which won the *Los Angeles Times* Book Award for Poetry in 2002, and five books for children. Her work has also appeared in *Architectural Digest,* the *New York Times Book Review,* the *New York Times Magazine,* the *Paris Review,* and other journals and has been widely anthologized. She is a contributing editor at *Gourmet.* Zarin was educated at Harvard and received an MFA from Columbia University's School of the Arts.

Notable Travel Writing of 2006

SELECTED BY JASON WILSON

KURT ANDERSON
A Different Denmark. *Travel + Leisure,* May.
ROGER ARNOLD
The Metal Hunters. *Scrap,* January/February.

JIM BENNING
Lust in Translation. *WorldHum.com,* May 1.
BEN BRADLEE
A Return. *The New Yorker,* October 2.

TIM CAHILL
Along the Devil's Highway. *National Geographic Adventure,* August.
WAYNE CURTIS
Greetings from Airworld! *The Atlantic Monthly,* July/August.

JASON DALEY
"Gentlemen, Destroy Your Engines." *Outside,* April.
BILL DONAHUE
Wheels of Life. *Washington Post Magazine,* September 17.
SIMON DUMENCO
Tomorrowland. *Condé Nast Traveler,* May.

ELIZABETH EAVES
Girls Go Wild, Adventures in New Zealand. *Slate.com,* February 10.

James Fallows
Postcards from Tomorrow Square. *The Atlantic Monthly,* December.
Robert Finch
Flat Time. *The American Scholar,* Winter.
Bill Fink
Accidentally Enjoying Albania. *San Francisco Chronicle Magazine,* October 1.
Michael Finkel
Olympic Glory. *Backpacker,* June.
Brett Forrest
Midnight in Moscow. *Vanity Fair,* July.
Katherine Friedman
Live Without Me. I'll Understand. *New York Times,* December 17.

J. Malcolm Garcia
War Costs. *Missouri Review,* Summer.
Descent into Haiti. *Virginia Quarterly Review,* Spring.
Kristoffer A. Garin
A Foreign Affair. *Harper's Magazine,* June.
Alma Guillermoprieto
Venezuela According to Chavez. *National Geographic,* April.

Tom Haines
The New Spin on Shanghai. *Boston Globe,* September 10.
A New Place for Confucius. *Boston Globe,* September 17.
Circle Game. *Boston Globe,* September 24.
Ayun Halliday
Monkey Brains and Mangosteens. *PerceptiveTravel.com,* May.
Steve Hendrix
Charge of the Bus Brigade. *Washington Post,* July 16.

Pico Iyer
Let's Go (Slightly) Crazy. *Condé Nast Traveler,* September.

Mark Jenkins
Above and Beyond. *Outside,* October.
Sebastian Junger
Welcome Stranger. *National Geographic Adventure,* May.

Wendy Knight
Dangerous Minds. *PerceptiveTravel.com,* July.

Anthony Lane
High and Low. *The New Yorker,* April 24.
David Lansing
Hopscotching the Inner Hebrides. *Islands,* March.

TONI MARTIN
Almost Algerian. *Threepenny Review,* Summer.
DIANE LAWSON MARTINEZ
The Road to Kotor Varos. *Bellevue Literary Review,* Spring.
ANDREW MCCARTHY
The Longest Way Home. *National Geographic Traveler,* November/December.
MARTHA MCPHEE
Journeys Along the Edge of the Underworld. *Condé Nast Traveler,* June.
DANIEL MENDELSOHN
Find Your Roots. *Travel + Leisure,* September.

TIM NEVILLE
Greetings from Happy Valley. *Skiing,* January.

ANN PATCHETT
The Paris Match. *New York Times Magazine,* November 26.
MICHAEL PATERNITI
How to Disappear. *GQ,* July.
STEPHANIE PEARSON
Cosmic Whiplash. *Outside,* June.
MATTHEW POLLY
Caipirinha Nights: An American in Rio. *Slate.com,* August 14–18.
ROLF POTTS
Cycladian Rhythms. *Outside Traveler,* Spring/Summer.
India's Isle of Ghosts. *San Francisco Chronicle Magazine,* March 19.

PAUL RAFFAELE
In John They Trust. *Smithsonian,* February.
EDWARD READICKER-HENDERSON
The Quietest Place on Earth. *National Geographic Traveler,* September.
Uses for Dirty Underwear. *PerceptiveTravel.com,* September.
ALAN RICHMAN
Putting on the Dog. *Condé Nast Traveler,* November.
ELIZABETH RUBIN
In the Land of the Taliban. *New York Times Magazine,* October.
ALAN PETER RYAN
Feckless and Reckless. *The American Scholar,* Summer.

KIRA SALAK
Hell and Back. *National Geographic Adventure,* March.
Myanmar's River of Spirits. *National Geographic,* May.
Iran: Travels in Hostile Territory. *National Geographic Adventure,* November.
DAVID SEDARIS
In the Waiting Room. *The New Yorker,* September 18.
JAKE SILVERSTEIN
Highway Run. *Harper's Magazine,* July.

Julie Solis
Exploring Paris's Urban Underground. *National Geographic Adventure,* April.
Peter Stark
Halfway House. *New York Times Magazine,* July 9.
Rob Story
Know When to Fold Them. *Skiing,* November.
Hank Stuever
The Roads Most Traveled. *Washington Post,* June 29.
Mimi Swartz
Once Upon a Time in Laredo. *National Geographic,* November.
Thomas Swick
Heaven to Bavarians. *South Florida Sun-Sentinel,* December 3 and 10.
Patrick Symmes
The Sweetest Villains. *Outside,* February.

Jeffrey Tayler
Escape to Old Russia. *The Atlantic Monthly,* October.
Catherine Texier
To Russia with Notions. *New York Times Magazine,* March 26.
Bill Thomas
The Finnish Line. *Washington Post Magazine,* March 26.
Calvin Trillin
With the Grain. *Gourmet,* August.
Kristin Van Tassel
The Places We Find Ourselves. *WorldHum.com,* May 31.

Catherine Watson
Unlocking Beirut. *WorldHum.com,* December 29.
Kerri Westenberg
Appalachian Trail Magic. *Minneapolis Star Tribune,* November 19.

THE B·E·S·T AMERICAN SERIES®

THE BEST AMERICAN SHORT STORIES® 2007. STEPHEN KING, editor, HEIDI PITLOR, series editor. This year's most beloved short fiction anthology is edited by Stephen King, author of sixty books, including *Misery, The Green Mile, Cell,* and *Lisey's Story,* as well as about four hundred short stories, including "The Man in the Black Suit," which won the O. Henry Prize in 1996. The collection features stories by Richard Russo, Alice Munro, William Gay, T. C. Boyle, Ann Beattie, and others.

ISBN-13: 978-0-618-71347-9 • ISBN-10: 0-618-71347-6 $28.00 CL
ISBN-13: 978-0-618-71348-6 • ISBN-10: 0-618-71348-4 $14.00 PA

THE BEST AMERICAN NONREQUIRED READING™ 2007. DAVE EGGERS, editor, introduction by SUFJAN STEVENS. This collection boasts the best in fiction, nonfiction, alternative comics, screenplays, blogs, and "anything else that defies categorization" (*USA Today*). With an introduction by singer-songwriter Sufjan Stevens, this volume features writing from Alison Bechdel, Scott Carrier, Miranda July, Lee Klein, Matthew Klam, and others.

ISBN-13: 978-0-618-90276-7 • ISBN-10: 0-618-90276-7 $28.00 CL
ISBN-13: 978-0-618-90281-1 • ISBN-10: 0-618-90281-3 $14.00 PA

THE BEST AMERICAN COMICS™ 2007. CHRIS WARE, editor, ANNE ELIZABETH MOORE, series editor. The newest addition to the Best American series—"A genuine salute to comics" (*Houston Chronicle*)—returns with a set of both established and up-and-coming contributors. Edited by Chris Ware, author of *Jimmy Corrigan: The Smartest Kid on Earth,* this volume features pieces by Lynda Barry, R. and Aline Crumb, David Heatley, Gilbert Hernandez, Adrian Tomine, Lauren Weinstein, and others.

ISBN-13: 978-0-618-71876-4 • ISBN-10: 0-618-71876-1 $22.00 CL

THE BEST AMERICAN ESSAYS® 2007. DAVID FOSTER WALLACE, editor, ROBERT ATWAN, series editor. Since 1986, *The Best American Essays* has gathered outstanding nonfiction writing, establishing itself as the premier anthology of its kind. Edited by the acclaimed writer David Foster Wallace, this year's collection brings together "witty, diverse" (*San Antonio Express-News*) essays from such contributors as Jo Ann Beard, Malcolm Gladwell, Louis Menand, and Molly Peacock.

ISBN-13: 978-0-618-70926-7 • ISBN-10: 0-618-70926-6 $28.00 CL
ISBN-13: 978-0-618-70927-4 • ISBN-10: 0-618-70927-4 $14.00 PA

THE BEST AMERICAN MYSTERY STORIES™ 2007. CARL HIAASEN, editor, OTTO PENZLER, series editor. This perennially popular anthology is sure to appeal to mystery fans of every variety. The 2007 volume, edited by best-selling novelist Carl Hiaasen, features both mystery veterans and new talents. Contributors include Lawrence Block, James Lee Burke, Louise Erdrich, David Means, and John Sandford.

ISBN-13: 978-0-618-81263-9 • ISBN-10: 0-618-81263-6 $28.00 CL
ISBN-13: 978-0-618-81265-3 • ISBN-10: 0-618-81265-2 $14.00 PA

THE B·E·S·T AMERICAN SERIES®

THE BEST AMERICAN SPORTS WRITING™ 2007. DAVID MARANISS, editor, GLENN STOUT, series editor. "An ongoing centerpiece for all sports collections" (*Booklist*), this series stands in high regard for its extraordinary sports writing and topnotch editors. This year David Maraniss, author of the critically acclaimed biography *Clemente*, brings together pieces by, among others, Michael Lewis, Ian Frazier, Bill Buford, Daniel Coyle, and Mimi Swartz.

ISBN-13: 978-0-618-75115-0 • ISBN-10: 0-618-75115-7 $28.00 CL
ISBN-13: 978-0-618-75116-7 • ISBN-10: 0-618-75116-5 $14.00 PA

THE BEST AMERICAN TRAVEL WRITING™ 2007. SUSAN ORLEAN, editor, JASON WILSON, series editor. Edited by Susan Orlean, staff writer for *The New Yorker* and author of *The Orchid Thief*, this year's collection, like its predecessors, is "a perfect mix of exotic locale and elegant prose" (*Publishers Weekly*) and includes pieces by Elizabeth Gilbert, Ann Patchett, David Halberstam, Peter Hessler, and others.

ISBN-13: 978-0-618-58217-4 • ISBN-10: 0-618-58217-7 $28.00 CL
ISBN-13: 978-0-618-58218-1 • ISBN-10: 0-618-58218-5 $14.00 PA

THE BEST AMERICAN SCIENCE AND NATURE WRITING™ 2007. RICHARD PRESTON, editor, TIM FOLGER, series editor. This year's collection of the finest science and nature writing is edited by Richard Preston, a leading science writer and author of *The Hot Zone* and *The Wild Trees*. The 2007 edition features a mix of new voices and prize-winning writers, including James Gleick, Neil deGrasse Tyson, John Horgan, William Langewiesche, Heather Pringle, and others.

ISBN-13: 978-0-618-72224-2 • ISBN-10: 0-618-72224-6 $28.00 CL
ISBN-13: 978-0-618-72231-0 • ISBN-10: 0-618-72231-9 $14.00 PA

THE BEST AMERICAN SPIRITUAL WRITING™ 2007. PHILIP ZALESKI, editor, introduction by HARVEY COX. Featuring an introduction by Harvey Cox, author of the groundbreaking *Secular City*, this year's edition of this "excellent annual" (*America*) contains selections that gracefully probe the role of faith in modern life. Contributors include Robert Bly, Adam Gopnik, George Packer, Marilynne Robinson, John Updike, and others.

ISBN-13: 978-0-618-83333-7 • ISBN-10: 0-618-83333-1 $28.00 CL
ISBN-13: 978-0-618-83346-7 • ISBN-10: 0-618-83346-3 $14.00 PA

THE B·E·S·T AMERICAN SERIES®

THE BEST AMERICAN SPORTS WRITING™ 2007. DAVID MARANISS, editor, GLENN STOUT, series editor. "An ongoing centerpiece for all sports collections" (*Booklist*), this series stands in high regard for its extraordinary sports writing and topnotch editors. This year David Maraniss, author of the critically acclaimed biography *Clemente*, brings together pieces by, among others, Michael Lewis, Ian Frazier, Bill Buford, Daniel Coyle, and Mimi Swartz.

ISBN-13: 978-0-618-75115-0 • ISBN-10: 0-618-75115-7 $28.00 CL
ISBN-13: 978-0-618-75116-7 • ISBN-10: 0-618-75116-5 $14.00 PA

THE BEST AMERICAN TRAVEL WRITING™ 2007. SUSAN ORLEAN, editor, JASON WILSON, series editor. Edited by Susan Orlean, staff writer for *The New Yorker* and author of *The Orchid Thief*, this year's collection, like its predecessors, is "a perfect mix of exotic locale and elegant prose" (*Publishers Weekly*) and includes pieces by Elizabeth Gilbert, Ann Patchett, David Halberstam, Peter Hessler, and others.

ISBN-13: 978-0-618-58217-4 • ISBN-10: 0-618-58217-7 $28.00 CL
ISBN-13: 978-0-618-58218-1 • ISBN-10: 0-618-58218-5 $14.00 PA

THE BEST AMERICAN SCIENCE AND NATURE WRITING™ 2007. RICHARD PRESTON, editor, TIM FOLGER, series editor. This year's collection of the finest science and nature writing is edited by Richard Preston, a leading science writer and author of *The Hot Zone* and *The Wild Trees*. The 2007 edition features a mix of new voices and prize-winning writers, including James Gleick, Neil deGrasse Tyson, John Horgan, William Langewiesche, Heather Pringle, and others.

ISBN-13: 978-0-618-72224-2 • ISBN-10: 0-618-72224-6 $28.00 CL
ISBN-13: 978-0-618-72231-0 • ISBN-10: 0-618-72231-9 $14.00 PA

THE BEST AMERICAN SPIRITUAL WRITING™ 2007. PHILIP ZALESKI, editor, introduction by HARVEY COX. Featuring an introduction by Harvey Cox, author of the groundbreaking *Secular City*, this year's edition of this "excellent annual" (*America*) contains selections that gracefully probe the role of faith in modern life. Contributors include Robert Bly, Adam Gopnik, George Packer, Marilynne Robinson, John Updike, and others.

ISBN-13: 978-0-618-83333-7 • ISBN-10: 0-618-83333-1 $28.00 CL
ISBN-13: 978-0-618-83346-7 • ISBN-10: 0-618-83346-3 $14.00 PA

HOUGHTON MIFFLIN COMPANY www.houghtonmifflinbooks.com

THE B·E·S·T AMERICAN SERIES®

THE BEST AMERICAN SHORT STORIES® 2007. STEPHEN KING, editor, HEIDI PITLOR, series editor. This year's most beloved short fiction anthology is edited by Stephen King, author of sixty books, including *Misery, The Green Mile, Cell,* and *Lisey's Story,* as well as about four hundred short stories, including "The Man in the Black Suit," which won the O. Henry Prize in 1996. The collection features stories by Richard Russo, Alice Munro, William Gay, T. C. Boyle, Ann Beattie, and others.

ISBN-13: 978-0-618-71347-9 • ISBN-10: 0-618-71347-6 $28.00 CL
ISBN-13: 978-0-618-71348-6 • ISBN-10: 0-618-71348-4 $14.00 PA

THE BEST AMERICAN NONREQUIRED READING™ 2007. DAVE EGGERS, editor, introduction by SUFJAN STEVENS. This collection boasts the best in fiction, nonfiction, alternative comics, screenplays, blogs, and "anything else that defies categorization" (*USA Today*). With an introduction by singer-songwriter Sufjan Stevens, this volume features writing from Alison Bechdel, Scott Carrier, Miranda July, Lee Klein, Matthew Klam, and others.

ISBN-13: 978-0-618-90276-7 • ISBN-10: 0-618-90276-7 $28.00 CL
ISBN-13: 978-0-618-90281-1 • ISBN-10: 0-618-90281-3 $14.00 PA

THE BEST AMERICAN COMICS™ 2007. CHRIS WARE, editor, ANNE ELIZABETH MOORE, series editor. The newest addition to the Best American series— "A genuine salute to comics" (*Houston Chronicle*)—returns with a set of both established and up-and-coming contributors. Edited by Chris Ware, author of *Jimmy Corrigan: The Smartest Kid on Earth,* this volume features pieces by Lynda Barry, R. and Aline Crumb, David Heatley, Gilbert Hernandez, Adrian Tomine, Lauren Weinstein, and others.

ISBN-13: 978-0-618-71876-4 • ISBN-10: 0-618-71876-1 $22.00 CL

THE BEST AMERICAN ESSAYS® 2007. DAVID FOSTER WALLACE, editor, ROBERT ATWAN, series editor. Since 1986, *The Best American Essays* has gathered outstanding nonfiction writing, establishing itself as the premier anthology of its kind. Edited by the acclaimed writer David Foster Wallace, this year's collection brings together "witty, diverse" (*San Antonio Express-News*) essays from such contributors as Jo Ann Beard, Malcolm Gladwell, Louis Menand, and Molly Peacock.

ISBN-13: 978-0-618-70926-7 • ISBN-10: 0-618-70926-6 $28.00 CL
ISBN-13: 978-0-618-70927-4 • ISBN-10: 0-618-70927-4 $14.00 PA

THE BEST AMERICAN MYSTERY STORIES™ 2007. CARL HIAASEN, editor, OTTO PENZLER, series editor. This perennially popular anthology is sure to appeal to mystery fans of every variety. The 2007 volume, edited by best-selling novelist Carl Hiaasen, features both mystery veterans and new talents. Contributors include Lawrence Block, James Lee Burke, Louise Erdrich, David Means, and John Sandford.

ISBN-13: 978-0-618-81263-9 • ISBN-10: 0-618-81263-6 $28.00 CL
ISBN-13: 978-0-618-81265-3 • ISBN-10: 0-618-81265-2 $14.00 PA

